IN WAR AND PEACE

IN WAR AND PEACE

An American Military History Anthology

EDWARD K. ECKERT

Saint Bonaventure University

Wadsworth Publishing Company
Belmont, California
A Division of Wadsworth, Inc.

History Editor: Peggy Adams
Production Editor: Cece Munson
Print Buyer: Randy Hurst
Designer: Carolyn Deacy
Copy Editor: Steven Bailey
Compositor: TCSystems, Inc., Shippensburg, Penn.
Cover Designer: Harry Voigt
Cover Painting: Hassam: Flag Day, 1917,
The White House Collection; Scala/Art Resource, N.Y.

Printed in the United States of America
1 2 3 4 5 6 7 8 9 10—94 93 92 91 90

Library of Congress Cataloging-in-Publication Data

In war and peace: an American military history anthology/[compiled by] Edward K. Eckert.

    p.   cm.

   ISBN 0-534-12516-6

   1. United States—History, Military.   I. Eckert, Edward K., 1943–

E181.I5   1989

973—dc20   89-36447

                                                   CIP

For the Veterans of History 203

CONTENTS

Preface   xvii

1 THE COLONIAL WARS   *1*

1 *Of Plymouth Plantation* • **William Bradford**   5

Portrays an early colonial campaign against nearby Indians and
the colonists' prejudices toward their native allies and enemies.

**2 The Siege of St. Augustine (1740) • Don Manuel de
Montiano**   **11**

Describes an unsuccessful eighteenth-century colonial siege of a
Spanish fort in Florida.

3 Self-Defense and Moral Scruples • Franklin   15

Franklin asks Pennsylvania's Quaker leaders who will protect the
colony from attack and help pay the cost of defending it?

**4 France and England in North America • Francis
Parkman   21**

This classic account of colonial warfare by one of America's
greatest historians discusses the French attack and slaughter of
the British garrison at Fort William Henry.

Annotated Bibliography   **33**

2   THE AMERICAN REVOLUTION   35

5 Two Shots Heard 'Round the World (1775)   39
Presents both the colonial and British side of the battles of
Lexington and Concord, and permits students to decide which
account was more objective.

6 Battle of Long Island (1776) • Joseph P. Martin   43
Shares the feelings of pride, fear, cowardice, and honor that
every soldier experiences before his first battle.

7 Valley Forge (1777–1778) • Albigence Waldo   49
Examines the meaning of personal sacrifice and the purpose for
the soldiers' suffering during the army's winter encampment at
Valley Forge.

8 New Jersey Naval Militia • Thomas Brown   52
Narration of life on board a small coastal vessel along the
Atlantic seaboard, portraying partisan fighting between loyalists
and patriots.

**9 The *Bonhomme Richard's* Defeat of the *Serapis*
(1779) • John Paul Jones   56**
One of the founders of the American navy describes his famous
battle against a British fleet off the coast of England.

**10 Hospitals and Prisons • James Thacher and Thomas
Dring   61**
Two articles focus on the often overlooked side of the
Revolution—the primitive medical care and life on board the
stifling hulls of prison ships in New York harbor.

11 Partisan Warfare • Moses Hall   66
Tells of the hatred between Southern loyalists and patriots and
the massacres it spawned.

12 Yorktown (1781) • James Thacher   71
Describes the final battle of the Revolution and the pride felt by
American forces when the British army surrendered.

Annotated Bibliography   75

3 THE EARLY REPUBLIC   *77*

13 The Constitution of the United States of America   79
Provides the essential parts of the U.S. Constitution that deal
with military matters.

14 Frontier War • Micah McDonough   82
Narrates the lack of training and discipline in the army that
caused one of the worst defeats in U.S. military history, as well
as the horrors of frontier warfare.

**15 A Kentucky Soldier's Account of the Battle of New
Orleans   88**
Portrays the excitement behind Andrew Jackson's lopsided
victory over British regulars in the battle that created the legend
of the invincible militia and helped establish American
nationalism.

16 The Expansible Army (1820) • John C. Calhoun   95
Argument that the United States will always be unprepared to
fight wars until a better way can be found to ensure greater
professionalism in the army.

**17 The Militia Company Drill • Augustus Baldwin
Longstreet   99**
A classic account of frontier humor, describing a militia day drill
when an inept company tries to follow a manual for close-order
drill.

**18 *White Jacket, or the World in a Man-of-War*
(1849) • Herman Melville   104**
Melville's autobiographical novel of life on board a man-of-war,
one that helped end the brutal punishment of flogging in the
navy.

19 Battle of Vera Cruz • George Ballentine   110
Narrates American landings and the siege of Vera Cruz, one of
the most successful battles of the War with Mexico, and raises
the question, Are civilians proper targets for armies?

20 **A Mean and Infamous War (1847)** • **Theodore Parker**   116

Challenges and motives behind American participation in the Mexican War, and advises citizens to follow their consciences, not the orders of the national government.

Annotated Bibliography   120

4   *The Civil War*   123

21 **Fort Donelson** • **Ulysses S. Grant**   124

Grant forces his opponent to agree to an "unconditional surrender" of a Confederate fort on the Cumberland River in Tennessee, thereby earning an enviable nickname and reputation.

22 **The Valley Campaign** • **Richard Taylor**   132

Recounts "Stonewall" Jackson's famous campaign, one of the most studied in history, and describes Jackson's personality and idiosyncrasies.

23 **Ironclad Warfare** • **Franklin Buchanan**   139

Reports the first clash between the Confederate ironclad *Virginia* and the wooden-hulled Union fleet guarding Hampton Roads.

24 **Pickett's Charge** • **Frank A. Haskell**   143

Lieutenant Haskell places the reader alongside him at the center of the Union line on the afternoon of the greatest assault of the Civil War.

25 *Hardtack and Coffee* • **John D. Billings**   152

Describes rations and everyday life of Civil War soldiers.

26 **The Fort Pillow Massacre**   160

Provides testimony by Union soldiers who had survived the Confederate attack on Fort Pillow, which they call a massacre.

27 **The Burning of Atlanta** • **William T. Sherman**   173

Warns the people of Atlanta to leave their homes before they are destroyed, and opens new moral issues about modern war.

Annotated Bibliography   176

5   *THE RISE OF PROFESSIONALISM*   *179*

28 The Freedmen at West Point • John M. Schofield   181
Portrays the racial prejudice that existed in the United States in
the late nineteenth century, and the difficulties it presented to
blacks who wanted to become army officers.

29 Battle of Bear Paw Mountain • Edward McClernand   185
Describes one of the last battles of the American Indian wars
when the Nez Perce tribe, fleeing to Canada, was caught by U.S.
cavalry.

**30 *The Influence of Sea Power Upon History* • Alfred Thayer
Mahan   190**
Contends that all great nations have protected their economic
resources by a powerful navy, and recommends that the United
States become a first-rate naval power.

**31 *The Military Policy of the United States* • Emory
Upton   194**
Argues that all past American wars have seen a needless waste of
life and money because the federal government had failed to
maintain a strong, professional army.

**32 The Spanish-American War • Richard Harding
Davis   200**
Reports the first significant land battle in Cuba, during which the
Rough Riders successfully defended themselves from a Spanish
ambush.

Annotated Bibliography   208

6   *WORLD WAR I   211*

33 The Moral Equivalent of War • William James   213
James raised the ire of fellow pacifists when he agreed with
military men that there are virtues in martial service and war that
cannot easily be duplicated in civilian life.

**34 The Reserve Officers Training Corps • Leonard
Wood   219**
Proposes a national reserve force to take the place of the
National Guard, and training on college campuses for officers to
command the reserves.

35 **Marines in the Trenches** • **Clifton B. Cates** 226

Enthusiastically reports a combat experience in Western Europe during the First World War, and comments on the effects of gas, tanks, and airplanes on military tactics.

36 **An Aerial Battle** • **E. C. Leonard** 239

Describes a World War I bombing mission and dogfight over enemy lines.

37 **The Body of an American** • **John Dos Passos** 246

Challenges the government's selection of a single body to exemplify the Unknown Soldier of World War I, and portrays the United States as a melting pot of many races and ethnic groups that are unrepresented by the selection.

Annotated Bibliography 252

7 *WORLD WAR II* 255

38 **The God-Damned Infantry** • **Ernie Pyle** 257

America's favorite war correspondent writes about life on the frontlines in North Africa with the infantry.

39 **A Bombing Run** • **"An Officer"** 261

Describes the flight of a B-17 squadron into the heartland of Germany and aerial battles against enemy fighters.

40 **Submarine Warfare** • **D. H. McClintock** 266

Recalls submarine duty in the Pacific from the Japanese attack on Pearl Harbor to the invasion of the Philippines.

41 **The Beaches and the Hedgerows** 276

Recounts the 90th Division's landing and breakout at Normandy to the battles across France, fighting both Germans and the weather.

42 **Prison Memoirs** • **Lewis C. Beebe** 285

A personal account of life in a Japanese camp, where prisoners were forced to work for their inadequate meals and to try to celebrate Christmas away from home.

43 **On Board a Fighting Ship** • **Ernie Pyle** 291

Pyle describes the marvels of American technology on board an aircraft carrier in the Pacific.

44 Today's Target: Nagasaki • William L. Laurence   296
A graphic, Pulitzer Prize–winning account of the dropping of the
atomic bomb on Nagasaki by *The New York Times*' science editor.

**45 The Ones That Stink the Worst • Donald Haguall and
Ralph G. Martin   305**
Predicts that if everyone could smell death on the battlefield,
mankind would soon end all wars.

Annotated Bibliography   306

8   KOREA AND THE COLD WAR   *309*

46 Blacks in the Military   311
Shows the racial discrimination that exists in the American
armed forces after World War II and suggests programs to end it.

47 Trouble in the Pass • S. L. A. Marshall   316
Places the reader on the ground with a unit trapped in a pass and
surrounded by the enemy, with all the confusion and uncertainty
of battle.

48 A Korean War Diary • Robert A. Howes   326
Follows an artillery officer on his first patrol behind enemy lines.

49 B-26s Wipe Out Red Stronghold • Dick Bartlett   331
Describes the thrill of flying over enemy territory to obliterate a
small North Korean village using the latest American technology.

**50 Old Soldiers Never Die, They Just Fade Away • Douglas
MacArthur   334**
MacArthur presents his controversial views on global strategy and
bids farewell to the army and the nation.

**51 The Military-Industrial Complex • Dwight D.
Eisenhower   338**
Warns the public that the costs of military defense might
bankrupt the nation's moral and economic resources.

52 Ethics at the Shelter Doorway • L. C. McHugh, S.J.   344
Presents a rationale for building—and defending—a backyard
fallout shelter, basing his arguments on traditional Judeo-
Christian morality.

Annotated Bibliography   348

9 THE VIETNAM WAR   349

53 A Vietnam War Journal • King J. Coffman   352

Justifies the American presence in Vietnam, and describes his frustration over strategic decisions that restrict his ability to defend his men.

54 The Grunts' War • Arthur E. Woodley, Jr., and Wallace Terry   359

Portrays the war from the perspective of a black soldier who delights in participating in long-range patrols but finds his wartime experiences did not prepare him to return to the United States.

55 War Is Hell • James Brady   370

Initially enthusiastic over the experience of war, Brady eventually discovers its hidden, evil nature when he finds it has killed his best friend.

56 An Unjust and Immoral War • Dale Noyd   377

An Air Force pilot requests separation from the service because he believes that the Vietnam War violates American and humanitarian values.

Annotated Bibliography   381

10 CONTEMPORARY ISSUES   383

57 M-16: A Bureaucratic Horror Story • James Fallows   384

Army bureaucrats rely on rules to hinder the performance of a perfectly fine new rifle, causing men to die in Vietnam from the mistakes they made but still deny.

58 The Grenada Operation   403

A U.S. Senate committee report exposes some of the problems encountered by the military during one of its most successful invasions, and warns that these same errors would mean defeat if the military were to face a better prepared enemy.

59 Women Cadets at West Point • Helen Rogan   411

Discloses the sexual discrimination and harassment the first female cadets experienced at the U.S. Military Academy.

60 The All-Volunteer Army • **Charles C. Moskos, Jr.**   **420**

A renowned sociologist discusses the problems and successes
spawned by an all-volunteer armed force.

Annotated Bibliography   **429**

EPILOGUE: THE ROMANCE OF WAR   430

61 Why Men Love War • **William Broyles, Jr.**   **431**

Captures the thrill that many men experience in war, one so
great and fearful that it reveals the heart of darkness in everyone.

PREFACE

In December 1862, Robert E. Lee stood on Marye's Heights outside Fredericksburg, Virginia. The vast field that lay beneath his feet was littered with Union dead, the remains of the men who had thrown themselves against his entrenched Confederates. "It is well that war is so terrible," Lee remarked, or "men would love it too much."

War, like religion, politics, and education, is a social institution, an organized effort by human beings to work in concert. But no other human activity requires greater cooperation, expends so much money, or demands so often the ultimate sacrifice. Our children play "war" to prepare them to fight in them as adults. Yet, despite its horror—its destruction, death, and despair—some men do love war. Few have experienced it personally. What most men (and some women, too) love is not war itself, but stories about war that enable them to experience combat vicariously. The thrill and the test of battle can be felt by reading about the leaders and soldiers who have fought in them.

Some war stories are on everyone's list of the world's best literature. A nation's earliest history is often the story of its wars. Israel's holy scriptures, the Greeks' *Iliad*, the *Song of Roland* of the French, and Spain's *El Cid* are literary and historical classics, and they are very much about people at war.

This anthology includes some of the finest writings on American wars. Memoirs, letters, journals, and historical tales of war are included, along with documents that raise important economic, ethical, and cultural questions. I tried to do two things in this anthology. First, I attempted to give students a taste of battle—a whiff of shot—by including selections from diaries, journals, letters, and memoirs. Second, I included documents of primary importance to American military history, documents that are not easily found elsewhere. Thus I included Alfred Thayer Mahan's study of naval power, John C. Calhoun's rationale for an expansible army, the United States Constitution, and President Dwight D. Eisenhower's farewell address to the nation. These two goals may occasionally clash in the mind of a purist looking for only one focus. Perhaps a more accurate description of this anthology is that it is a collection of essential documents on U.S. military history, one that emphasizes the personal experience of war.

In some cases, the purpose of the reading is to introduce students to great historical literature. The sheer majesty of Francis Parkman's account of the titanic struggle between France and Britain in North America or the clear, crisp analysis of war in Ulysses S. Grant's Civil War memoirs opens the reader's mind to the real drama of military campaigns. In fact, military history offers some of the best literature in the English language.

Other selections, especially diaries and letters, were chosen so that readers could experience what combat felt like through the words of its participants. Confusion, terror, and pride mingle in these accounts, echoing feelings shared by every man when he faces the enemy.

Still other selections were chosen to challenge some students' pre-conceived notions of war. Basic questions about conscience and ethics, economics and finance, racial and sexual equality, and political democracy have not changed much in more than two centuries of American wars. Hopefully, these documents will open students' minds to new ideas.

Any anthology always faces a question of balance. My concerns were to give equal emphasis to the four major American wars (Revolution, Civil War, World War II, and Vietnam) and to use the other chapters to link these four periods. Furthermore, I decided not to give equal weight to the navy because far more men have served in the army than the navy and because all major American wars have primarily been land wars. This does not take away the heroism of naval service; it just accepts the fact that more American money and lives have been expended on land than in the water. Once I reached the twentieth century, I had to give some attention to air power and the air force.

Wherever possible I have left the original document alone. I have corrected spelling or added punctuation marks or explanatory notes only when it was necessary to make the meaning clear. A brief introduction provides essential background for each selection.

I would like to thank the publisher's reviewers of this book: Larry Cable of the University of North Carolina, Wilmington; David T. Childress of Jacksonville State University; Joseph G. Dawson, III, of Texas A&M University; Randolph Hennes of the University of Washington; and Brian Linn of Old Dominion University.

I have been greatly aided by colleagues, friends, and students who helped me acquire documents, corrected the manuscript, or made critical suggestions. I thank St. Bonaventure University for permitting me a sabbatical leave to develop this project and a faculty research grant to travel to archives; Francis Householter and Jennifer Coleman, who helped me obtain Captain Noyd's letter of resignation; Dr. Richard J. Sommers, archivist at the U.S. Army Military History Institute; Michael Miller, Curator of Personal Papers at the U.S. Marine Corps Museum; and the research staff at the U.S. Navy Historical Branch for their skillful aid in locating suitable documents to include; Sandra Goodliff and Elizabeth Anne Schroder for typing portions of the manuscript; Professors Paul V. Joliet of St. Bonaventure University and Craig Symonds and Bill Roberts at the U.S. Naval Academy, who read the manuscript and offered valuable suggestions; St. Bonaventure University graduate students Michael Gabriel and Robert Kasbohm, who proofread parts of the manuscript; my editor, R. Jackson Wilson of Smith College, whose suggested changes improved my work; and the students in my U.S. military history course in the fall of 1987, who critiqued the selections: James T. Benson, Anthony M. Bimonte, Paul W. Caprio, Carolyn N. Dowd, Timothy J. Dunn, Mark R. Havers, Christopher J. Heil, John D. Kivari, Jeffrey L. Mills, Patrick E. Plaehn, Eileen M. Regan, and William J. Stephens. Lastly, my thanks to my son, Christopher K. Eckert, who accompanied me to archives and then helped me choose illustrations; and to my wife, Linda Corroum Eckert, who read the entire manuscript and offered many helpful suggestions.

C H A P T E R   1

THE COLONIAL WARS

When the first English settlers came to America, they clearly understood that they were undertaking a military incursion on land claimed by others. While their ships waited offshore, they built a crude palisaded fort before constructing any other building. Fortunately for the settlers, the natives had a long history of intertribal warfare. The Indians failed to offer any coordinated opposition to the first English colonists. Other European nations did not actively oppose the English settlements because they had enough difficulty governing their own colonies.

England provided no military or naval protection to the colonists. The settlers hired professional soldiers to teach them how to defend themselves, and adapted an old English institution, the militia, to the American environment. The militia required most males, teenagers to middle-aged men, to defend their homes. These amateur soldiers were the colonies' primary military force for more than a century. Yet, as a defensive force, the part-time militia was weak because it could not prevent surprise attacks. Offensively, however, the militia was powerful, because it obligated almost every free man to become a soldier.

The colonial military posture of a weak defense and a strong offense soon created a distinct cycle in American warfare. First, a surprise attack would catch colonists off-guard. Men from nearby towns quickly responded to chase away the Indians. The settlers would then raise a sizable militia army to remove or exterminate the attackers. Such total military goals were reasonable in a wilderness where the natives did not understand the finer points of European "diplomacy" and the settlers were so vulnerable. By the end of the seventeenth century, the Indian threat had been largely eliminated east of the Appalachian mountains.

Just as the English settlers were ending their wars against the Indians, a series of conflicts broke out in Europe. These pitted the Protestant nations of England and Germany against Catholic Spain and France. In Europe, these wars had limited political or dynastic goals, but in America they were fought to gain dominance over vast and valuable territories. The colonists again found themselves vulnerable to surprise attacks, this time from French or Spanish soldiers accompanied by Indian allies. The first three of the four colonial wars were inconclusive, but the final one, called the French and Indian War by the colonists, gave England a worldwide empire. The Peace of Paris (1763), which concluded this last war, forced France to cede Canada, and Spain, Florida, to England.

By 1763, the colonists had obtained a total strategic solution. All foreign enemies had been removed, and only a few thousand English troops remained along the colonial frontier and in important ports.

Indian massacre in Virginia (Library of Congress). This woodcut shows an early Indian massacre. It had originally appeared in the first volume of Johann Theodor de Bry's America series (Frankfurt am Main, 1590), which was published in Latin, English, French, and German. De Bry and other Europeans published books about life in the New World. They usually mixed fiction with fact, but in either case colonial life was dangerous. In this print, de Bry's ferocious Indians appear larger than the seemingly innocent Europeans. The colonists are passive and largely unarmed. Although the man in the lower right wields a large axe, he has not noticed the ferocious attack. This was de Bry's way of portraying the total innocence and victimization of the colonists by the Indians. The Indians in the foreground have metal daggers and wooden clubs, indicative of the transitional cultural stage in which they found themselves as they moved from primitive to modern weapons. In the background are four large canoes full of Indians with bows and arrows, preparing to land and attack the fortress, which is firing its cannons at the attackers. Early English settlements did build wooden stockades around the dwellings for protection, but de Bry's fortress and buildings are German in design, not American or English. They are far too large and grand for this early period of colonization. From drawings like this and descriptions of colonial life in travel books, Europeans realized that hostility and violence awaited them in the New

World. Yet these same sources also told of bountiful food, comfortable homes, and ample land. Both the hazards and benefits of colonial American life had to be weighed by every emigrant.

OF PLYMOUTH PLANTATION

William Bradford

O*f Plymouth Plantation* is the history of the first three decades of Pilgrim settlement in New England. Its author, William Bradford (1590–1657), was the principal figure behind the colony's success and was elected governor thirty times. *Of Plymouth Plantation* is Bradford's classic account of colonial America.

The following chapter tells of Plymouth's problems with the Pequot Indians and shows the bloody nature of early colonial warfare. By 1637, the New Englanders had prevented an alliance between the Narragansett Indians and the Pequots. The colonists had accused the Pequots of killing two unsavory merchant captains, and the militia set out to "punish" the culprits. Two previous expeditions to Connecticut and Block Island had failed. Now the Massachusetts colonists agreed to cooperate with the Connecticut militia to destroy the Pequots once and for all. They succeeded with such vengeance that the results shocked the colonists' Narragansett allies, who had hoped to return with valuable Pequot captives.

The colonists' success left the Narragansetts alone and vulnerable. Thirty years later, they too would be unable to save themselves from an inevitable war that destroyed their tribe.

Bradford's spelling and prose is difficult for the modern reader. Although Bradford was an educated man, spelling and consistency were not important to most seventeenth-century writers. The differences in spelling and grammar between this document and the rest of the selections in this section demonstrate how close the first American colonists still were to the Middle Ages. This selection may be easier to understand if it is read aloud.

SOURCE: William T. Davis (Ed.), *Bradford's History of Plymouth Plantation, 1606–1646* (New York: Charles Scribner's Sons, 1908).

Anno Dom: 1637

In the fore part of this year, the Pequents [Pequots] fell openly upon the English at Conightecutte [Connecticut], in the lower parts of the river, and slew sundry of them, (as they were at work in the feilds,) both men and women, to the great terrour of the rest; and wente away in great pride and triumph, with many high threats. They allso assalted a fort at the rivers mouth, though strong and well defended; and though they did not their prevaile, yet it struk them with much fear and astonishmente to see their bould attempts in the face of danger; which made them in all places to stand upon their gard and to prepare for resistance, and ernestly to solisit their friends and confederats in the Bay of Massachusetts to send them speedy aid, for they looked for more forcible assaults. Mr. Vane, being then Govr [governor], write from their Generall Courte [colonial assembly] to them here, to joyne with them in this Warr; to which they were cordially willing, but tooke opportunitie to write to them aboute some former things, as well as presente, considerable hereaboute. . . .

In the mean time, the Pequents, espetially in the winter before, sought to make peace with the Narigansets [Narragansetts], and used very pernicious arguments to move them thereunto: as that the English were stranegers and begane to overspread their countrie, and would deprive them therof in time, if they were suffered to grow and increse; and if the Narigansets did assist the English to subdue them, they did but make way for their owne overthrow, for if they were rooted out, the English would soone take occasion to subjugate them; and if they would hearken to them, they should not neede to fear the strength of the English; for they would not come to open battle with them, but fire their houses, kill their katle [cattle], and lye in ambush for them as they went abroad upon their occasions; and all this they might easily doe without any or litle danger to them selves. The which course being held, they well saw the English could not long subsiste but they would either be starved with hunger, or be forced to forsake the countrie; with many the like things; insomuch that the Narigansets were once wavering, and were halfe minded to have made peace with them, and joyned against the English. But againe, when they considered, how much wrong they had received from the Pequents, and what an oppertunitie they now had by the help of the English to right them selves, revenge was so sweete unto them, as it prevailed above all the rest, so as they resolved to joyne with the English against them, and did. . . .

From Conightecutte, (who were most sencible of the hurt sustained, and the present danger), they sett out a partie of men, and an other partie mett them from the [Massachusetts] Bay, at the Narigansets', who were to joyne with them. The Narigansets were earnest to be gone before the

English were well rested and refreshte, espetially some of them which came last. It should seeme their desire was to come upon the enemie sudenly, and undiscovered. There was a barke of this place, newly put in there, which was come from Conightecutte, who did incourage them to lay hold of the Indeans' forwardnes, and to shew as great forwardnes as they, for it would incourage them, and expedition might prove to their great advantage. So they went on, and so ordered their march, as the Indeans brought them to a forte of the enimie's (in which most of the cheefe men were) before day. They approached the same with great silence, and surrounded it both with English and Indeans, that they might not breake out; and so assaulted them with great courage, shooting amongst them, and entered the forte with all speed; and those that first entered found sharp resistance from the enimie who both shott at and grapled with them; others rane into their howses and brought out fire, and sett them on fire, which soone tooke in their matts, and, standing close together, with the wind, all was quickly on a flame, and thereby more were burnte to death then was otherwise slain; it burnte their bowstrings, and made them unserviseable. Those that scaped the fire were slaine with the sword; some hewed to peeces, others run throw with their rapiers [light, thin swords used for thrusting], so as they were quickly dispatchte and very few escaped. It was conceived they thus destroyed about 400 at this time. It was a fearfull sight to see them thus frying in the fyer [fire] and the streams of blood quenching the same, and horrible was the stinck and scent there of; but the victory seemed a sweete sacrifice, and they gave the praise thereof to God, who had wrought so wonderfully for them, thus to inclose their enimies in their hands, and give them so speedy a victory over so proud and insulting an enimie. The Narragansett Indeans, all this while, stood round aboute, but aloofe from all danger, and left the whole execution to the English, except it were the stoping of any that broke away, insulting over their enimies in this their ruine and miserie, when they saw them dancing in the flames, calling them by a word in their owne language, signifying O brave Pequents! which they used familierly among them selves in their own praise, in songs of triumph after their victories. After this service was thus happily accomplished, they marcht to the water side, wher they mett with some of their vessells, by which they had refreishing with victualls [food] and other necessaries. But in their march the rest of the Pequents drew into a body, and acoasted them, thinking to have some advantage against them by reason of a neck of land; but when they saw the English prepare for them, they kept aloofe, so as they neither did hurt, nor could receive any. After their refreishing and repair to gether for further counsell and directions, they resolved to pursue their victory, and follow the warr against the rest; but the Narigansett Indeans most of them forsooke them, and such of them as they had with them for guides, or otherwise, they found them very cold and backward in the busines, either out of envie, or that they saw the English would make more profite of the victorie then they were willing they should, or else deprive them of such advantage as them selves desired by having them become tributaries unto them, or the like. . . .

That I may make an end of this matter: this Sassacouse (the Pequents' chief sachem) being fled to the Mohawkes, they cutt off his head, with some other of the cheefe of them, whether to satisfie the English, or rather the Narigansets (who, as I have since heard, hired them to doe it,) or for their owne advantage, I well know not; but thus this warr tooke end. The rest of the Pequents were wholy driven from their place, and some of them submitted them selves to the Narigansets and lived under them; others of them betooke them selves to the Monhiggs [Mohicans] under Uncass, their sachem, with the approbation of the English of Conightecutte, under whose protection Uncass lived, and he and his men had been faithful to them in this warr, and done them very good service.

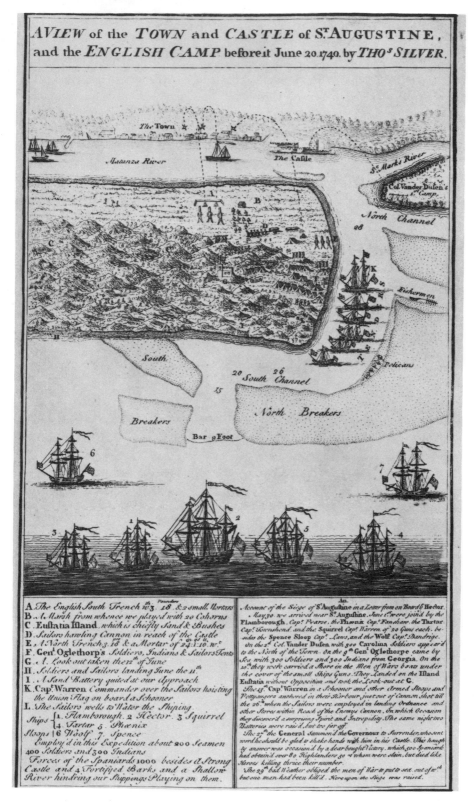

Siege of St. Augustine, 1740 (Library of Congress). This sketch of St. Augustine was drawn by Thomas Silver shortly after the battle. Topographical maps and road maps both are nineteenth-century innovations. Before then, maps were usually sketches that lacked detailed topographical information or proportion. Early cartographers were more concerned with creating a pleasing pictographic rendition of a site than an accurate one. They used pictures of soldiers, ships, castles, animals, and weapons to portray a battle. This sketch showed how the siege of St. Augustine might have appeared to an observer, located several miles away and several thousand feet above the battle. Modern maps, in contrast, place the reader directly above the site. In the foreground of this drawing, an English fleet of seven major ships blocks the main channel to St. Augustine. Six tenders or supply ships reinforce General Oglethorpe's camp while his soldiers bombard the town and fort (Castillo de San Marcos) with mortars and artillery pieces. What the drawing does not show is the south channel (to the left), which permitted Spanish reinforcements to relieve the besieged defenders.

THE SIEGE OF ST. AUGUSTINE (1740)

Don Manuel de Montiano

Georgia was the last of the thirteen English colonies to be established. In 1733, a corporation headed by General James E. Oglethorpe founded the southernmost colony. Georgia served as a refuge for British debtors and a military buffer to protect the valuable port of Charleston, South Carolina, from the Spanish in Florida. Spain had been involved in Florida since Ponce de Leon had first explored it in 1513. Florida's chief importance to Spain was as the last safe harbor for its merchantmen from pirates, storms, or European enemies before they crossed the Atlantic. The inlet from Matanzas in the south to St. Augustine formed a natural harbor. Spain built a stone fort at each end to protect it.

In 1739, the third war between England and her Catholic neighbors in Europe began. Don Manuel de Montiano, the governor of Florida, had expected the Georgia militiamen to attack him. When General Oglethorpe's force of almost 900 soldiers and sailors, along with their Indian allies, sailed into the waters off St. Augustine, more than 2,000 Spanish settlers sought refuge in the large fort, the Castillo de San Marcos, protected by Montiano's garrison of 750 soldiers. The fort's soft limestone walls absorbed cannon balls and gave protection to everyone until a relief force arrived from Havana. The arrival of the Spanish fleet prompted Oglethorpe to lift the siege and return to Georgia.

The following document is part of a letter that the victorious and jubilant Montiano wrote to the governor of Havana on 28 July 1740. In it,

SOURCE: Albert C. Manucy (ed.), *The History of Castillo de San Marcos & Fort Matanzas from Contemporary Narratives and Letters* (Washington, DC: 1955).

Montiano reported on the repulse of the Georgians and heaped priase on all his soldiers, including the blacks and Indians, who helped defend the fort.

[On the night of July 7, 1740,] Louis Gomez arrived at this place, with intelligence that he left within the bar of Mosquitoes [Ponce de León Inlet], three sloop, one small sloop, and two schooners, with provisions sent by Your Excellency, in charge of Juan de Oxeda, and addressed to the Captain Don Manuel de Villasante. The pleasure with which I received this news is indescribable; but the joy subsisted but a short time in my heart; for I was also informed, that when Pedro Chepuz, and the French sloop in which he came as pilot, arrived off this bar, he was seen and chased by an English ship, and packet, which did no harm, but got notice of our provisions, and of their whereabouts. At the same time came a deserter from the enemy's camp, who said that on some night, during spring tides, it was the intention of General Oglethorpe, to make an attack on this place by sea and land. On this I suspended the execution of the plan I had fixed on for bringing the provisions, little by little, and applied myself entirely to the purpose of resisting whatever attempts his pride and arrogance might undertake; but the days of opportunity, passed, without his executing his idea, and I turned my eyes upon our relief vessels, which were manifestly in danger. Using only the launches and the boat, we carried on the work of unloading and transporting to this place; for although I also sent with them a priogue [canoe] of considerable capacity for the same purpose, it so happened that on making that bar, four boats and launches, one frigate and a despatch boat crossed their path, separating them and attacking the small ones. But our people defended themselves stoutly, from four of the afternoon until nightfall, suffering only the loss of our pirogue, which splintered itself against the launches; the crew having shifted over, they continued their journey, and returned happily loaded with flour, and continued their task until it was no longer necessary, for on the 20th, the enemy having raised his camp, and taken to hasty and shameful flight, I promptly ordered our bilander* after making the most careful inspection to see if the pass was open and the coast clear, to resume their voyage and come in by Matanzas, if they had at least a moral certainty of safety. This they accordingly did on the 25th; and to-day the sloop from Campeche and the two schooners have completely discharged their cargo. And I have consequently directed Palomarez, Captain of one of them, to prepare to take this news to Your Excellency.

    I assure Your Excellency, that I cannot arrive at a comprehension of the conduct, or rules of this General; for I am informed by at least twelve

---

* Small boats with two masts.

deserters from him present here, that his camp was composed of 370 men of his regiment, 600 militia of Carolina, 130 Indians, and 200 sailors armed, and encamped on the Island of Santa Anastacia, and as many more sailors for the management of the sloops, schooners, and launches. My wonder is inexpressible that this gentleman should make his retreat with such precipitation, as to leave abandoned, four 6-pounders on the battery on the point of San Mateo [north shore of St. Augustine Inlet], one schooner, two kegs of gunpowder, several muskets and escopettes [carbines], and to set fire to a quantity of provisions, such as boxes of bacon, cheese, lard, dried beef, rice and beans, to a schooner, and to an excellent mortar carriage; besides many things that have profited the Indians, and galley slaves who have had the fortune to pick up several barrels of lard and flour, and some pork. Notwithstanding all this, I can assure Your Excellency that all the deserters, and two squaws of ours, prisoners of theirs that escaped, agree in saying that Don Diego [James] Oglethorpe is going to reorganize his forces, and make a great effort to stir up the Indians. And although I appraise this rumor as something to placate and leave in doubt his people, moderating the fire that may be burning among them, and especially the Carolinians and Scotchmen as having been the hardest hit, yet I believe there would be no harm in taking precautions, and in Your Excellency sending me such reenforcements as may be suitable, and the munitions and stores as set forth in memorandum herewith. I shall send a post at once to the Uchises [Uchee Indians], to draw them, in view of all this news, from their allegiance to the English, and I shall offer to treat them handsomely if it will please them to come see me.

The formal siege has continued 38 days, counting from the 13th of June, to the 20th of July, and the fire of the batteries and bombardment 27 days, from the 24th of June, to the said 20th of July. The batteries were three; one in the pool [*pozo*] on the Island of Santa Anastacia, of four 18-pounders and one 9-pounder; another on the point of the hammock on said island, of two 18-pounders, and the other on the coast of the interior part of the point San Mateo, of seven 6-pounders, five of iron, and two of brass. The mortars, and small mortars were thirty-four, two mortars throwing shell of half a quintal, and two others of about a quintal [100 lbs.]. The thirty small mortars, which the deserters call cow horns [cohorns], were, some small hand grenades, and others for those of ten or twelve pounds.

The loss we have suffered is reduced to two men killed, and wounded. Those (wounded) by gun fire who died were [. . .] artilleryman and the convict, son of Ordonez, whom with the other one named Contreras I received in the first launch-loads from Mosquito. Of the other two wounded by shellfire, to wit, a soldier and a negro, the negro is perfectly well, and the other has a good chance of pulling through, though with one leg fewer.

The constancy, valor and glory of the officers here are beyond all praise; the patriotism, courage and steadiness of the troops, militia, free negroes, and convicts, have been great. These last I may say to Your Excellency, have borne themselves like veteran soldiers. I especially commend their humble devotion, for without ceasing work by day, they have persevered by night with the care and vigilance of old soldiers.

Even among the slaves a particular steadiness has been noticed, and a desire not to await the enemy within the place but to go out to meet him. In short, I have been thoroughly satisfied with all during the siege, and especially with the circumstance that during the entire siege no one has deserted. And lastly, Your Excellency may believe that the galliots* have been of great service to me: for if the siege had caught me without them, the English would have given me much work to do, as the launches could have been used for nothing but the guard of this port, to say nothing of the necessity of taking other indispensable measures, at great cost. And so I renew my thanks to Your Excellency for having sent them to my relief, even against the common opinion of the entire torrent of members of the Junta held by you to decide whether or no they should be sent.

---

* Small, swift boats propelled either by oars or sail.

SELF-DEFENSE AND MORAL SCRUPLES

Benjamin Franklin

By 1754, there were 777 militia laws in the colonies establishing military organizations in almost every community. In fact, militia companies rivaled religious congregations as the most uniform institutional feature of colonial society. Exemptions were granted for critical occupations, handicaps, and religious beliefs. Some men, usually slaves, criminals, or Indians, were forbidden to join. But in general, all colonies required military service from men between the ages of 16 and 60.

Quaker Pennsylvania was the only colony without any laws requiring militia service. Benjamin Franklin (1706–1790), a pragmatic politician as well as a highly successful businessman, feared that the colony would be unable to defend itself from French privateers and their Indian allies during the French and Indian War (1754–1763). Franklin wrote a pamphlet that addressed these dangers, along with two other important issues: the freedom of religion, or the right to dissent from military service and support, and how to fund an army.

Many Quaker leaders were unable to reconcile their religious beliefs with their duties as provincial legislators. When they were finally confronted with war, they resigned their political offices. Some American historians contend that their resignations deprived the future United States of an effective heritage of pacifism.

Non-Quakers took over the offices and prepared the colony for war. They not only had to raise an army but also had to decide who was going to pay for it. People who are wealthy are often more willing to draft young men

SOURCE: Leonard W. Larrabee (Ed.), *The Papers of Benjamin Franklin,* Vol. 3 (New Haven, CT: Yale University Press, 1961). © Yale University Press. Reprinted by permission.

for military service than to tax old men to pay for the costs of war. "A rich man's war, but a poor man's fight" is a complaint that has been heard in many American wars. Franklin's solution (and that of most politicians for most of America's history) was to organize a popular army backed by general taxation.

War, at this Time, rages over a great Part of the known World; our News-Papers are Weekly filled with fresh Accounts of the Destruction it every where occasions. Pennsylvania, indeed, situate in the Center of the Colonies, has hitherto enjoy'd profound Repose; and tho' our Nation is engag'd in a bloody War, with two great and powerful Kingdoms, yet, defended, in a great Degree, from the French on the one Hand by the Northern Provinces, and from the Spaniards on the other by the Southern, at no small Expence to each, our People have, till lately, slept securely in their Habitations.

There is no British Colony excepting this, but has made some Kind of Provision for its Defence; many of them have therefore never been attempted by an Enemy; and others that were attack'd, have generally defended themselves with Success. The length and difficulty of our Bay and River has been thought so effectual a Security to us, that hitherto no Means have been entered into that might discourage an Attempt upon us, or prevent its succeeding. . . .

Perhaps some in the City, Towns and Plantations near the River, may say to themselves, *An Indian War on the Frontiers will not affect us; the Enemy will never come near our Habitations; let those concern'd take Care of themselves.* And others who live in the Country, when they are told of the Danger the City is in from Attempts by Sea, may say, *What is that to us? The Enemy will be satisfied with the Plunder of the Town, and never think it worth his while to visit our Plantations: Let the Town take care of itself.* These are not mere Suppositions, for I have heard some talk in this strange Manner. But are these the Sentiments of true Pennsylvanians, of Fellow-Countrymen, or even of Men that have common Sense or Goodness? Is not the whole Province one Body, united by living under the same Laws, and enjoying the same Priviledges? . . . When New-England, a distant Colony, involv'd itself in a grievous Debt to reduce Cape-Breton, we freely gave *Four Thousand Pounds* for *their* Relief. And at another Time, remembering that Great Britain, still more distant, groan'd under heavy Taxes in Supporting the War, we threw in our Mite to their Assistance, by a free Gift of *Three Thousand Pounds:* And shall Country and Town join in helping Strangers (as those comparatively are) and yet refuse to assist each other? . . .

The Enemy, no doubt, have been told, That the People of Pennsylvania are Quakers, and against all Defence, from a Principle of Conscience; this, tho' true of a Part, and that a small Part only of the Inhabitants, is commonly said of the Whole; and what may make it look probable to Strangers, is, that in Fact, nothing is done by any Part of the People towards their Defence. . . .

'Tis true, with very little Notice, the Rich may shift for themselves. The Means of speedy Flight are ready in their Hands; and with some previous Care to lodge Money and Effects in distant and secure Places, tho' they should lose much, yet enough may be left them, and to spare. But most unhappily circumstanced indeed are we, the middling People, the Trades-men, Shopkeepers, and Farmers of this Province and City! We cannot all fly with our Families; and if we could, how shall we subsist? No; we and they, and what little we have gained by hard Labour and Industry, must bear the Brunt: The Weight of Contributions, extorted by the Enemy (as it is of Taxes among ourselves) must be surely borne by us. Nor can it be avoided as we stand at present; for tho' we are numerous, we are quite defenceless, having neither Forts, Arms, Union, nor Discipline. And tho' it were true, that our Trade might be protected at no great Expence, and our Country and our City easily defended, if proper Measures were but taken; yet who shall take these Measures? Who shall pay that Expence? On whom may we fix our Eyes with the least Expectation that they will do any one Thing for our Security? Should we address that wealthy and powerful Body of People, who have ever since the war governed our Elections, and filled almost every Seat in our Assembly? . . . They have already been by great Numbers of the People petitioned in vain. Our late Governor did for Years sollicit, request, and even threaten them in vain. Their religious Prepossessions are un-changeable, their Obstinacy invincible. Is there then the least Hope remaining, that from that Quarter any Thing should arise for our Security?

And is our Prospect better, if we turn our Eyes to the Strength of the *opposite Party*, those Great and rich Men, Merchants and others, who are ever railing at Quakers for doing what their Principles seem to require, and what in Charity we ought to believe they think their Duty, but take no one Step themselves for the Publick Safety? . . . *Rage* at the Disappointment of their little Schemes for Power, gnaws their Souls, and fills them with such cordial Hatred to their Opponents, that every Proposal, by the Execution of which *those* may receive Benefit as well as themselves, is rejected with Indignation. *What,* say they, *shall we lay out our Money to protect the Trade of Quakers? Shall we fight to defend Quakers? No; Let the Trade perish, and the City burn; let what will happen, we shall never lift a Finger to prevent it.* Yet the Quakers have *Conscience* to plead for their Resolution not to fight, which these Gentlemen have not. . . .

Thus unfortunately are we circumstanc'd at this Time, my dear

Countrymen and Fellow-Citizens; we, I mean, the middling People, the Farmers, Shopkeepers and Tradesmen of this City and Country. Thro' the Dissensions of our Leaders, thro' *mistaken Principles of Religion,* join'd with a Love of Worldly Power, on the one Hand; thro *Pride, Envy* and *implacable Resentment* on the other; our Lives, our Families and little Fortunes, dear to us as any Great Man's can be to him, are to remain continually expos'd to Destruction, from an enterprizing, cruel, now well-inform'd, and by Success encourag'd Enemy. . . . Our Case indeed is dangerously bad; but perhaps there is yet a Remedy, if we have but the Prudence and the Spirit to apply it.

If this now flourishing City, and greatly improving Colony, is destroy'd and ruin'd, it will not be for want of Numbers of Inhabitants able to bear Arms in its Defence. 'Tis computed that we have at least (exclusive of the Quakers) 60,000 Fighting Men, acquainted with Fire-Arms, many of them Hunters and Marksmen, hardy and bold. All we want is Order, Discipline, and a few Cannon. At present we are like the separate Filaments of Flax before the Thread is form'd, without Strength because without Connection; but UNION would make us strong and even formidable: . . . The Way to secure Peace is to be prepared for War. They that are on their Guard, and appear ready to receive their Adversaries, are in much less Danger of being attack'd, than the supine, secure and negligent. We have yet a Winter before us, which may afford a good and almost sufficient Opportunity for this, if we seize and improve it with a becoming Vigour. . . .

A TRADESMAN *of Philadelphia*

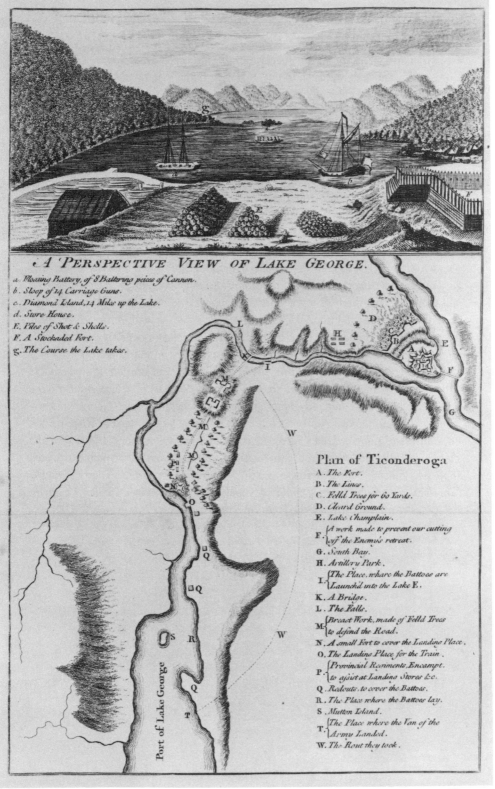

A PERSPECTIVE VIEW OF LAKE GEORGE.

a. Floating Battery, of 8 Battering peices of Cannon.
b. Sloop of 14 Carriage Guns.
c. Diamond Island, 14 Miles up the Lake.
d. Store House.
E. Piles of Shot & Shells.
F. A Stockaded Fort.
g. The Course the Lake takes.

Port of Lake George

Plan of Ticonderoga

A. The Fort.
B. The Lines.
C. Felld Trees for 60 Yards.
D. Cleard Ground.
E. Lake Champlain.
F. A work made to prevent our cutting off the Enemis retreat.
G. South Bay.
H. Artillery Park.
I. The Place where the Battoes are Launch'd into the Lake E.
K. A Bridge.
L. The Falls.
M. Breast Work, made of Felld Trees to defend the Road.
N. A small Fort to cover the Landing Place.
O. The Landing Place for the Train.
P. Provincial Renments Encampt. to assist at Landing Stores &c.
Q. Redouts to cover the Battoes.
R. The Place where the Battoes lay.
S. Mutton Island.
T. The Place where the Van of the Army Landed.
W. The Rout they took.

19

A *perspective view of Lake George and plan of Ticonderoga (Library of Congress). The axis between New York City and Montreal was the critical invasion route in the colonial Franco-English wars. Men and supplies traveled from New York City up the Hudson to Albany, Lake George, Lake Champlain, the Richelieu, and St. Lawrence Rivers to Montreal, or vice versa. Along the water route were several nonnavigable spots. There vessels had to be unloaded and the cargo and men taken overland to the next body of water. These transshipment routes were protected by forts. One of the most important—and most heavily defended—was the portage from the northern shore of Lake George to the southern end of Lake Champlain. This map combines a pictograph of Lake George (like the sketch of St. Augustine) with a more modern, vertical topographic map. In the center of the map is the transshipment route marked by the letter M. A small wooden fort (N) protected the southern landing place (O) and the route was guarded by breastworks alongside the trail. The falls and rapids (which the boats had to avoid) were from N to the northern landing spot at I. This tributary (called "the Creek") flowed into Lake Champlain (E), which was protected by Fort Ticonderoga, a formidable stone structure that controlled a bend in the waterway that was difficult to navigate. This engraving appeared in the London* Universal Magazine *(November 1759) during the French and Indian War. It offered readers a map to help them understand the campaign, along with a pictograph of the American landscape that only hints at the narrowness of Lake George and the formidable mountainous Adirondack terrain. In some places, such as Rogers Rock on the western shore of Lake George near Mutton (now Prisoners) Island (S), the sheer wall of the mountain drops hundreds of feet into the lake. The map and sketch show why control of the waterways was such an important part of military strategy. No eighteenth-century army could be supplied and maintained in the American wilderness except by way of the lakes and rivers.*

FRANCE AND ENGLAND IN NORTH AMERICA

Francis Parkman

T he French and Indian War was the climactic struggle between England and its European enemies for a worldwide empire. After more than a half century of almost continuous warfare, England concentrated its military forces to come to the aid of its American colonies. The results were decisive. The war destroyed the Franco-Spanish threat in North America, and by 1763 had left England as master of the continent east of the Mississippi River.

Fortunately, this epic struggle found a historian worthy of its grandeur. Francis Parkman (1823–1893), from a wealthy New England family, made it his life's work to tell the story of the conflict between England and France in North America. Despite a disabling nervous disorder that left him partially blind and unable to concentrate for more than brief periods, Parkman eventually wrote eight volumes of history so vivid that it has a place among the classics of American literature. Before he wrote, Parkman studied original documents and visited many of the places he would later describe. Although his Englishmen are too noble, his Frenchmen too devious, and his Indians too barbaric, Parkman's narrative is still considered by many historians to be the greatest historical work ever written by an American.

The following excerpt comes from *Montcalm and Wolfe* (1884). It tells of the French invasion of Lake Champlain in their effort to split New England from New York. The massacre at Fort William Henry already had been used by James Fenimore Cooper in *The Last of the Mohicans* (1826), his classic tale of the colonial frontier.

SOURCE: Francis Parkman, *Montcalm and Wolfe* (Boston: Macmillan, 1884).

1757, FORT WILLIAM HENRY

Canadians and Indians, were moving by detachments up Lake Champlain. Fleets of bateaux [boats] and canoes followed each other day by day along the capricious lake, in calm or storm, sunshine or rain, till, towards the end of July, the whole force was gathered at Ticonderoga, the base of the intended movement. . . .

Ticonderoga is a high rocky promontory between Lake Champlain on the north and the mouth of the outlet of Lake George on the south. Near its extremity and close to the fort were still encamped the two battalions under Bourlamaque, while bateaux and canoes were passing incessantly up the river of the outlet. There were scarcely two miles of navigable water, at the end of which the stream fell foaming over a high ledge of rock that barred the way. Here the French were building a saw-mill; and a wide space had been cleared to form an encampment defended on all sides by an abatis.*
. . . Above the cascade the stream circled through the forest in a series of beautiful rapids, and from the camp of Lévis a road a mile and a half long had been cut to the navigable water above. At the end of this road there was another fortified camp, formed of colony regulars, Canadians, and Indians, under Rigaud. It was scarcely a mile farther to Lake George, where on the western side there was an outpost, chiefly of Canadians and Indians; while advanced parties were stationed at Bald Mountain, now called Rogers Rock, and elsewhere on the lake, to watch the movements of the English. The various encampments just mentioned were ranged along a valley extending four miles from Lake Champlain to Lake George, and bordered by mountains wooded to the top.

Here was gathered a martial population of eight thousand men, including the brightest civilization and the darkest barbarism: from the scholar-soldier Montcalm and his no less accomplished aide-de-camp; from Lévis, conspicuous for graces of person; from a throng of courtly young officers, who would have seemed out of place in that wilderness had they not done their work so well in it; from these to the foulest man-eating savage of the uttermost northwest. . . .

The Mission Indians were better allies than these heathen of the west; and their priests, who followed them to the war, had great influence over them. They were armed with guns, which they well knew how to use. Their dress, though savage, was generally decent, and they were not cannibals; though in other respects they retained all their traditional ferocity and most of their traditional habits. They held frequent war-feasts, one of which is

---

* A defensive position formed from felled, pointed trees facing the enemy.

described by Roubaud, Jesuit missionary of the Abenakis of St. Francis, whose flock formed a part of the company present.

"Imagine," says the father, "a great assembly of savages adorned with every ornament most suited to disfigure them in European eyes, painted with vermilion, white, green, yellow, and black made of soot and the scrapings of pots. A single savage face combines all these different colors, methodically laid on with the help of a little tallow, which serves for pomatum [ointment]. The head is shaved except at the top, where there is a small tuft, to which are fastened feathers, a few beads of wampum, or some such trinket. Every part of the head has its ornament. Pendants hang from the nose and also from the ears, which are split in infancy and drawn down by weights till they flap at last against the shoulders. The rest of the equipment answers to this fantastic decoration: a shirt bedaubed with vermilion, wampum collars, silver bracelets, a large knife hanging on the breast, moose-skin moccasins, and a belt of various colors always absurdly combined. The sachems and war-chiefs are distinguished from the rest: the latter by a gorget [armor to protect the throat], and the former by a medal, with the King's portrait on one side, and on the other Mars and Bellona joining hands with the device, *Virtus et Honor.*"

Thus attired, the company sat in two lines facing each other, with kettles in the middle filled with meat chopped for distribution. To a dignified silence succeeded songs, sung by several chiefs in succession, and compared by the narrator to the howling of wolves. Then followed a speech from the chief orator, highly commended by Roubaud, who could not help admiring this effort of savage eloquence. "After the harangue," he continues, "they proceeded to nominate the chiefs who were to take command. As soon as one was named he rose and took the head of some animal that had been butchered for the feast. He raised it aloft so that all the company could see it, and cried, 'Behold the head of the enemy!' Applause and cries of joy rose from all parts of the assembly. . . ."

Roubaud was one day near the fort, when he saw the shore lined with a thousand Indians, watching four or five English prisoners, who, with the war-party that had captured them, were approaching in a boat from the farther side of the water. Suddenly the whole savage crew broke away together and ran into the neighboring woods, whence they soon emerged, yelling diabolically, each armed with a club. The wretched prisoners were forced to "run the gauntlet," which would probably have killed them. They were saved by the chief who commanded the war party, and who, on the persuasion of a French officer, claimed them as his own and forbade the game; upon which, according to rule in such cases, the rest abandoned it. On this same day the missionary met troops of Indians conducting several bands of English prisoners along the road that led through the forest from the camp of Lévis. Each of the captives was held by a cord made fast about the neck; and the sweat was starting from their brows in the extremity of their horror and distress. Roubaud's tent was at this time in the camp of the Ottawas. He presently saw a large number of them squatted about a fire, before which meat was roasting on sticks stuck in the ground; and, approaching, he saw that it was the flesh of an Englishman, other parts of which were boiling in a kettle, while near by sat eight or ten of the prisoners, forced to see their comrade devoured. The horror-stricken priest began to remonstrate; on which a young savage fiercely replied in broken French: "You have French taste; I have Indian. This is good meat for me"; and the feasters pressed him to share it.

Bougainville says that this abomination could not be prevented; which only means that if force had been used to stop it, the Ottawas would have gone home in a rage. They were therefore left to finish their meal undisturbed. Having eaten one of their prisoners, they began to treat the rest with the utmost kindness, bringing them white bread, and attending to all their wants,—a seeming change of heart due to the fact that they were a valuable commodity, for which the owners hoped to get a good price at Montreal. Montcalm wished to send them thither at once, to which after long debate the Indians consented, demanding, however, a receipt in full, and bargaining that the captives should be supplied with shoes and blankets.

These unfortunates belonged to a detachment of three hundred provincials, chiefly New Jersey men, sent from Fort William Henry under command of Colonel Parker to reconnoiter the French outposts. Montcalm's scouts discovered them; on which a band of Indians, considerably more numerous, went to meet them under a French partisan named Corbiere, and ambushed themselves not far from Sabbath Day Point. Parker had rashly divided his force; and at daybreak of the twenty-sixth of July three of his boats fell into the snare, and were captured without a shot. Three others followed, in ignorance of what had happened, and shared the fate of the first. . . .

Preparations were urged on with the utmost energy. Provisions, camp equipage, ammunition, cannon, and bateaux were dragged by gangs of men up the road from the camp of Lévis to the head of the rapids. The work went on through heat and rain, by day and night, till, at the end of July, all was done. Now, on the eve of departure, Montcalm, anxious for harmony among his red allies, called them to a grand council near the camp of Rigaud. Forty-one tribes and sub-tribes, Christian and heathen, from the east and from the west, were represented in it. . . . All sat in silence, decked with ceremonial paint, scalp-locks, eagle plumes, or horns of buffalo; and the dark and wild assemblage was edged with white uniforms of officers from France, who came in numbers to the spectacle. Other officers were also here, all belonging to the colony. They had been appointed to the command of the Indian allies, over whom, however, they had little or no real authority. First among them was the bold and hardy Saint-Luc de la Corne, who was called general of the Indians; and under him were others, each assigned to some tribe or group of tribes, . . .

The bateaux lay ready by the shore, but could not carry the whole force; and Lévis received orders to march by the side of the lake with twenty-five hundred men, Canadians, regulars, and Iroquois. He set out at daybreak of the thirtieth of July, his men carrying nothing but their knapsacks, blankets, and weapons. Guided by the unerring Indians, they climbed the steep gorge at the side of Rogers Rock, gained the valley beyond, and marched southward along a Mohawk trail which threaded the forest in a course parallel to the lake. The way was of the roughest; many straggled from the line, and two officers completely broke down. The first destination of the party was the mouth of Ganouskie Bay, now called Northwest Bay, where they were to wait for Montcalm, and kindle three fires as a signal that they had reached the rendezvous.

Montcalm left a detachment to hold Ticonderoga; and then, on the first of August, at two in the afternoon, he embarked at the Burned Camp with all his remaining force. Including those with Lévis, the expedition counted about seven thousand six hundred men, of whom more than sixteen hundred were Indians. At five in the afternoon they reached the place where the Indians, having finished their rattlesnake hunt, were smoking their pipes and waiting for the army. The red warriors embarked, and joined the French flotilla; and now, as evening drew near, was seen one of those wild pageantries of war which Lake George has often witnessed. A restless multitude of birch canoes, filled with painted savages, glided by shores and islands, like troops of swimming water-fowl. Two hundred and fifty bateaux came next, moved by sail and oar, some bearing the Canadian militia, and some the battalions of Old France in trim and gay attire: . . . So, under the flush of sunset, they held their course along the romantic lake, to play their part in the historic drama that lends a stern enchantment to its fascinating scenery. They passed the Narrows in mist and darkness; and when, a little before dawn, they rounded the high promontory of Tongue Mountain, they saw, far on the right, three fiery sparks shining through the gloom. These were the signal-fires of Lévis, to tell them that he had reached the appointed spot.

Lévis had arrived the evening before, after his hard march through the sultry midsummer forest. His men had now rested for a night, and at ten in the morning he marched again. Montcalm followed at noon, and coasted the western shore, till, towards evening, he found Lévis waiting for him by the margin of a small bay not far from the English fort, though hidden from it by a projecting point of land. Canoes and bateaux were drawn up on the beach, and the united forces made their bivouac together.

The earthen mounds of Fort William Henry still stand by the brink of Lake George; and seated at the sunset of an August day under the pines that cover them, one gazes on a scene of soft and soothing beauty, where dreamy waters reflect the glories of the mountains and the sky. As it is to-day, so it was then; all breathed repose and peace. The splash of some leaping trout, or the dipping wing of a passing swallow, alone disturbed the summer calm of that unruffled mirror. . . .

As the sun rose above the eastern mountains the French camp was all astir. The column of Lévis, with Indians to lead the way, moved through the forest towards the fort, and Montcalm followed with the main body; then the artillery boats rounded the point that had hid them from the sight of the English, saluting them as they did so with musketry and cannon; while a host of savages put out upon the lake, ranged their canoes abreast in a line from shore to shore, and advanced slowly, with measured paddle-strokes and yells of defiance.

The position of the enemy was full in sight before them. At the head of the lake, towards the right, stood the fort, close to the edge of the water. On its left was a marsh; then the rough piece of ground where Johnson had encamped two years before; then a low, flat, rocky hill crowned with an intrenched camp; and, lastly, on the extreme left, another marsh. Far around to the fort and up the slopes of the western mountain the forest had been cut down and burned, and the ground was cumbered with blackened stumps and charred carcasses and limbs of fallen trees, strewn in savage disorder one upon another. This was the work of Winslow in the autumn before. Distant shouts and war-cries, the clatter of musketry, white puffs of smoke in the dismal clearing and along the scorched edge of the bordering forest, told that Lévis' Indians were skirmishing with parties of the English, who had gone out to save the cattle roaming in the neighborhood, and burn some out-buildings that would have favored the besiegers. Others were taking down the tents that stood on a plateau near the foot of the mountain on the right, and moving them to the intrenchment on the hill. The garrison sallied from the fort to support their comrades, and for a time the firing was hot.

Fort William Henry was an irregularly bastioned square, formed by embankments of gravel surmounted by a rampart of heavy logs, laid in tiers crossed one upon another, the interstices filled with earth. The lake protected it on the north, the marsh on the east, and ditches with *chevaux-de-frise** on the south and west. Seventeen cannon, great and small,

---

* An obstacle made of logs with spikes on four sides along the trunk that is designed to stop infantry and cavalry.

besides several mortars and [smaller cannon on] swivels, were mounted upon it; and a brave Scotch veteran, Lieutenant-Colonel Monro, of the thirty-fifth regiment, was in command.

General Webb lay fourteen miles distant at Fort Edward, with twenty-six hundred men, chiefly provincials. On the twenty-fifth of July he had made a visit to Fort William Henry, examined the place, given some orders, and returned on the twenty-ninth. He then wrote the governor of New York, telling him that the French were certainly coming, begging him to send up the militia, and saying: "I am determined to march to Fort William Henry with the whole army under my command as soon as I shall hear of the farther approach of the enemy." Instead of doing so, he waited three days, and then sent up a detachment of two hundred regulars under Lieutenant-Colonel Young, and eight hundred Massachusetts men under Colonel Frye. This raised the force at the lake to two thousand and two hundred, including sailors and mechanics, and reduced that of Webb to sixteen hundred, besides half as many more distributed at Albany and the intervening forts. . . .

When the skirmishing around the fort was over, La Corne, with a body of Indians, occupied the road that led to Fort Edward, and Lévis encamped hard by to support him, while Montcalm proceeded to examine the ground and settle his plan of attack. He made his way to the rear of the intrenched camp and reconnoitered it, hoping to carry it by assault; but it had a breastwork of stones and logs, and he thought the attempt too hazardous . . . he resolved to besiege the fort in form.

He chose for the site of his operations the ground now covered by the village of Caldwell. A little to the north of it was a ravine, beyond which he formed his main camp, while Lévis occupied a tract of dry ground beside the marsh, whence he could easily move to intercept succors from Fort Edward on the one hand, or repel a sortie from Fort William Henry on the other. A brook ran down the ravine and entered the lake at a small cove protected from the fire of the fort by a point of land; and at this place, still called Artillery Cove, Montcalm prepared to debark his cannon and mortars.

Having made his preparations, he sent Fontbrune, one of his aides-de-camp, with a letter to Monro. "I owe it to humanity," he wrote, "to summon you to surrender. At present I can restrain the savages, and make them observe the terms of a capitulation, as I might not have power to do under other circumstances; and an obstinate defence on your part could only retard the capture of the place a few days, and endanger an unfortunate garrison which cannot be relieved, in consequence of the dispositions I have made. I demand a decisive answer within an hour." Monro replied that he and his soldiers would defend themselves to the last. While the flags of truce were flying, the Indians swarmed over the fields before the fort; and when they learned the result, an Abenaki chief shouted in broken French: "You won't surrender, eh! Fire away then, and fight your best; for if I catch you, you shall get no quarter." Monro emphasized his refusal by a general discharge of his cannon.

The trenches were opened on the night of the fourth,—a task of extreme difficulty, as the ground was covered by a profusion of half-burned stumps, roots, branches, and fallen trunks. Eight hundred men toiled till daylight with pick, spade, and axe, while the cannon from the fort flashed through the darkness, and grape and round-shot whistled and screamed over their heads. Some of the English balls reached the camp beyond the ravine, and disturbed the slumbers of the officers off duty, as they lay wrapped in their blankets and bear-skins. Before daybreak the first parallel was made; a battery was nearly finished on the left, and another was begun on the right. The men now worked under cover, safe in their burrows; one gang relieved another, and the work went on all day.

The Indians were far from doing what was expected of them. Instead of scouting in the direction of Fort Edward to learn the movements of the enemy and prevent surprise, they loitered about the camp and in the trenches, or amused themselves by firing at the fort from behind stumps and logs. Some, in imitation of the French, dug little trenches for themselves, in which they wormed their way towards the rampart, and now and then picked off an artilleryman, not without loss on their own side. . . .

About sunrise the battery of the left opened with eight heavy cannon and a mortar, joined, on the next morning, by the battery of the right, with eleven pieces more. The fort replied with spirit. The cannon thundered all day, and from a hundred peaks and crags the astonished wilderness roared back the sound. The Indians were delighted. They wanted to point the guns; and to humor them, they were now and then allowed to do so. Others lay behind logs and fallen trees, and yelled their satisfaction when they saw the splinters fly from the wooden rampart.

Day after day the weary roar of the distant cannonade fell on the ears of Webb in his camp at Fort Edward. "I have not yet received the least reinforcement," he writes to Loudon; "this is the disagreeable situation we are at present in. The fort, by the heavy firing we hear from the lake, is still in our possession; but I fear it cannot long hold out against so warm a cannonading if I am not reinforced by a sufficient number of militia to march to their relief." The militia were coming; but it was impossible that many could reach him in less than a week. . . .

The sappers [combat engineers] had worked their way to the angle of the lake, where they were stopped by a marshy hollow, beyond which was a tract of high ground, reaching to the fort and serving as the garden of the garrison. Logs and fascines* in large quantities were thrown into the hollow, and hurdles were laid over them to form a causeway for the cannon. Then the sap [trench] was continued up the acclivity beyond, a trench was opened in the garden, and a battery begun, not two hundred and fifty yards from the fort. The Indians, in great number, crawled forward among the beans, maize, and cabbages, and lay there ensconced. On the night of the seventh, two men came out of the fort, apparently to reconnoiter, with a view to a sortie, when they were greeted by a general volley and a burst of yells which echoed among the mountains; followed by responsive whoops pealing through the darkness from the various camps and lurking-places of the savage warriors far and near.

The position of the besieged was now deplorable. More than three hundred of them had been killed and wounded; small-pox was raging in the fort; the place was a focus of infection, and the casemates [outer walls of the fort] were crowded with the sick. A sortie from the intrenched camp and another from the fort had been repulsed with loss. All their large cannon and mortars had been burst, or disabled by shot; only seven small pieces were left fit for service; and the whole of Montcalm's thirty-one cannon and fifteen mortars and howitzers† would soon open fire, while the walls were already breached, and an assault was imminent. Through the night of the eighth they fired briskly from all their remaining pieces. In the morning the officers held a council, and all agreed to surrender if honorable terms could be had. A white flag was raised, a drum was beat, and Lieutenant-Colonel Young, mounted on horseback, for a shot in the foot had disabled him from walking, went, followed by a few soldiers, to the tent of Montcalm.

It was agreed that the English troops should march out with the honors of war, and be escorted to Fort Edward by a detachment of French troops; that they should not serve for eighteen months; and that all French prisoners captured in America since the war began should be given up within three months. The stores, munitions, and artillery were to be the prize of the victors, except one field-piece, which the garrison were to retain in recognition of their brave defence.

Before signing the capitulation Montcalm called the Indian chiefs to council, and asked them to consent to the conditions, and promise to restrain their young warriors from any disorder. They approved everything and promised everything. The garrison then evacuated the fort, and marched to join their comrades in the intrenched camp, which was included

---

* Bundles of sticks used to construct a temporary fort, or bridge ditches.
† Mortars and howitzers are high trajectory artillery used to fire into a town or fort.

in the surrender. No sooner were they gone than a crowd of Indians clambered through the embrasures [small openings in the wall for guns] in search of rum and plunder. All the sick men unable to leave their beds were instantly butchered. "I was witness of this spectacle," says the missionary Roubaud; "I saw one of these barbarians come out of the casemates with a human head in his hand, from which the blood ran in streams, and which he paraded as if he had got the finest prize in the world." There was little left to plunder; and the Indians, joined by the more lawless of the Canadians, turned their attention to the intrenched camp, where all the English were now collected.

The French guard stationed there could not or would not keep out the rabble. By the advice of Montcalm the English stove their rum-barrels; but the Indians were drunk already with homicidal rage, and the glitter of their vicious eyes told of the devil within. They roamed among the tents, intrusive, insolent, their visages besmirched with war-paint; grinning like fiends as they handled, in anticipation of the knife, the long hair of cowering women, of whom, as well as of children, there were many in the camp, all crazed with fright. Since the last war the New England border population had regarded Indians with a mixture of detestation and horror. Their mysterious warfare of ambush and surprise, their midnight onslaughts, their butcheries, their burnings, and all their nameless atrocities, had been for years the theme of fireside story; and the dread they excited was deepened by the distrust and dejection of the time. . . . "The Marquis de Montcalm ran thither immediately, and used every means to restore tranquility: prayers, threats, caresses, interposition of the officers and interpreters who have some influence over these savages." "We shall be but too happy if we can prevent a massacre. Detestable position! of which nobody who has not been in it can have any idea, and which makes victory itself a sorrow to the victors. The Marquis spared no efforts to prevent the rapacity of the savages and, I must say it, of certain persons associated with them, from resulting in something worse than plunder. At last, at nine o'clock in the evening, order seemed restored. The Marquis even induced the Indians to promise that, besides the escort agreed upon in the capitulation, two chiefs for each tribe should accompany the English on their way to Fort Edward." He also ordered La Corne and the other Canadian officers attached to the Indians to see that no violence took place. He might well have done more. In view of the disorders of the afternoon, it would not have been too much if he had ordered the whole body of regular troops, whom alone he could trust for the purpose, to hold themselves ready to move to the spot in case of outbreak, and shelter their defeated foes behind a hedge of bayonets. . . .

The English in their camp had passed a troubled night, agitated by strange rumors. In the morning something like a panic seized them; for they distrusted not the Indians only, but the Canadians. In their haste to be gone they got together at daybreak, before the escort of three hundred regulars had arrived. They had their muskets, but no ammunition; and few or none of the provincials had bayonets. Early as it was, the Indians were on the alert; and, indeed, since midnight great numbers of them had been prowling about the skirts of the camp, showing, says Colonel Frye, "more than usual malice in their looks." Seventeen wounded men of his regiment lay in huts, unable to join the march. In the preceding afternoon Miles Whitworth, the regimental surgeon, had passed them over to the care of a French surgeon, according to an agreement made at the time of the surrender; but, the Frenchman being absent, the other remained with them attending to their wants. The French surgeon had caused special sentinels to be posted for their protection. These were now removed, at the moment when they were needed most; upon which, about five o'clock in the morning, the Indians entered the huts, dragged out the inmates, tomahawked and scalped them all, before the eyes of Whitworth, and in presence of La Corne and other Canadian officers, as well as of a French guard stationed within forty feet of the spot; and, declares the surgeon under oath, "none, either officer or soldier, protected the said wounded men." The opportune butchery relieved them of a troublesome burden.

A scene of plundering now began. The escort had by this time arrived, and Monro complained to the officers that the capitulation was broken; but got no other answer than advice to give up the baggage to the Indians in order to appease them. To this the English at length agreed; but it only increased the excitement of the mob. They demanded rum; and some of the soldiers, afraid to refuse gave it to them from their canteens, thus adding fuel to the flame. When, after much difficulty, the column at last got out of the camp and began to move along the road that crossed the rough plain between the intrenchment and the forest, the Indians crowded upon them, impeded their march, snatched caps, coats, and weapons from men and officers, tomahawked those that resisted, and seizing upon shrieking women and children, dragged them off or murdered them on the spot. It is said that some of the interpreters secretly fomented the disorder. Suddenly there rose the screech of the war-whoop. At this signal of butchery, which was given by Abenaki Christians from the mission of the Penobscot, a mob of savages rushed upon the New Hampshire men at the rear of the column, and killed or dragged away eighty of them. A frightful tumult ensued, when Montcalm, Lévis, Bourlamaque, and many other French officers, who had hastened from their camp on the first news of disturbance, threw themselves among the Indians, and by promises and threats tried to allay their frenzy. "Kill me, but spare the English who are under my protection," exclaimed Montcalm. He took from one of them a young officer whom the savage had seized; upon which several other Indians immediately tomahawked their prisoners, lest they too should be taken from them. . . .

The bonds of discipline seemed for the time to have been completely broken; for while Montcalm and his chief officers used every effort to restore order, even at the risk of their lives, many other officers, chiefly of the militia, failed atrociously to do their duty. How many English were killed it is impossible to tell with exactness. Roubaud says that he saw forty or fifty corpses scattered about the field. Lévis says fifty; which does not include the sick and wounded before murdered in the camp and fort. It is certain that six or seven hundred persons were carried off, stripped, and otherwise maltreated. Montcalm succeeded in recovering more than four hundred of them in the course of the day; and many of the French officers did what they could to relieve their wants by buying back from their captors the clothing that had been torn from them. Many of the fugitives had taken refuge in the fort, whither Monro himself had gone to demand protection for his followers; and here Roubaud presently found a crowd of half-frenzied women, crying in anguish for husbands and children. All the refugees and redeemed prisoners were afterwards conducted to the intrenched camp, where food and shelter were provided for them and a strong guard set for their protection until the fifteenth, when they were sent under an escort to Fort Edward. Here cannon had been fired at intervals to guide those who had fled to the woods, whence they came dropping in from day to day, half dead with famine.

On the morning after the massacre the Indians decamped in a body and set out for Montreal, carrying with them their plunder and some two hundred prisoners, who, it is said, could not be got out of their hands. The soldiers were set to the work of demolishing the English fort; and the task occupied several days. The barracks were torn down, and the huge pine-logs of the rampart thrown into a heap. The dead bodies that filled the casemates were added to the mass, and fire was set to the whole. The mighty funeral pyre blazed all night. Then, on the sixteenth, the army re-embarked. The din of ten thousand combatants, the rage, the terror, the agony, were gone; and no living thing was left but the wolves that gathered from the mountains to feast upon the dead.

ANNOTATED BIBLIOGRAPHY

Although the number of primary sources on the colonial wars is large, the documents are often difficult to read because of antiquated spellings and the lack of consistent grammatical rules. War and peace, life and death, were less segmented in the seventeenth century. Early colonial accounts accepted the reality of Indian raids on isolated settlements and the close proximity of privateers and pirates to coastal villages. Colonial journals do not separate peacetime activities from military service; both were part of everyday life in the colonies.

States have published editions of their colonial records. Some mix laws and judicial decisions with militia regulations and reports of campaigns filed by officers. Charles M. Andrews separated military accounts from other material in his *Narratives of the Insurrections, 1675–1690* (1915). Another important primary collection is *Privateering and Piracy in the Colonial Period: Illustrative Documents* (1923), edited by John Franklin Jameson. To support twentieth-century conscription, the U.S. Selective Service System collected the colonial militia laws in a two-volume series (Volume 2 has nine separate parts) entitled *Backgrounds of Selective Service* (1947), edited by Arthur Vollmer. Samuel Eliot Morison edited John Winthrop's *History of Plimouth Plantation* (1942) with a unique blend of scholarly adherence to the flavor of the original supported by modern spelling and punctuation.

No serious reader should overlook Francis Parkman's magnificent history of *France and England in North America*, eight volumes (1865–1892). *The Library of America* recently republished the entire work in two volumes (1983). An equally ambitious undertaking is Lawrence H. Gipson's *The British Empire Before the American Revolution*, fifteen volumes (1936–1970). Gipson's work surpasses Parkman's in breadth of coverage of colonial life, but his prose lacks Parkman's brilliance.

The best one-volume history of the colonial wars is Douglas E. Leach's *Arms for Empire: A Military History of the British Colonies in North America, 1607–1763* (1973). Like other volumes in the Macmillan *History of American Wars*, Leach's book examines the military in the context of American life. A shorter, but equally competent, account of early American wars can be found in Howard H. Peckham's *The Colonial Wars, 1689–1762* (1964). Readers interested in more detail on the tactics of colonial warfare should consult "Anglo-American Methods of Indian Warfare, 1676–1794" by John K. Mahon in the *Mississippi Valley Historical Review* 45 (1958).

George Washington played a critical role in the last colonial war. Two good biographies exist of young Washington. Volume 2 of Douglas Southall Freeman's *George Washington* (1950) and James Flexner's *George Washington: The Forge of Experience, 1732–1775* (1965) deal with Washington's part in the French and Indian War. Readers should also consult *The Diaries of George Washington*, four volumes, edited by John C. Fitzpatrick (1925).

THE AMERICAN REVOLUTION

The Anglo-American success in the French and Indian War had sown the seeds of colonial conflict with Britain. The war with France and Spain had made Britain aware that it would have to devise better means of governing and defending its worldwide empire. For more than 150 years, American colonials had lived with little British interference. Then, in the 1760s, they resented Britain's new demands that they help pay the cost of maintaining the empire. When the British government tried to force compliance, some colonists reacted by abusing tax collectors, freeing smugglers, and dumping tea. Britain decided to make an example of its most recalcitrant colony, Massachusetts. Parliament suspended civil government, closed Boston Harbor, and placed a regular army general over the colony as its governor.

Some Americans, calling themselves "patriots," responded by collecting arms and supplies in magazines and preparing to defend themselves by designating a portion of the militia "Minutemen." In 1775, Minutemen and British regulars fought a bloody battle outside Boston, and the new intercolonial Continental Congress, meeting in Philadelphia, created an American army. The following spring, this Continental army drove all the British troops out of Massachusetts. Although the war would drag on for another seven years, British strategy rarely rose above its limited objective of occupying major American seaports and gaining loyalist support.

Meanwhile, certain key American military leaders, especially George Washington and Nathanael Greene, eventually devised an effective counterstrategy that focused not only on winning major battles or holding particular places but also on maintaining the colonial armies at all costs.

They knew that so long as the patriot forces could survive to fight another day, the war could not be lost.

Despite such gifted leaders, the Americans were badly divided by the Revolution. A civil war soon broke out in many areas, especially in the South. The lack of wholehearted support often made soldiers' lives unnecessarily hard and this provoked soldiers to use increasingly savage tactics.

By 1778, England's traditional enemy, France, had formally joined with the colonists, and began to send fleets loaded with armies and war chests full of gold to America. The French aid had made the local rebellion part of a new world war. Because the colonies lacked a naval tradition, they had to rely on foreign aid (and the daring of a few former merchant captains) to gain any advantage over the seafaring British.

To Britain, the American Revolution became only one theater in its global fight. But to the American patriots, the war had one essential purpose—the establishment of independence. In 1781, Britain tired of the war on the American mainland and focused its attention on the far more valuable sugar colonies in the Caribbean. Two years later, England recognized the United States as an independent nation. The Western world was surprised to learn that an amateur army had succeeded in driving Britain's professional soldiers off American soil.

"The Boston Massacre" by Paul Revere (National Archives). This engraving is one of the best known pieces of American propaganda. Master engraver Paul Revere had copied a drawing by Henry Pelham which had shown disciplined and cool British soldiers firing into a group of unarmed, and apparently peaceful, citizens. The French threat to the colonies had been removed by the Peace of Paris (1763), which had ended the French and Indian War. Most Americans felt that they had no need of further "protection" by the British army. English soldiers and their officers were caught between their orders to enforce the imperial laws and the hostile contempt of some of the colonists, who frequently subjected soldiers to verbal and physical abuse. The British soldiers soon tired of their precarious position. On the night of 5 March 1770, one detachment fired into an angry mob of colonists, killing five, including Crispus Attucks, who was identified as both black and

Indian. Excessive force, however, rarely gains allies. More often it alienates moderates who had preached patience and compromise. The "Boston Massacre" forced people to choose sides. One newspaper reported that more than 10,000 people from the surrounding countryside later joined the citizens of Boston to mourn the victims on the day of the funeral.

TWO SHOTS HEARD 'ROUND THE WORLD (1775)

*H*istorians work with documents that recount what other people have experienced. But like those of eyewitnesses to an automobile accident or a crime, such accounts are at best only partially accurate. Hindsight permits historians to evaluate events more objectively than contemporaries, so history books are usually more accurate than original accounts.

The following selections provide both an American and an English account of the opening battles of the Revolutionary War at Lexington and Concord. The American report was published soon after these incidents had occurred. It aroused public ire both in England and in the colonies against British military excesses. The British account was part of the official military record, and never received the same publicity or success.

ACCOUNT BY THE PROVINCIAL CONGRESS OF MASSACHUSETTS, WATERTOWN, 26 APRIL 1775

Friends and fellow subjects—Hostilities are at length commenced in this colony by the troops under the command of general Gage, and it being of the greatest importance, that an early, true, and authentic account of the inhuman proceeding should be known to you, the congress of this colony have transmitted the same, . . .

By the clearest depositions relative to this transaction, it will appear that on the night preceding the nineteenth of April instant [this year], a body of the king's troops, under the command of colonel Smith, were secretly landed at Cambridge, with an apparent design to take or destroy the

SOURCE: H. Niles (Ed.), *Principles and Acts of the Revolution* (Baltimore, MD: W. O. Niles, 1822).

military and other stores, provided for the defence of this colony, and deposited at Concord—that some inhabitants of the colony, on the night aforesaid, whilst traveling peaceably on the road, between Boston and Concord, were seized and greatly abused by armed men, who appeared to be officers of general Gage's army; that the town of Lexington, by these means, was alarmed, and a company of the inhabitants mustered on the occasion— that the regular troops on their way to Concord, marched into the said town of Lexington, and the said company, on their approach, began to disperse—that, notwithstanding this, the regulars rushed on with great violence and first began hostilities, by firing on said Lexington company, whereby they killed eight, and wounded several others—that the regulars continued their fire, until those of said company, who were neither killed nor wounded, had made their escape—that colonel Smith, with the detachment then marched to Concord, where a number of provincials [colonists] were again fired on by the troops, two of them killed and several wounded, before the provincials fired on them, and provincials were again fired on by the troops, produced an engagement that lasted through the day, in which many of the provincials and more of the regular troops were killed and wounded.

To give a particular account of the ravages of the troops, as they retreated from Concord to Charlestown, would be very difficult, if not impracticable; let it suffice to say, that a great number of the houses on the road were plundered and rendered unfit for use, several were burnt, women in child-bed were driven by the soldiery naked into the streets, old men peaceably in their houses were shot dead, and such scenes exhibited as would disgrace the annals of the most uncivilized nation. . . .

By order,

John Warren, President

ACCOUNT OF LIEUTENANT COLONEL FRANCIS SMITH TO GOVERNOR-GENERAL GAGE

22 April 1775

SIR,—In obedience to your Excellency's commands, I marched on the evening of the 18th inst. with the corps of grenadiers* and light infantry for

---

* Technically, grenadiers are soldiers who throw grenades, but the term usually denotes the tallest and strongest, hence the finest and most feared soldiers.
SOURCE: Massachusetts Historical Society, *Proceedings* (May, 1876).

Concord, to execute your Excellency's orders with respect to destroying all ammunition, artillery, tents, &c., collected there, which was effected, having knocked off the trunnions [supports on the sides of a cannon] of three pieces of iron ordnance, some new gun-carriages, a great number of carriage-wheels burnt, a considerable quantity of flour, some gun-powder and musquet-balls, with other small articles thrown into the river. Notwithstanding we marched with the utmost expedition and secrecy, we found the country had intelligence or strong suspicion of our coming, and fired many signal guns, and rung the alarm bells repeatedly; and were informed, when at Concord, that some cannon had been taken out of the town that day, that others, with some stores, had been carried three days before, which prevented our having an opportunity of destroying so much as might have been expected at our first setting off.

I think it proper to observe, that when I had got some miles on the march from Boston, I detached six light infantry companies to march with all expedition to seize the two bridges on different roads beyond Concord. On these companies' arrival at Lexington, I understand, from the report of Major Pitcairn, who was with them, and from many officers, that they found on a green close to the road a body of the country people drawn up in military order, with arms and accoutrements [military supplies], and, as appeared after, loaded; and that they had posted some men in a dwelling and Meeting-house. Our troops advanced towards them, without any intention of injuring them, further than to inquire the reason of their being thus assembled, and, if not satisfactory, to have secured their arms; but he in confusion went off, principally to the left, only one of them fired before they went off, and three or four more jumped over a wall and fired from behind it among the soldiers; on which the troops returned it, and killed several of them. They likewise fired on the soldiers from the Meeting and dwelling houses. . . . Rather earlier than this, on the road, a countryman from behind a wall had snapped his piece at Lieutenants Adair and Sutherland, but it flashed and did not go off. After this we saw some in the woods, but marched on to Concord without anything further happening. While at Concord, we saw vast numbers assembling in many parts; at one of the bridges they marched down, with a very considerable body, on the light infantry posted there. On their coming pretty near, one of our men fired on them, which they returned; on which an action ensued, and some few were killed and wounded. In this affair, it appears that, after the bridge was quitted, they scalped and otherwise ill-treated one or two of the men who were either killed or severely wounded. . . . On our leaving Concord to return to Boston, they began to fire on us from behind the walls, ditches, trees, &c., which, as we marched, increased to a very great degree, and continued without the intermission of five minutes altogether, for, I believe, upwards of eighteen miles; so that I can't think but it must have been a preconcerted scheme in them, to attack the King's troops the first favourable opportunity that offered, otherwise, I think they could not, in so short a time as from our marching out, have raised such a numerous body, and for so great a space of ground. Notwithstanding the enemy's numbers, they did not make one gallant attempt during so long an action, though our men were very much fatiqued, but kept under cover.

I have the honor, &c.,

F. Smith, Lieutenant-Colonel 10th Foot.

BATTLE OF LONG ISLAND (1776)

Joseph P. Martin

In 1776, Britain decided to capture New York City. When British troops landed on Staten Island, George Washington recommended that the city be abandoned. The Continental Congress rejected his strategy, which was to save the army and abandon the city. Instead, Congress ordered Washington to defend New York and its magnificent harbor. Washington placed his army on Brooklyn Heights, across the East River from Manhattan. The British easily turned Washington's line, which lacked cavalry to protect its flanks, and drove the patriot army to the water's edge.

The previous year at Bunker Hill outside Boston, British officers had attempted a deadly frontal assault. This time they decided to wait. That night Washington and his army escaped. Britain had gained a vital port, but its real target, the Continental army, had escaped. Never again would British generals have the opportunity to destroy Washington's army, and as long as it existed, Britain could not claim victory in America.

In old age, men often want to leave behind a record of their lives. This is especially true of veterans, whose wartime experiences usually surpass any other event in their lives. The following memoir was written by a man who styled himself a common soldier. It provides a graphic description of the emotions shared by all men before their first taste of battle. Readers should recall that it is a universal human trait to embellish some events, and to forget others.

SOURCE: Joseph P. Martin, *A Narrative of Some of the Adventures, Dangers and Sufferings of a Revolutionary Soldier* (Hallowell, ME: Glazier, Masters & Co., 1830).

I remained in New-York two or three months, in which time several things occurred, but so trifling that I shall not mention them. When, sometime in the latter part of August, I was ordered on a fatique [work] party, we had scarcely reached the grand parade when I saw our sergeant-major directing his course up Broadway toward us in rather an unusual step for him. He soon arrived and informed us, and then the commanding officer of the party, that he had offers to take off all belonging to our regiment and march us to our quarters, as the regiment was ordered to Long-Island, the British having landed in force there. Although this was not unexpected to me, yet it gave me rather a disagreeable feeling, as I was pretty well assured I should have to sniff a little gunpowder. However I kept my cogitations to myself, went to my quarters, packed up my clothes, and got myself in readiness for the expedition as soon as possible. I then went to the top of the house where I had a full view of that part of the island; I distinctly saw the smoke of the field-artillery, but the distance and unfavorableness of the wind prevented my hearing their report, at least but faintly.

The horrors of battle there presented themselves to my mind in all their hideousness. I must come to it now, thought I—well, I will endeavor to do my duty as well as I am able and leave the event with Providence. We were soon ordered to our regimental parade, from which, as soon as the regiment was formed, we were marched off for the ferry. At the lower end of the street were placed several casks of sea-bread, made, I believe, of canel [cinnamon] and peas-meal, nearly hard enough for musket flints; the casks were unheaded and each man was allowed to take as many as he could as he marched by. As my good luck would have it, there was a momentary halt made; I improved the opportunity thus offered me, as every good soldier should upon all important occasions, to get as many of the biscuit as I possibly could. No one said any thing to me, and I filled my bosom, and took as many as I could hold in my hand, a dozen or more in all, and when we arrived at the ferry-stairs I stowed them away in my knapsack.

We quickly embarked on board of the boats. As each boat started, three cheers were given by those on board, which was returned by the numerous spectators who thronged the wharves; they all wished us good luck apparently; although it was, with most of them, perhaps nothing more than ceremony. We soon landed at Brooklyn, upon the island, marched up the ascent from the ferry to the plain.

We now began to meet the wounded men, another sight I was unacquainted with, some with broken legs and some with broken heads. The sight of these a little daunted me and made me think of home, but the sight and thought vanished together. We marched a short distance when we halted to refresh ourselves. Whether we had any other victuals besides the hard bread I do not remember, but I remember my gnawing at them; they were hard enough to break the teeth of a rat. One of the soldiers complaining of thirst to his officer, "Look at that man," said he, pointing to me; "he is not thirsty, I will warrant it." I felt a little elevated to be stiled a man. While resting here, which was not more than twenty minutes or half an hour, the Americans and British were warmly engaged within sight of us.

What were the feelings of most or all the young soldiers at this time I know not, but I know what were mine; but let mine or theirs be what they might, I saw a lieutenant who appeared to have feelings not very enviable. Whether he was actuated by fear or the canteen I cannot determine now; I thought it fear at the time, for he ran round among the men of his company, snivelling and blubbering, praying each one if he had aught against him, or if *he* had injured any one, that they would forgive him, declaring at the same time that he, from his heart, forgave them if they had offended him, and I gave him full credit for his assertion, for had he been at the gallows with a halter about his neck, he could not have shown more fear or penitence. A fine soldier you are, I thought, a fine officer, an exemplary man for young soldiers! I would have then suffered anything short of death rather than have made such an exhibition of myself. . . .

The officers of the new levies wore cockades [hat ribbons] of different colours to distinguish them from the standing forces, as they were called; the field officers wore red, the captains white, and the subaltern officers [lieutenants] green. While we were resting here our lieutenant-colonel and major (our colonel not being with us) took their cockades from their hats; being asked the reason, the lieutenant-colonel replied that he was willing to risk his life in the cause of his country, but was unwilling to stand a particular mark for the enemy to fire at. He was a fine officer and a brave soldier.

We were called upon to fall in and proceed. We had not gone far, about half a mile, when I heard one in the rear ask another where his musket was. I looked around and saw one of the soldiers stemming off without his gun, having left it where we last halted; he was inspecting his side as if undetermined whether he had it or not; he then fell out of the ranks to go in search of it. One of the company who had brought it on (wishing to see how far he would go before he missed it), gave it to him. The reader will naturally enough conclude that he was a brave soldier. Well, he was a brave fellow for all this accident, and received two severe wounds by musket balls while fearlessly fighting for his country at the battle of White Plains. . . .

We overtook a small party of the artillery here dragging a heavy twelve-pounder upon a field carriage, sinking half way to the naves in the sandy soil. They plead hard for some of us to assist them to get in their piece; our officers, however, paid no attention to their entreaties, but pressed forward towards a creek, where a large party of Americans and British were engaged. By the time we arrived, the enemy had driven our men into the creek, or rather millpond (the tide being up), where such as could swim got across; those that could not swim, and could not procure anything to buoy them up, sunk. The British, having several fieldpieces [artillery] stationed by a brick house, were pouring the canister and grape [artillery rounds with the effect of giant shotgun shells] upon the Americans like a shower of hail. They would doubtless have done them much more damage than they did but for the twelve-pounder mentioned above; the men, having gotten it within sufficient distance to reach them, and opening a fire upon them, soon obliged them to shift their quarters.

There was in this action a regiment of Maryland troops (volunteers), all young gentlemen. When they came out of the water and mud to us, looking like water rats, it was a truly pitiful sight. Many of them were killed in the pond, and more were drowned. Some of us went into the water after the fall of the tide and took out a number of corpses and a great many arms that were sunk in the pond and creek.

"Battle of Bunker Hill" (17 June 1775) by Bernard Romans (National Archives). In April 1775, British soldiers set out to destroy American arms stored at Concord. Two months later, militiamen from Massachusetts and other New England colonies responded to the English presence by seizing an unoccupied British redoubt on Bunker Hill, overlooking Charlestown, just across the bay from Boston. For reasons that are unclear today, the militiamen moved to Breed's Hill. Although the English navy controlled the seas and could easily have bagged the patriot army from the rear, three British generals conferred (which is always a bad sign), and decided to attack the colonial army head-on. Seldom have generals shown such stupid and disastrous contempt. Twice the British regulars marched toward the American line. They carried full packs and loaded muskets, but expected to drive the defenders out with their bayonets. The patriots' musket fire destroyed the British line and stacked the soldiers like cordwood. At last, the British generals called for their reserves and permitted them to discard their packs before a third attack. By then, the colonials had almost run out of ammunition. Once the British reached the parapet, the colonists abandoned their positions. This patriotic engraving, which calls the battle by its eighteenth-century name (Charlestown), shows the British line on the right marching up Breed's Hill against the American defenders. British ships fired into the American line, and British artillery on Copp's Hills lobbed red hot cannon balls to burn the abandoned buildings in Charlestown, which harbored American snipers. General John Burgoyne watched the battle from Copp's Hill (at approximately the focal point of this engraving). A week later he

described what he had seen: "And now ensued one of the greatest scenes that can be conceived; if we look to the height, Howe's corps ascending the hill in the face of entrenchments and in the face of a very disadvantageous ground, was much engaged; to the left the enemy pouring in fresh troops by thousands over the land, and in the arm of the sea our ships and floating batteries cannonading them; straight before us a large and noble town in one great blaze; the church steeples being of timber, were great pyramids of fire above the rest; behind us the church steeples and heights of our own camp, covered with spectators of the rest of our army who were not engaged; the hills round the country covered with spectators, the enemy all in anxious suspense; the roar of cannon, mortars, and musketry, the crash of churches, ships upon the stocks, and whole streets falling together in ruin to fill the ear; the storm of the redoubts with the objects above described to fill the eye, and the reflections that perhaps a defeat was the final loss to the British empire in America, to fill the mind, made the whole a picture and a complication of horror and importance beyond anything that ever came to my lot to be witness to." The British had won the battle, but it was a phyrric victory at best. They not only lost 1,054 men (compared to 440 American casualties) but also had lost momentum. The patriots' stand at "Bunker Hill," which the battle later came to be called, inspired their fellow countrymen to join their cause, placed renewed confidence in the colonial militia, and forced the British out of Boston the following spring.

VALLEY FORGE (1777–1778)

Albigence Waldo

After Washington had abandoned New York City, the British chased his army across New Jersey to Pennsylvania before both sides went into winter quarters. On the day after Christmas 1776, Washington surprised an enemy garrison at Trenton, and proved that his army still had plenty of fight left. The following summer (1777) one British army was defeated at Saratoga while Washington met another near Philadelphia. There he was defeated again, but Washington once more managed to keep his army intact. That winter, they camped at Valley Forge, where officers and men alike suffered from the harsh weather. British troops, housed in nearby Philadelphia, enjoyed the fruits of victory.

War sometimes encourages men to reflect upon fundamental values. Few have revealed their thoughts as well as Dr. Albigence Waldo, a surgeon with the Connecticut Line, the regular infantry from that state. In his diary, Dr. Waldo meditated on the meaning of the sacrifices he and the other soldiers suffered during the cold winter of 1777–1778 at Valley Forge.

December 11. At four o'clock the Whole Army were Order'd to March to Swede's Ford on the River Schuylkill, about 9 miles N.W. of Chestnut Hill, and 6 from White Marsh, our present Encampment. At sun an hour high the whole were mov'd from the lines and on their march with baggage. This Night encamped in a Semi circle nigh the ford. The enemy had march'd up the West side of Schuylkill—Potter's Brigade of Pennsylvania Militia were

SOURCE: Albigence Waldo, "Valley Forge, 1777–1778. Diary of Surgeon Albigence Waldo, of the Connecticut Line." *Pennsylvania Magazine of History and Biography 21*, 299–323 (October 1897).

already there, & had several skirmishes with them with some loss on his side and considerable on the Enemies. . . .

I am prodigious Sick and cannot get anything comfortable—what in the name of Providence am I to do with a fit of Sickness in this place where nothing appears pleasing to the Sicken'd Eye & nausiating stomach. But I doubt not Providence will find out a way for my relief. But I cannot eat Beef if I starve, for my stomach positively refuses to entertain such Company, and how can I help that?

December 12.   A Bridge of Waggons made across the Schuylkill last Night consisting of 36 waggons, with a bridge of Rails between each. Some skirmishing over the River. Militia and dragoons [mounted infantry or light cavalry] brought into camp several Prisoners. Sun Set—We were order'd to march over the River—It snows—I'm Sick—eat nothing—No Whiskey— No Forage—Lord—Lord—Lord. The army were 'till Sun Rise crossing the River—some at the Waggon Bridge & some at the Raft Bridge below. Cold & uncomfortable. . . .

December 14.   Prisoners & Deserters are continually coming in. The Army which has been surprisingly healthy hitherto, now begins to grow sickly from the continued fatiques they have suffered this Campaign. Yet they still show a spirit of Alacrity & Contentment not to be expected from so young Troops. I am Sick—discontented—and out of humour. Poor food—hard lodging—Cold Weather—fatique—Nasty Cloaths—nasty Cookery— —Vomit half my time—smoak'd out of my senses—the Devil's in't—I can't Endure it—Why are we sent here to starve and Freeze—What sweet Felicities have I left at home; a charming Wife—pretty Children—Good Beds—good food—good Cookery—all agreeable—all harmonious. Here all Confusion—smoke & Cold—hunger & filthyness—A pox on my bad luck. There comes a bowl of beef soup—full of burnt leaves and dirt, sickish enough to make a Hector spue—away with it Boys—I'll live like the Chameleon upon Air. Poh! Poh! crys Patience with me—you talk like a fool. Your being sick Covers your mind with a Melanchollic Gloom, which makes everything about you appear gloomy. See the poor Soldier, when in health—with what cheerfulness he meets his foes and encounters every hardship—if barefoot, he labours thro' the Mud & Cold with a Song in his mouth extolling War & Washington—if his food be bad, he eats it notwithstanding with seeming content—blesses God for a good Stomach and Whistles it into digestion. But harkee Patience, a moment—There comes a Soldier, his bare feet are seen thro' his worn out Shoes, his legs nearly naked from the tatter'd remains of an only pair of stockings, his Breeches not sufficient to cover his nakedness, his Shirt hanging in Strings, his hair dishevel'd, his face meagre; his whole appearance pictures a person forsaken & discouraged. He comes, and crys with an air of wretchedness & despair, I am Sick, my feet lame, my legs are sore, my body cover'd with this tormenting Itch—my Cloaths are worn out, my Constitution is broken, my former Activity is exhausted by fatique, hunger & cold, I fail fast I shall soon be no more! and all the reward I shall get will be "Poor Will is dead." People who live at home in Luxury and Ease, quietly possessing their habitations, Enjoying their Wives & Families in peace, have but a very faint Idea of the unpleasing sensations, and continual Anxiety the Man endures who is in a Camp, and is the husband and parent of an agreeable family. These same People are willing we should suffer every thing for their Benefit & advantage, and yet are the first to Condemn us for not doing more!!

December 15. Quiet. Eat Pesimmens, found myself better for their Lenient Operation. Went to a house, poor & small, but good food within—eat too much from being so long Abstemious, thro' want of palatables. Mankind are never truly thankfull for the Benefits of Life until they have experienc'd the want of them. The Man who has seen misery knows best how to enjoy good. He who is always at ease & has enough of the Blessings of common life is an Impotent Judge of the feelings of the unfortunate. . . .

December 22. Lay excessive Cold & uncomfortable last Night—my eyes are started out from their Orbits like a Rabbit's eyes, occasion'd by a great Cold & Smoke.

What have you got for Breakfast, Lads? "Fire Cake & Water, Sir." The Lord send that our Commissary of Purchases may live [on] Fire Cake & Water 'till their glutted Gutts are turned to Pasteboard.

Our Division are under Marching Orders this morning. I am ashamed to say it, but I am tempted to steal Fowls if I could find them, or even a whole Hog, for I feel as if I could eat one. But the Impoverish'd Country about us, affords but little matter to employ a Thief, or keep a Clever Fellow in good humour. But why do I talk of hunger & hard usage, when so many in the World have not even fire Cake & Water to eat. . . .

NEW JERSEY NAVAL MILITIA

Thomas Brown

W hile some men served in famous battles, others fought in smaller, but no less important, actions. The following account of naval service on board a militia gunboat off the New Jersey coast was filed by a veteran who sought a federal pension. To establish his eligibility, Thomas Brown had to describe his wartime experiences. Written military records were scarce before the twentieth century, and Revolutionary War veterans had to submit lengthy accounts of their service to qualify for pensions.

Brown's petition recalled many minor skirmishes that illustrated the partisan nature of the Revolutionary War. He described a type of militia service that was required from men who lived along the seacoast. Brown's application, and other official records, are kept in the National Archives. They are a treasure trove of historical information.

This deponent is the son of Samuel Brown, who resided at the time of the commencement of the revolutionary war, at Forked river, in the Township of Dover (according to the present bounds of the township so designated), in the County of Monmouth and State of New Jersey, aforesaid, which river empties into Barnegat bay was navigable for boats and galleys of not more than three feet draught of water, and with which there was a communication from the Atlantic Ocean through Barnegat bay and Barnegat Inlet.

That those parts of the said counties of Monmouth and Burlington either bordering upon the sea, or upon the bays and rivers, immediately communicating therewith, and which were separated from the improved and

---

SOURCE: Military Pension Record, National Archives, Group 15, records of The Veterans Administration: Microfilm Publication 804; reel no. 379.

cultivated parts of the said State by an immense tract of uncultivated and uninhabited land covered with forests and swamps, in many parts almost impassable, were taken possession of by that portion of the inhabitants of the State, who had abandoned the standards of their country, and flown to the British for refuge from their justly incensed countrymen, the forests and swamps furnishing fastnesses from which it was difficult to dislodge them. And from their retreats they made incursions into the cultivated parts of the State, committed every species of depredations, carried the plunder seized in these incursions into the woods, from which they could conveniently transport it by water on board the British vessels.

In this state of things, it became necessary for the whigs [the patriots] inhabiting those parts of the said counties to associate themselves together for self defense, and at Forked river a company of about thirty men was formed, who chose the said Samuel Brown as their Captain, Joseph Bell Lieutenant, and William Holmes ensign. This company were called minute men, their duty being understood to be to hold themselves continually in readiness, to turn out at a moments warning to resist the depredations of the tories and refugees in whatever place their services might be required.

The said Samuel Brown received a commission under the authority of the State of New Jersey to act as Captain of this Company. This deponent, being then between the age of sixteen and seventeen years entered as a volunteer in the said company and his name was the first inscribed on the list of the privates of the said company. From the time of the Organization of the said Company until the month of October of the same year, the Company was stationed at the mouth of Forked river, about one mile and an half from the residence of the said Samuel Brown, in order to watch the motions of then enemy.

During which period the said Samuel Brown commenced building a heavy gun boat, on the said river and no more than a mile from the place where the said Company was stationed. This boat was intended to be used for the annoyance of the enemy, and a part of the duty assigned to the privates of the said company while so stationed at the mouth of Forked river, was by turns, to aid in the construction of the said boat and watch over her safety. . . .

The boat . . . was called "The Civil Usage" and was launched sometime in the month of May [1777]. . . . She was armed with one long six pounder, four swivels, and two wale pieces [small cannons], and muskets for each of the crew . . . consisting of from thirty six to forty men. The duty assigned to the said gun boat after she was so armed, equipped and manned, was to guard Barnegat bay and inlet, and prevent as far as practicable, aggressions of the enemy through these sources. . . .

While the boat was repairing [in 1779] Captain Brown and this deponent paid a visit to their family leaving the rest of the Company with the boat. We arrived at home a little while before dark and slept there. The next morning as the sun was rising, we were alarmed by the dog barking fiercely, and immediately running to the window, this deponent saw a large number of men, whom he supposed to be refugees engaged in fording a creek about thirty paces from the house. This deponent immediately informed his father Captain Brown of what he saw, and he and this deponent, feeling their danger immediately left the house &, with all the speed they had, made for the woods. They were under the necessity in making their escape to pass thro' a cleared level field of thirty acres and no obstructions intervened between this field and the position occupied by the refugees but a slight fence. Captain Brown and this deponent left the house with no other garments than their shirts, and though fired at by the whole body of the refugees were so fortunate as to reach their gun boat at Toms River unhurt.

When we reached our boat, we learnt that the refugees who had attacked us were bodies of men under two refugee captains, known as Captain Davenport and Captain Roch who were supposed to have come up the bay in two boats from Clam Town, and information was brought to us that they designed to pass out to sea through Barnegat Inlet and go to New York. Their number was estimated at one hundred and sixty men. The repairs of our boat being then completed, we immediately put to sea to watch them, and if possible to attack and capture them. Capt. Andrew Brown and Capt. Joshua Studson being then at Toms River and each in command of an armed boat, and tendering us their aid.

We stationed our boats between Cranberry Inlet and Sandy hook, & there watched for the refugee boats. But we watched in vain. The refugees, a few days after their attack upon Captain Brown and this deponent, taking advantage of our absence, and having probably learnt the position of our boats, and that it would be dangerous for them to attempt to reach New York, returned to Forked River and finding Captain Brown's house without other guard than his wife and younger children, they robbed it of everything of value that it contained, forced his wife and children to leave it, and then burnt the house, barn, shop, and other out buildings to ashes. And at the same time they burnt a valuable Schooner belonging to Captain Brown of forty or fifty tons burthen, then lying in Forked river. . . .

In the fall of the year seventeen hundred and eighty, a considerable body of refugees and tories being located at Clam Town in the township of Little Egg Harbour . . . , parties of them were dispatched from thence to penetrate into & commit depredations in the cultivated parts of the Counties of Burlington and of Monmouth. By these marauding parties, Clayton Newbold, John Black, & Caleb Shreve of the County of Burlington, and John Holmes of the County of Monmouth were robbed of large quantities of silver plate, money, clothing and other articles, and of a number of negroes. The marauders took their booty to Clam town, and put the same on board a lumber sloop lying there under the controul of the refugees, to be transported to New York as soon as the navigation should open in the spring.

Captain Swain the captain of the said gun boat being in the interior of the County of Burlington at the time these robberies were committed, and by that means becoming informed of the same, conceived the idea of intercepting the booty in its passage to New York. He rejoined his crew & ordered his gun boat to Shrewsbury Inlet to watch the motions of the enemy.

Early in the spring following, in the year seventeen hundred and eighty one, we proceeded to Barnegat Inlet and on our way we fell in with and captured the Schooner containing the booty which had been taken by the refugees in the previous fall as before set forth, and had the satisfaction of restoring the same to its owners. Immediately after the capture of the Schooner we fell in with a Captain Gray from Rhode Island, commanding an American Privateer. With him we concerted the plan of dispersing the refugees established at Clam Town.

It was agreed that he should approach Clam Town from the sea through Egg Harbour Inlet and decoy them out to sea in their boats, and that we should approach the same inlet thro' the bay, keeping ourselves concealed, and in case he should succeed in decoying them out, we were to follow and support him in the engagement, placing the enemy between two fires. Captain Gray accordingly approached within sight with covered guns, putting about as soon as he perceived he was observed by the enemy affecting to fly with all the sail he could make. The ruse succeeded. The refugees pursued in their galley commanded by Captain Davenport. When they were out at sea, Captain Gray hove about & stood for them. The vessels engaged. Captain Davenport and eight or nine of his men were killed by the first broad side from the privateer, when the galley of the refugees struck and was immediately taken possession of by Captain Gray and sunk. The survivors of the galley's crew were received on board the privateer & from thence sent to the gaol [jail] of Burlington County.

After this defeat the refugees & tories broke up their establishment at Clam Town, and we returned with our gun boat to the Raritan River. In the same year we were joined by Capt. John Storey, commander of another gun boat, and in a thick fog in the fall of that year, the two gun boats, Captain Storey's & "The Civil Usage" boarded and captured the British guard galley that lay in Prince's Bay & sent her into New Brunswick. After this occurrence we continued with our boat on the same station, in service, until peace was proclaimed.

THE BONHOMME RICHARD'S DEFEAT OF THE SERAPIS (1779)

John Paul Jones

American naval hero John Paul Jones (1747–1792) renamed a failing merchantman the *Bonhomme Richard* in honor of Benjamin Franklin. ("Bonhomme Richard" was a French expression that meant, roughly, "Poor Richard," the fictitious author of Franklin's famous *Almanack*.) Jones commanded a Franco-American squadron. On 23 September 1779, off Flamborough Head on the east coast of England, he fought a British convoy protected by two 50-gun frigates. Jones replied to the British captain's premature demand that he surrender, with the words, "I have not yet begun to fight!" Unable to outsail them, Jones lashed his flagship to the British frigate *Serapis*. With the two ships tied together, muzzle-to-muzzle, an American sailor dropped a grenade onto the *Serapis*'s deck and killed many of its gunners; the British captain panicked and struck his colors.

A month later, Jones wrote the following report to Franklin, the American minister to France. Jones colorfully described the most famous American naval battle of the Revolution, and vented his anger at French Captain Pierre Landais who commanded the *Alliance*. Historians generally have accepted Jones's claim that Landais had tried to sink the *Bonhomme Richard* along with the *Serapis* to reap all the glory for himself. But other evidence, recently uncovered in letters written by Denis-Nicolas de Cottineau, captain of another frigate in Jones's squadron, reveal that Jones's vitriolic report may have been motivated by pettiness and egotism. In any

---

SOURCE: Charles W. Stewart (Ed.), *John Paul Jones Commemoration at Annapolis* (Washington, DC: U.S. Government Printing Office, 1907).

event, the naval battle off Flamborough Head had initiated a proud American naval tradition.

On the morning of that day, the 23, . . . we chaced a brigantine that appeared Laying too to Windward. About noon We Saw and chaced a large ship that appeared Coming around Flamborough Head, from the Northward, and at the same time I manned and armed one of the pilot boats to send in pursuit of the brigantine, Which now appeared to be the Vessel that I had forced ashore. Soon after this a fleet of 41 Sail appeared off Flamborough Head, bearing N.N.E.; this induced me to abandon the Single Ship Which had then anchored in Burlington Bay; I also called back the pilot boat and hoisted a Signal for a general chace. When the fleet discovered us bearing down, all the merchant ships Crowded Sail towards the Shore. The two Ships of War that protected the fleet, at the Same time Steered from the land, and made the disposition for the battle. In approaching the Enemy I crowded Every possible Sail, and made the Signal for the line of battle, to Which the *Alliance* Showed no attention. Earnest as I Was for the action, I could not reach the Commodore's Ship until Seven in the evening, being then within pistol shot. While he hailed the *B. H. R.* [*Bonhomme Richard*], we answered him by firing a Whole broadside.

The battle being thus begun, Was continued With unremitting fury. Every method was practised on both Sides to gain an advantage, and rake Each other; and I must Confess that the Enemie's Ship being much more manageable than the *B. H. R.*, gained thereby several times an advantageous situation, in spite of my best endeavors to prevent it. As I had to deal with an Enemy of *greatly Superior force,* I was under the necessity of Closing with him, to prevent the advantage Which he had over me in point of manoeuvre. It was my intention to lay the *B. H. R.* athwart the enemie's bow, but as that operation required great dexterity in the management of both Sails and helm, and Some of our braces being Shot away, it did not exactly succeed to my Wishes, the Enemie's bowsprit [a spar off the ship's bow] however, came over the *B. H. R.*'s bow, so that the Ships lay Square along side of each other, the yards being all entangled, and the cannon of Each Ship touching the opponent's Side. When this position took place it Was 8 o'clock [P.M.], previous to which the *B. H. R.* had received sundry eighteen pounds shot below the water, and Leaked Very much. My battery of 12 pounders, on Which I had placed my chief dependence, being commanded by Lieut. Deal [Dale] and Col. Weibert, and manned principally with American seamen, and French Volunteers, Were entirely silenced and abandoned. As to the six old eighteen pounders that formed the Battery of the Lower gun-deck, they did no Service Whatever: two out of three of them burst at the first fire, and killed almost all the men Who Were stationed to manage them. Before this time too, Col. de Chamillard, Who Commanded a party of 20 soldiers on the poop [deck at the ship's stern] had abandoned that Station, after having lost some of his men. I had now only two pieces of Cannon, nine pounders, on the quarter deck that Were not silenced, and not one of the heavyer Cannon Was fired during the rest of the action. The purser, Mr. Mease, Who Commanded the guns on the quarter deck, being dangerously Wounded in the head, I was obliged to fill his place, and With great difficulty rallied a few men, and Shifted over one of the Lee quarter-deck guns, So that We afterward played three pieces of 9 pounders upon the Enemy. The tops alone Seconded the fire of this little battery, and held out bravely during the Whole of the action; Especially the main top, Where Lieut. Stack commanded. I directed the fire of one of the three Cannon against the mainmast, With double-headed Shot, While the other two Were exceedingly Well Served With Grape and Canister Shot to Silence the Enemie's musquetry, and clear her decks, Which Was at last Effected. The Enemy Were, as i have Since understood, on the instant of Calling for quarters, When the Cowardice or treachery of three of my under officers induced them to Call to the Enemy. The English Commodore asked me if I demanded quarters, and I having answered him in the most determined negative, they renewed the battle with Double fury; they Were unable to Stand the deck, but the fire of their Cannon, especially the lower battery, Which Was Entirely formed of 18 pounders, Was incessant, both Ships Were Set on fire in Various places, and the Scene was dreadful beyond the reach of Language. To account for the timidity of my three under officers, I mean the gunner. the carpenter, and the master-at-arms, I must observe that the two first Were Slightly Wounded, and as the Ship had received Various Shots under Water, and one of the pumps being Shot away, the Carpenter expressed his fear that she Should Sink, and the other two concluded that She Was Sinking; Which occasioned the gunner to run aft on the poop without my Knowledge, to Strike the Colours. Fortunately for me, a Cannon ball had done that before, by carrying away the ensign staff: he was therefore reduced to the necessity of Sinking, as he Supposed, or of Calling for quarter, and he preferred the Latter.

All this time the B. H. R. had sustained the action alone, and the Enemy, though much Superior in force, Would have been Very glad to have got clear, as appears by their own acknowledgments, and by their having let go an anchor the instant that I laid them on board, by Which means they Would have escaped had I not made them Well fast to the B. H. R.

At last, at half past 9 o'clock, the *Alliance* appeared, and I now thought the battle was at an End; but, to my utter astonishment, he discharged a broadside full into the stern of the B. H. R. We called to him for God's Sake to forbear firing into the B. H. R.; yet he passed along the off Side of the Ship and continued firing. There was no possibility of his mistaking the Enemie's Ship for the B. H. R., there being the most essential difference in their appearance and Construction; besides, it Was then full moon Light, and the Sides of the B. H. R. Were all black, while the Sides of the prizes Were yellow. Yet, for the greater Security, I Shewed the Signal of our reconnaissance, by putting out three Lanthorns [lanterns], one at the head, (Bow,) another at the Stern, (Quarter,) and the third in the middle, in a horizontal line. Every tongue Cried that he Was firing into the Wrong Ship, but nothing availed; he passed round, firing into the B. H. R.'s head, stern, and broadside, and by one of his Vollies Killed several of my best men, and mortally wounded a good officer on the forecastle. My Situation Was really deplorable. The B. H. R. received various Shot under Water from the *Alliance;* the Leack gained on the pump, and the fire increased much on board both Ships. Some officers persuaded me to strike, of Whose Courage and good sense I entertain an high opinion. My treacherous master-at-arms let Loose all my prisoners without my Knowledge, and my prospect became gloomy indeed. I would not, however, give up the point. The Enemie's main-mast begain to shake, their firing decreased, ours Rather increased, and the British colours Were Struck at half an hour past 10 o'clock.

This prize proved to be the British Ship of War the *Serapis,* a New Ship of 44 guns, built on their most approved Construction, With two compleat batteries, one of them of 18 pounders, and commanded by the brave Commodore Richard Pearson. I had yet two enemies to encounter far more formidable than the britons; I mean fire and Water. The *Serapis* Was attacked only by the first, but the B. H. R. Was assailed by both: there Was five feet Water in the hould, and Tho it Was moderate from the Explosion of so much gunpowder, yet the three pumps that remained Could With difficulty only Keep the Water from gaining. The fire broke out in Various parts of the Ship, in spite of all the Water that could be thrown to quench it, and at length broke out as low as the powder magazine, and Within a few inches of the powder. In that dilemma, I took out the powder upon the deck, ready to be thrown overboard at the Last Extremity, and it was 10 o'clock the next day, the 24, before the fire Was entirely Extinguished. With respect to the situation of the B. H. R., the rudder Was Cut entirely off, the stern frame, and the transoms Were almost Entirely Cut away, the timbers by the lower Deck especially, from the mainmast to the Stern, being greatly decayed with age, Were mangled beyond my power of description, and a person must have been an Eye-Witness to form a just idea of the tremendous scene of Carnage, Wreck, and ruin, that Every Where appeared. Humanity Cannot but recoil from the prospect of Such finished horror, and Lament that War Should produce Such fatal consequences. . . .

It Was impossible to prevent the good old Ship from Sinking. They did not abandon her till after 9 o'clock: the Water Was then up to the Lower deck; and a little after ten, I saw With inexpressible grief the last glimpse of the *B. H. R.* . . .

HOSPITALS AND PRISONS

Revolutionary War armies were composed of three types of soldiers: militiamen participating in a single battle or campaign, volunteers serving for a year or more, and "continentals" who had joined the American regular army. The records that survive indicate that 4,435 Americans died in the Revolutionary War, and another 6,188 suffered nonfatal wounds. Thousands of other soldiers either had their wounds treated locally, or their remains were buried quickly and forgotten. They were never included in the official statistics.

Many veterans contend that the soldiers who died on the battlefield, especially before modern antiseptics and anesthesia, were the lucky ones. Nowhere is human suffering more apparent than in military hospitals and prisons. Men wounded in body or mind are condemned to suffer every day for the rest of their lives, and the American government has not been overly generous in rewarding its wounded veterans. Until the twentieth century, postwar medical care has been minimal, and frequently the government has denied any responsibility to help veterans overcome some service-related problems. The Vietnam War's "Agent Orange" casualties are only the latest example. When a war has ended, most people only want to remember the victories and forget the defeats. Veterans with unhealed wounds are awkward reminders of the high price of military glory.

HOSPITALS

Dr. James Thacher

October 24th, 1777. This hospital is now crowded with officers and soldiers from the field of battle; those belonging to the British and Hessian

SOURCE: James Thacher, M.D., *A Military Journal During the American Revolutionary War, from 1775–1783; describing interesting events and transactions of this period, with numerous historical facts and anecdotes, from the original manuscript, to which is added, an appendix containing biographical sketches of several general officers.* 2nd ed. (Boston: Cottons & Barnard, 1827).

troops are accommodated in the same hospital with our own men, and receive equal care and attention. The foreigners are under the care and management of their own surgeons. I have been present at some of their capital operations, and remarked that the English surgeons perform with skill and dexterity, but the Germans, with a few exceptions, do no credit to their profession; some of them are the most uncouth and clumsy operators I ever witnessed, and appear to be destitute of all sympathy and tenderness towards the suffering patient. Not less than one thousand wounded and sick are now in this city [Saratoga]; the Dutch church and several private houses are occupied as hospitals. We have about thirty surgeons and mates; and all are constantly employed. I am obliged to devote the whole of my time, from eight o'clock in the morning to a late hour in the evening, to the care of our patients.

Here is a fine field for professional improvement. Amputating limbs, trepanning fractured skulls, and dressing the most formidable wounds, have familiarized my mind to scenes of woe. A military hospital is peculiarly calculated to afford example for profitable contemplation, and to interest our sympathy and commiseration. If I turn from beholding mutilated bodies, mangled limbs, and bleeding, incurable wounds, a spectacle no less revolting is presented, of miserable objects languishing under afflicting diseases of every description—here, are those in a mournful state of despair, exhibiting the awful harbingers of approaching dissolution—there, are those with emaciated bodies and ghastly visage, who begin to triumph over grim disease and just lift their feeble heads from the pillow of sorrow. . . .

It is my lot to have twenty wounded men committed to my care by Dr. Potts, our surgeon-general; one of whom, a young man, received a musket-ball through his cheeks, cutting its way through the teeth on each side and the substance of the tongue; his sufferings have been great, but he now begins to articulate tolerably well. Another had the whole side of his face torn off by a cannon-ball, laying his mouth and throat open to view. A brave soldier received a musket-ball in his forehead; observing that it did not penetrate deep, it was imagined that the ball rebounded and fell out; but after several days, on examination, I detected the ball lying flat on the bone, and spread under the skin, which I removed. No one can doubt that he received his wound while facing the enemy, and it is fortunate for the brave fellow that his skull proved too thick for the ball to penetrate. But in another instance, a soldier's wound was not so honorable; he received a ball in the bottom of his foot, which could not have happened unless when in the act of running from the enemy. This poor fellow had been held in derision by his comrades, and is made a subject of their wit for having the mark of a coward.

PRISONS

Thomas Dring

The first night on board. We had now reached the accommodation-ladder, which led to the gangway on the larboard [port] side of the *Jersey*, and my station in the boat, as she hauled alongside, was exactly opposite to one of the air-ports in the side of the ship. From this aperture proceeded a strong current of foul vapor, of a kind to which I had been before accustomed while confined on board the *Good Hope;* the peculiarly disgusting smell of which I then recollected, after a lapse of three years. This was, however, far more foul and loathsome than anything which I had ever met with on board that ship; and it produced a sensation of nausea far beyond my powers of description.

Here, while waiting for orders to ascend on board, we were addressed by some of the prisoners, from the air-ports. We could not, however, discern their features, as it had now become so dark that we could not distinctly see any object in the interior of the ship. After some questions whence we came and respecting the manner of our capture, one of the prisoners said to me that it was "a lamentable thing to see so many young men in full strength, with the flush of health upon their countenances, about to enter that infernal place of abode." He then added in a tone and manner but little fitted to afford us much consolation: "Death has no relish for such skeleton carcasses as we are, but he will now have a feast upon you fresh-comers."

After lanterns had been lighted on board, for our examination, we ascended the accommodation-ladder to the upper deck, and passed through the barricade door, where we were examined and our bags of clothes inspected. These we were permitted to retain, provided they contained no money or weapons of any kind.

After each man had given his name and the capacity in which he had served on board the vessel in which he was captured, and the same had been duly registered, we were directed to pass through the other barricade door, on the starboard side, down the ladder leading to the main hatchway. I was detained but a short time with the examination, and was permitted to take my bag of clothes with me below; and passing down the hatchway, which was still open, through a guard of soldiers, I found myself among the wretched and disgusting multitude, a prisoner on board the *Jersey*.

SOURCE: Captain Thomas Dring, *Recollections of the Jersey Prison-Ship; from the Original Manuscripts,* rewritten by Albert Greene; edited by Henry Dawson (Morrisania, NY: Alvord, 1865).

The gratings were soon after placed over the hatchways and fastened down for the night; and I seated myself on the deck, holding my bag with a firm grasp, fearful of losing it among the crowd. I had now ample time to reflect on the horrors of the scene, and to consider the prospect before me. It was impossible to find out one of my former shipmates in the darkness; and I had, of course, no one with whom to speak during the long hours of that dreadful night—surrounded by I knew not whom, except that they were beings as wretched as myself; with dismal sounds meeting my ears from every direction; a nauseous and putrid atmosphere filling my lungs at every breath; and a stiffling and suffocating heat, which almost deprived me of sense, and even of life. . . .

The thought of sleep did not enter my mind. At length, discovering a glimmering of light through the iron gratings of one of the air-ports, I felt that it would indeed be a luxury if I could but obtain a situation near that place, in order to gain one breath of the exterior air. Clenching my hand firmly around my bag, which I dared not leave, I began to advance towards the side of the ship, but was soon greeted with the curses and imprecations of those who were lying on the deck, and whom I had disturbed in attempting to pass over them. I, however, persevered and at length arrived near the desired spot, but found it already occupied, and no persuasion would induce a single individual to relinquish his place for a moment.

Thus I passed the first dreadful night, waiting with sorrowful forebodings for the coming day. The dawn at length appeared, but came only to present new scenes of wretchedness, disease and woe. I found myself surrounded by a crowd of strange and unknown forms, with the lines of death and famine upon their faces. My former shipmates were all lost and mingled among the multitude, and it was not until we were permitted to ascend the deck, at eight o'clock, that I could discern a single individual whom I had ever seen before. Pale and meager, the throng came upon deck to view, for a few moments, the morning sun, and then to descend again, to pass another day of misery and wretchedness.

The first day. After passing the weary and tedious night, to whose accumulated horrors I have but slightly alluded, I was permitted to ascend to the upper deck, where other objects, even more disgusting and loathsome, met my view. I found myself surrounded by a motley crew of wretches, with tattered garments and pallid visages, who had hurried from below for the luxury of a little fresh air. Among them I saw one ruddy and healthful countenance, and recognized the features of one of my late fellow-prisoners on board the *Belisarius*. But how different did he appear from the group around him, who had here been doomed to combat with disease and death! Men who, shrunken and decayed as they stood around him, had been but a short time before as strong, as healthful, and as vigorous as himself—men who had breathed the pure breezes of the ocean, or danced lightly in the flower-scented air of the meadow and the hill, and had from thence been hurried into the pent-up air of a crowded prison ship, pregnant with putrid fever, foul with deadly contagion; here to linger out the tedious and weary day, the disturbed and anxious night; to count over the days and weeks and months of a wearying and degrading captivity, unvaried but by new scenes of painful suffering, and new inflictions of remorseless cruelty—their brightest hope and their daily prayer, that death would not long delay to release them from their torments.

In the wretched groups around me, I saw but too faithful a picture of our own almost certain fate; and found that all which we had been taught to fear of this terrible place of abode was more than realized.

During the night, in addition to my other sufferings, I had been tormented with what I supposed to be vermin; and on coming upon deck, I found that a black silk handkerchief, which I wore around my neck, was completely spotted with them. Although this had often been mentioned as one of the miseries of the place, yet, as I had never before been in a situation to witness anything of the kind, the sight made me shudder; as I knew, at once, that so long as I should remain on board, these loathsome creatures would be my constant companions and unceasing tormentors.

The next disgusting object which met my sight was a man suffering with the smallpox; and in a few minutes I found myself surrounded by many others laboring under the same disease, in every stage of its progress.

As I have never had the smallpox, it became necessary that I should be inoculated; and there being no proper person on board to perform the operation, I concluded to act as my own physician. On looking about me, I soon found a man in the proper stage of the disease, and desired him to favor me with some of the matter for that purpose. He readily complied, observing that it was a necessary precaution on my part, and that my situation was an excellent one in regard to *diet*, as I might depend upon finding that *extremely moderate*. The only instrument which I could procure, for the purpose of inoculation, was a common pin. With this, having scarified the skin of my hand, between the thumb and forefinger, I applied the matter and bound up my hand. The next morning I found that the wound had begun to fester; a sure symptom that the application had taken effect.

Many of my former shipmates took the same precaution and were inoculated during the day. In my case the disorder came on but lightly, and its progress was favorable; and without the least medical advice or attention, by the blessing of Divine Providence, I soon recovered. . . .

PARTISAN WARFARE
Moses Hall

The Revolutionary War in the Southern colonies pitted neighbor against neighbor. Guerrilla tactics and partisan raids were conducted by both loyalists and patriots. The presence of British regulars exacerbated the ill feelings. At Waxhaws, South Carolina (29 May 1780), Colonel Banastre Tarleton permitted his Tory legion to slaughter a contingent of 400 Virginians commanded by Colonel Abraham Burford, who had asked for the customary "quarter" that professional commanders gave defeated enemies.

That same year, Nathanael Greene took command of the Southern department. He embraced a strategy of partisan warfare, comparing his army's movements to a crab "that could run either way." By then the British were tied to a strategy of place. They could not hope to win against Greene's strategy.

The following account of the Battle of Haw River (23 February 1781) is a frightening story about civil war in the South. Loyalists, some 400 strong under Colonel John Pyle, were defeated and slaughtered by a patriot force commanded by Major Joseph Dixon and General "Light Horse" Harry Lee. The atrocities that Moses Hall describes in this document are found in all wars, but are most common in civil wars over clashing ideologies.

To the best of his recollections it was in the year 1779 or 1780, he thinks in the fall season of the year. Then living in said County of Rowan in the said State of North Carolina, he entered the service in the militia of said State in company of mounted men or mounted infantry commanded by Hugh Hall. . . .

SOURCE: Military Pension Record, National Archives, Group 15, records of The Veterans Administration: Microfilm Publication 804; reel no. 1164.

They, this applicant & said company, marched in an expedition to and through the counties of Wilkes and Surry in said State against the Tories. They [the Tories] dispersed before we reached their resorting places. We turned and without going home marched down by Moravian Town or Salem through Guilford County, Hawfields etc in pursuit of Cornwallis. We were marched in circuitous routes around and about Hillsborough and that part of the State. A little after a skirmish on the Alimance and not far from Haw River we were joined by Colonel Lee & his Light Horse [cavalry]. I was on picket guard at the time. Our said Company belonged to and was joined to a higher [one, under] their captain's command. They were (our said company) commanded by Major Joseph Dixon. . . .

When I ordered those in front of Colonel Lee's troops to halt and give the countersign they were unable to do so and I proposed to Colonel Lee not being certain who they were whether friends or foes that I would send my comrade who was standing guard next to me and one of his men into Major Dixon whilst the Colonel Lee should stand with me which was done. During this time perhaps half an hour or more I had the satisfaction of an intimate and familiar conversation with Colonel Lee. He was one of the finest looking men and best riders on horseback.

Shortly after this, and during my said . . . (this) tour, a body of Tories had raised as was the information with the view of reinforcing Colonel Tarleton. Our troops and this body of Tories and Colonel Tarleton all being in the same neighborhood, our troops on the march met said body of Tories at a place called the Race Paths. [They] mistaking our troops for Tarleton's, Colonel Lee and officers kept up the deception and Colonel Lee and his Light Horse marching in one column or line, and Major or Colonel Dixon's command in another, some interval apart. The Tories passed into this interval between our lines, or perhaps which is the fact, the Tories having halted our lines passed one on each side of them, whilst marching along to cover them so as to place them between our said lines. They frequently uttered salutations of a friendly kind believing us to be British.

Colonel Lee knew what he was about and so did Major Dixon. But I recollect that (our) my Captain Hall, perceiving they were Tories and thinking that Colonel Lee did not know it, & was imposed upon by their cries of friendship & misunderstood them to be our friends instead of the British, he called to Colonel Lee across the Tories' line and told him "Colonel Lee they are every blood of them Tories." Colonel Lee gave him a sign to proceed on with the execution of the command which was to march on untill a different command was given.

In a few minutes or less time, and at the instant they, the Tories, were completely covered by our lines upon both flanks, on front and rear, as the case may have been. The bugle sounded to attack and the slaughter began.

The Tories crying out "Your own men, your own men, as good subjects of his Majesty as in America."

It was said that upwards of two hundreds of these Tories were slain on the ground. They were I think headed by a Colonel Pile [Pyle] or Piles. Tarleton at this time was in a few miles of us and . . . in pursuing him next morning we found he had encamped in four or five miles of the said Race Paths (where we met the Tories under Colonel Piles) the night after that affair.

The evening after our battle with the Tories we having a considerable number of prisoners I recollect a scene which made a lasting impression upon my mind. I was invited by some of my comrades to go and see some of the prisoners. We went to where six were standing together. Some discussion taking place, I heard some of our men cry out "Remember Buford," and the prisoners were immediately hewed to pieces with broadswords.

At first I bore the scene without any emotion, but upon a moments reflection, I felt such horror as I never did before nor have since, and, returning to my quarters and throwing myself upon my blanket I contemplated the cruelties of war untill overcome and unmanned by a distressing gloom from which I was not relieved untill commencing our march next morning before day by moon light. I came to Tarleton's camp which he had just abandoned leaving lovely rail fires. Being on the left of the road as we marched along I discovered lying upon the ground something with appearance of a man. Upon approaching him he proved to be a youth about sixteen who having come out to view the British through curiosity for fear he might give information to our troops they had run him through with a bayonet and left him for dead, though able to speak, he was mortally wounded. The sight of this unoffending boy, butchered rather than be encumbered in the least on the march, I assume, relieved me of my distressful feelings for the slaughter of the Tories and I desired nothing so much as the opportunity of participating in their destruction.

Yorktown (Library of Congress). This commemorative map was a gift to the Marquis de Lafayette, probably at the time of his triumphant visit to the United States in 1824. Compare this map with those shown earlier in this anthology (St. Augustine and Fort Ticonderoga). Here, north is clearly marked by the fleur-de-lis above the Y in "York River," and a scale (in yards), at the lower right, gives approximate distances. Except for the ships, a few buildings, and a couple of ranks of men, symbols have replaced miniatures to depict positions. The original also used colors to add interest and distinguish the British and American lines. Roads and trails are carefully drawn through woods and fields. Still lacking are symbols for elevation that would permit a user to determine whether the land was flat, hilly, or mountainous.

YORKTOWN (1781)

Dr. James Thacher

After France officially entered the war in 1778, it became possible for Washington to consider engaging British forces in major battles. The arrival of French soldiers and ships permitted Washington to plan a combined Franco-American campaign to gain a dramatic victory to end the war quickly. His chance came in the fall of 1781 when Lord Cornwallis's army of about 7,000 men was trapped on a peninsula in Virginia. A French naval squadron had stopped the British fleet from sailing up the Chesapeake and into the York River to rescue Cornwallis. Meanwhile, the Franco-American army mounted a formal siege of Yorktown, where the British army was encamped.

Dr. James Thacher, the physician whose Saratoga hospital journal we have already read, continued his entries to the end of the war. Dr. Thacher's journal permits us to follow the story of the siege at Yorktown and the British surrender.

From the 10th to the 15th [of October], a tremendous and incessant firing from the American and French batteries is kept up, and the enemy return the fire, but with little effect. A red hot shell from the French battery set fire to the Charon, a British 44 gun ship, and two or three smaller vessels at anchor in the river, which were consumed in the night. From the bank of the river, I had a fine view of this splendid conflagration. The ships were enwrapped in a torrent of fire, which spreading with vivid brightness among the combustible rigging, and running with amazing rapidity to the tops of

---

SOURCE: James Thacher, M.D., A Military Journal During the American Revolutionary War, 2nd ed. (Boston: Cottons & Barnard, 1827).

the several masts, while all around was thunder and lightning from our numerous cannon and mortars, and in the darkness of night, presented one of the most sublime and magnificent spectacles which can be imagined. Some of our shells, overreaching the town, are seen to fall into the river, and bursting, throw up columns of water like the spouting of the monsters of the deep. We have now made further approaches to the town, by throwing up a second parallel line, and batteries within about three hundred yards; this was effected in the night, and at daylight the enemy were roused to the greatest exertions, the engines of war have raged with redoubled fury and destruction on both sides, no cessation day or night. The French had two officers wounded, and fifteen men killed or wounded, and among the Americans, two or three were wounded. I assisted in amputating a man's thigh. The siege is daily becoming more and more formidable and alarming, and his Lordship must view his situation as extremely critical, if not desperate.

Being in the trenches every other night and day, I have a fine opportunity of witnessing the sublime and stupendous scene which is continually exhibiting. The bombshells from the besiegers and the besieged are incessantly crossing each others' path in the air. They are clearly visible in the form of a black ball in the day, but in the night, they appear like fiery meteors with blazing tails, most beautifully brilliant, ascending majestically from the mortar to a certain altitude, and gradually descending to the spot where they are destined to execute their work of destruction. It is astonishing with what accuracy an experienced gunner will make his calculations, that a shell shall fall within a few feet of a given point, and burst at the precise time, though at a great distance. When a shell falls, it whirls round, burrows, and excavates the earth to a considerable extent, and bursting, makes dreadful havoc around. I have more than once witnessed fragments of the mangled bodies and limbs of the British soldiers thrown into the air by the bursting of our shells, and by one from the enemy, Captain White, of the seventh Massachusetts regiment, and one soldier were killed, and another wounded near where I was standing. About twelve or fourteen men have been killed or wounded within twenty-four hours; I attended at the hospital, amputated a man's arm, and assisted in dressing a number of wounds. . . .

19th.—This is to us a most glorious day, but to the English, one of bitter chagrin and disappointment. Preparations are now making to receive as captives, that vindictive, haughty commander, and that victorious army, who by their robberies and murders have so long been a scourge to our brethren of the southern states. Being on horseback, I anticipate a full share of satisfaction in viewing the various movements in the interesting scene.

The stipulated terms of capitulation are similar to those granted to

General Lincoln at Charleston the last year. The captive troops are to march out with shouldered arms, colors cased, and drums beating a British or German march, and to ground their arms at a place assigned for the purpose. The officers are allowed their side arms and private property, and the generals and such officers as desire it, are to go on parole to England or New York. The marines and seamen of the king's ships are prisoners of war to the navy of France, and the land forces to the United States. All military and artillery stores to be delivered up unimpaired. The royal prisoners to be sent into the interior of Virginia, Maryland and Pennsylvania, in regiments, to have rations allowed them equal to the American soldiers, and to have their officers near them. Lord Cornwallis to man and despatch the Bonetta sloop of war with despatches to Sir Henry Clinton at New York without being searched, the vessel to be returned and the hands accounted for.

At about twelve o'clock, the combined army was arranged and drawn up in two lines extending more than a mile in length. The Americans were drawn up in a line on the right side of the road, and the French occupied the left. At the head of the former the great American commander, mounted on his noble courser, took his station, attended by his aides. At the head of the latter was posted the excellent Count Rochambeau and his suite. The French troops, in complete uniform, displayed a martial and noble appearance, their band of music, of which the timbrel formed a part, is a delightful novelty, and produced while marching to the ground, a most enchanting effect. The Americans though not all in uniform nor their dress so neat, yet exhibited an erect soldierly air, and every countenance beamed with satisfaction and joy. The concourse of spectators from the country was prodigious, in point of numbers probably equal to the military, but universal silence and order prevailed.

It was about two o'clock when the captive army advanced through the line formed for their reception. Every eye was prepared to gaze upon Lord Cornwallis, the object of peculiar interest and solicitude; but he disappointed our anxious expectations; pretending indisposition, he made General O'Harra his substitute as the leader of his army. This officer was followed by the conquered troops in a slow and solemn step, with shouldered arms, colors cased and drums beating a British march. Having arrived at the head of the line, General O'Harra, elegantly mounted, advanced to his Excellency the Commander in Chief [Washington], taking off his hat, and apologized for the non-appearance of Earl Cornwallis. With his usual dignity and politeness His Excellency pointed to Major General Lincoln for directions, by whom the British army was conducted into a spacious field, where it was intended they should ground their arms.

The royal troops, while marching through the line formed by the allied army, exhibited a decent and neat appearance, as respects arms and clothing, for their commander opened his store and directed every soldier to be furnished with a new suit complete, prior to the capitulation. But in their line of march we remarked a disorderly and unsoldierly conduct, their step was irregular and their ranks frequently broken. But it was in the field when they came to the last act of the drama, that the spirit and pride of the British soldier was put to the severest test, here their mortification could not be concealed. Some of the platoon officers appeared to be exceedingly chagrined when giving the word "*ground arms,*" and I am a witness that they performed this duty in a very unofficerlike manner, and that many of the soldiers manifested a *sullen temper,* throwing their arms on the pile with violence, as if determined to render them useless. This irregularity, however, was checked by the authority of General Lincoln. After having grounded their arms and divested themselves of their accoutrements, the captive troops were conducted back to Yorktown and guarded by our troops till they could be removed to the place of their destination. The British troops that were stationed at Gloucester surrendered at the same time, and in the same manner to the command of the French general de Choise.

ANNOTATED BIBLIOGRAPHY

The American Revolution produced the first body of military memoirs and collections. Unlike the colonial wars, the Revolution marked a historical watershed. It would change the future of humankind. The people who participated in it wanted to leave a record. Although most Americans were unaffected by the war, all recognized its significance.

One of the best collections of documents from an American war is *The Spirit of '76: The Story of the American Revolution as Told by Participants*, two volumes, edited by Henry Steele Commager and Robert B. Morris (1958). Another collection of primary sources is *The Revolution Remembered, Eyewitness Accounts of the War for Independence*, edited by John C. Dann (1980). Dann relies on pension records in the National Archives for his sources. Additional accounts of wartime experiences are collected in *A Salute to Courage: The American Revolution as Seen Through Wartime Writings of the Continental Army and Navy*, edited by Dennis P. Ryan et al. (1979).

The best military history of the Revolution is Don Higginbotham's *The War of American Independence: Military Attitudes, Policies, and Practices* (1971), which goes far beyond the battlefield, examining the social, economic, and diplomatic ramifications. John Shy's *Toward Lexington: The Role of the British Army in the Coming of the American Revolution* (1965) offers important ideas on how British military policy influenced American life. In addition, there are five reliable and sprightly accounts of the war: Willard Wallace's *Appeal to Arms* (1951); Lynn Montross's *Rag, Tag, and Bobtail: The Story of the Continental Army* (1952); Christopher Ward's *The War of the Revolution* (1952); George F. Scheer's and Hugh F. Rankin's *Rebels and Redcoats* (1957); and Howard Peckham's *The War for Independence: A Military History* (1958). An account of the war from the British perspective can be found in Piers Mackesy's *The War for America, 1775–1783* (1964). A short summary of the Revolution with excellent, uncluttered battle maps is in *A Battlefield Atlas of the American Revolution* (1986) by Craig L. Symonds, with maps by William J. Clipson.

The most complete naval account of the Revolutionary War is Gardner W. Allen's *The Naval History of the American Revolution*, two volumes (1913). William W. Fowler's *Rebels Under Sail* (1976) is a readable and accurate modern history. One of the best biographies on the war is Samuel Eliot Morison's *John Paul Jones: A Sailor's Biography* (1958). Jack Coggins has written and delightfully illustrated *Ships and Seamen of the American Revolution: Vessels, Crews, Weapons, Gear, Naval Tactics, and Actions of the War for Independence* (1969).

In addition to the biographies of Washington mentioned earlier, students should consult later volumes of his life by the same authors, and Dave R. Palmer's *The Way of the Fox: American Strategy in the War for America* (1975). Palmer is the foremost modern defender of Washington's strategy in the war. Another particularly fine biography is Theodore

Thayer's *Nathanael Green: Strategist of the Revolution* (1960), who contends that Green's southern strategy is among the most creative ever conceived.

For many the best approach to American history is fiction. There are several fine historical novels dealing with the war. Several were written by Kenneth Roberts in the 1930s. Although his work is both dramatic and accurate, he writes from an unabashedly patriotic stance. Despite this shortcoming, *Arundel* (1930) and *Rable in Arms* (1933), to name only two, are worth reading. A fascinating story about a British regular in the American Revolution was spun by Robert Graves in *Sergeant Lamb's America* (1940), which offers a fresh look at the common soldier's life.

THE EARLY REPUBLIC

The revolution was a success, but, at the same time, it had revealed some fundamental problems. The wartime national government could not raise enough money to finance the war, and so went heavily into debt. During the two years between Yorktown and the final peace settlement, some soldiers threatened a mutiny if not paid, and officers talked of forcing Congress to meet their demands. George Washington quelled these threats and worked for a stronger national government. Personally, he had sacrificed much to gain independence and did not want a government too weak to protect itself.

The new Constitution of 1787 was ratified by representatives of the people of the United States, meeting in state conventions (representatives, at least, of the white males who were qualified to vote). It had created a national government with independent powers to tax and control commerce. This stronger frame was accepted just in time to meet the threat of renewed European war. England and France were fighting again, and both demanded American support.

The new U.S. administrations not only had to devise military and diplomatic strategies to deal with the European war but also they had to protect overseas commerce and settlers on the frontier. Few American politicians were opposed to protecting the frontiers, but there was widespread disagreement over foreign policy. The Federalists, led by Alexander Hamilton and John Adams, favored a strong military and naval program to protect trade and discourage any conceivable enemy from invading the United States. The Republicans, the party of Thomas Jefferson and James Madison, argued that distance alone provided adequate protection from foreign enemies and that the militia would be able to deal with all domestic threats.

However, as the world's richest neutral nation, the United States could not stay out of European problems. The French and British navies interfered with American commerce, and both refused to negotiate trade disputes or to agree on what exactly were the trading rights of a neutral nation during wartime. By 1815, the United States was forced to fight a separate war against each of the two greatest military powers in the world—one a declared war, the other undeclared. The "Quasi-War" with France and the War of 1812 with England proved to the rest of the world that the young American republic could successfully defend itself. In the future, both nations would treat the United States more carefully, preferring diplomacy to war.

The War of 1812 not only had enhanced the nation's reputation but also had destroyed most of the Indian threat east of the Mississippi River. Once again, Americans had removed an enemy and enjoyed uncontested peace. The most intangible result of these two wars was a feeling of nationalism—a sense of an American community.

The first half of the nineteenth century marked rapid growth in the United State's population, industry, and railroads, but only moderate growth in its military might. Despite the militia's successes in the War of 1812, it had shown itself to be ineffective in coordinating a national, wartime military strategy. After the war, Congress improved the Military Academy at West Point, New York, and eventually established a Naval Academy at Annapolis, Maryland, in 1845. These schools would produce professional officers to replace the popularly elected leaders of the militia. A few young men who enjoyed the splendor of martial uniforms and drill but who did not want to serve full-time in the army, formed elite military units, especially cavalry and artillery. They called themselves the national guard. (Later in the century, these volunteer companies would be recognized as replacements for the defunct militia.)

The growing prosperity of the United States combined with a sense of national destiny to fuel the notion that Americans had a "manifest destiny" to control the fate of the western hemisphere. Many Americans coveted sparsely settled land in the West. After the northern American border had been adjusted with England, and Florida had been acquired from Spain, attention focused on the Southwest, where a large number of Americans had settled on Mexican territory. This land, including the fertile California coast, tempted adventurers to try to expand the U.S. borders to what they described as their "natural limits." In the 1840s, these expansionist tendencies brought the United States and the newly independent Republic of Mexico to war. It was the first major test of American military might in a generation. But the Americans had overwhelming advantages of population and economic development along with a highly trained army and navy cadre. The result was a crushing defeat for the Mexicans. Some Americans, however, questioned the expansionists' motives. Opponents spoke of "moral" issues, and challenged the legitimacy of what they considered an immoral war against Mexico.

THE CONSTITUTION OF THE UNITED STATES OF AMERICA

The United States government under the Articles of Confederation was too fragile to succeed. One problem was its military weakness. When Daniel Shays led a revolt of indebted farmers in western Massachusetts in 1786, the national government could not help quell the riot. Clearly, a more powerful government was needed if the great experiment in popular rule was to succeed.

When the authors of the Constitution met in Philadelphia in the summer of 1787 they knew what was needed. They wanted a national military force that combined a small regular army with the militia. What they did not want was centralized military tyranny. Therefore, they divided military powers in two ways: between the legislature and the executive, and between the states and the national government. The following reading consists of the portions of the United States Constitution that deal specifically with military powers.

THE CONSTITUTION OF THE UNITED STATES OF AMERICA

We The People of the United States, in Order to form a more perfect Union, establish Justice, insure domestic Tranquility, provide for the common defence, promote the general Welfare, and secure the Blessings of Liberty to ourselves and our Posterity, do ordain and establish this Constitution for the United States of America.

Article I

Section 8. The Congress shall have Power To lay and collect Taxes, Duties, Imposts and Excises, to pay the Debts and provide for the common Defence and general Welfare of the United States; but all Duties, Imposts and Excises shall be uniform throughout the United States. . . .

To define and punish Piracies and Felonies committed on the high Seas, and Offences against the Law of Nations;

To declare War, grant Letters of Marque and Reprisal,* and make Rules concerning Captures on Land and Water;

To raise and support Armies, But no Appropriation of Money to that Use shall be for a longer Term than two Years;

To provide and maintain a Navy;

To make Rules for the Government and Regulation of the land and naval Forces;

To provide for calling forth the Militia to execute the Laws of the Union, suppress Insurrections and repel Invasions;

To provide for organizing, arming and disciplining, the Militia, and for governing such Part of them as may be employed in the Service of the United States, reserving to the States respectively, the Appointment of the Officers, and the Authority of training the Militia according to the discipline prescribed by Congress;

To exercise exclusive Legislation in all Cases whatsoever, over such District (not exceeding ten Miles square) as may, by Cession of particular States, and the Acceptance of Congress, become the Seat of the Government of the United States, and to exercise like Authority over all Places purchased by the Consent of the Legislature of the State in which the Same shall be, for the Erection of Forts, Magazines, Arsenals, dock-Yards, and other needful Buildings;—And

To make all Laws which shall be necessary and proper for carrying into Execution the foregoing Powers, and all other Powers vested by this Constitution in the Government of the United States, or in any Department or Officer thereof. . . .

Article II

Section 2.   The President shall be Commander in Chief of the Army and Navy of the United States, and of the Militia of the several States, when called into the actual Service of the United States. . . .

Article IV

Section 4.   The United States shall guarantee to every State in this Union a Republican Form of Government, and shall protect each of them against Invasion; and on Application of the Legislature, or of the Executive (when the Legislature cannot be convened) against domestic Violence.

---

* Letters of Marque and Reprisal permitted merchantmen to act as warships and capture enemy vessels in wartime. Without a Letter of Marque and Reprisal, such a ship would be a pirate.

Amendment II

A well regulated Militia, being necessary to the security of a free State, the right of the people to keep and bear Arms, shall not be infringed.

Amendment III

No Soldier shall, in time of peace be quartered in any house, without the consent of the Owner, nor in time of war, but in a manner to be prescribed by law.

Amendment V

No person shall be held to answer for a capital, or otherwise infamous crime, unless on a presentment or indictment of a Grand Jury, except in cases arising in the land or naval forces, or in the Militia, when in actual service in time of War or public danger. . . .

FRONTIER WAR

Micah McDonough

Clearly, the new nation had an obligation to protect American settlers in the old Northwest from the Indians. In order to provide this protection and to show the government's control over its own borders, President Washington sent three expeditions to Ohio to confirm American claims in that territory and to "awe" the Indians. The first expedition, under Josiah Harmar in 1790, was repulsed with heavy losses. Harmar, most recently a major in the Pennsylvania militia, blamed his defeat on his men's drunkenness and desertions. Washington then ordered Governor Arthur St. Clair to lead a second expedition the following year. St. Clair failed to plan adequately and suffered one of the worst American defeats at the hands of the Indians. Furious over this humiliating and costly loss, Washington had St. Clair court-martialed, and ordered yet another expedition.

The third army—called a *legion* because it combined artillery and cavalry with infantry—was led by Anthony Wayne. General Wayne had studied Caesar's *Gallic Wars* to prepare for the campaign. Marching slowly into the interior in order to give the weakening Indian alliance time to fall apart, Wayne finally met Little Turtle and his braves at Fallen Timbers in Ohio (20 August 1794). After winning the battle, Wayne devastated Indian villages and crops. The Indians were forced to sign the Treaty of Greenville, which gave the United States all of Ohio and some of Indiana and ensured peace on the northern frontier for more than a decade.

The following account of St. Clair's defeat is from a letter written by Lieutenant Micah McDonough to his brother Patrick. The McDonoughs

SOURCE: Letter of Micah McDonough to Patrick McDonough in the Thomas Macdonough Collection, Historical Society of Delaware, Wilmington. Courtesy of the Historical Society of Delaware.

were a Delaware family whose most famous son, Thomas Macdonough, would later defeat a British fleet on Lake Champlain during the War of 1812.

Fort. Washington Nov. 10th 1791

D[ear] Patt

Be assured, it's a pleasure for me to embrace an opportunity of informing you that I am ALIVE, and well, altho such a great number of my acquaintances & friends, have lately changed their place of abode, and that without the hair of their heads. The American Arms never meet with such a defeat. Bradocks is not to be compared considering ye [the] numbers of each Army.

Shall endeavour to give you the particulars. Genl. St Clair left this place ye 12th of August with about Twelve Hundred Troops, four Hundred of which belonged to ye first U.S. Regt. the rest excepting Kirk's company, where ye Jersey & Maryland Levies. We marched six miles out to a place called Ludlows Station there encamp, and continued for two weeks. Expecting to be join'd by Genl. Butler, with ye remaining Levies & second U.S. Regt., Butlers not arriving, St Clair proceeded on with us, to ye great Miamie River, Twenty three miles, And began erecting a Fort. In five days Major Genl. Butler join'd us, with about one Thousand Levies & two Hundred & fifty of ye second U.S. Regt., which enabled us, to finish ye Fort in a short time. Called Fort Hamilton, Left about one hundred & fifty Troops in it consisting of ye sick, Lame, and lazy of ye army.

Proceeded on ye fourth of Octr., Our army consisting of about Eighteen Hundred effectives, infantry—one Hundred & fifty artillery, & Eighty Light Dragoons—our movements were very slow, and attended with ye greatest fatiegue imaginable, in cutting a road through such a Wilderness. We halted forty four miles from Fort Hamilton (*Delighte full country*) and erected a well constructed strong Garisson, called Fort Jefferson. During which time we were almost starved to death, The duty being severe and on half allowance, from Fort Jefferson, we proceeded on with a fresh supply of provision, slowly, through a low swampy (tho fertile) Country scarcely passable, thirty three miles, to the place of action which happened on ye fourth of this inst [month].

He could have attacked us, at no better time, the first U.S. Regt. consisting of four Hundred, & old veterans, were detach'd back, to meet & escort a quantity of provision, that was on ye way, that detachment together with many of the Levies being discharged (*their times being up*) and the commands, at ye different garissons, with ye sick list and desertions, Reduced our Army to about Twelve Hundred, two hundred & fifty militia from Kentuck, excepted, the third of Nov. We encamp, on a rising peace of ground on some of ye Wabash waters, surrounded with low swampy Land, full of under brush & old logs, which answered their purpose very well, during ye night ye keep us awake, by their constant stir around our Camp. We supposed no attack, expected it was as usuall, their endeavouring to steal our Horses, and many they did get during our line of march, with a few scalps.

Just as ye Revelie [reveille], was done playing, on ye morning of ye fourth inst. all under arms, as usual, We heard ye Damndest noise imaginable, in fact we supposed their was ten thousand & one bells around us. But alas, we were soon convinced it was ye tawny sons of ye West who attacked ye Militia Camp a little in our front. They run like ye Devil and through our line, in some confusion, by their breaking through us, they pushed for ye Officers Tents & many of them done nothing but plunder. In ten minutes ye attack became general, and they were all round us, as thick as Bees and scalp'd from ye very onset, at our very feet. The action continued three hours, during which time all ye leading officers fell, St Clair finding he had a few men left, and them without officers, ordered a retreat, which was done without form, every man for himself, they followed us eight miles, Butchering many that couldn't get out of their way. We left every thing behind, Eight pieces of Cannon, cattle, horses, flour, officers, & soldiers, Baggage, Officers private property in Cash, supposed to be ten thousand pounds, besides all their cloathing, we retreated, day & night, for this place, without provision, which is Ninety Eight Miles and arrived at this place on ye Eight inst.

Inclosed is a list of the many brave Officers, that fell. The number of Non Commissioned Officers, Music[ians] and privates, that fell on ye field is upwards of six hundred, Sixty odd women were killed, and I see some of them cut in two, their bubbies cut off, and burning, with a number of Officers, on our own fires, before I left ye field of action, what must they have done to a number that was badly wounded, when ye had leasure to torture them, I believe most of ye Officers were scalped (as ye were conspicuous) before we retreated, I saw a Capt. Smith, just after he was scalped, sitting on his backside, his head smoaking like a Chimney & he asked me if ye battle was a most over, some soldiers have come in with all ye skin & Hare taken clean off, of their heads. There was two hundred and fifty eight, Non Commissioned Officers, & privates nine Commissioned officers of our Regt. in the action, out of which, there's only one Hundred & Eleven escaped & forty two of them wounded, two Officers, Mr. Bissell & myself escaped fortunately for poor Platt. he was in Comm'd escorting some hack Horses to the Army.

My God, I shall say no more about it, only add, that as their were such havock made in our Regt. I shall in the course of six or eight months, write Captain after my name, and that I am yr.

affectionate Brother

M. M *Donough*
Lieut. 2nd U.S. Regt.

N.b. among ye troops that got in, one Hundred & thirty three are wounded, some, nay, many of them dangerously so. Out of Twelve Hundred near Eight Hundred officers, men, & women, were killed & wounded. My kindest wishes to my Father, yr. family and all ye pretty Girls.

MD

Jackson quelling the mutiny (Library of Congress). In 1813, Andrew Jackson led an army of some 2,500 volunteers and Tennessee militia against Creek Indians in Alabama. After several successful skirmishes, the soldiers became tired of the march, poor rations, and cold. First the militia and then the volunteers tried to head for home. Jackson had to use threats and force to keep his army together. Twice he rode to the front of the rebellious line, aimed his musket at the mutineers, and threatened to shoot the next man who took a step toward home. Jackson's threats were effective with the help of some loyal followers. But the grumbling had not ended. On 9 December 1813, an entire brigade planned to desert. Jackson placed his artillery—two small, brass cannons—at the front and rear of the mutinous volunteers while loyal militiamen deployed themselves on hills covering the road home. Once again, Jackson rode before his armed soldiers to implore them to remain with him until reinforcements arrived. When he saw that his words were having little effect, Jackson ordered his artillerymen to light their matches to fire the cannons. The volunteers knew that Jackson had a hair-trigger temper. They decided to be prudent and remain until a relief force arrived. After the force's arrival three days later, Jackson permitted his unhappy volunteers to return to Nashville. He complained to a friend that this brigade was so weary of the fighting that they "had swore that if they were marched and in front of the Indians and had their guns up with their fingers on the trickers [triggers] and their times that moment expired they would take down their guns and not fire, but march directly home." In this engraving, the artist took pains to show that the cannons (one is apparently broken and faces away from the volunteers) had less effect than Jackson's personal

fortitude. Although he has help coming from the right, it is Jackson himself who not only tames the powerful horse he rides but also the men he commands. This sketch first appeared in the Life of Andrew Jackson *(1843) by Amos Kendall, a member of President Jackson's "Kitchen Cabinet."*

A KENTUCKY SOLDIER'S ACCOUNT OF THE BATTLE OF NEW ORLEANS

The War of 1812 gave the United States little to cheer about; it had lacked a clear cause, astute leadership, or an attainable strategy. It was a splendid example of how not to fight a war.

During the first year of the war, American armies suffered severe losses on the Canadian front. In the fall of 1813, a combined land–sea force did manage to regain the western end of Lake Erie while another army held onto posts along the Niagara River. Most of the war's scant glory was reaped by the navy in a series of splendid single-ship duels fought on the high seas. These battles captured the imagination of the American public. But England soon learned its lesson and dispatched hundreds of ships to blockade the American coast, thereby sealing most of the tiny U.S. navy in port.

By 1814, Great Britain and its allies had defeated Napoleon and sent him into exile on the island of Elba. British military planners now could concentrate their manpower and materiel against the United States. A combined British army–naval force invaded the Chesapeake and burned the American capital before finally being stopped at Baltimore. A second invasion was defeated by the brilliant naval strategy of Thomas Macdonough on Lake Champlain.

A third British army targeted New Orleans, the valuable commercial center near the mouth of the Mississippi River. There Andrew Jackson enlisted every willing man into his army: young and old, black and white, pirates, gamblers, and rivermen. All manned Jackson's defensive line just

SOURCE: "A Contemporary Account of the Battle of New Orleans by a Soldier in the Ranks," *Louisiana Historical Quarterly* 9, 11–15 (January 1926). Courtesy of The Louisiana Historical Society.

south of the city. Hemmed in by the river on one side and a formidable cypress swamp on the other, Sir Edward Packenham attacked the defenders head-on across an open field. When the smoke had cleared, more than 2,000 British veterans were dead or seriously wounded. Fewer than 50 Americans had been hurt. Word of Jackson's victory reached the east coast of the United States before the news of the peace treaty. (The treaty had been signed two weeks before the battle, but many Americans assumed that the victory at New Orleans had contributed to the successful negotiations.)

The following selection is an account of the Battle of New Orleans by a Kentucky militiaman. The River Raisin that he mentions was the site where Kentucky militiamen were massacred by a British–Indian army. The author's enthusiastic memoir is evidence of the renewed national pride felt by most Americans, who regarded Jackson and his militia army as heroes.

Col. Smiley, from Bardstown, was the first one who gave us orders to fire from our part of the line; and then, I reckon, there was a pretty considerable noise. There were also brass pieces [cannon] on our right, the noisest kind of varmints, that began blaring away as hard as they could, while the heavy iron cannon, toward the river, and some thousands of small arms, joined in the chorus and made the ground shake under our feet. Directly after the firing began, Capt. Patterson, I think he was from Knox County, Kentucky, but an Irishman born, came running along. He jumped upon the brestwork and stooping a moment to look through the darkness as well as he could, he shouted with a broad North of Ireland brogue, "shoot low, boys! shoot low! rake them—rake them! They're comin' on their all fours!"

The official report said that the action lasted two hours and five minutes, but it did not seem half that length of time to me. It was so dark that little could be seen, until just about the time the battle ceased. The morning had dawned to be sure, but the smoke was so thick that every thing seemed to be covered up in it. Our men did not seem to apprehend any danger, but would load and fire as fast as they could, talking, swearing, and joking all the time. All ranks and sections were soon broken up. After the first shot, every one loaded and banged away on his own hook. Henry Spillman did not load and fire quite so often as some of the rest, but every time he did fire he would go up to the brestwork, look over until he could see something to shoot at, and then take deliberate aim and crack away. Lieut. Ashby was as busy as a nailor and it was evident that, the River Raisin was uppermost in his mind all the time. He kept dashing about and every now and then he would call out, with an oath, "We'll pay you now for the River Raisin! We'll give you something to remember the River Raisin!" When the British had come up to the opposite side of the brestwork, having no gun, he picked up an empty barrel and flung it at them. Then finding an iron bar, he jumped up on the works and hove that at them.

At one time I noticed, a little on our right, a curious kind of a chap named Ambrose Odd, one of Captain Higdon's company, and known among the men by the nickname of "Sukey," standing cooly on the top of the brestworks and peering into the darkness for something to shoot at. The balls were whistling around him and over our heads, as thick as hail, and Col. Slaughter coming along, ordered him to come down. The Colonel told him there was policy in war, and that he was exposing himself too much. Sukey turned around, holding up the flap of his old broad brimmed hat with one hand, to see who was speaking to him, and replied: "Oh! never mind Colonel—here's Sukey—I don't want to waste my powder, and I'd like to know how I can shoot until I see something?" Pretty soon after, Sukey got his eye on a red coat, and, no doubt, made a hole through it, for he took deliberate aim, fired and then coolly came down to load again.

During the action, a number of the Tennessee men got mixed with ours. One of them was killed about five or six yards from where I stood. I did not know his name. A ball passed through his head and he fell against Ensign Weller. I always thought, as did many others who were standing near, that he must have been accidentally shot by some of our own men. From the range of the British balls, they could hardly have passed over the brestwork without passing over our heads, unless we were standing very close to the works, which were a little over brest high, and five or six feet wide on the top. This man was standing a little back and rather behind Weller. After the battle, I could not see that any of the balls had struck the oak tree lower than ten or twelve feet from the ground. Above that height it was thickly peppered. This was the only man killed near where I was stationed.

It was near the close of the firing. About the time that I observed three or four men carrying his body away or directly after, there was a white flag raised on the opposite side of the brestwork and the firing ceased.

The white flag, before mentioned, was raised about ten or twelve feet from where I stood, close to the brestwork and a little to the right. It was a white handkerchief, or something of the kind, on a sword or stick. It was waved several times, and as soon as it was perceived, we ceased firing. Just then the wind got up a little and blew the smoke off, so that we could see the field. It then appeared that the flag had been raised by a British Officer wearing epaulets. It was told he was a Major. He stepped over the brestwork and came into our lines. Among the Tennesseeans who had got mixed with us during the fight, there was a little fellow whose name I do not know; but he was a cadaverous looking chap and went by that of Paleface. As the British Officer came in, Paleface demanded his sword. He hesitated about giving it to him, probably thinking it was derogatory to his dignity, to surrender to a private all over begrimed with dust and powder and that some Officer should show him the courtesy to receive it. Just at that moment, Col. Smiley came up and cried, with a harsh oath, "Give it up—give it up to him in a minute!" The British Officer quickly handed his weapon to Paleface, holding it in both hands and making a very polite bow.

A good many others came in just about the same time. Among them I noticed a very neatly dressed young man, standing on the edge of the brestwork, and offering his hand, as if for some one to assist him. He appeared to be about nineteen or twenty years old, and, as I should judge from his appearance, was an Irishman. He held his musket in one hand, while he was offering the other. I took hold of his musket and set it down, and then giving him my hand, he jumped down quite lightly. As soon as he got down, he began trying to take off his cartouch [cartridge] box, and then I noticed a red spot of blood on his clean white under jacket. I asked him if he was wounded, he said that he was and he feared pretty badly. While he was trying to disengage his accounterments [accoutrements], Capt. Farmer came up, and said to him, "Let me help you my man!" The Captain and myself then assisted him to take them off. He begged us not to take his canteen, which contained his water. We told him we did not wish to take anything but what was in his way and cumbersome to him. Just then one of the Tennesseeans, who had run down to the river, as soon as the firing had ceased, for water, came along with some in a tin coffee-pot. The wounded man observed him, asked if he would please give him a drop. "O! Yes," said the Tenneessean, "I will treat you to anything I've got." The young man took the coffee-pot and swallowed two or three mouthfuls out of the spout. He then handed back the pot, and in an instant we observed him sinking backward. We eased him down against the side of a tent, when he gave two or three gasps and was dead. He had been shot through the breast.

On the opposite side of the brestwork there was a ditch about ten feet wide, made by the excavation of the earth, of which the work was formed. In it, was about a foot or eighteen inches of water, and to make it the more difficult of passage, a quantity of thornbush had been cut and thrown into it. In this ditch a number of British soldiers were found at the close under the brestwork, as a shelter from our fire. These, of course, came in and surrendered.

When the smoke had cleared away and we could obtain a fair view of the field, it looked, at the first glance, like a sea of blood. It was not blood itself which gave it this appearance but the red coats in which the British soldiers were dressed. Straight out before our position, for about the width of space which we supposed had been occupied by the British column, the field was entirely covered with prostrate bodies. In some places they were laying in piles of several, one on the top of the other. On either side, there was an interval more thinly sprinkled with the slain; and then two other dense rows, one near the levee and the other towards the swamp. About two hundred yards off, directly in front of our position, lay a dark dapple gray horse, which we understood had been Packenham's.

Something about half way between the body of the horse and our brestwork there was a very large pile of dead, and at this spot, as I was afterward told, Packenham had been killed; his horse having staggered off to a considerable distance before he fell. I have no doubt that I could . . . have walked on the bodies from the edge of the ditch to where the horse was laying, without touching the ground. I did not notice any other horse on the field.

When we first got a fair view of the field in our front, individuals could be seen in every possible attitude. Some laying quite dead, others mortally wounded, pitching and tumbling about in the agonies of death. Some had their heads shot off, some their legs, some their arms. Some were laughing, some crying, some groaning, and some screaming. There was every variety of sight and sound. Among those that were on the ground, however, there were some that were neither dead nor wounded. A great many had thrown themselves down behind piles of slain, for protection. As the firing ceased, these men were every now and then jumping up and either running off or coming in and giving themselves up.

Among those that were running off, we observed one stout looking fellow, in a red coat, who would every now and then stop and display some gestures toward us, that were rather the opposite of complimentary. Perhaps fifty guns were fired at him, but as he was a good way off, without effect. "Hurra, Paleface! load quick and give him a shot. The infernal rascal is patting his butt at us!" Sure enough, Paleface rammed home his bullet, and taking a long sight, he let drive. The fellow, by this time, was from two to three hundred yards off, and somewhat to the left of Packenham's horse. Paleface said as he drew sight on him and then run it along up his back until the sight was lost over his head, to allow for the sinking of the ball in so great a distance, and then let go. As soon as the gun cracked, the fellow was seen to stagger. He ran forward a few steps, and then pitched down on his head, and moved no more. As soon as he fell, George Huffman, a big stout Dutchman, belonging to our Company, asked the Captain if he might go and see where Paleface hit him. The Captain said he didn't care and George jumping from the brestwork over the ditch, ran over the dead and wounded until he came to the place where the fellow was lying. George rolled the body over until he could see the face and then turning round to us, shouted at the top of his voice, "Mine Gott! he is a nagar!" He was a mulatto and he was quite dead. Paleface's ball had entered between the shoulders and passed out through his breast. George, as he came back, brought three or four muskets which he had picked up. By this time, our men were running out in all directions, picking up muskets and sometimes watches and other plunder. One man who had got a little too far out on the field was fired at from the British brestwork and wounded in the arm. He came running back a good deal faster than he had gone out. He was not much hurt but pretty well scared.

Hunting Indians in Florida with bloodhounds (Library of Congress). What Americans call the Seminole Wars were fought against Indians in Florida, who included original natives from there along with remnants of other Southeastern tribes who had opposed the removal policies of the government and fled into Florida. In three separate "wars," the American government was unable to destroy Seminole control over south Florida. The Seminole Wars are a classic example of successful guerrilla war strategy—wars fought by a people well-protected by hostile terrain and climate as well as supported by a noncombatant population sympathetic to their cause. This lithograph (published by J. Baillie in 1848) shows American soldiers marching in perfect alignment against an encampment of Seminoles (dressed in the costumes of Western Indians, outside tepees, which also were not found in Florida). The Florida governor and territorial legislature had suggested that the army use bloodhounds to track Indians. A Tallahassee newspaper expressed hope that the dogs would "tear to pieces" the "red devils." In 1840, General Zachary Taylor (shown here on horseback) unsuccessfully tried to use two bloodhounds against the Seminoles. This drawing criticizes the army's controversial decision. In order to evoke sympathy, the Indians are shown appealing for mercy from soldiers who ignore their pleas, maintain military discipline, and permit the dogs to attack the Seminoles. Although the army used bloodhounds (which in this lithograph look more like mongrels), the dogs were muzzled and found only two Indians. Despite its failure, this policy provoked some congressional opposition. Former president John Quincy Adams, then a member of the House of Representatives, offered a resolution that required the secretary of war to report "the natural, political, and martial history of the bloodhounds . . . and whether he deems it expedient to extend to the said bloodhounds and their posterity the benefits of the pension laws." Almost two decades later, the still unsuccessful army (and navy) declared that they had gained a victory over the Indians (although they knew they had not), and left them alone in their swampy home.

THE EXPANSIBLE ARMY (1820)

John C. Calhoun

*T*he three decades from the end of the War of 1812 to the beginning of the Mexican War are called the "germinal period" of American military history. These thirty years germinated the seeds of military professionalism in the United States. Amateur armies made up of militia units were no longer practical as cities and manufacturing grew.

Instrumental in the transformation from the militia to a professional army was John C. Calhoun (1782–1850), secretary of war from 1817 to 1825. When Congress asked him for a plan to cut the army in half, Calhoun devised the novel idea of an "expansible" army. Calhoun's plan went hand-in-hand with a revitalized military academy. According to his proposal, most officers would be retained so that they could maintain their professional skill and prepare for future wars. In wartime, privates would be enrolled and quickly trained by the professional cadre. Calhoun hoped that his expansible army would not only provide an environment of professionalism but also would cut defense costs. Calhoun's plan, however, bucked American military tradition. Congress rejected the expansible army concept and continued to rely upon the state militias backed by a small, but professional, national army.

The following selection is from Calhoun's proposal. His plan is considered by many military historians to be one of the most creative designs ever submitted by a secretary of war to reduce military costs while maintaining professional competence.

SOURCE: *American State Papers, Military Affairs*, 16th Cong., 2nd Session, Vol. 2 (Washington, DC: 1820).

The necessity of a standing army in peace is not believed to be involved in the subject under consideration, as the resolution presupposes the propriety of maintaining one; and in fact its necessity is so apparent, that, even those least friendly to the army have never attempted to abolish it, or even to reduce it, since the late war, much below the number proposed in the resolution. . . .

However remote our situation from the great powers of the world, and however pacific our policy, we are, notwithstanding, liable to be involved in war; and, to resist, with success, its calamities and dangers, a standing army in peace, in the present improved state of the military science, is an indispensable preparation. The opposite opinion cannot be adopted, without putting to hazard the independence and safety of the country. I am aware that the militia is considered, and in many respects justly, as the great national force; but, to render them effective, every experienced officer must acknowledge, that they require the aid of regular troops. Supported by a suitable corps of regular artillerists, and by a small well-disciplined body of infantry, they may be safely relied on to garrison our forts, and to act in the field as light troops. In these services, their zeal, courage, and habit of using fire-arms, would be of great importance, and would have their full effect. To rely on them beyond this, to suppose our militia capable of meeting in the open field the regular troops of Europe, would be to resist the most obvious truth, and the whole of our experience as a nation. War is an art, to attain perfection in which, much time and experience, particularly for the officers, are necessary. It is true, that men of great military genius occasionally appear, who, though without experience, may, when an army is already organized and disciplined, lead it to victory; yet I know of no instance, under circumstances nearly equal, in which the greatest talents have been able, with irregular and undisciplined troops, to meet with success those that were regularly trained. Genius without much experience may command, but it cannot go much further. It cannot at once organize and discipline an army, and give it that military tone and habit which only, in the midst of imminent danger, can enable it to perform the most complex evolutions with precision and promptitude. Those qualities which essentially distinguish an army from an equal assemblage of untrained individuals, can only be acquired by the instruction of experienced officers. If they, particularly the company and regimental officers, are inexperienced, the army must remain undisciplined, in which case, the genius, and even experience of the commander, will be of little avail. The great and leading objects, then, of a military establishment in peace, ought to be to create and perpetuate military skill and experience; so that, at all times, the country may have at its command a body of officers, sufficiently numerous, and well instructed in every branch of duty, both of the line and staff; and the organization of the army ought to be such as to enable the Government, at the commencement of hostilities, to obtain a regular force, adequate to the emergencies of the country, properly organized and prepared for actual service. It is thus only that we can be in the condition to meet the first shocks of hostilities with unyielding firmness; and to press on an enemy, while our resources are yet unexhausted. But if, on the other hand, disregarding the sound dictates of reason and experience, we should in peace neglect our military establishment, we must, with a powerful and skilful enemy, be exposed to the most distressing calamities. Not all the zeal, courage, and patriotism of our militia, unsupported by regularly trained and disciplined troops, can avert them. Without such troops, the two or three first campaigns would be worse than lost. The honor of our arms would be tarnished, and the resources of the country uselessly lavished; for, in proportion to the want of efficiency, and a proper organization, must, in actual service, be our military expenditures. When taught by sad experience, we would be compelled to make redoubled efforts, with exhausted means, to regain those very advantages which were lost for the want of experience and skill. In addition to the immense expenditure which would then be necessary, exceeding manifold what would have been sufficient to put our peace establishment on a respectable footing, a crisis would be thus brought on of the most dangerous character. If our liberty should ever be endangered by the military power gaining the ascendancy, it will be from the necessity of making those mighty and irregular efforts to retrieve our affairs, after a series of disasters, caused by the want of adequate military knowledge; just as, in our physical system, a state of the most dangerous excitement and paroxysm follows that of the greatest debility and prostration. To avoid these dangerous consequences, and to prepare the country to meet a state of war, particularly at its commencement, with honor and safety, much must depend on the organization of our military peace establishment, and I have, accordingly, in a plan about to be proposed for the reduction of the army, directed my attention mainly to that point, believing it to be of the greatest importance.

To give such an organization the leading principles in its formation ought to be, that, at the commencement of hostilities, there should be nothing either to new model or to create. The only difference, consequently, between the peace and the war formation of the army ought to be in the increased magnitude of the latter; and the only change in passing from the former to the latter, should consist in giving to it the augmentation which will then be necessary.

It is thus, and thus only, the dangerous transition from peace to war may be made without confusion or disorder; and the weakness and danger, which otherwise would be inevitable, be avoided. Two consequences result from this principle. First, the organization of the staff in a peace establishment ought to be such, that every branch of it should be completely formed, with such extension as the number of troops and posts occupied may render necessary; and, secondly, that the organization of the line ought, as far as practicable, to be such that, in passing from the peace to the war formation, the force may be sufficiently augmented; without adding new regiments or battalions; thus raising the war on the basis of the peace establishment, instead of creating a new army to be added to the old, as at the commencement of the late war. The next principle to be observed is, that the organization ought to be such as to induce, in time of peace, citizens of adequate talents and respectability of character to enter and remain in the military service of the country, so that the Government may have officers at its command, who, to the requisite experience, would add the public confidence. The correctness of this principle can scarcely be doubted; for, surely, if it is worth having an army at all, it is worth having it well commanded.

These are the general principles upon which I propose to form the organization of the army, as proposed to be reduced under the resolution.

THE MILITIA COMPANY DRILL

Augustus Baldwin Longstreet

After the War of 1812, few states enforced their militia laws. By then, it was no longer feasible to expect all males to arm themselves and report for regular drill. In many cities, some men began voluntary associations to practice military drill and ceremony because they liked the fraternal contact and splendid martial uniforms. These voluntary units were the nucleus of the future National Guard.

In rural areas, annual muster days provided country folk with an excuse for partying, "rasslin'," and turkey shoots with little formal drill and less discipline. Few politicians pretended any longer that the primary defense of the United States rested upon the unorganized militia.

By the time Augustus Baldwin Longstreet (1790–1870) wrote *Georgia Scenes* in 1835, the militia had become a sad joke. Longstreet's account of a muster day is American folk humor at its best. Its publication was a clear indication of the disrepute into which the hallowed militia tradition had fallen.

I happened, not long since, to be present at the muster of a captain's company, in a remote part of one of the counties; and as no general description could convey an accurate idea of the achievements of that day, I must be permitted to go a little into detail, as well as my recollection will serve me.

The men had been notified to meet at nine o'clock, "armed and equipped as the law directs"; that is to say, with a gun and cartridge box at least, but, as directed by the law of the United States, "with a good firelock

SOURCE: Augustus Baldwin Longstreet, *Georgia Scenes* (Augusta, GA: S. R. Sentinel, 1835).

[flintlock], a sufficient bayonet and belt, and a pouch with a box to contain no less than twenty-four sufficient cartridges of powder and ball."

At twelve, about one third, perhaps one half, of the men had collected, and an inspector's return of the number present, and of their arms, would have stood nearly thus: 1 captain, 1 lieutenant, ensign, none; fifers, none; privates, present 24; ditto, absent 40; guns, 14; gunlocks, 12; ramrods, 10; rifle pouches, 3; bayonets, none; belts, none; spare flints, none; cartridges, none; horsewhips, walking canes and umbrellas, 10. A little before one, the captain, whom I shall distinguish by the name of Clodpole, gave directions for forming the line of parade. In obedience to this order, one of the sergeants, whose lungs had long supplied the place of a drum and fife, placed himself in front of the house, and began to ball with great vehemence, "All Captain Clodpole's company parade here! Come GENTLE-MEN, parade here!" says he—"all you that has n't got guns fall into the lower *end.*" He might have bawled till this time, with as little success as the syrens sung to Ulysses, had he not changed his post to a neighboring shade. There he was immediately joined by all who were then at leisure; the others were at that time engaged as parties or spectators at a game of fives, and could not just then attend. However, in less than half an hour the game was finished, and the captain enabled to form his company, and proceed in the duties of the day.

Look to the right and dress!

They were soon, by the help of the non-commissioned officers, placed in a straight line; but, as every man was anxious to see how the rest stood, those on the wings pressed forward for that purpose till the whole line assumed nearly the form of a crescent.

"Why, look at 'em," says the captain; "why, gentlemen, you are all a crooking in at both *ends,* so that you will get on to me bye and bye! Come, gentlemen, *dress, dress!*"

This was accordingly done; but, impelled by the same motives as before, they soon resumed their former figure, and so they were permitted to remain.

"Now, gentlemen," says the captain, "I am going to carry you through the *revolutions* of the manual exercise, and I want you, gentlemen, if you please, to pay particular attention to the word of command, just exactly as I give it out to you. I hope you will have a little patience, gentlemen, if you please, and if I should be agoing wrong, I will be much obliged to any of you, gentlemen, to put me right again, for I mean all for the best, and I hope you will excuse me if you please. And one thing, gentlemen, I caution you against, in particular—and that is this—not to make any *mistakes* if you can possibly help it; and the best way to do this, will be to do all the motions right at first; and that will help us to get along so much the faster; and I will try to have it over as soon as possible.—Come boys, come to a shoulder."

Poise, foolk [contraction of flintlock]!
Cock foolk! Very handsomely done.
Take aim!

Ram down cartridge! No! No! *Fire!* I recollect now that firing comes next after taking aim, according to Steuben; but, with your permission, gentlemen, I'll *read* the words of command just exactly as they are printed in the book, and then I shall be sure to be right. "Oh yes! read it Captain, read it!" (exclaimed twenty voices at once:) "that will save time."

" '*Tention the whole!* Please to observe, gentlemen, that at the word "fire!" you must fire; that is, if any of your guns are *loaden'd,* you must not shoot in *yearnest,* but only make pretence like; and you, gentlemen fellow soldiers, who's armed with nothing but sticks, riding switches and corn stalks, need n't go through the firings, but stand as you are, and keep yourselves to yourselves. . . .

Present arms! Very handsomely done! only hold your gun over t'other knee—t'other hand up—turn your hands round a little and raise them up higher—draw t'other foot back—now you are nearly right—very well done.

"Gentlemen, we now come to the *revolutions.* Men, you have all got into a sort of snarl, as I may say; how did you get all into such a higglet pigglety?

The fact was, the shade had moved considerably to the eastward, and had exposed the right wing of these hardy veterans to a galling fire of the sun. Being poorly provided with umbrellas at this end of the line, they found it convenient to follow the shade, and in huddling to the left for this purpose, they changed the figure of their line from that of a crescent to one which more nearly resembled a pair of pothooks.

"Come, gentlemen," (says the captain,) "spread yourselves out again in a straight line; and let us get into the wheelings and other matters as soon as possible."

But this was strenuously opposed by the soldiers.—They objected going into the *revolutions* at all, inasmuch as the weather was extremely hot, and they had already been kept in the field upwards of three quarters of an hour. They reminded the captain of his repeated promise to be as short as he possibly could, and it was clear he could dispense with all this same wheeling and flourishing, if he chose. They were already very thirsty, and if he would not dismiss them, they declared they would go off without dismission, and get something to drink, and he might fine them if that would do him any good; they were able to pay their fine, but would not go without drink to please any body; and they swore they would never vote for another captain who wished to be so unreasonably strict.

The captain behaved with great spirit upon the occasion, and a smart colloquy ensued; when at length becoming exasperated to the last degree, he roundly asserted that no soldier ought ever to *think hard* of the orders of his officer; and, finally, he went so far as to say that he did not think any gentleman on that ground had any just cause to be offended with him. The dispute was finally settled by the captain sending for some grog for their present accommodation, and agreeing to omit reading the military law, and the performance of all the manoeuvres, except two or three such easy and simple ones as could be performed within the compass of the shade. After they had drank their grog, and had "spread themselves," they were divided into platoons.

'Tention the whole!—To the right wheel! Each man faced to the right about. . . .

"Now, boys, you must try to wheel by divisions; and there is one thing in particular which I have to request of you, gentlemen, and that is, not to make any blunder in your wheeling. You must mind and keep at a wheeling distance, and not talk in the ranks, nor get out of fix again; for I want you to do this motion well, and not to make any blunder now."

'Tention the whole! By divisions, to the right wheel, march!

In doing this, it seemed as if Bedlam had broke loose: every man took the command. Not so fast on the right!—Slow now?—Haul down those umbrellas!—Faster on the left!—Keep back a little there!—Don't *scrouge* so!—Hold up your gun Sam!—Go faster there!—faster! Who trod on my——? d--n your huffs!—Keep back! Stop us, Captain—do stop us! Go faster there! I've lost my shoe! Get up again, Ned! Halt! halt! halt!—Stop, gentlemen! stop! stop!

By this time they had got into utter and inextricable confusion, and so I left them.

Massachusetts militia on parade (United States Army Military History Institute). Although compulsory, universal militia service was ignored by most Americans, some young men contributed their time and money to form elite units. Precision drill was a popular form of entertainment in the mid-nineteenth century. Some voluntary militia units chose the name "National Guard" to honor the visit of the Marquis de Lafayette, who had commanded the Guarde Nationale in France. This unit, the 43rd Massachusetts Regiment, was photographed on parade in New York City, about 1858. The photographer, Charles D. Fredericks, had to wait until the regiment stopped because the new photographic techniques could only work with still subjects. Viewers watch the parade from the sidewalks and businesses along the route, including the Santa Claus Concert & Billiard Saloon in the center. The colorful uniforms of the men of the "Tiger Regiment," as they preferred to be called, were designed to attract attention and build esprit off the battlefield. Bearskin hats and chalked cross-belts were reminiscent of the close-order maneuvers of traditional warfare. They would not last long in the new style of combat that came with the Civil War, which would begin a few years after this photograph was taken. The commanders of these regiments were often prominent politicians or men of wealth. When the Civil War began many volunteered for active duty. Some of them had more command time with larger units than most regular officers.

WHITE JACKET, OR THE WORLD IN A MAN-OF-WAR (1849)

Herman Melville

During the three decades between the War of 1812 and the Mexican War, American naval captains maintained their professional skills by studying trade routes and ocean currents, exploring the Arctic and Pacific, and protecting overseas commerce. The haphazard training of midshipmen on board ships was regularized with the establishment of the Naval Academy at Annapolis, Maryland.

These accomplishments helped promote reform in the navy. The most glaring challenge to a free American's rights as a sailor was the nearly absolute power held by captains at sea. Although corporal punishment was widely accepted in the United States at the time, opponents focused on the brutal naval custom of flogging men with crude whips—the cat-o'-nine-tails. No sailor who had witnessed this barbaric ritual ever forgot it and the public humiliation it cast on its victims.

Herman Melville (1819–1891), best known for his epic novel *Moby Dick* and his moral tale *Billy Budd*, had experienced life at sea on merchantmen and the frigate *United States. White Jacket* was an autobiographical novel that protested the severe discipline on American warships. By this time, England had outlawed flogging in its navy, and Melville and others hoped to accomplish the same in the American navy. A copy of *White Jacket* was sent to every member of Congress when it was first published in 1849. Although eighty of the eighty-three captains in the navy favored continued flogging, Congress outlawed it the following year.

SOURCE: Herman Melville, *White Jacket* (New York: Grove Press, 1850).

White Jacket was a loosely written narrative about the life of a crew on board the American frigate *Neversink*. Its story is told by "White Jacket," a common seaman who gained his nickname from the homemade canvas coat he wore. As the ship sailed from Peru around Cape Horn to Brazil and on to its home port in Virginia, the narrator described the boredom of shipboard life, which was punctuated by occasional dramatic scenes of men falling overboard, a visit by the Emperor of Brazil to the ship, or a crude amputation. The most dramatic incident White Jacket recounts is the brutal flogging of sailors for minor offenses.

"A Flogging"

If you begin the day with a laugh, you may, nevertheless, end it with a sob and a sigh.

Among the many who were exceedingly diverted with the scene between the Down Easter and the Lieutenant, none laughed more heartily than John, Peter, Mark, and Antone—four sailors of the starboard-watch. The same evening these four found themselves prisoners in the "brig," with a sentry standing over them. They were charged with violating a well-known law of the ship—having been engaged in one of those tangled, general fights sometimes occurring among sailors. They had nothing to anticipate but a flogging, at the captain's pleasure.

Toward evening of the next day, they were startled by the dread summons of the boatswain* and his mates at the principal hatchway—a summons that ever sends a shudder through every manly heart in a frigate:

"All hands witness punishment, ahoy!"

The hoarseness of the cry, its unrelenting prolongation, its being caught up at different points, and sent through the lowermost depths of the ship; all this produces a most dismal effect upon every heart not calloused by long habituation to it.

However much you may desire to absent yourself from the scene that ensues, yet behold it you must; or, at least, stand near it you must; for the regulations enjoin the attendance of the entire ship's company, from the corpulent Captain himself to the smallest boy who strikes the bell.

"All hands witness punishment, ahoy!"

To the sensitive seaman that summons sounds like a doom. He knows that the same law which impels it—the same law by which the culprits of the day must suffer; that by that very law he also is liable at any time to be judged and condemned. And the inevitableness of his own presence at the

---

* The boatswain is the petty officer in charge of the deck crew as well as the ship's rigging and lines.

scene; the strong arm that drags him in view of the scourge, and holds him there till all is over; forcing upon his loathing eye and soul the sufferings and groans of men who have familiarly consorted with him, eaten with him, battled out watches with him—men of his own type and badge—all this conveys a terrible hint of the omnipotent authority under which he lives. Indeed, to such a man the naval summons to witness punishment carries a thrill, somewhat akin to what we may impute to the quick and the dead, when they shall hear the Last Trump, that is to bid them all arise in their ranks, and behold the final penalties inflicted upon the sinners of our race.

But it must not be imagined that to all men-of-war's-men this summons conveys such poignant emotions; but it is hard to decide whether one should be glad or sad that this is not the case; whether it is grateful to know that so much pain is avoided, or whether it is far sadder to think that, either from constitutional hard-heartedness or the multiplied searings of habit, hundreds of men-of-war's-men have been made proof against the sense of degradation, pity, and shame.

As if in sympathy with the scene to be enacted, the sun, which the day previous had merrily flashed upon the tin pan of the disconsolate Down Easter, was now setting over the dreary waters, veiling itself in vapors. The wind blew hoarsely in the cordage; the seas broke heavily against the bows; and the frigate, staggering under whole top-sails, strained as in agony on her way.

"*All hands witness punishment, ahoy!*"

At the summons the crew crowded round the main-mast; multitudes eager to obtain a good place on the booms, to overlook the scene; many laughing and chatting, others canvassing the case of the culprits; some maintaining sad, anxious countenances, or carrying a suppressed indignation in their eyes; a few purposely keeping behind to avoid looking on; in short, among five hundred men, there was every possible shade of character.

All the officers—midshipmen included—stood together in a group on the starboard side of the main-mast; the First Lieutenant in advance, and the surgeon, whose special duty it is to be present at such times, standing close by his side.

Presently the Captain came forward from his cabin, and stood in the centre of this solemn group, with a small paper in his hand. That paper was the daily report of offences, regularly laid upon his table every morning or evening, like the day's journal placed by a bachelor's napkin at breakfast.

"Master-at-arms, bring up the prisoners," he said.

A few moments elapsed, during which the Captain, now clothed in his most dreadful attributes, fixed his eyes severely upon the crew, when suddenly a lane formed through the crowd of seamen, and the prisoners advanced—the master-at-arms, rattan in hand, on one side, and an armed marine on the other—and took up their stations at the mast.

"You John, you Peter, you Mark, you Antone," said the Captain, "were yesterday found fighting on the gun-deck. Have you anything to say?"

Mark and Antone, two steady, middle-aged men, whom I had often admired for their sobriety, replied that they did not strike the first blow; that they had submitted to much before they had yielded to their passions; but as they acknowledged that they had at least defended themselves, their excuse was overruled.

John—a brutal bully, who, it seems, was the real author of the disturbance—was about entering into a long extenuation, when he was cut short by being made to confess, irrespective of circumstances, that he had been in the fray.

Peter, a handsome lad about nineteen years old, belonging to the mizzentop,* looked pale and tremulous. He was a great favorite in his part of the ship, and especially in his own mess, principally composed of lads his own age. That morning two of his young mess-mates had gone to his bag, taken out his best clothes, and, obtaining the permission of the marine sentry at the "brig," had handed them to him, to be put on against being summoned to the mast. This was done to propitiate the Captain, as most captains love to see a tidy sailor. But it would not do. To all his supplications the Captain turned a deaf ear. Peter declared that he had been struck twice before he had returned a blow. "No matter," said the Captain, "you struck at last, instead of reporting the case to an officer. I allow no man to fight on board here but myself. *I* do the fighting."

"Now, men," he added, "you all admit the charge; you know the penalty. Strip! Quarter-masters, are the gratings rigged?"

The gratings are square frames of barred wood-work, sometimes placed over the hatch-ways. One of these squares was now laid on the deck, close to the ship's bulwarks,† and while the remaining preparations were being made, the master-at-arms assisted the prisoners in removing their jackets and shirts. This done, their shirts were loosely thrown over their shoulders.

At a sign from the Captain, John, with a shameless leer, advanced, and stood passively upon the grating, while the bare-headed old quarter-master, with gray hair streaming in the wind, bound his feet to the cross-bars, and stretching out his arms over his head, secured them to the hammock-nettings above. He then retreated a little space, standing silent.

Meanwhile, the boatswain stood solemnly on the other side, with a green bag in his hand, from which taking four instruments of punishment,

---

* The mizzen mast is the third mast on a ship with three or more masts.
† The ship's sides above the deck.

he gave one to each of his mates; for a fresh "cat," applied by a fresh hand, is the ceremonious privilege accorded to every man-of-war culprit.

At another sign from the Captain, the master-at-arms, stepping up, removed the shirt from the prisoner. At this juncture a wave broke against the ship's side, and dashed the spray over his exposed back. But though the air was piercing cold, and the water drenched him, John stood still, without a shudder.

The Captain's finger now lifted, and the first boatswain's-mate advanced, combing out the nine tails of his *cat* with his hand, and then, sweeping them round his neck, brought them with the whole force of his body upon the mark. Again, and again, and again; and at every blow, higher and higher rose the long, purple bars on the prisoner's back. But he only bowed over his head, and stood still. Meantime, some of the crew whispered among themselves in applause of their ship-mate's nerve; but the greater part were breathlessly silent as the keen scourge hissed through the wintry air, and fell with a cutting, wiry sound upon the mark. One dozen lashes being applied, the man was taken down, and went among the crew with a smile, saying, "D--n me! it's nothing when you're used to it! Who wants to fight?"

The next was Antone, the Portuguese. At every blow he surged from side to side, pouring out a torrent of involuntary blasphemies. Never before had he been heard to curse. When cut down, he went among the men, swearing to have the life of the Captain. Of course, this was unheard by the officers.

Mark, the third prisoner, only cringed and coughed under his punishment. He had some pulmonary complaint. He was off duty for several days after the flogging; but this was partly to be imputed to his extreme mental misery. It was his first scourging, and he felt the insult more than the injury. He became silent and sullen for the rest of the cruise.

The fourth and last was Peter, the mizzen-top lad. He had often boasted that he had never been degraded at the gangway. The day before his cheek had worn its usual red, but now no ghost was whiter. As he was being secured to the gratings, and the shudderings and creepings of his dazzlingly white back were revealed, he turned round his head imploringly; but his weeping entreaties and vows of contrition were of no avail. "I would not forgive God Almighty!" cried the Captain. The fourth boatswain's-mate advanced, and at the first blow, the boy, shouting *"My God! Oh! my God!"* writhed and leaped so as to displace the gratings, and scatter the nine tails of the scourge all over his person. At the next blow he howled, leaped, and raged in unendurable torture.

"What are you stopping for, boatswain's-mate?" cried the Captain. "Lay on!" and the whole dozen was applied.

"I don't care what happens to me now!" wept Peter, going among the crew, with blood-shot eyes, as he put on his shirt. "I have been flogged once, and they may do it again, if they will. Let them look out for me now!"

"Pipe down!" cried the Captain, and the crew slowly dispersed.

Let us have the charity to believe them—as we do—when some Captains in the Navy say, that the thing of all others most repulsive to them, in the routine of what they consider their duty, is the administration of corporal punishment upon the crew; for, surely, not to feel scarificed to the quick at these scenes would argue a man but a beast.

You see a human being, stripped like a slave; scourged worse than a hound. And for what? For things not essentially criminal, but only made so by arbitrary laws.

BATTLE OF VERA CRUZ

George Ballentine

The Mexican War marked a notable change in American foreign policy. For the first time, the sole purpose of a war was to take another nation's territory. A professionally trained and led American army was ready to fight. The success of the U.S. forces was impressive; the only thing that prevented a quicker victory was the absence of a stable Mexican government willing to surrender nearly half its territory to the United States. The professionalism of the American army and navy had paid off. Careful preparation and training, along with remarkable army–navy cooperation, made the American losses tiny and its military success overwhelming.

George Ballentine, a Scot with some prior experience in the British army, had emigrated to the United States to find work as a weaver. Unable to find a civilian job, he joined General Winfield Scott's Mexican expedition. Ballentine's memoirs provide a colorful account of the Mexican War. They also raise one of the key issues of modern warfare: Are civilians proper targets for armed violence?

On the morning of the third [March 1847], General Scott summoned the city and castle of Vera Cruz to surrender; and after a delay of several days, consumed in discussion by the military governor and the civil authorities, the latter of whom were in favour of a surrender, a definitive answer was returned to General Scott that he might come and take them if he could. San Juan is a very strong fortification built upon a small island in the bay, about three quarters of a mile from the pier at Vera Cruz. It had a garrison of

---

SOURCE: George Ballentine, *Autobiography of an English Soldier in the United States Army* (New York: Hurst & Blackett, 1853).

between five and six thousand men, was well supplied with ammunition, and bristling with cannon, of which it had about a hundred, some of them of very heavy calibre. The buildings in the castle are all bombproof, and with the sea wall, are built of a soft species of coral, in which cannon balls are imbedded without producing the usual shattering and crumbling effect of these missiles on stone of a harder quality, and which is necessary to cause a breach. It was generally considered impregnable, and could only be approached by vessels on one side, a coral reef stretching round it on every side except the one facing the town. The city of Vera Cruz is surrounded with a wall about twelve or fifteen feet high, but which could be easily breached, and there are a number of half moon batteries round it well manned with guns; it is about three miles in circumference. . . .

The surfboats used for our disembarkation, had been expressly made for the purpose, for which they were admirably adapted, being strong, light, and roomy, and carrying about a hundred men with ease. . . .

As our regiment belonged to the second division, we had an excellent opportunity of witnessing the landing of the first party—an interesting spectacle, as we fully expected they would receive a warm reception from the Mexicans, who we imagined were stationed behind the sand-hills. A little above high-water mark, on the coast, in the neighbourhood of Vera Cruz, there is a series of sand-hills, formed by the drifting of the fine sand by the violent north gales that blow during the winter months. These sand-hills are thirty or forty feet to a hundred feet in height, the highest being in the vicinity of the city. It was on the highest of these that our batteries were erected for its bombardment. Immediately opposite where we were to land, they formed a sloping acclivity, varying from thirty to fifty feet in height, covered with short scrubby brushwood, and the prickly pear cactus. While the troops were getting into the landing-boats, an operation which, though using all possible despatch, occupied about half an hour, the gunboats sailed as close as they could to the shore, throwing an occasional shell into the brushwood, for the purpose of ascertaining if the Mexicans had any masked batteries erected, as we supposed. There being no indication of any enemy in the vicinity, and the boats being now filled, everything was ready for landing the first party. . . .

When the boats, which contained fully two thousand men, were drawn up in line and ready to start, so strong was the feeling of contagious sympathy elicited and communicated by the sight, surrounded as it was by all the glorious pomp and circumstance of war, that I believe that there were few of the army who did not envy their position, or would not gladly have incurred the hazard of the enterprise, for the shadow of glory which the distinction conferred. The scene was certainly exciting and imposing: the military bands of different regiments stationed on the decks of the steamers, transports, and men-of-war, played the national airs of "Yankee Doodle," "Hail Columbia," and the "Star Spangled Banner." Ten thousand of our own troops were anxious and eager spectators, and the English, French, and Spanish fleets, had each their representative, scanning our operations with a critical eye, and all looking with curiosity to see the issue of the exploit.

At a signal from the vessel having General Scott on board, the boats simultaneously gave way for shore, leaving a considerable space vacant in front of our men-of-war, who were anchored next to the shore, and had their guns double shotted, ready to open upon the enemy, should they make their appearance. The gun-boats, meanwhile, continued to tack backwards and forwards, almost close to the shore, for the same purpose. Under the circumstances, it was plain that the Mexicans could not prevent us from landing, but, by waiting until the first party were fairly on the sands, they might assault them with a very superior force, when our gun-boats and men-of-war would be prevented from firing, by the fear of injuring our own men. This was the event we almost expected to witness, and, as the boats neared the shore, all straining their energies for the honour of being the first to land, we watched the result with intense anxiety, expecting each moment to see a body of Mexican cavalry charge over the sand-hills. But no such event occurred; on coming to within about a hundred yards of the shore, the boats grounded on a small sandbar. The men and officers immediately leaped into the water, the former carrying their muskets on their shoulders, and holding their cartridge boxes well up, as the water reached to their hips while wading ashore. As the boats successively arrived, the men were formed on the beach; the boats making all expedition back to the vessels for more men. All of the first party having formed into line, several regimental colours were displayed, and a charge made to the heights in front, but not a single Mexican was to be seen. The American flag was immediately planted amidst loud and prolonged cheers, which were enthusiastically echoed by the troops on board. All idea of there being any fighting for that day, at least, was now at an end, piquets [pickets, or forward guards] were thrown out, and sentries posted on the most advantageous points of the heights to guard against a surprise; the men began to make themselves at home; we could observe fires were kindled, and camp kettles swinging on them, in less than an hour after they had landed, and before evening the beach had all the appearance of a camp. . . .

From the landing of siege material and heavy ordnance, which had busily commenced, we now perceived that the intention of General Scott was to bombard the city.

A great deal of virtuous indignation has been exhibited by the English press on the subject of the bombardment of Vera Cruz, which it has generally stigmatized as a barbarous slaughter of women and children, having no parallel in modern history. . . . Now all that sort of twaddle seems excessively weak to any one at all acquainted with the circumstances; the truth being notorious that General Scott, besides being one of the most skillful and scientific generals of modern times, is also one of the most humane men in the world. . . . The real fact being, that his humanity, and a desire to spare a needless effusion of blood, caused him to adopt the method he took for the reduction of Vera Cruz; being anxious to avoid a repetition of the horrible and savagely barbarous scenes consequent on the storming of a city. . . . To understand this apparent paradox, one should know a few of the facts of the case. In the first place, Vera Cruz, so far from being an open city, is very well fortified, having a wall and ditch all round it, and a series of half-moon batteries, not deficient in the requisite ordnance to make a stout resistance. These batteries sweep a perfectly level plain, extending from half a mile to a mile between the walls and the sand-hills, and would have proved very destructive to an assaulting party. Now, if the inhabitants, receiving, as they did, two or three weeks' previous notice to quit, preferred remaining in the city, General Scott having plainly signified that, for certain economical reasons, he declined taking their batteries with the bayonet, and intended to try a game at the long bowls, which the Mexicans are so fond of themselves—if, being duly warned, they chose to remain and be killed, I do not see how General Scott should be blamed for the result. But let us suppose that, with the intention of sparing the lives of the inhabitants, by the very disinterested sacrifice of the lives of a few of the troops under his command, he had decided on carrying the place by assault, which would probably have cost the assaulting force from 1,000 to 1,500 men; does any person, in the possession of sound intellect, imagine that, in the latter event, General Scott could have prevented scenes of plunder, the resistance of inhabitants, and the commission of deeds of crime and horror, fearful to contemplate? Those who think that troops, even of well-disciplined armies (a character I would by no means claim for the army under General Scott), can be held in subordinate check by any amount of exertion on the part of their officers, on an occasion of the above nature, are not likely, I apprehend, to form a correct idea on the subject. But to any impartial person, taking an unprejudiced view of the case, I think it will appear tolerably obvious, that the method adopted by General Scott was the most humane even for the inhabitants. . . .

Next day a schooner arrived loaded with provisions, saving the men a very laborious task of carrying them round from the beach. Still the duties of guards, piquets, and fatigue parties, harassed the men greatly; and many of them were soon prostrated by disease—especially with that scourge of armies on a campaign, diarrhea. About a week after our arrival, we also got tents pitched—our regimental baggage having been brought round from Sacrificios by light sailing vessels. Our knapsacks also arrived at the same time; but the plight in which we received them, was the cause of loud and general complaint; many of them being rifled of their most valuable contents, and some completely gutted, while but a small number had escaped untouched. They had been left on the beach, at the place where we had landed, for the previous eight or ten days, during which time they had been in charge of different hordes of volunteers, who, as might have been expected, had made rather too free with their contents. But there was no help for it; and the bursting choler of many found vent in a storm of imprecations and maledictions, while the more cool and reflective only hoped they would have an opportunity of serving out a volunteer before the end of the campaign. . . .

The erection of the batteries on the sand hills, and the conveyance of so much heavy ammunition to places convenient, was a very laborious task for our army in such a warm and exhausting climate. But all the troops took their share of the duty, each regiment working so many hours in succession, under its officers. At last, by dint of prodigious and untiring exertion, parties of our men having been employed in working day and night ever since our landing, on the 22nd of March, all being ready for operations, the town was formally summoned, and the governor having refused to surrender, the work of havoc and destruction was ordered to be commenced. For three successive days and nights, with short periods of intermission, the thunders of our guns and mortars, and the enemy's batteries in the city, were most deafening and incessant. On a height near our camp at Vergara, a number of our men frequently stood watching the shells at night; their appearance resembled that of the meteors called shooting or falling stars; and they were distinctly visible from the time when they began to ascend in their circling course until they disappeared among the roofs of the buildings. At length, on the 26th, after shot and shell to the number of seven thousand of those destructive missiles had been poured into the unfortunate city, they displayed a white flag, and after a day or two spent in negotiating, the following terms were finally agreed on. The town and castle were to be surrendered on the 29th, the garrison to march out of the central city gate and lay down their arms, and to be furnished with four days' provisions. The officers to be allowed to retain their arms, and to have five days to return to their native homes; all public property and *materiel* of war to belong to the American forces, the sick and wounded to be allowed to remain in the city, and no private property or building to be taken possession of by the Americans. On the 29th, the Mexicans, amounting to between four and five thousand, marched out of the city, and deposited their arms in front of a strong body of the American army drawn up to receive them. A brigade under General Quitman marched in and occupied the garrisons forthwith, and the

American flag floated over San Juan d'Ulloa and the city of Vera Cruz. . . .

The whole of the south-west side of the city, which, lying nearest our batteries, was most exposed to the storm of destructive missiles, was a scene of desolation calculated to make the most strenuous advocates of physical force pause and reflect. . . . Whole streets were crumbled to ruins, and they told us the killed and wounded inhabitants amounted to between five and six hundred, while the soldiers who had been employed at their batteries during the whole time of the bombardment had as many more; the entire killed and wounded being over a thousand.

A MEAN AND INFAMOUS WAR (1847)

Theodore Parker

*L*ike the War of 1812 and the Vietnam War, the Mexican War provoked a torrent of opposition. In all three, most opponents were not pacifists who opposed all wars, but people who opposed a particular war on humanitarian, ethical, or moral grounds. Opposition to the Mexican War focused on what its opponents called its "illegal" nature, what they described as the blatant American greed to obtain Mexican land, along with the likely spread of slavery into this territory.

By 1845, abolitionism had become an important political and moral force in the United States. Most opponents of slavery were willing to let it die a natural death in the southern states but violently opposed any possibility of allowing its spread into new territory. Theodore Parker (1810–1860), a prominent abolitionist and minister, attacked the Mexican War in a speech at Faneuil Hall in Boston on 4 February 1847. Parker eloquently spoke on the twin evils of greed and slavery. He challenged his listeners neither to pay taxes to support the war nor to enlist in the armies fighting it.

We are in a war; the signs of war are seen here in Boston. Men, needed to hew wood and honestly serve society, are marching about your streets; they are learning to kill men, men who never harmed us nor them; learning to kill their brothers. It is a mean and infamous war we are fighting. It is a great

SOURCE: Theodore Parker, *The Slave Power*, ed. by James K. Hosmer (Boston: American Unitarian Association, 1907). Used by permission of the Unitarian Universalist Association.

boy fighting a little one, and that little one feeble and sick. What makes it worse is, the little boy is in the right, and the big boy is in the wrong, and tells solemn lies to make his side seem right. He wants, besides, to make the small boy pay the expenses of the quarrel.

The friends of the war say, "Mexico has invaded our territory!" When it is shown that it is we who have invaded hers, then it is said, "Ay, but she owes us money." Better say outright, "Mexico has land, and we want to steal it!"

This war is waged for a mean and infamous purpose, for the extension of slavery. It is not enough that there are fifteen slave States, and 3,000,000 men here who have no legal rights—not so much as the horse and the ox have in Boston; it is not enough that the slaveholders annexed Texas, and made slavery perpetual therein, extending even north of Mason and Dixon's line, covering a territory forty-five times as large as the State of Massachusetts. Oh, no; we must have yet more land to whip negroes in!

The war had a mean and infamous beginning. It began illegally, unconstitutionally. The Whigs say, "The President made the war." Mr. Webster says so! It went on meanly and infamously. Your Congress lied about it. Do not lay the blame on the Democrats; the Whigs lied just as badly. Your Congress has seldom been so single-mouthed before. Why, only sixteen voted against the war, or the lie. I say this war is mean and infamous, all the more because waged by a people calling itself democratic and Christian. . . .

The Government had made war; the Congress voted the dollars, voted the men, voted a lie. Your representative men of Boston voted for all three—the lie, the dollars, and the men; all three, in obedience to the slave power! Let him excuse that to the conscience of his party; it is an easy matter. I do not believe he can excuse it to his own conscience. To the conscience of the world it admits of no excuse. Your President called for volunteers, 50,000 of them. Then came an opportunity such as offers not once in a hundred years, an opportunity to speak for freedom and the rights of mankind! Then was the time for Massachusetts to stand up in the spirit of '76, and say, "We won't send a man, from Cape Ann to Williamstown—not one Yankee man, for this wicked war." Then was the time for your Governor to say, "Not a volunteer for this wicked war." Then was the time for your merchants to say, "Not a ship, not a dollar, for this wicked war"; for your manufacturers to say, "We will not make you a cannon, nor a sword, nor a kernel of powder, nor a soldier's shirt, for this wicked war." Then was the time for all good men to say, "This is a war for slavery, a mean and infamous war; an aristocratic war, a war against the best interests of mankind. If God please, we will die a thousand times, but never draw blade in this wicked war." . . .

That is what a democratic nation, a Christian people ought to have said, ought to have done. But we did not say so; the Bay State did not say so, nor your Governor, nor your merchants, nor your manufacturers, nor your good men; the Governor accepted the President's decree, issued his proclamation calling for soldiers, recommended men to enlist, appealing to their "patriotism" and "humanity." . . .

I think there is a good deal to excuse the volunteers. I blame them, for some of them know what they are about. Yet I pity them more, for most of them, I am told, are low, ignorant men; some of them drunken and brutal. From the uproar they make here to-night, arms in their hands, I think what was told me is true! I say, I pity them. They are my brothers; not the less brothers because low and misguided. If they are so needy that they are forced to enlist by poverty, surely I pity them. If they are of good families, and know better, I pity them still more! I blame most the men that have duped the rank and file! I blame the captains and colonels, who will have least of the hardships, most of the pay, and all of the "glory." I blame the men that made the war; the men that make money out of it. I blame the great party men of the land. . . .

It is time for the people of Massachusetts to instruct their servants in Congress to oppose this war; to refuse all supplies for it; to ask for the recall of the army into our own land. It is time for us to tell them that not an inch of slave territory shall ever be added to the realm. Let us remonstrate; let us petition; let us command. If any class of men have hitherto been remiss, let them come forward now and give us their names—the merchants, the manufacturers, the Whigs and the Democrats. If men love their country better than their party or their purse, now let them show it.

Let us ask the General Court of Massachusetts to cancel every commission which the Governor has given to the officers of the volunteers. Let us ask them to disband the companies not yet mustered into actual service; and then, if you like that, ask them to call a convention of the people of Massachusetts, to see what we shall do in reference to the war; in reference to the annexation of more territory; in reference to the violation of the Constitution. . . .

Your President tells us it is treason to talk so! treason, is it? Treason to discuss a war which the Government made, and which the people are made to pay for? If it be treason to speak against the war, what was it to make the war, to ask for 50,000 men and $74,000,000 for the war? Why, if the people cannot discuss the war they have got to fight and to pay for, who under heaven can? Whose business is it, if it is not yours and mine? If my country is in the wrong, and I know it, and hold my peace, then I am guilty of treason, moral treason. . . .

Now is the time to act! . . . Let it be infamous for a New England man to enlist; for a New England merchant to loan his dollars, or to let his ships in aid of this wicked war; let it be infamous for a manufacturer to make a cannon, a sword, or a kernel of powder to kill our brothers with, while we all know that they are in the right, and we in the wrong. . . .

I call on the men of Boston, on the men of the old Bay State, to act worthy of their fathers, worthy of their country, worthy of themselves! Men and brothers, I call on you all to protest against this most infamous war, in the name of the State, in the name of the country, in the name of man—yes, in the name of God; leave not your children saddled with a war debt, to cripple the nation's commerce for years to come. Leave not your land cursed with slavery, extended and extending, palsying the nation's arm and corrupting the nation's heart. Leave not your memory infamous among the nations, because you feared men, feared the Government; because you loved money got by crime, land plundered in war, loved land unjustly bounded; because you debased your country by defending the wrong she dared to do; because you loved slavery, loved war, but loved not the eternal justice of all-judging God. If my counsel is weak and poor, follow one stronger and more manly. I am speaking to men; think of these things, and then act like men!

ANNOTATED BIBLIOGRAPHY

The early republic is rich in sources that detail military policy and campaigns, and is the only time in American history that the intimate connection between military power and human liberty is fully discussed. Arguments in support of a strong military in a democratic republic appear in several of *The Federalist Papers*, coauthored by Alexander Hamilton, James Madison, and John Jay to encourage New York to ratify the Constitution. These men envisaged a strong central government with a clear foreign policy backed by a credible army and navy. Opponents, collectively known as Anti-Federalists, wanted a weak, agrarian republic with political power concentrated in local communities. They felt that no national navy was necessary and the militia was sufficient to defend a peaceful republic. Their views, along with Federalists' arguments, have been collected by Jonathan Eliot in *The Debates in the Several State Conventions on the Adoption of the Federal Constitution*, five volumes (1888). Other early papers relating to the army and navy in the new nation have been collected by the U.S. Government in a series entitled the *American State Papers*.

Several important general works deserve mention. Walter Millis's *Arms and Men: A Study in American Military History* (1956) is the best introduction to the branch of military history that deals with the effects of war on finance, society, and government. Sometimes known as "new" military history, its practitioners try to understand the broad cultural effects of war on humankind. There is no better book to begin to explore these issues than Millis's *Arms and Men*. Russell Weigley's *The American Way of War: A History of United States Military Strategy and Policy* (1973) traces U.S. strategy from the American Revolution to the Vietnam War. Weigley's *History of the United States Army* is the best work on the army as an institution from colonial times to the 1960s. Allan R. Millett does the same for the marines in *Semper Fidelis: The History of the United States Marine Corps* (1980). No similar history exists for the navy. Harold and Margaret Sprout's *The Rise of American Naval Power, 1776–1918* (1939) discusses the role of sea power in American foreign policy, and Edward L. Beach's *The United States Navy, 200 Years* (1986) is an individualistic and highly interpretative account. A collection of scholarly biographies of naval captains written by leading naval historians can be found in two volumes edited by James C. Bradford, *Command Under Sail: Makers of American Naval Tradition, 1775–1850* (1985) and *Captains of the Old Steam Navy: Makers of American Naval Tradition, 1840–1880* (1986). John K. Mahon's *History of the Militia and the National Guard* (1983) traces these institutions from their precolonial roots to the present day. Life inside the army is ably discussed in Edward M. Coffman's *The Old Army: A Portrait of the American Army in Peacetime, 1784–1898* (1986).

Books that deal specifically with this period include *Soldiers & Civilians: The Martial Spirit in America, 1775–1865* (1968) by Marcus

Cunliffe, who contends that Americans are more militaristic than they like to admit. Richard H. Kohn's *Eagle and Sword: The Beginnings of the Military Establishment in America, 1783–1802* (1975) is the best work on how the Federalists managed to foment an aggressive domestic and foreign policy to insure their control over the national government. Other important works dealing with the early administration of the army and navy are James R. Jacobs's *The Beginnings of the U.S. Army* (1947) and Marshall Smelser's *The Congress Founds the Navy* (1959). William J. Fowler traces the early history of the American navy in his scholarly *Jack Tars & Commodores: The American Navy, 1783–1815* (1984). Other important naval histories include Fletcher Pratt's *Preble's Boys* (1940), which details the influence of Commodore Edward Preble on young naval captains, and David F. Long's *Nothing Too Daring: A Biography of Commodore David Porter, 1780–1843* (1970).

The best histories of the frontier wars are Francis Prucha's *The Sword of the Republic: The United States Army on the Frontier, 1783–1846* (1969) and Robert M. Utley's *Frontiersmen in Blue: The United States Army and the Indian, 1848–1865* (1967). The only complete, modern military history of the War of 1812 is John K. Mahon's *The War of 1812* (1972). A shorter account may be found in Harry L. Coles's *The War of 1812* (1969). The best naval history of this war is in C. S. Forester's *Age of Fighting Sail: The Naval War of 1812* (1956), but still valuable is Theodore Roosevelt's *The Naval War of 1812* (1882). The Canadian view of the war is masterfully told by Pierre Berton in *The Invasion of Canada, 1812–1813* (1980) and *Flames Across the Border: The Canadian-American Tragedy, 1813–1814* (1981). John K. Mahon has written the best history of the Seminole wars in the *History of the Second Seminole War* (1967). The Mexican War is covered in two excellent works, a short one by Otis Singletary entitled *The Mexican War* (1960) and K. Jack Bauer's more detailed study, *The Mexican War (1846–1848)* (1974). Bauer's *Surfboats and Horse Marines: U.S. Naval Operations in the Mexican War* (1969) is the best history of the navy in that conflict.

Besides these general histories are several good biographies and memoirs. James R. Jacobs's *Tarnished Warrior* (1938) recounts the life of the arch-scoundrel James Wilkinson, the commanding general of the U.S. Army, governor of Louisiana, and Spanish spy. Included in most lists of great American biographies is Marquis James's life of *Andrew Jackson: The Border Captain* (1933). Charles W. Elliot's *Winfield Scott: The Soldier and the Man* (1937) is a fine biography of the man who many military historians consider to be the greatest American general between the Revolution and the Civil War. Holman Hamilton's *Zachary Taylor: Soldier of the Republic* (1941) is the best biography of "Old Rough and Ready," the common soldier's general. Glenn Tucker's *Tecumseh: Vision of Glory* (1956) is a sympathetic look at America's most important Indian leader. Samuel Eliot

Morison's *"Old Bruin": Commodore Matthew C. Perry, 1794–1858* (1967) and Frances L. Williams's *Matthew Fontaine Maury: Scientist of the Sea* (1963) are excellent biographies of naval captains whose careers spanned battle, commerce, and experimentation.

Published primary accounts of the early republic include *The Journals of Lewis and Clark*, edited by Bernard DeVoto (1953), which illustrates the diverse roles played by the frontier army. An excellent narrative of the military's frustrating attempt to control the Indians can be found in John Bemrose's *Reminiscences of the Second Seminole War* (1966), edited by John K. Mahon. Winfield Scott's *Memoirs*, two volumes (1864), recall his service in the American army from the War of 1812 to the beginning of the Civil War. There are three good collections of Mexican War memoirs written by junior officers and enlisted men. These are *Zach Taylor's Little Army*, edited by Edward J. Nichols (1963); *Chronicles of the Gringoes: The U.S. Army in the Mexican War, 1846–1848: Accounts of Eyewitnesses and Combatants*, edited by George Winston Smith and Charles Judah (1968); and *To Mexico with Scott and Taylor, 1845–1847*, edited by Grady and Sue McWhiney (1969). The properly named warrior Napoleon Jackson Tecumseh Dana's Mexican War letters to his wife were published as *Monterrey Is Ours!* (1989), edited by Robert H. Ferrell. Cadet life at West Point and service with the cavalry in the Indian wars in the desert Southwest after the Mexican War are recounted by William Woods Averell in *Ten Years in the Saddle: The Military Memoir of William W. Averell*, edited by Edward K. Eckert and Nicholas J. Amato (1979). An enlisted man's view of frontier service can be found in Percival Lowe's *Five Years a Dragoon ('49 to '54) and Other Adventures on the Great Plains* (1906).

THE CIVIL WAR

The territory that was added to the United States as a result of the Mexican War soon became one of the primary causes of antagonism between North and South. Residents in both slave and free states demanded the right to take their social and economic institutions into the new lands. The controversy over slavery had been growing since the earliest days of the republic. Nineteenth-century romanticism changed what had been a political issue into a moral one, and eventually further political compromise over slavery became impossible.

Both Northerners and Southerners saw the future of the nation and of popular government at stake. Old constitutional issues were raised and debated again. Could the majority in a republic force a minority to live a certain way? Could a nation dedicated to the ideal that "all men are created equal" continue to support slavery?

In 1860, some Southern states left the Union—in peace, they hoped. But Abraham Lincoln, the new president had endorsed the idea that liberty and union were one and inseparable. When South Carolina's forces fired on Fort Sumter in Charleston Harbor in April 1861, they united the Northern states behind Lincoln's philosophy and so ignited the conflict. Soon after, the largest armies ever to appear in the Western hemisphere marched off to war. Initially both Northerners and Southerners were ecstatic about the fight. Many viewed it as a glorious pageant. But bitter and bloody battles at Manassas, Shiloh, Malvern Hill, Antietam, Vicksburg, Gettysburg, Atlanta, and Cold Harbor eventually transformed their romantic dreams of glory into the real nightmare of modern war. By 1865, much of the Southeast lay in ruin. More than 600,000 soldiers were dead, and a stronger national government had been forged in the crucible of war.

FORT DONELSON

Ulysses S. Grant

Ulysses S. Grant (1822–1885) is on almost everyone's list of great American generals. Apart from the war, the rest of his life was a failure: prior military service, farming, clerking. Even his two terms as president after the war ended in scandal, corruption, and ineffective administration. But during the Civil War, Grant had the ability to see what was needed to win a battle and the courage to carry it out.

Four years after he had left the White House in 1877, Grant learned that he was dying of cancer. By then, all his financial investments had failed, and he realized that his wife would be left penniless. In one final, heroic campaign, General Grant wrote his military memoirs, finishing the last chapter on his death bed. These memoirs (some say written with the aid of his friend Mark Twain) are the best to come from any American war, and among the best in all literature. Grant's prose was candid and objective. His vivid descriptions recalled bittersweet memories shared by all veterans. The two volumes were an immediate literary and financial success, earning enough royalties to guarantee Grant's widow a comfortable life.

The following selection describes the Union success at Fort Donelson in northern Tennessee. In January 1862, Lincoln had ordered all federal armies to begin marching against the enemy. Up to that point, no Union commander had gained a significant victory. Early in February, Grant's tenacity and creativity were rewarded when the Confederate defenders of Forts Henry and Donelson surrendered to him, thereby opening the way into Tennessee and the heartland of the Confederacy. Grant's demand for "unconditional surrender" from his Confederate opponent linked his own initials with his terms, and began his rise to fame.

SOURCE: Ulysses S. Grant, *Personal Memoirs*, Vol. 1 (New York: C. L. Webster, 1885).

FORT DONELSON

Fort Donelson is two miles north, or down the [Cumberland] river, from Dover. The fort, as it stood in 1861, embraced about one hundred acres of land. On the east it fronted the Cumberland; to the north it faced Hickman's creek, a small stream which at that time was deep and wide because of the back-water from the river; on the south was another small stream, or rather a ravine, opening into the Cumberland. This also was filled with back-water from the river. The fort stood on high ground, some of it as much as a hundred feet above the Cumberland. Strong protection to the heavy guns in the water batteries had been obtained by cutting away places for them in the bluff. To the west there was a line of rifle-pits some two miles back from the river at the farthest point. This line ran generally along the crest of high ground, but in one place crossed a ravine which opens into the river between the village and the fort. The ground inside and outside of this intrenched line was very broken and generally wooded. The trees outside of the rifle-pits had been cut down for a considerable way out, and had been felled so that their tops lay outwards from the intrenchments. The limbs had been trimmed and pointed, and thus formed an abatis in front of the greater part of the line. Outside of this intrenched line, and extending about half the entire length of it, is a ravine running north and south and opening into Hickman creek at a point north of the fort. The entire side of this ravine next to the works was one long abatis. . . .

I was very impatient to get to Fort Donelson because I knew the importance of the place to the enemy and supposed he would reinforce it rapidly. I felt that 15,000 men on the 8th [of February] would be more effective than 50,000 a month later. I asked Flag-officer Foote, therefore, to order his gunboats still about Cairo to proceed up the Cumberland River and not to wait for those gone to Eastport and Florence; but the others got back in time and we started on the 12th. I had moved McClernand out a few miles the night before so as to leave the road as free as possible. . . .

It was midwinter and during the siege we had rain and snow, thawing and freezing alternately. It would not do to allow camp-fires except far down the hill out of sight of the enemy, and it would not do to allow many of the troops to remain there at the same time. In the march over from Fort Henry numbers of the men had thrown away their blankets and overcoats. There was therefore much discomfort and absolute suffering.

During the 12th and 13th, and until the arrival of Wallace and Thayer on the 14th, the National forces, composed of but 15,000 men, without intrenchments, confronted an intrenched army of 21,000, without conflict further than what was brought on by ourselves. Only one gunboat had arrived. There was a little skirmishing each day, brought on by the movement of our troops in securing commanding positions; but there was no actual fighting during this time except once, on the 13th, in front of McClernand's command. That general had undertaken to capture a battery of the enemy which was annoying his men. Without orders or authority he sent three regiments to make the assault. The battery was in the main line of the enemy, which was defended by his whole army present. Of course the assault was a failure, and of course the loss on our side was great for the number of men engaged. In this assault Colonel William Morrison fell badly wounded. Up to this time the surgeons with the army had no difficulty in finding room in the houses near our line for all the sick and wounded; but now hospitals were overcrowded. Owing, however, to the energy and skill of the surgeons the suffering was not so great as it might have been. The hospital arrangements at Fort Donelson were as complete as it was possible to make them, considering the inclemency of the weather and the lack of tents, in a sparsely settled country where the houses were generally of but one or two rooms. . . .

The plan was for the troops to hold the enemy within his lines, while the gunboats should attack the water batteries at close quarters and silence his guns if possible. Some of the gunboats were to run the batteries, get above the fort and above the village of Dover. I had ordered a reconnaissance made with the view of getting troops to the river above Dover in case they should be needed there. That position attained by the gunboats it would have been but a question of time—and a very short time, too—when the garrison would have been compelled to surrender.

By three in the afternoon of the 14th Flag-officer Foote was ready, and advanced upon the water batteries with his entire fleet. After coming in range of the batteries of the enemy the advance was slow, but a constant fire was delivered from every gun that could be brought to bear upon the fort. I occupied a position on shore from which I could see the advancing navy. The leading boat got within a very short distance of the water battery, not further off I think than two hundred yards, and I soon saw one and then another of them dropping down the river, visibly disabled. Then the whole fleet followed and the engagement closed for the day. The gunboat which Flag-officer Foote was on, besides having been hit about sixty times, several of the shots passing through near the water-line, had a shot enter the pilot-house which killed the pilot, carried away the wheel and wounded the flag-officer himself. The tiller-ropes of another vessel were carried away and she, too, dropped helplessly back. Two others had their pilot-houses so injured that they scarcely formed a protection to the men at the wheel.

The enemy had evidently been much demoralized by the assault, but they were jubilant when they saw the disabled vessels dropping down the river entirely out of the control of the men on board. Of course I only witnessed the falling back of our gunboats and felt sad enough at the time over the repulse. Subsequent reports, now published, show that the enemy telegraphed a great victory to Richmond. The sun went down on the night of the 14th of February, 1862, leaving the army confronting Fort Donelson anything but comforted over the prospects. The weather had turned intensely cold; the men were without tents and could not keep up fires where most of them had to stay, and, as previously stated, many had thrown away their overcoats and blankets. Two of the strongest of our gunboats had been disabled, presumably beyond the possibility of rendering any present assistance. I retired this night not knowing but that I would have to intrench my position, and bring up tents for the men or build huts under the cover of the hills.

On the morning of the 15th, before it was yet broad day, a messenger from Flag-officer Foote handed me a note, expressing a desire to see me on the flag-ship and saying that he had been injured the day before so much that he could not come himself to me. I at once made my preparations for starting. . . .

When I reached the fleet I found the flag-ship was anchored out in the stream. A small boat, however, awaited my arrival and I was soon on board with the flag-officer. He explained to me in short the condition in which he was left by the engagement of the evening before, and suggested that I should intrench while he returned to Mound City with his disabled boats, expressing at the time the belief that he could have the necessary repairs made and be back in ten days. I saw the absolute necessity of his gunboats going into hospital and did not know but I should be forced to the alternative of going through a siege. But the enemy relieved me from this necessity.

When I left the National line to visit Flag-officer Foote I had no idea that there would be any engagement on land unless I brought it on myself. The conditions for battle were much more favorable to us than they had been for the first two days of the investment. From the 12th to the 14th we had but 15,000 men of all arms and no gunboats. Now we had been reinforced by a fleet of six naval vessels, a large division of troops under General L. Wallace and 2,500 men brought over from Fort Henry belonging to the division of C. F. Smith. The enemy, however, had taken the initiative. Just as I landed I met Captain Hillyer of my staff, white with fear, not for his personal safety, but for the safety of the National troops. He said the enemy had come out of his lines in full force and attacked and scattered McClernand's division, which was in full retreat. The roads, as I have said, were unfit for making fast time, but I got to my command as soon as possible. The attack had been made on the National right. I was some four or five miles north of our left. The line was about three miles long. In reaching the point where the disaster had occurred I had to pass the divisions of Smith and Wallace. I saw no sign of excitement on the portion of the line held by Smith; Wallace was nearer the scene of conflict and had taken part in it. He had, at an opportune time, sent Thayer's brigade to the support of McClernand and thereby contributed to hold the enemy within his lines.

I saw everything favorable for us along the line of our left and centre. When I came to the right appearances were different. The enemy had come out in full force to cut his way out and make his escape. McClernand's division had to bear the brunt of the attack from this combined force. His men had stood up gallantly until the ammunition in their cartridge-boxes gave out. There was abundance of ammunition near by lying on the ground in boxes, but at that stage of the war it was not all of our commanders of regiments, brigades, or even divisions, who had been educated up to the point of seeing that their men were constantly supplied with ammunition during an engagement. When the men found themselves without ammunition they could not stand up against troops who seemed to have plenty of it. The division broke and a portion fled, but most of the men, as they were not pursued, only fell back out of range of the fire of the enemy. It must have been about this time that Thayer pushed his brigade in between the enemy and those of our troops that were without ammunition. At all events the enemy fell back within his intrenchments and was there when I got on the field.

I saw the men standing in knots talking in the most excited manner. No officer seemed to be giving any directions. The soldiers had their muskets, but no ammunition, while there were tons of it close at hand. I heard some of the men say that the enemy had come out with knapsacks, and haversacks filled with rations. They seemed to think this indicated a determination on his part to stay out and fight just as long as the provisions held out. I turned to Colonel J. D. Webster, of my staff, who was with me, and said: "Some of our men are pretty badly demoralized, but the enemy must be more so, for he has attempted to force his way out, but has fallen back: the one who attacks first now will be victorious and the enemy will have to be in a hurry if he gets ahead of me." I determined to make the assault at once on our left. It was clear to my mind that the enemy had started to march out with his entire force, except a few pickets, and if our attack could be made on the left before the enemy could redistribute his forces along the line, we would find but little opposition except from the intervening abatis. I directed Colonel Webster to ride with me and call out to the men as we passed: "Fill your cartridge-boxes, quick, and get into line; the enemy is trying to escape and he must not be permitted to do so." This acted like a charm. The men only wanted some one to give them a command. We rode rapidly to Smith's quarters, when I explained the situation to him and directed him to charge the enemy's works in his front with his whole division, saying at the same time that he would find nothing but a very thin line to contend with. The general was off in an incredibly short time, going in advance himself to keep his men from firing while they were working their way through the abatis intervening between them and the enemy. The outer line of rifle-pits was passed, and the night of the 15th General Smith, with much of his division, bivouacked within the lines of the enemy. There was now no doubt but that the Confederates must surrender or be captured the next day.

There seems from subsequent accounts to have been much consternation, particularly among the officers of high rank, in Dover during the night of the 15th. General Floyd, the commanding officer, who was a man of talent enough for any civil position, was no soldier and, possibly, did not possess the elements of one. He was further unfitted for command, for the reason that his conscience must have troubled him and made him afraid. As Secretary of War he had taken a solemn oath to maintain the Constitution of the United States and to uphold the same against all its enemies. He had betrayed that trust. As Secretary of War he was reported through the northern press to have scattered the little army the country had so that the most of it could be picked up in detail when secession occurred. About a year before leaving the Cabinet he had removed arms from northern to southern arsenals. He continued in the Cabinet of President Buchanan until about the 1st of January, 1861, while he was working vigilantly for the establishment of a confederacy made out of United States territory. Well may he have been afraid to fall into the hands of National troops. He would no doubt have been tried for misappropriating public property, if not for treason, had he been captured. General Pillow, next in command, was conceited, and prided himself much on his services in the Mexican war. He telegraphed to General Johnston, at Nashville, after our men were within the rebel rifle-pits, and almost on the eve of his making his escape, that the Southern troops had had great success all day. Johnston forwarded the dispatch to Richmond. While the authorities at the capital were reading it Floyd and Pillow were fugitives.

A council of war was held by the enemy at which all agreed that it would be impossible to hold out longer. General Buckner, who was third in rank in the garrison but much the most capable soldier, seems to have regarded it a duty to hold the fort until the general commanding the department, A. S. Johnston, should get back to his headquarters at Nashville. Buckner's report shows, however, that he considered Donelson lost and that any attempt to hold the place longer would be at the sacrifice of the command. Being assured that Johnston was already in Nashville, Buckner too agreed that surrender was the proper thing. Floyd turned over the command to Pillow, who declined it. It then devolved upon Buckner, who accepted the responsibility of the position. Floyd and Pillow took possession of all the river transports at Dover and before morning both were on their way to Nashville, with the brigade formerly commanded by Floyd and some other troops, in all about 3,000. Some marched up the east bank of the Cumberland; others went on the steamers. During the night Forrest also, with his cavalry and some other troops, about a thousand in all, made their way out, passing between our right and the river. They had to ford or swim over the back-water in the little creek just south of Dover.

Before daylight General Smith brought to me the following letter from General Buckner: . . .

"Sir:—In consideration of all the circumstances governing the present situation of affairs at this station, I propose to the Commanding Officer of the Federal forces the appointment of Commissioners to agree upon terms of capitulation of the forces and fort under my command, and in that view suggest an armistice until 12 o'clock to-day. . . ."

To this I responded as follows: . . .

"Sir:—Yours of this date, proposing armistice and appointment of Commissioners to settle terms of capitulation, is just received. No terms except an unconditional and immediate surrender can be accepted. I propose to move immediately upon your works. . . ."

To this I received the following reply: . . .

"Sir:—The distribution of the forces under my command, incident to an unexpected change of commanders, and the overwhelming force under your command, compel me, notwithstanding the brilliant success of the Confederate arms yesterday, to accept the ungenerous and unchivalrous terms which you propose. . . ."

General Buckner, as soon as he had dispatched the first of the above letters, sent word to his different commanders on the line of rifle-pits, notifying them that he had made a proposition looking to the surrender of the garrison, and directing them to notify National troops in their front so that all fighting might be prevented. White flags were stuck at intervals along the line of rifle-pits, but none over the fort. As soon as the last letter from Buckner was received I mounted my horse and rode to Dover. . . .

Union artillery near Petersburg, Virginia (National Archives). The Civil War was the first major war recorded in photographs. In this one, Matthew Brady has posed the First Pennsylvania Light Artillery as if they are ready for action during the siege of Petersburg (21 June 1864). Brady is the best known Civil War photographer even though his failing eyesight prevented him from taking many pictures. Brady was more an entrepreneur than a photographer. He employed teams of photographers to record wartime events, the photos of which he would later sell to a receptive public. Brady often could not resist the temptation to place himself in the photographs. In this print, he stands in the center in a casual pose, with a slouch hat and his hands in his jacket pockets. Under actual fire, the muskets would not be stacked so neatly or the cannons aligned so perfectly. A Civil War cannon required a crew of six or more men to load, aim, and fire and then to sponge the gun. The cannons were aimed by sighting along the barrel while the trail was shifted right or left. Elevation was by trial and error.

THE VALLEY CAMPAIGN

Richard Taylor

The list of outstanding Civil War memoirs is almost endless. By the time the United States celebrated its centennial in 1876, the wounds of the fractured nation had begun to heal, and the Civil War had been transformed into the great national epic. Veterans penned their experiences so that their descendants would never forget the sacrifices they had made. Their memoirs also played an important role in the national healing process. Northerners and Southerners alike relished reading these war stories, which to them only showed that all Americans, Union and Confederate, had been brave and noble.

Destruction and Reconstruction by Confederate General Richard Taylor (1826–1879) is one of the best memoirs of the war. Taylor was the son of President Zachary Taylor and a brother-in-law of Jefferson Davis, president of the Confederacy. He was a wealthy planter and an influential Louisiana politician. The first portion of his memoirs appeared in the *North American Review* (significantly, a Northern journal) in 1876, the centennial of the Declaration of Independence. Taylor expanded these chapters into a book, which was published shortly before his death three years later. The following excerpt is from his chapter titled "The Valley Campaign." It offers a fascinating glimpse into the personality of the legendary Southern leader, Thomas J. "Stonewall" Jackson, and traces what many historians consider to be one of the most brilliant military campaigns of all time—Jackson's Valley Campaign.

SOURCE: Richard Taylor, *Destruction and Reconstruction: Personal Experiences of the Late War*, (New York: D. Appleton & Co., 1879).

The great valley of Virginia was before us in all its beauty. Fields of wheat spread far and wide, interspersed with woodlands, bright in their robes of tender green. Wherever appropriate sites existed, quaint old mills, with turning wheels, were busily grinding the previous year's harvest; and grove and eminence showed comfortable homesteads. The soft vernal influence shed a languid grace over the scene. The theatre of the war in this region was from Staunton to the Potomac, one hundred and twenty miles, with an average width of some twenty-five miles; and the Blue Ridge and Alleghanies bounded it east and west. Drained by the Shenandoah with its numerous affluents, the surface was nowhere flat, but a succession of graceful swells, occasionally rising into abrupt hills. Resting on limestone, the soil was productive, especially of wheat, and the underlying rock furnished abundant metal for the construction of roads. Railway communication was limited to the Virginia Central, which entered the Valley by a tunnel east of Staunton and passed westward through that town; to the Manassas Gap, which traversed the Blue Ridge at the pass of that name and ended at Strasburg; and to the Winchester and Harper's Ferry, thirty miles long. The first extended to Richmond by Charlottesville and Gordonsville, crossing at the former place the line from Washington and Alexandria to Lynchburg; the second connected Strasburg and Front Royal, in the Valley, with the same line at Manassas Junction; and the last united with the Baltimore and Ohio at Harper's Ferry. Frequent passes or gaps in the mountains, through which wagon roads had been constructed, afforded easy access from east and west; and pikes were excellent, though unmetaled roads became heavy after rains.

But the glory of the Valley is Massanutten. Rising abruptly from the plain near Harrisonburg, twenty-five miles north of Staunton, this lovely mountain extends fifty miles, and as suddenly ends near Strasburg. Parallel with the Blue Ridge, and of equal height, its sharp peaks have a bolder and more picturesque aspect, while the abruptness of its slopes gives the appearance of greater altitude. Midway of Massanutten, a gap with good road affords communication between Newmarket and Luray. The eastern or Luray valley, much narrower than the one west of Massanutten, is drained by the east branch of the Shenandoah which is joined at Front Royal, near the northern end of the mountain, by its western affluent, whence the united waters flow north, at the base of the Blue Ridge, to meet the Potomac at Harper's Ferry. . . .

Our position was near a pike leading south of west to Harrisonburg, whence to gain Newmarket, the great Valley pike ran due north. All roads near our camp had been examined and sketched, and among them was a road running northwest over the southern foot-hills of Massanutten, and joining the Valley pike some distance to the north of Harrisonburg. It was called the Keazletown road, from a little German village on the flank of Massanutten; and as it was the hypotenuse of the triangle, and reported good except at two points, I decided to take it. That night a pioneer party was sent forward to light fires and repair the road for artillery and [wagon] trains. Early dawn saw us in motion, with lovely weather, a fairish road, and men in high health and spirits.

Later in the day a mounted officer was dispatched to report our approach and select a camp, which proved to be beyond Jackson's forces, then lying in the fields on both sides of the pike. Over three thousand strong, neat in fresh clothing of gray with white gaiters, bands playing at the head of their regiments, not a straggler, but every man in his place, stepping jauntily as on parade, though it had marched twenty miles and more, in open column with arms at "right shoulder shift," and rays of the declining sun flaming on polished bayonets, the brigade moved down the broad, smooth pike, and wheeled on to its camping ground. Jackson's men, by thousands, had gathered on either side of the road to see us pass. Indeed, it was a martial sight, and no man with a spark of sacred fire in his heart but would have striven hard to prove worthy of such a command. . . .

The mounted officer who had been sent on in advance pointed out a figure perched on the topmost rail of a fence overlooking the road and field, and said it was Jackson. Approaching, I saluted and declared my name and rank, then waited for a response. Before this came I had time to see a pair of cavalry boots covering feet of gigantic size, a mangy cap with visor drawn low, a heavy, dark beard, and weary eyes—eyes I afterward saw filled with intense but never brilliant light. A low, gentle voice inquired the road and distance marched that day. "Keazletown road, six and twenty miles." "You seem to have no stragglers." "Never allow straggling." "You must teach my people; they straggle badly." A bow in reply. Just then my creoles started their band and a waltz. After a contemplative suck at a lemon, "Thoughtless fellows for serious work" came forth. I expressed a hope that the work would not be less well done because of the gayety. A return to the lemon gave me the opportunity to retire. Where Jackson got his lemons "no fellow could find out," but he was rarely without one. . . .

Quite late that night General Jackson came to my camp fire, where he stayed some hours. He said we would move at dawn, asked a few questions about the marching of my men, which seemed to have impressed him, and then remained silent. If silence be golden, he was a "bonanza." He sucked lemons, ate hard-tack, and drank water, and praying and fighting appeared to be his idea of the "whole duty of man."

In the gray of the morning, as I was forming my column on the pike, Jackson appeared and gave the route—north—which, from the situation of its camp, put my brigade in advance of the army. After moving a short distance in this direction, the head of the column was turned to the east and took the road over Massanutten gap to Luray. Scarce a word was spoken on the march, as Jackson rode with me. From time to time a courier would gallop up, report, and return toward Luray. An ungraceful horseman, mounted on a sorry chestnut with a shambling gait, his huge feet with outturned toes thrust into his stirrups, and such parts of his countenance as the low visor of his shocking cap failed to conceal wearing a wooden look, our new commander was not prepossessing. That night we crossed the east branch of the Shenandoah by a bridge, and camped on the stream, near Luray. Here, after three long marches, we were but a short distance below Conrad's store, a point we had left several days before. I began to think that Jackson was an unconscious poet, and, as an ardent lover of nature, desired to give strangers an opportunity to admire the beauties of his Valley. It seemed hard lines to be wandering like sentimental travelers about the country, instead of gaining "kudos" on the [Virginia] Peninsula.

Off the next morning, my command still in advance, and Jackson riding with me. The road led north between the east bank of the river and the western base of the Blue Ridge. Rain had fallen and softened it, so as to delay the wagon trains in rear. Past midday we reached a wood extending from the mountain to the river, when a mounted officer from the rear called Jackson's attention, who rode back with him. A moment later, there rushed out of the wood to meet us a young, rather well-looking woman, afterward widely known as Belle Boyd. Breathless with speed and agitation, some time elapsed before she found her voice. Then, with much volubility, she said we were near Front Royal, beyond the wood; that the town was filled with Federals, whose camp was on the west side of the river, where they had guns in position to cover the wagon bridge, but none bearing on the railway bridge below the former; that they believed Jackson to be west of Massanutten, near Harrisonburg; that General Banks, the Federal commander, was at Winchester, twenty miles northwest of Front Royal, where he was slowly concentrating his widely scattered forces to meet Jackson's advance, which was expected some days later. All this she told with the precision of a staff officer making a report, and it was true to the letter. Jackson was possessed of these facts before he left Newmarket, and based his movements upon them; but, as he never told anything, it was news to me, and gave me an idea of the strategic value of Massanutten—pointed out, indeed, by Washington before the Revolution. There also dawned on me quite another view of our leader than the one from which I had been regarding him for two days past.

Convinced of the correctness of the woman's statements, I hurried forward at "a double," hoping to surprise the enemy's idlers in the town, or swarm over the wagon bridge with them and secure it. Doubtless, this was rash, but I felt immensely "cocky" about my brigade, and believed that it would prove equal to any demand. Before we had cleared the wood Jackson came galloping from the rear, followed by a company of horse. He ordered me to deploy my leading regiment as skirmishers on both sides of the road and continue the advance, then passed on. We speedily came in sight of Front Royal, but the enemy had taken the alarm, and his men were scurrying over the bridge to their camp, where troops could be seen forming. The situation of the village is surpassingly beautiful. It lies near the east bank of the Shenandoah, which just below unites all its waters, and looks directly on the northern peaks of Massanutten. The Blue Ridge, with Manassas Gap, through which passes the railway, overhangs it on the east; distant Alleghany bounds the horizon to the west; and down the Shenandoah, the eye ranges over a fertile, well-farmed country. Two bridges spanned the river—a wagon bridge above, a railway bridge some yards lower. A good pike led to Winchester, twenty miles, and another followed the river north, whence many cross-roads united with the Valley pike near Winchester. The river, swollen by rain, was deep and turbulent, with a strong current. The Federals were posted on the west bank, here somewhat higher than the opposite, and a short distance above the junction of waters, with batteries bearing more especially on the upper bridge.

Under instructions, my brigade was drawn up in line, a little retired from the river, but overlooking it—the Federals and their guns in full view. So far, not a shot had been fired. I rode down the river's brink to get a better look at the enemy through a field-glass, when my horse, heated by the march, stepped into the water to drink. Instantly a brisk fire was opened upon me, bullets striking all around and raising a little shower-bath. Like many a foolish fellow, I found it easier to get into than out of a difficulty. I had not yet led my command into action, and, remembering that one must "strut" one's little part to the best advantage, sat my horse with all the composure I could muster. A provident camel, on the eve of a desert journey, would not have laid in a greater supply of water than did my thoughtless beast. At last he raised his head, looked placidly around, turned and walked up the bank.

This little incident was not without value, for my men welcomed me with a cheer; upon which, as if in response, the enemy's guns opened, and, having the range, inflicted some loss on my line. We had no guns up to reply, and, in advance as has been mentioned, had outmarched the troops behind us. Motionless as a statue, Jackson, sat his horse some few yards away, and seemed lost in thought. . . . I approached him with the suggestion that the railway bridge might be passed by stepping on the cross-ties, as the enemy's guns bore less directly on it than on the upper bridge. He nodded approval. The 8th regiment was on the right of my line, near at hand; and dismounting, Colonel Kelly led it across under a sharp musketry fire. Several men fell to disappear in the dark water beneath; but the movement continued with great rapidity, considering the difficulty of walking on ties, and Kelly with his leading files gained the opposite shore. Thereupon the enemy fired combustibles previously placed near the center of the wagon bridge. The loss of this structure would have seriously delayed us, as the railway bridge was not floored, and I looked at Jackson, who, near by, was watching Kelly's progress. Again he nodded, and my command rushed at the bridge. Concealed by the cloud of smoke, the suddenness of the movement saved us from much loss; but it was rather a near thing. My horse and clothing were scorched, and many men burned their hands severely while throwing brands into the river. We were soon over, and the enemy in full flight to Winchester, with loss of camp, guns, and prisoners. Just as I emerged from the flames and smoke, Jackson was by my side. How he got there was a mystery, as the bridge was thronged with my men going at full speed; but smoke and fire had decidedly freshened up his costume. . . .

Late in the night Jackson came out of the darkness and seated himself by my camp fire. He mentioned that I would move with him in the morning, then relapsed into silence. I fancied he looked at me kindly, and interpreted it into an approval of the conduct of the brigade. . . . For hours he sat silently and motionless, with eyes fixed on the fire. I took up the idea that he was inwardly praying, and he remained throughout the night.

Off in the morning, Jackson leading the way, my brigade, a small body of horse, and a section of the Rockbridge (Virginia) artillery forming the column. Major Wheat with his battalion of "Tigers," was directed to keep close to the guns. Sturdy marchers, they trotted along with the horse and artillery at Jackson's heels, and after several hours were some distance in advance of the brigade, with which I remained.

A volley in front, followed by wild cheers, stirred us up to a "double," and we speedily came upon a moving spectacle. Jackson had struck the Valley pike at Middletown, twelve miles south of Winchester, along which a large body of federal horse, with many wagons, was hastening north. He had attacked at once with his handful of men, overwhelmed resistance, and captured prisoners and wagons. The gentle Tigers were looting right merrily, diving in and out of wagons with the activity of rabbits in a warren; but this occupation was abandoned on my approach, and in a moment they were in line, looking as solemn and virtuous as deacons at a funeral. Prisoners and spoil were promptly secured. The horse was from New England, a section in which horsemanship was an unknown art, and some of the riders were strapped to their steeds. Ordered to dismount, they explained their condition, and were given time to unbuckle. Many breastplates and other protective devices were seen here, and later at Winchester. . . . I saw a poor fellow lying dead on the pike, pierced through breastplate and body by a rifle ball. Iron-clad men are of small account before modern weapons.

The Monitor *versus the* Merrimac *(United States Army Military History Institute). The face of naval war changed forever on 9 March 1862 when the Confederate ironclad* Virginia *(built on the recovered hull of the* Merrimac) *faced the* Monitor, *the Union's "cheese box on a raft." In the background of this contemporary drawing floats some of the wreckage from the Union ships that the* Virginia *had fought at Hampton Roads the previous day. The Confederate ship carried more guns, but its design was not as innovative as the* Monitor's. *The* Virginia's *guns were fixed, while the* Monitor's *two guns were mounted in a moveable turret. This meant that the* Monitor *could fire at an enemy from any direction. Four hours of close fighting only dented the armor on both ships. The* Virginia *left the* Monitor *in control of Hampton Roads and steamed back to the mouth of the James River, which it protected until the Confederate army evacuated Norfolk in May. Then the* Virginia *was destroyed by its own crew to prevent its capture. On the way to North Carolina, the* Monitor *foundered in a storm off Cape Hatteras on 30 December 1862, taking with it four officers and twelve men. Its hull was found 111 years later in 220 feet of water. It still rests on the same spot, which is now an underwater National Park.*

IRONCLAD WARFARE

Franklin Buchanan

The following document is called an "after action report." Army and navy officers are still required to file reports like it promptly after any engagement. In recognition of the historic importance of the Civil War, Congress ordered the War Department to collect all official Union and Confederate reports and correspondence. These documents were published in a seventy-volume series called *The War of the Rebellion: A Compilation of the Official Records of the Union and Confederate Armies*. Later it was expanded to include three other series. The *Official Records*, as they are usually called, are an indispensable reference collection of more than 120 volumes. They are the world's finest collection of documents on nineteenth-century warfare and the starting point for any serious scholarship on the war.

Franklin Buchanan (1800–1874) was a career navy officer. He resigned his commission in April 1861, expecting his native state of Maryland to secede. When Maryland remained with the Union, Buchanan tried to regain his commission. Rejected by the North, Buchanan then offered his services to the Confederacy—determined to fight on one side or the other. He was placed in command of naval defenses on the James River, where he made the ironclad *Virginia* (formerly the *Merrimac*) his flagship.

Buchanan's ship attacked the federal base at Newport News, Virginia, without any aid from the Confederate army. The enormous damage the *Virginia* did to the wooden-hulled Union fleet guarding Hampton Roads demonstrated the vulnerability of wooden ships to ironclads. Buchanan suffered a bullet wound in his thigh during this fight. His injury prevented him from commanding the *Virginia* the next day when the Confederate ship met its match in the Union's own ironclad, the *Monitor*. The battle of Hampton Roads had inaugurated a new era in naval warfare.

SOURCE: U.S. War Department, *Official Records*, Series I, Vol. 9 (Washington, DC: 1883).

On the 8th instant [April], at 11 a.m., the *Virginia* left the navy-yard (Norfolk), accompanied by the *Raleigh* and *Beaufort,* and proceeded to Newport News, to engage the enemy's frigates *Cumberland* and *Congress,* gunboats, and shore batteries. When within less than a mile of the *Cumberland* the *Virginia* commenced the engagement with that ship with her bow gun, and the action soon became general, the *Cumberland, Congress,* gunboats, and shore batteries concentrating upon us their heavy fire, which was returned with great spirit and determination. The *Virginia* stood rapidly on toward the *Cumberland,* which ship I had determined to sink with our prow if possible. In about fifteen minutes after the action commenced we ran into her on her starboard bow. The crash below the water was distinctly heard, and she commenced sinking, gallantly fighting her guns as long as they were above water. She went down with her colors flying.

During this time the shore batteries, *Congress,* and gunboats kept up their heavy concentrated fire upon us, doing us some injury. Our guns, however, were not idle; their fire was very destructive to the shore batteries and vessels, and we were gallantly sustained by the rest of the squadron. . . .

Having sunk the *Cumberland,* I turned our attention to the *Congress.* We were some time in getting our proper position in consequence of the shoalness of the water and the great difficulty of managing the ship when in or near the mud. To succeed in my object I was obliged to run the ship a short distance above the batteries on James River in order to wind [turn] her. During all the time her keel was in the mud; of course she moved but slowly. Thus we were subjected twice to the heavy guns of all the batteries in passing up and down the river, but it could not be avoided. We silenced several of the batteries and did much injury on shore. A large transport steamer alongside the wharf was blown up, one schooner sunk, and another captured and sent to Norfolk. The loss of life on shore we have no means of ascertaining.

While the *Virginia* was thus engaged in getting her position for attacking the *Congress* the prisoners state it was believed on board that ship that we had hauled off. The men left their guns and gave three cheers. They were soon sadly undeceived, for a few minutes after we opened upon her again, she having run on shore in shoal water. The carnage, havoc, and dismay caused by our fire compelled them to haul down their colors and to hoist a white flag. . . . The crew instantly took to their boats and landed. Our fire immediately ceased, and a signal was made for the *Beaufort* to come within hail. I then ordered Lieutenant-Commanding Parker to take possession of the *Congress,* secure the officers as prisoners, allow the crew to land, and burn the ship. He ran alongside, received her flag and surrender from Commander William Smith and Lieutenant Pendergrast, with the side-arms of those officers. They delivered themselves as prisoners of war on board the *Beaufort,* and afterward were permitted at their own request to return to the *Congress* to assist in removing the wounded to the *Beaufort.* They never returned, and I submit to the decision of the Department whether they are not our prisoners. While the *Beaufort* and *Raleigh* were alongside the *Congress,* and the surrender of that vessel had been received from the commander, she having two white flags flying, hoisted by our own people, a heavy fire was opened upon them from the shore and from the *Congress,* killing some valuable officers and men. Under this fire the steamers left the *Congress,* but as I was not informed that any injury had been sustained by those vessels at that time, Lieutenant-Commanding Parker having failed to report to me, I took it for granted that my order to him to burn her had been executed, and waited some minute to see the smoke ascending from her hatches. During this delay we were still subject to the heavy fire from the batteries, which was always promptly returned.

The steam frigates *Minnesota* and *Roanoke* and the sailing frigate *St. Lawrence* had previously been reported as coming from Old Point [Comfort, or Fort Monroe], but as I was determined that the *Congress* should not again fall into the hands of the enemy, I remarked to that gallant young officer Flag-Lieutenant Minor, "That ship must be burned." He promptly volunteered to take a boat and burn her, and the *Teazer,* Lieutenant-Commanding Webb, was ordered to cover the boat. Lieutenant Minor had scarcely reached within 50 yards of the *Congress* when a deadly fire was opened upon him, wounding him severely and several of his men. On witnessing this vile treachery I instantly recalled the boat and ordered the *Congress* destroyed by hot shot and incendiary shell. About this period I was disabled, and transferred the command of the ship to that gallant, intelligent officer Lieut. Catesby Jones, with orders to fight her as long as the men could stand to their guns.

The ships from Old Point opened their fire upon us. The *Minnesota* grounded in the north channel, where, unfortunately, the shoalness of the channel prevented our near approach. We continued, however, to fire upon her until the pilots declared it was no longer safe to remain in that position, and we accordingly returned by the south channel (the middle ground being necessarily between the *Virginia* and *Minnesota,* and *St. Lawrence* and the *Roanoke* having retreated under the guns of Old Point), and again had an opportunity of opening upon the *Minnesota,* receiving her heavy fire in return, and shortly afterward upon the *St. Lawrence,* from which vessel was received several broadsides. It had by this time become dark and we soon after anchored off Sewell's Point. The rest of the squadron followed our movements, with the exception of the *Beaufort,* Lieutenant-Commanding Parker, who proceeded to Norfolk with the wounded and prisoners as soon as he had left the *Congress*, without reporting to me. The *Congress*, having been set on fire by our hot shot and incendiary shell, continued to burn, her loaded guns being successively discharged as the flames reached them, until a few minutes past midnight, when her magazine exploded with a tremendous report.

PICKETT'S CHARGE

Frank A. Haskell

N o other American battle has had more books written about it than Gettysburg. It has come to be known as the "High Tide" of the Confederacy, and its ground is considered to be among the most hallowed—and popular—of American shrines. It was not only the size of the battle that has caused it to be remembered but also the desperate tragedy of Lee's decision to risk everything on that hot July afternoon among the gently rolling fields of a small Pennsylvania town. "What if?" is the question asked by both professional historians and casual visitors when they look across the mile-wide field where 8,000 Confederates fell in less than an hour.

Lee had come to Pennsylvania in the summer of 1863 to fight and defeat the Union army on its own soil. The Confederate commander knew that the war had been fought in Virginia too long. Now the Old Dominion could gain some respite, and the North would taste the war's bitter fruit. The battle began accidentally on 1 July 1863 when Union cavalry and Confederate infantry ran into each other just west of Gettysburg. That night, both sides rushed reinforcements onto the fields south of town. The following day, Lee tried to drive the Union army off the hills, but George G. Meade, the Union commander, held the better position and meant to keep it. Disregarding the advice of his trusted lieutenant, James Longstreet, to place the Confederate army between Meade and Washington, D.C., Lee chose to fight at Gettysburg. On 3 July 1863, after more than two hours of intense artillery fire, 12,000 of the South's finest soldiers left the comparative safety of a wooded ridge and marched toward the mouths of flaming cannon and muskets. Forty minutes later, Lee recognized the consequences; he had asked

SOURCE: Dartmouth College Class of 1854, *A History of the Class of 1854 in Dartmouth College, including Col. Haskell's Narrative of the Battle of Gettysburg,* Henry A. Hazen and S. Lewis B. Speare, Eds. (Boston: A. Mudge, 1898).

too much of his men. Never again would he be able to mount an offensive campaign. The best the Confederacy could do was to hold off the inevitable.

The following memoir of Pickett's Charge was written by a lieutenant in the Union's Army of the Potomac. Frank A. Haskell, a Vermont native, had moved to Wisconsin in 1854, where he joined Company I of the 6th Wisconsin Infantry, part of the famed "Iron Brigade" commanded by Brigadier General John Gibbon. On the afternoon of July 3rd, Haskell and the men of the Iron Brigade stood just behind the copse of trees where the Confederates had aimed their assault. Haskell saw it all. Shortly afterward, he wrote down his fresh memories and sent a copy to his brother. Unfortunately, Frank Haskell never saw his stirring words in print. He died almost a year later, on 3 June 1864, leading an assault at Cold Harbor, a charge even more futile than the one that he had witnessed at Gettysburg.

We dozed in the heat, and lolled upon the ground, with half-open eyes. Our horses were hitched to the trees munching some oats. A great lull rests upon all the field. Time was heavy, and for want of something better to do, I yawned, and looked at my watch. It was five minutes before one o'clock. I returned my watch to my pocket, and thought possibly that I might go to sleep, and stretched myself upon the ground accordingly. . . .

What sound was that? There was no mistaking it. The distinct sharp sound of one of the enemy's guns, square over to the front, caused us to open our eyes and turn them in that direction, when we saw directly above the crest the smoke of the bursting shell, and heard its noise. In an instant, before a word was spoken, as if that was the signal gun for general work, loud, startling, booming, the report of gun after gun in rapid succession smote our ears and their shells plunged down and exploded all around us. We sprang to our feet. In briefest time the whole Rebel line to the West was pouring out its thunder and its iron upon our devoted crest. The wildest confusion for a few moments obtained sway among us. The shells came bursting all about. The servants ran terror-stricken for dear life and disappeared. The horses, hitched to the trees or held by the slack hands of the orderlies, neighed out in fright and broke away and plunged riderless through the fields. The General [Gibbon] at the first had snatched his sword, and started on foot for the front. I called for my horse; nobody responded. I found him tied to a tree, nearby, eating oats, with an air of the greatest composure, which under the circumstances, even then struck me as exceedingly ridiculous. He alone, of all beasts or men near, was cool. I am not sure but that I learned a lesson then from a horse. Anxious alone for his oats, while I put on the bridle and adjusted the halter, he delayed me by keeping his head down, so I had time to see one of the horses of our mess

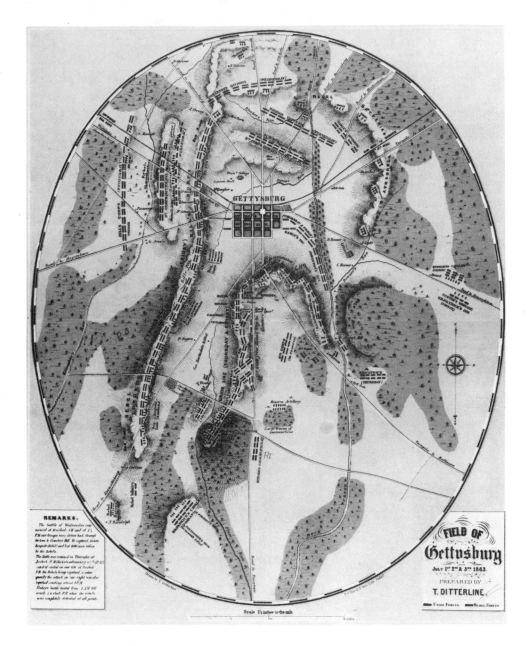

Field of Gettysburg (Library of Congress). This detailed map of the Battle of Gettysburg was drawn by Theodore Ditterline for inclusion in a book (Sketch of the Battle of Gettysburg) published a few months after the battle. The field of Pickett's Charge is in the center. Confederate soldiers had marched out of the woods along Seminary Ridge (on the left) across the open field just below Gettysburg toward the Union line on Cemetery Ridge. Frank A. Haskell's division stood near the spot where the word "GIBBON" is drawn on the map. Compare this map with the three earlier ones (St. Augustine, Fort Ticonderoga, and Yorktown). Note how much more accurately this map is drawn. Not only are all the roads

shown but also the fields of battle are clearly drawn, units carefully marked, a practical scale used, and comparative elevations shown by lines drawn closer together as steepness increases. A person using this map would have some idea of the terrain. Unfortunately for Civil War commanders, almost all maps were drawn after a battle had occurred. Both armies relied on spies or cavalry to find their way through the still largely uncharted American terrain.

wagon struck and torn by a shell. The pair plunge—the driver has lost the reins—horses, driver and wagon go into a heap by a tree. Two mules close at hand, packed with boxes of ammunition, are knocked all to pieces by a shell. . . .

The mighty din that now rises to heaven and shakes the earth is not all of it the voice of the rebellion; for our guns, the guardian lions of the crest, quick to awake when danger comes, have opened their fiery jaws and begun to roar—the great hoarse roar of battle. I overtake the General half way up to the line. Before we reach the crest his horse is brought by an orderly. Leaving our horses just behind a sharp declivity of the ridge, on foot we go up among the batteries. How the long streams of fire spout from the guns, how the rifled shells hiss, how the smoke deepens and rolls. But where is the infantry? Has it vanished in smoke? Is this a nightmare or a juggler's devilish trick? All too real. The men of the infantry have seized their arms, and behind their works, behind every rock, in every ditch, wherever there is any shelter, they hug the ground, silent, quiet, unterrified, little harmed. The enemy's guns now in action are in position at their front of the woods along the second ridge that I have before mentioned and towards their right, behind a small crest in the open field, where we saw the flags this morning. Their line is some two miles long, concave on the side towards us, and their range is from one thousand to eighteen hundred yards. A hundred and twenty-five rebel guns, we estimate, are now active, firing twenty-four pound, twenty, twelve and ten-pound projectiles, solid shot and shells, spherical, conical, spiral.

The enemy's fire is chiefly concentrated upon the position of the Second Corps. From the Cemetery to Round Top, with over a hundred guns, and to all parts of the enemy's line, our batteries reply, of twenty and ten-pound Parrotts, ten-pound rifled ordnance, and twelve-pound Napoleons, using projectiles as various in shape and name as those of the enemy. . . .

Who can describe such a conflict as is raging around us? To say that it was like a summer storm, with the crash of thunder, the glare of lightning, the shrieking of the wind, and the clatter of hailstones, would be weak. The thunder and lightning of these two hundred and fifty guns and their shells, whose smoke darkens the sky, are incessant, all pervading, in the air above our heads, on the ground at our feet, remote, near, deafening, ear-piercing, astounding; and these hailstones are massy iron, charged with exploding fire. And there is little of human interest in a storm; it is an absorbing element of this. You may see flame and smoke, and hurrying men, and human passion at a great conflagration; but they are all earthly and nothing more. . . . The projectiles shriek long and sharp. They hiss, they scream, they growl, they sputter; all sounds of life and rage; and each has its different note, and all are discordant. Was ever such a chorus of sound before? We note the effect of the enemies' fire among the batteries and along the crest. We see the solid shot strike axle, or pole, or wheel, and the tough iron and heart of oak snap and fly like straws. The great oaks there by Woodruff's guns heave down their massy branches with a crash, as if the lightning smote them. The shells swoop down among the battery horses standing there apart. A half a dozen horses start, they tumble, their legs stiffen, their vitals and blood smear the ground. And these shot and shells have no respect for men either. We see the poor fellows hobbling back from the crest, or unable to do so, pale and weak, lying on the ground with the mangled stump of an arm or leg, dripping their life-blood away; or with a cheek torn open or a shoulder mashed. And many, alas! hear not the roar as they stretch upon the ground with upturned faces and open eyes, though a shell should burst at their very ears. Their ears and their bodies this instant are only mud. We saw them but a moment since there among the flame, with brawny arms and muscles of iron, wielding the rammer and pushing home the cannon's plethoric load. . . .

Half-past two o'clock, an hour and a half since the commencement, and still the cannonade did not in the least abate; but soon thereafter some signs of weariness and a little slacking of fire began to be apparent upon both sides. . . .

None on that crest now need be told that *the enemy is advancing.* Every eye could see his legions, an overwhelming resistless tide of an ocean of armed men sweeping upon us! Regiment after regiment and brigade after brigade move from the woods and rapidly take their places in the lines forming the assault. . . . The first line at short interval is followed by a second, and that a third succeeds; and columns between support the lines. More than half a mile their front extends; more than a thousand yards the dull gray masses deploy, man touching man, rank pressing rank, and line supporting line. The red flags wave, their horsemen gallop up and down; the arms of eighteen thousand men, barrel and bayonet, gleam in the sun, a sloping forest of flashing steel. Right on they move, as with one soul, in perfect order, without impediment of ditch, or wall or stream, over ridge and slope, through orchard and meadow, and cornfield, magnificent, grim, irresistible.

All was orderly and still upon our crest; no noise and no confusion. The men had little need of commands, for the survivors of a dozen battles knew well enough what this array in front portended, and, already in their places, they would be prepared to act when the right time should come. The click of the locks as each man raised the hammer to feel with his fingers that the cap was on the nipple; the sharp jar as a musket touched a stone upon the wall when thrust in aiming over it, and the clicking of the iron axles as the guns were rolled up by hand a little further to the front, were quite all the sounds that could be heard. Cap-boxes were slid around to the front of the body; cartridge boxes opened, officers opened their pistol-holsters. . . .

General Gibbon rode down the lines, cool and calm, and in an unimpassioned voice he said to the men, "Do not hurry, men, and fire too fast, let them come up close before you fire, and then aim low and steadily." The coolness of their General was reflected in the faces of his men. Five minutes has elapsed since first the enemy have emerged from the woods—no great space of time surely, if measured by the usual standard by which men estimate duration—but it was long enough for us to note and weigh some of the elements of mighty moment that surrounded us. . . . Should these advancing men pierce our line and become the entering wedge, driven home, that would sever our army asunder, what hope would there be afterwards, and where the blood-earned fruits of yesterday? It was long enough for the Rebel storm to drift across more than half the space that had at first separated us. None, or all, of these considerations either depressed or elevated us. They might have done the former, had we been timid; the latter had we been confident and vain. But, we were there waiting, and ready to do our duty—that done, results could not dishonor us.

Our skirmishers open a spattering fire along the front, and, fighting, retire upon the main line—the first drops, the heralds of the storm, sounding on our windows. Then the thunders of our guns, first Arnold's then Cushing's and Woodruff's and the rest, shake and reverberate again through the air, and their sounding shells smite the enemy. The General said I had better go and tell General Meade of this advance. To gallop to General Meade's headquarters, to learn there that he had changed them to another part of the field, to dispatch to him by the Signal Corps in General Gibbon's name the message, "The enemy is advancing his infantry in force upon my front," and to be again upon the crest, were but the work of a minute. All our available guns are now active, and from the fire of shells, as the range grows shorter and shorter, they change to shrapnel, and from shrapnel to canister; but in spite of shells, and shrapnel and canister, without wavering or halt, the hardy lines of the enemy continue to move on. The Rebel guns make no reply to ours, and no charging shout rings out to-day, as is the Rebel wont; but the courage of these silent men amid our shots seems not to need the stimulus of other noise. The enemy's right flank sweeps near Stannard's bushy crest, and his concealed Vermonters rake it with a well-delivered fire of musketry. The gray lines do not halt or reply, but withdrawing a little from that extreme, they still move on.

And so across all that broad open ground they have come, nearer and nearer, nearly half the way, with our guns bellowing in their faces, until now a hundred yards, no more, divide our ready left from their advancing right.

The eager men there are impatient to begin. Let them. First, Harrow's breastworks flame; then Hall's; then Webb's. As if our bullets were the fire coals that touched off their muskets, the enemy in front halts, and his countless level barrels blaze back upon us. . . .

The jostling, swaying lines on either side boil, and roar, and dash their flamy spray, two hostile billows of a fiery ocean. Thick flashes stream from the wall, thick volleys answer from the crest. No threats or expostulation now, only example and encouragement. All depths of passion are stirred, and all combatives fire, down to their deep foundations. Individuality is drowned in a sea of clamor, and timid men, breathing the breath of the multitude, are brave. The frequent dead and wounded lie where they stagger and fall—there is no humanity for them now, and none can be spared to care for them. The men do not cheer or shout; they growl, and over that uneasy sea, heard with the roar of musketry, sweeps the muttered thunder of a storm of growls. Webb, Hall, Devereux, Mallon, Abbott among the men where all are heroes, are doing deeds of note. Now the loyal wave rolls up as if it would overleap its barrier, the crest. Pistols flash with the muskets. My "Forward to the wall" is answered by the Rebel counter-command, "Steady, men!" and the wave swings back. Again it surges, and again it sinks. . . .

Many things cannot be described by pen or pencil—such a fight is one. Some hints and incidents may be given, but a description or picture never. From what is told the imagination may for itself construct the scene; otherwise he who never saw can have no adequate idea of what such a battle is. . . .

Just as the fight was over, and the first outburst of victory had a little subsided, when all in front of the crest was noise and confusion—prisoners being collected, small parties in pursuit of them far down into the fields, flags waving, officers giving quick, sharp commands to their men—I stood apart for a few moments upon the crest, by that group of trees which ought to be historic forever, a spectator of the thrilling scene around. Some few musket shots were still heard in the Third Division; and the enemy's guns, almost silent since the advance of his infantry until the moment of his defeat, were dropping a few sullen shells among friend and foe upon the crest. Rebellion fosters such humanity. Near me, saddest sight of the many of such a field and not in keeping with all this noise, were mingled alone the thick dead of Maine and Minnesota, and Michigan and Massachusetts, and the Empire and Keystone States, who, not yet cold, with the blood still oozing from their death-wounds, had given their lives to the country upon that stormy field.

So mingled upon that crest let their honored graves be. Look with me about us. These dead have been avenged already. Where the long lines of the enemy's thousands so proudly advanced, see how thick the silent men of gray are scattered. It is not an hour since these legions were sweeping along so grandly; now sixteen hundred of that fiery mass are strewn among the trampled grass, dead as the clods they load; more than seven thousand, probably eight thousand, are wounded, some there with the dead, in our hands, some fugitive far towards the woods, among them Generals Pettigrew, Garnett, Kemper and Armistead, the last three mortally, and the last one in our hands. "Tell General Hancock," he said to Lieutenant Mitchell, Hancock's aide-de-camp, to whom he handed his watch, "that I know I did my country a great wrong when I took up arms against her, for which I am sorry, but for which I cannot live to atone." Four thousand, not wounded, are prisoners of war. More in number of the captured than the captors. Our men are still "gathering them in." Some hold up their hands or a handkerchief in sign of submission; some have hugged the ground to escape our bullets and so are taken; few made resistance after the first moment of our crossing the wall; some yield submissively with good grace, some with grim, dogged aspect, showing that but for the other alternative they could not submit to this. Colonels, and all less grades of officers, in the usual proportion are among them, and all are being stripped of their arms. Such of them as escaped wounds and capture are fleeing routed and panic stricken, and disappearing in the woods. Small arms, more thousands than we can count, are in our hands, scattered over the field. And these defiant battle-flags, some inscribed with "First Manassas," the numerous battles of the Peninsula, "Second Manassas," "South Mountain," "Sharpsburg" (our Antietam), "Fredericksburg," "Chancellorsville," and many more names, our men have, and are showing about, *over thirty of them.*

Such was really the closing scene of the grand drama of Gettysburg. After repeated assaults upon the right and the left, where and in all of which repulse had been his only success, this persistent and presuming enemy forms his chosen troops, the flower of his army, for a grand assault upon our center.

HARDTACK AND COFFEE

John D. Billings

Not all Civil War memoirs recounted battlefield action. Some veterans took the time to write about other aspects of soldier life: hospitals, recruiting stations, basic training, or military prisons. Aided by a daily journal and the hundreds of detailed letters he had sent home during the war, John D. Billings (1842–1933), a private in the 10th Massachusetts Light Artillery, compiled his memories of everyday life in the Union army. First published in 1887, *Hardtack and Coffee* was an immediate success and soon became a best seller. Billings's straightforward narrative is tinged with good-natured criticism and humor. *Hardtack and Coffee* is a virtual encyclopedia of information on recruiting, ambulances, punishment, hospitals, food—and even army mules. The following excerpt describes army food and echoes the complaints made by every soldier in all wars.

I will speak of the rations more in detail, beginning with the hard bread, or, to use the name by which it was known in the Army of the Potomac, *Hardtack*. What was hardtack? It was a plain flour-and-water biscuit. Two which I have in my possession as mementos measure three and one-eighth by two and seven-eighths inches, and are nearly half an inch thick. Although these biscuits were furnished to organizations by weight, they were dealt out to the men by number, nine constituting a ration in some regiments, and ten in others; but there were usually enough for those who wanted more, as some men would not draw them. While hardtack was nutritious, yet a hungry man could eat his ten in a short time and still be hungry. When they were poor and fit objects for the soldiers' wrath, it was due to one of three conditions:

SOURCE: John D. Billings, *Hardtack and Coffee, or The Unwritten Story of Army Life* (Boston: G. M. Smith & Co., 1887).

First, they may have been so hard that they could not be bitten; it then required a very strong blow of the fist to break them. The cause of this hardness it would be difficult for one not an expert to determine. This variety certainly well deserved their name. They could not be *soaked* soft, but after a time took on the elasticity of gutta-percha [rubber].

The second condition was when they were mouldy or wet, as sometimes happened, and should not have been given to the soldiers. I think this condition was often due to their having been boxed up too soon after baking. It certainly was frequently due to exposure to the weather. It was no uncommon sight to see thousands of boxes of hard bread piled up at some railway station or other place used as a base of supplies, where they were only imperfectly sheltered from the weather, and too often not sheltered at all. The failure of inspectors to do their full duty was one reason that so many of this sort reached the rank and file of the service.

The third condition was when from storage they had become infested with maggots and weevils. These weevils were, in my experience, more abundant than the maggots. They were a little, slim, brown bug an eighth of an inch in length, and were great *bores* on a small scale, having the ability to completely riddle the hardtack. I believe they never interfered with the hardest variety.

When the bread was mouldy or moist, it was thrown away and made good at the next drawing, so that the men were not the losers; but in the case of its being infested with the weevils, they had to stand it as a rule; for the biscuits had to be pretty thoroughly alive, and well covered with the webs which these creatures left, to insure condemnation. An exception occurs to me. Two cargoes of hard bread came to City Point [Virginia], and on being examined by an inspector were found to be infested with weevils. This fact was brought to Grant's attention, who would not allow it landed, greatly to the discomfiture of the contractor, who had been attempting to bulldoze the inspector to pass it.

The quartermasters did not always take as active an interest in righting such matters as they should have done; and when the men growled at them, of course they were virtuously indignant and prompt to shift the responsibility to the next higher power, and so it passed on until the real culprit could not be found.

But hardtack was not so bad an article of food, even when traversed by insects, as may be supposed. Eaten in the dark, no one could tell the difference between it and hardtack that was untenanted. It was no uncommon occurrence for a man to find the surface of his pot of coffee swimming with weevils, after breaking up hardtack in it, which had come out of the fragments only to drown; but they were easily skimmed off, and left no distinctive flavor behind. If a soldier cared to do so, he could expel the weevils by heating the bread at the fire. The maggots did not budge in that way. The most of the hard bread was made in Baltimore, and put up in boxes of sixty pounds gross, fifty pounds net; and it is said that some of the storehouses in which it was kept would swarm with weevils in an incredibly short time after the first box was infested with them, so rapidly did these pests multiply.

Having gone so far, I know the reader will be interested to learn of the styles in which this particular article was served up by the soldiers. I say *styles* because I think there must have been at least a score of ways adopted to make this simple *flour tile* more edible. Of course, many of them were eaten just as they were received—hardtack *plain;* then I have already spoken of their being crumbed in coffee, giving the "hardtack and coffee." Probably more were eaten in this way than in any other, for they thus frequently furnished the soldier his breakfast and supper. But there were other and more appetizing ways of preparing them. Many of the soldiers, partly through a slight taste for the business but more from force of circumstances, became in their way and opinion experts in the art of cooking the greatest variety of dishes with the smallest amount of capital.

Some of these crumbed them in soups for want of other thickening. For this purpose they served very well. Some crumbed them in cold water, then fried the crumbs in the juice and fat of meat. A dish akin to this one, which was said to "make the hair curl," and certainly was indigestible enough to satisfy the cravings of the most ambitious dyspeptic, was prepared by soaking hardtack in cold water, then frying them brown in pork fat, salting to taste. Another name for this dish was "skillygalee." Some liked them toasted, either to crumb in coffee, or, if a sutler* was at hand whom they could patronize, to butter. The toasting generally took place from the end of a split stick, and if perchance they dropped out of it into the camp-fire, and were not recovered quickly enough to prevent them from getting pretty well charred, they were not thrown away on that account, being then thought good for weak bowels.

Then they worked into milk-toast made of condensed milk at seventy-five cents a can; but only a recruit with a big bounty, or an old vet the child of wealthy parents, or a re-enlisted man did much in that way. A few who succeeded by hook or by crook in saving up a portion of their sugar ration spread *it* upon hardtack. The hodge-podge of lobscouse [stew] also contained this edible among its divers other ingredients; and so in various ways the ingenuity of the men was taxed to make this plainest and

---

* Sutlers were civilian merchants authorized to accompany a unit to sell an approved list of supplies to soldiers. They were the Civil War's version of the modern post exchange, or PX.

commonest yet most serviceable of army food to do duty in every conceivable combination. . . .

I began my description of the rations with the bread as being the most important one to the soldier. Some old veterans may be disposed to question the judgment which gives it this rank, and claim that *coffee*, of which I shall speak next, should take first place in importance; in reply to which I will simply say that he is wrong, because coffee being a stimulant, serves only a temporary purpose, while the bread has nearly or quite all the elements of nutrition necessary to build up the wasted tissues of the body, thus conferring a permanent benefit. Whatever words of condemnation or criticism may have been bestowed on other government rations, there was but one opinion of the coffee which was served out, and that was of unqualified approval.

The rations may have been small, the commissary or quartermaster may have given us a short allowance, but what we got was good. And what a perfect Godsend it seemed to us at times! How often, after being completely jaded by a night march,—and this is an experience common to thousands,—have I had a wash, if there was water to be had, made and drunk my pint or so of coffee, and felt as fresh and invigorated as if just arisen from a night's sound sleep! At such times it could seem to have had no substitute.

It would have interested a civilian to observe the manner in which this ration was served out when the army was in active service. It was usually brought to camp in an oatsack, a regimental quartermaster receiving and apportioning his among the ten companies, and the quartermaster-sergeant of a battery apportioning his to the four or six detachments. Then the orderly-sergeant of a company or the sergeant of a detachment must devote himself to dividing it. One method of accomplishing this purpose was to spread a rubber blanket on the ground,—more than one if the company was large,—and upon it were put as many piles of the coffee as there were men to receive rations; and the care taken to make the piles of the same size to the eye, to keep the men from growling, would remind one of a country physician making his powders, taking a little from one pile and adding to another. The sugar which always accompanied the coffee was spooned out at the same time on another blanket. When both were ready, they were given out, each man taking a pile, or, in some companies, to prevent any charge of unfairness or injustice, the sergeant would turn his back on the rations, and take out his roll of the company. Then, by request, some one else would point to a pile and ask, "Who shall have this?" and the sergeant, without turning, would call a name from his list of the company or detachment, and the person thus called would appropriate the pile specified. This process would be continued until the last pile was disposed of. There were other plans for distributing the rations; but I have described this one because of its being quite common.

The manner in which each man disposed of his coffee and sugar ration after receiving it is worth noting. Every soldier of a month's experience in campaigning was provided with some sort of bag into which he spooned his coffee; but the *kind* of bag he used indicated pretty accurately, in a general way, the length of time he had been in the service. For example, a raw recruit just arrived would take it up in a paper, and stow it away in that well known receptacle for all eatables, the soldier's haversack, only to find it a part of a general mixture of hardtack, salt pork, pepper, salt, knife, fork, spoon, sugar, and coffee by the time the next halt was made. A recruit of longer standing, who had been through this experience and had begun to feel his wisdom-teeth coming, would take his up in a bag made of a scrap of rubber blanket or a *poncho;* but after a few days carrying the rubber would peel off or the paint of the *poncho* would rub off from contact with the greasy pork or boiled meat ration which was its travelling companion, and make a black, dirty mess, besides leaving the coffee-bag unfit for further use. Now and then some young soldier, a little starchier than his fellows, would bring out an oil-silk bag lined with cloth, which his mother had made and sent him; but even oil-silk couldn't stand everything, certainly not the peculiar inside furnishings of the average soldier's haversack, so it too was not long in yielding. But your plain, straightforward old veteran, who had shed all his poetry and romance, if he had ever possessed any, who had roughed it up and down "Old Virginny," man and boy, for many months, and who had tried all plans under all circumstances, took out an oblong plain cloth bag, which looked as immaculate as the every-day shirt of a coal-heaver, and into it scooped without ceremony both his sugar and coffee, and stirred them thoroughly together.

There was method in this plan. He had learned from a hard experience that his sugar was a better investment thus disposed of than in any other way; for on several occasions he had eaten it with his hardtack a little at a time, had got it wet and melted in a rain, or, what happened fully as often, had sweetened his coffee to his taste when the sugar was kept separate, and in consequence had several messes of coffee to drink *without* sweetening, which was *not* to his taste. There was now and then a man who could keep the two separate, sometimes in different ends of the same bag, and serve them up proportionally. The reader already knows that milk was a luxury in the army. It was a new experience for all soldiers to drink coffee without milk. But they soon learned to make a virtue of a necessity, and I doubt whether one man in ten, before the war closed, would have used the lactic fluid in his coffee from choice. Condensed milk of two brands, the *Lewis* and *Borden,* was to be had at the sutler's when sutlers were handy, and occasionally milk was brought in from the udders of stray cows, the men milking them into their canteens; but this was early in the war. Later, war-swept Virginia afforded very few of these brutes, for they were regarded by the armies as more valuable for beef than for milking purposes, and only those survived that were kept apart from lines of march. In many instances they were the chief reliance of Southern families, whose able-bodied men were in the Rebel army, serving both as a source of nourishment and as beasts of burden.

When the army was in settled camp, company cooks generally prepared the rations. These cooks were men selected from the company, who had a taste or an ambition for the business. If there were none such, turns were taken at it; but this did not often happen as the office excused men from all other duty.

When company cooks prepared the food, the soldiers, at the bugle signal, formed single file at the cook-house door, in winter, or the cook's open fire, in summer, where, with a long-handled dipper, he filled each man's tin with coffee from the mess kettles, and dispensed to him such other food as was to be given out at that meal.

For various reasons, some of which I have previously hinted at, the coffee made by these cooks was of a very inferior quality and unpleasant to taste at times. It was not to be compared in excellence with what the men made for themselves. I think that when the soldiers were first thrown upon their own resources to prepare their food, they almost invariably cooked their coffee in the tin dipper with which all were provided, holding from a pint to a quart, perhaps. But it was an unfortunate dish for the purpose, forever tipping over and spilling the coffee into the fire, either because the coals burned away beneath, or because the Jonah upset it. Then if the fire was new and blazing, it sometimes needed a hand that could stand heat like a steam safe to get it when it was wanted, with the chance in favor of more than half of the coffee boiling out before it was rescued, all of which was conducive to ill-temper, so that such utensils would soon disappear, and a recruit would afterwards be seen with his pint or quart preserve can, its improvised wire bail held on the end of a stick, boiling his coffee at the camp-fire, happy in the security of his ration from Jonahs and other casualties. His can soon became as black as the blackest, inside and out. This was the typical coffee-boiler of the private soldier, and had the advantage of being easily replaced when lost, as canned goods were in very general use by commissioned officers and hospitals. Besides this, each man was generally supplied with a small tin cup as a drinking-cup for his coffee and water.

The coffee ration was most heartily appreciated by the soldier. When tired and foot-sore, he would drop out of the marching column, build his little camp-fire, cook his mess of coffee, take a nap behind the nearest shelter, and, when he woke, hurry on to overtake his company. Such men were sometimes called stragglers; but it could, obviously, have no offensive meaning when applied to them. Tea was served so rarely that it does not merit any particular description. In the latter part of the war, it was rarely seen outside of hospitals.

Confederate dead near Fredericksburg, May 1863 (National Archives). War is the use of organized violence to force an enemy to do your will. War is also death and destruction. More than a quarter of a million Confederates and more than 300,000 Northern men died in the Civil War. The rifles in this photograph were placed by the photographer to give a more dramatic effect. He also moved some of the bodies. This photograph of Marye's Heights above Fredericksburg, Virginia, was taken by the Union photographer A. J. Russell minutes after the spot had fallen to the Union army in May 1863. Only five months earlier, this same Confederate position had held in the battle of Fredericksburg. Herman Haupt, in charge of the Union's military railroads, accompanied Russell. General Haupt later recalled this moment: "I walked over the battle-ground, and examined the heights beyond Marye's house. I then realized the great strength of the position and the impossibility of taking it, if properly defended, by a direct assault in front, as had been attempted by [Union general Ambrose] Burnside with disastrous results [in the battle of Fredericksburg]. My photographic artist, Captain Russell, was with me and secured several large photographic negatives—one very good one of the stone wall, with the rebel dead lying behind it."

THE FORT PILLOW MASSACRE

*E*ven war, the most violent of all human acts, has its own code of ethics. Possibly its most ancient, solemn, and universally held precept is that once an enemy has surrendered and come under your control, you must protect him from further injury. Armies usually have abided by that principle, even if only because they realize that atrocities can be committed by either side, and once that horror has been unleashed, it is extremely difficult to regain control.

Blacks had been used by both sides since the start of the Civil War to build temporary fortifications, drive wagons, and cook food. Free blacks, along with their brothers in slavery, had asked Union commanders to permit them to serve as soldiers. At first, the Lincoln administration was opposed to this, but in March 1863, Lincoln accepted as policy what had already been begun in practice by some Union commanders. The Confederate government, fearing an armed slave rebellion, protested Lincoln's decision and threatened retaliation against all white officers commanding black regiments. Despite its threat, the Davis administration never instituted such draconian measures. Yet, its very pronouncement was clear indication of the emotionalism of the issue.

Fort Pillow was a dirt fort on the Mississippi River in Tennessee. Guarding it were 262 black soldiers of the 11th U.S. Colored Troops and the 6th U.S. Colored Heavy Artillery. They were joined by 295 whites, mostly in the 13th Tennessee cavalry, many of whom had earlier deserted from the Confederate army. On 12 April 1864, a Confederate cavalry force under Nathan Bedford Forrest captured the fort. Although the defenders quickly surrendered, only 168 whites and 58 blacks had been captured. Forrest's army, by comparison, had suffered only 100 casualties out of the 1,500 men

---

SOURCE: United States Congress, House Reports, No. 65, 38 Cong., 1 Sess., Joint Committee on the Conduct of the War, *Fort Pillow Massacre* (Washington, DC: 1864).

engaged. These unusual, suspiciously disproportionate numbers lent credence to the Union survivors' claims that the Confederates had massacred a large number of prisoners. The U.S. Congress sent Republican Senator Benjamin F. Wade of Ohio and Congressman Daniel W. Gooch of Massachusetts to investigate these charges. Not surprisingly, the Northern congressional committee concluded that the Confederates had not only massacred many prisoners but also committed other atrocities.

Confederates then, and many of their supporters ever since, have asserted that the congressional report of Confederate actions at Fort Pillow, issued by the Joint Committee on the Conduct of the War, were politically motivated. They contended that the reports of a massacre were political lies planted by Northern extremists intent on continuing the war. However, all reputable modern historians agree with Albert Castel's careful conclusions, which were published in his article in *Civil War History* (1958). Castel maintained that Forrest's cavalry had captured Fort Pillow fairly, but the climate of racial hatred had provoked an unjustifiable slaughter of a large number of Union prisoners, most of them black.

The following document consists of portions of the sworn testimony given by survivors of the Fort Pillow massacre to the Congressional committee.

Lieutenant McJ. Leming, sworn and examined.
By Mr. Gooch:
Question. Were you in the fight at Fort Pillow?
Answer. Yes, sir.
Question. What is your rank and position?
Answer. I am a first lieutenant and adjutant of the 13th Tennessee cavalry. A short time previous to the fight I was post adjutant at Fort Pillow, and during most of the engagement I was acting as post adjutant. After Major Booth was killed, Major Bradford was in command. The pickets were driven in just before sunrise, which was the first intimation we had that the enemy were approaching. I repaired to the fort, and found that Major Booth was shelling the rebels as they came up towards the outer intrenchments. They kept up a steady fire by sharpshooters behind trees, and logs, and high knolls. The major thought at one time they were planting some artillery, or looking for places to plant it. They began to draw nearer and nearer, up to the time our men were all drawn into the fort. Two companies of the 13th Tennessee cavalry were ordered out as sharpshooters, but were finally ordered in. We were pressed on all sides.

I think Major Booth fell not later than 9 o'clock. His adjutant, who was then acting post adjutant, fell near the same time. Major Bradford then took the command, and I acted as post adjutant. Previous to this, Major Booth had ordered some buildings in front of the fort to be destroyed, as the enemy's sharpshooters were endeavoring to get possession of them. There were four rows of buildings, but only the row nearest the fort was destroyed; the sharpshooters gained possession of the others before they could be destroyed. The fight continued, one almost unceasing fire all the time, until about three o'clock. They threw some shells, but they did not do much damage with their shells.

I think it was about three o'clock that a flag of truce approached. I went out, accompanied by Captain Young, the provost marshal of the post. There was another officer, I think, but I do not recollect now particularly who it was, and some four mounted men. The rebels announced that they had a communication from General Forrest. One of their officers there, I think, from his dress, was a colonel. I received the communication, and they said they would wait for an answer. As near as I remember, the communication was as follows:

"HEADQUARTERS CONFEDERATE CAVALRY,
"*Near Fort Pillow, April 12, 1864.*

"As your gallant defence of the fort has entitled you to the treatment of brave men, (or something to that effect,) I now demand an unconditional surrender of your force, at the same time assuring you that they will be treated as prisoners of war. I have received a fresh supply of ammunition, and can easily take your position.

"N. B. FORREST.

"Major L. F. BOOTH,
    "*Commanding United States Forces.*"

I took this message back to the fort. Major Bradford replied that he desired an hour for consultation and consideration with his officers, and the officers of the gunboat. I took out this communication to them, and they carried it back to General Forrest. In a few minutes another flag of truce appeared, and I went out to meet it. Some one said, when they handed the communication to me. "That gives you 20 minutes to surrender; I am General Forrest." I took it back. The substance of it was: "Twenty minutes will be given you to take your men outside of the fort. If in that time they are not out, I will immediately proceed to assault your works," or something of that kind. To this Major Bradford replied: "I will not surrender." I took it out in a sealed envelope, and gave it to him. The general opened it and read it. Nothing was said; we simply saluted, and they went their way, and I returned back into the fort.

Almost instantly the firing began again. We mistrusted, while this flag of truce was going on, that they were taking horses out at a camp we had. It was mentioned to them, the last time that this and other movements excited our suspicion, that they were moving their troops. They said that they had noticed it themselves, and had it stopped; that it was unintentional on their part, and that it should not be repeated.

It was not long after the last flag of truce had retired, that they made their grand charge. We kept them back for several minutes. What was called—brigade or battalion attacked the centre of the fort where several companies of colored troops were stationed. They finally gave way, and, before we could fill up the breach, the enemy got inside the fort, and then they came in on the other two sides, and had complete possession of the fort. In the mean time nearly all the officers had been killed, especially of the colored troops, and there was no one hardly to guide the men. They fought bravely, indeed, until that time. I do not think the men who broke had a commissioned officer over them. They fought with the most determined bravery, until the enemy gained possession of the fort. They kept shooting all the time. The negroes ran down the hill towards the river, but the rebels kept shooting them as they were running; shot some again after they had fallen; robbed and plundered them. After everything was all gone, after we had given up the fort entirely, the guns thrown away and the firing on our part stopped, they still kept up their murderous fire, more especially on the colored troops, I thought, although the white troops suffered a great deal. I know the colored troops had a great deal the worst of it. I saw several shot after they were wounded; as they were crawling around, the secesh would step out and blow their brains out.

About this time they shot me. It must have been four or half-past four o'clock. I saw there was no chance at all, and threw down my sabre. A man took deliberate aim at me, but a short distance from me, certainly not more than 15 paces, and shot me.

Question. With a musket or pistol?

Answer. I think it was a carbine; it may have been a musket, but my impression is that it was a carbine. Soon after I was shot I was robbed. A secesh soldier came along, and wanted to know if I had any greenbacks. I gave him my pocket-book. I had about a hundred dollars, I think, more or less, and a gold watch and gold chain. They took everything in the way of valuables that I had. I saw them robbing others. That seemed to be the general way they served the wounded, so far as regards those who fell in my vicinity. Some of the colored troops jumped into the river, but were shot as fast as they were seen. One poor fellow was shot as he reached the bank of the river. They ran down and hauled him out. He got on his hands and knees, and was crawling along, when a secesh soldier put his revolver to his head, and blew his brains out. It was about the same thing all along, until dark that night.

I was very weak, but I finally found a rebel who belonged to a society that I am a member of, (the Masons,) and he got two of our colored soldiers to assist me up the hill, and he brought me some water. At that time it was about dusk. He carried me up just to the edge of the fort, and laid me down. There seemed to be quite a number of dead collected there. They were throwing them into the outside trench, and I heard them talking about burying them there. I heard one of them say, "There is a man who is not quite dead yet." They buried a number there; I do not know how many.

I was carried that night to a sort of little shanty that the rebels had occupied during the day with their sharpshooters. I received no medical attention that night at all. The next morning early I heard the report of cannon down the river. It was the gunboat 28 coming up from Memphis; she was shelling the rebels along the shore as she came up. The rebels immediately ordered the burning of all the buildings, and ordered the two buildings where the wounded were to be fired. Some one called to the officer who gave the order and said there were wounded in them. The building I was in began to catch fire. I prevailed upon one of our soldiers who had not been hurt much to draw me out, and I think others got the rest out. They drew us down a little way, in a sort of gulley, and we lay there in the hot sun without water or anything.

About this time a squad of rebels came around, it would seem for the purpose of murdering what negroes they could find. They began to shoot the wounded negroes all around there, interspersed with the whites. I was lying a little way from a wounded negro, when a secesh soldier came up to him and said: "What in hell are you doing here?" The colored soldier said he wanted to get on the gunboat. The secesh soldier said: "You want to fight us again, do you? Damn you, I'll teach you," and drew up his gun and shot him dead. Another negro was standing up erect a little way from me; he did not seem to be hurt much. The rebel loaded his gun again immediately. The negro begged of him not to shoot him, but he drew up his gun and took deliberate aim at his head. The gun snapped, but he fixed it again, and then killed him. I saw this. I heard them shooting all around there—I suppose killing them. . . .

Surgeon Horace Wardner sworn and examined.

By the chairman:
Question. Have you been in charge of this hospital, Mound City hospital?
Answer. I have been in charge of this hospital continually since the 25th of April, 1863.
Question. Will you state, if you please, what you know about the persons who escaped from Fort Pillow? And how many have been under your charge?
Answer. I have received thirty-four whites, twenty-seven colored men, and

one colored woman, and seven corpses of those who died on their way here.

Question. Did any of those you have mentioned escape from Fort Pillow?

Answer. There were eight or nine men, I forget the number, who did escape and come here, the others were paroled. I learned the following facts about that: The day after the battle a gunboat was coming up and commenced shelling the place; the rebels sent a flag of truce for the purpose of giving over into our hands what wounded remained alive; a transport then landed and sent out details to look about the grounds and pick up the wounded there, and bring them on the boat. They had no previous attention.

Question. They were then brought under your charge?

Answer. They were brought immediately to this hospital.

Question. Who commanded that boat?

Answer. I forget the naval officer's name.

Question. How long after the capture of the place did he come along?

Answer. That was the next day after the capture.

Question. Did all who were paroled in this way come under your charge, or did any of them go to other hospitals?

Answer. None went to other hospitals that I am aware of.

Question. Please state their condition.

Answer. They were the worst butchered men I have ever seen. I have been in several hard battles, but I have never seen men so mangled as they were; and nearly all of them concur in stating that they received all their wounds after they had thrown down their arms, surrendered, and asked for quarters. They state that they ran out of the fort, threw down their arms, and ran down the bank to the edge of the river, and were pursued to the top of the bank and fired on from above.

Question. Were there any females there?

Answer. I have one wounded woman from there.

Question. Were there any children or young persons there?

Answer. I have no wounded children or young persons from there.

Question. Those you have received were mostly combatants, or had been?

Answer. Yes, sir, soldiers, white or colored.

Question. Were any of the wounded here in the hospital in the fort, and wounded while in the hospital?

Answer. I so understand them.

Question. How many in that condition did you understand?

Answer. I learned from those who came here that nearly all who were in the hospital were killed. I received a young negro boy, probably sixteen years old, who was in the hospital there sick with fever, and unable to get away. The rebels entered the hospital, and with a sabre hacked his head, no doubt with the intention of splitting it open. The boy put up his hand to protect his head, and they cut off one or two of his fingers. He was brought here insensible, and died yesterday. I made a post-mortem examination, and found that the outer table of the skull was incised, the inner table was fractured, and a piece driven into the brain.

Question. This was done while he was sick in the hospital?

Answer. Yes, sir, unable to get off his bed.

Question. Have you any means of knowing how many were murdered in that way?

Answer. No positive means, except the statment of the men.

Question. How many do you suppose from the information you have received?

Answer. I suppose there were about four hundred massacred—murdered there.

Question. What proportion white, and what proportion colored, as near as you could ascertain?

Answer. The impression I have, from what I can learn, is, that all the negroes were massacred except about eighty, and all the white soldiers were killed except about one hundred or one hundred and ten.

Question. We have heard rumors that some of these persons were buried alive; did you hear anything about that?

Answer. I have two in the hospital here who were buried alive.

Question. Both colored men?

Answer. Yes, sir.

Question. How did they escape?

Answer. One of them I have not conversed with personally, the other I have. He was thrown into a pit, as he states, with a great many others, white and black, several of whom were alive; they were all buried up together. He lay on the outer edge, but his head was nearer the surface; he had one well hand, and with that hand he was able to work a place through which he could breathe, and in that way he got his head out; he lay there for some twenty-four hours, and was finally taken out by somebody. The others, next to him, were buried so deep that they could not get out, and died.

Question. Did you hear anything about any of them having been thrown into the flames and burned?

Answer. I do not know anything about that myself. These men did not say much, and in fact I did not myself have time to question them very closely.

Question. What is the general condition now of the wounded men from Fort Pillow under your charge?

Answer. They are in as good condition as they can be, probably about one-third of them must die. . . .

Statement of William F. Mays, company B, 13th Tennessee cavalry.

In about five minutes after the disappearance of the flag of truce, a general assault was made upon our works from every direction. They were kept at bay for some time, when the negroes gave way upon the left and ran down the bluff, leaving an opening through which the rebels entered and immediately commenced an indiscriminate slaughter of both white and black. We all threw down our arms and gave tokens of surrender, asking for quarter. (I was wounded in the right shoulder and muscle of the back, and knocked down before I threw down my gun.) But no quarter was given. Voices were heard upon all sides, crying, "Give them no quarter; kill them; kill them; it is General Forrest's orders." I saw four white men and at least twenty-five negroes shot while begging for mercy; and I saw one negro dragged from a hollow log within ten feet of where I lay, and as one rebel held him by the foot another shot him. These were all soldiers. There were also two negro women and three little children standing within twenty-five steps from me, when a rebel stepped up to them and said, "Yes, God damn you, you thought you were free, did you," and shot them all. They all fell but one child, when he knocked it in the head with the breech of his gun. They then disappeared in the direction of the landing, following up the fugitives, firing at them wherever seen. They came back in about three-quarters of an hour, shooting and robbing the dead of their money and clothes. I saw a man with a canteen upon him and a pistol in his hand. I ventured to ask him for a drink of water. He turned around, saying, "Yes, God damn you, I will give you a drink of water," and shot at my head three different times covering my face up with dust, and then turned from me, no doubt thinking he had killed me, remarking, "God damn you, it's too late to pray now," then went on with his pilfering. I lay there until dark, feigning death, when a rebel officer came along, drawing his sabre and ordered me to get up, threatening to run his sabre into me if I did not, saying I had to march ten miles that night. I succeeded in getting up and got among a small squad he had already gathered up, but stole away from them during the night, and got among the dead, feigning death for fear of being murdered. The next morning the gunboat came up and commenced shelling them out, when I crawled out from among the dead, and with a piece of paper motioning to the boat, she came up and I crawled on board.

his

WM. F.   +   MAYS. . . .

mark.

Jacob Thompson, (colored,) sworn and examined.
      By Mr. Gooch:
Question. Were you a soldier at Fort Pillow?

Answer. No, sir, I was not a soldier; but I went up in the fort and fought with the rest. I was shot in the hand and the head.

Question. When were you shot?

Answer. After I surrendered.

Question. How many times were you shot?

Answer. I was shot but once; but I threw my hand up, and the shot went through my hand and my head.

Question. Who shot you?

Answer. A private.

Question. What did he say?

Answer. He said, "God damn you, I will shoot you, old friend."

Question. Did you see anybody else shot?

Answer. Yes, sir; they just called them out like dogs, and shot them down. I reckon they shot about fifty, white and black, right there. They nailed some black sergeants to the logs, and set the logs on fire.

Question. When did you see that?

Answer. When I went there in the morning I saw them; they were burning all together.

Question. Did they kill them before they burned them?

Answer. No, sir, they nailed them to the logs; drove the nails right through their hands.

Question. How many did you see in that condition?

Answer. Some four or five; I saw two white men burned.

Question. Was there any one else there who saw that?

Answer. I reckon there was; I could not tell who.

Question. When was it that you saw them?

Answer. I saw them in the morning after the fight; some of them were burned almost in two. I could tell they were white men, because they were whiter than the colored men.

Question. Did you notice how they were nailed?

Answer. I saw one nailed to the side of a house; he looked like he was nailed right through his wrist. I was trying them to get to the boat when I saw it.

Question. Did you see them kill any white men?

Answer. They killed some eight or nine there. I reckon they killed more than twenty after it was all over; called them out from under the hill, and shot them down. They would call out a white man and shoot him down, and call out a colored man ahd shoot him down; do it just as fast as they could make their guns go off.

Question. Did you see any rebel officers about there when this was going on?

Answer. Yes sir; old Forrest was one.

Question. Did you know Forrest?

Answer. Yes, sir; he was a little bit of a man. I had seen him before at Jackson.

Question. Are you sure he was there when this was going on?

Answer. Yes, sir.

Question. Did you see any other officers that you knew?

Answer. I did not know any other but him. There were some two or three more officers came up there.

Question. Did you see any buried there?

Answer. Yes, sir; they buried right smart of them. They buried a great many secesh, and a great many of our folks. I think they buried more secesh than our folks.

Question. How did they bury them?

Answer. They buried the secesh over back of the fort, all except those on Fort hill; them they buried up on top of the hill where the gunboats shelled them.

Question. Did they bury any alive?

Answer. I heard the gunboat men say they dug two out who were alive.

Question. You did not see them?

Answer. No, sir. . . .

Frank Hogan, (colored,) sworn and examined.

    By the chairman:

Question. Were you at Fort Pillow on the day of the fight?

Answer. Yes, sir.

Question. In what company and regiment?

Answer. Company A, 6th United States heavy artillery.

Question. What did you see there that day, especially after the fort was taken?

Answer. I saw them shoot a great many men after the fort was taken, officers and private soldiers, white and black.

Question. After they had given up?

Answer. Yes, sir. I saw them shoot a captain in our battalion, about a quarter of an hour after he had surrendered. One of the secesh called him up to him, and asked him if he was an officer of a nigger regiment. He said, "Yes," and then they shot him with a revolver.

Question. Did they say anything more at the time they shot him?

Answer. Yes, sir; one of them said, "God damn you, I will give you a nigger officer." They talked with him a little time before they shot him. They asked him how he came to be there, and several other questions, and then asked if he belonged to a nigger regiment, and then they shot him. It was a secesh officer who shot him. I was standing a little behind.

Question. What was the rank of the secesh officer?

Answer. He was a first lieutenant. I do not know his name.

Question. Do you know the name of the officer he shot?

Answer. Yes, sir; Captain Carson, company D.

Question. Why did they not shoot you?

Answer. I do not know why they didn't.

Question. How long did you stay with them?

Answer. I staid with them two nights and one day. They took me on Tuesday evening, and I got away from them Thursday morning, about two hours before daylight. They were going to make an early move that morning, and they sent me back for some water, and I left with another boy in the same company with myself.

Question. Where did you go then?

Answer. Right straight through the woods for about three or four miles, and then we turned to the right and came to a road. We crossed the road, went down about three miles, and crossed it again, and I kept on, backwards and forwards, until I got to a creek about five or six miles from here.

Question. Do you know anything of the rebels burning any of the tents that had wounded men in them?

Answer. I know they set some on fire that had wounded men in them, but I did not see them burn, because they would not let us go around to see.

Question. About what time of the day was that?

Answer. It was when the sun was about an hour or three-quarters on from the day of the battle.

Question. Did you hear the men in there after they set the building on fire?

Answer. Yes, sir; I heard them in there. I knew they were in there. I knew that they were there sick. I saw them shoot one or two men who came out of the hospital, and then they went into the tents, and then shot them right in the tents. I saw them shoot two of them right in the head. When they charged the fort they did not look into the tents, but when they came back afterwards they shot those sick men in the head. I knew the men, because they belonged to the company I did. One of them was named Dennis Gibbs, and the other was named Alfred Flag.

Question. How long had they been sick?

Answer. They had been sick at the hospital in Memphis, and had got better a little, and been brought up here, but they never did any duty here, and went to the hospital. They came out of the hospital and went into these tents, and were killed there. They were in the hospital the morning of the fight. When the fight commenced, they left the hospital and came into the tents inside the fort.

Question. Did you see them bury any of our men?

Answer. I saw them put them in a ditch. I did not see them cover them up.

Question. Were they all really dead or not?

Answer. I saw them bury one man alive, and heard the secesh speak about it as much as twenty times. He was shot in the side, but he was not dead, and was breathing along right good.

Question. Did you see the man?

Answer. Yes, sir.

Question. How came they to bury him when he was alive?

Answer. They said he would die any how, and they would let him stay. Every once in a while, if they put dirt on him, he would move his hands. I was standing right there, and saw him when they put him in, and saw he was not dead.

Ruins of Richmond, Virginia, 1865 (National Archives). Modern war makes all of a nation's resources into military objectives. One of the results of this kind of warfare is revealed in this photograph of a business section of Richmond. During the last year of the Civil War, Union armies burned towns to punish the supporters of the Confederacy. But in this case, Richmond's defenders had set fire to the warehouses shown here so that their supplies and machinery could not be used by the conquerors. In both cases, innocent people suffered.

THE BURNING OF ATLANTA

William T. Sherman

Although he may never have said, "War is hell," William Tecumseh Sherman (1820–1891) did say, "There is many a boy here to-day who looks on war as all glory, but boys, it is all hell." Sherman knew that modern war had brought the suffering and destruction of battle into the homes, farms, and shops of noncombatants.

Most military memoirs published after the Civil War were fond recollections of military service. They emphasized the romantic vision of camaraderie and bravery. They minimized suffering and emphasized heroism. But the Civil War had changed the face of war. Civilians now were as important as armies in sustaining the conflict. Civilian resources—farms, cities, and factories—had to be destroyed along with the armies they supplied. Generals on both sides recognized the need to bring the pain of war into the enemy's homes, but only the Northern generals had the resources to carry out this scorched-earth policy.

Few motion picture scenes are better remembered than *Gone with the Wind*'s portrayal of the burning of Atlanta. The man who ordered that destruction was General Sherman. By 1864, Sherman had become convinced that the only way to restore the Union—forcing the Confederacy to surrender unconditionally—was to destroy the economic base that supported the South's armies in the field. Sherman gave the people of Atlanta time to leave their homes before he issued the order to torch the city. When Atlanta's mayor and members of the city council begged for leniency, Sherman sent them the following letter.

SOURCE: William T. Sherman, *Memoirs of General William T. Sherman*, Vol. 2 (New York: D. Appleton & Co., 1875).

Gentlemen: I have your letter of the 11th, in the nature of a petition to revoke my orders removing all the inhabitants from Atlanta. I have read it carefully, and give full credit to your statements of the distress that will be occasioned, and yet shall not revoke my orders, because they were not designed to meet the humanities of the case, but to prepare for the future struggles in which millions of good people outside of Atlanta have a deep interest. We must have peace, not only at Atlanta, but in all America. To secure this, we must stop the war that now desolates our once happy and favored country. To stop war, we must defeat the rebel armies which are arrayed against the laws and Constitution that all must respect and obey. To defeat those armies, we must prepare the way to reach them in their recesses, provided with the arms and instruments which enable us to accomplish our purpose. Now, I know the vindictive nature of our enemy, that we may have many years of military operations from this quarter; and, therefore, deem it wise and prudent to prepare in time. The use of Atlanta for warlike purposes is inconsistent with its character as a home for families. There will be no manufactures, commerce, or agriculture here, for the maintenance of families, and sooner or later want will compel the inhabitants to go. Why not go now, when the arrangements are completed for the transfer, instead of waiting till the plunging shot of contending armies will renew the scenes of the past month? Of course, I do not apprehend any such thing at this moment, but you do not suppose this army will be here until the war is over. I cannot discuss this subject with you fairly, because I cannot impart to you what we propose to do, but I assert that our military plans make it necessary for the inhabitants to go away, and I can only renew my offer of services to make their exodus in any direction as easy and comfortable as possible.

You cannot qualify war in harsher terms than I will. War is cruelty, and you cannot refine it; and those who brought war into our country deserve all the curses and maledictions a people can pour out. I know I had no hand in making this war, and I know I will make more sacrifices to-day than any of you to secure peace. But you cannot have peace and a division of our country. If the United States submits to a division now, it will not stop, but will go on until we reap the fate of Mexico, which is eternal war. The United States does and must assert its authority, wherever it once had power; for, if it relaxes one bit to pressure, it is gone, and I believe that such is the national feeling. This feeling assumes various shapes, but always comes back to that of Union. Once admit the Union, once more acknowledge the authority of the national Government, and, instead of devoting your houses and streets and roads to the dread uses of war, I and this army become at once your protectors and supporters, shielding you from danger, let it come from what quarter it may. I know that a few individuals cannot resist a torrent of error and passion, such as swept the South into rebellion, but you can point out, so that we may know those who desire a government, and those who insist on war and its desolation.

You might as well appeal against the thunder-storm as against these terrible hardships of war. They are inevitable, and the only way the people of Atlanta can hope once more to live in peace and quiet at home, is to stop the war, which can only be done by admitting that it began in error and is perpetuated in pride.

We don't want your negroes, or your horses, or your houses, or your lands, or any thing you have, but we do want and will have a just obedience to the laws of the United States. That we will have, and if it involves the destruction of your improvements, we cannot help it.

You have heretofore read public sentiment in your newspapers, that live by flasehood and excitement; and the quicker you seek for truth in other quarters, the better. I repeat then that, by the original compact of Government, the United States had certain rights in Georgia, which have never been relinquished and never will be; that the South began war by seizing forts, arsenals, mints, custom-houses, etc., etc., long before Mr. Lincoln was installed, and before the South had one jot or tittle of provocation. I myself have seen in Missouri, Kentucky, Tennessee, and Mississippi, hundreds and thousands of women and children fleeing from your armies and desperadoes, hungry and with bleeding feet. In Memphis, Vicksburg, and Mississippi, we fed thousands upon thousands of the families of rebel soldiers left on our hands, and whom we could not see starve. Now that war comes home to you, you feel very different. You deprecate its horrors, but did not feel them when you sent car-loads of soldiers and ammunition, and moulded shells and shot, to carry war into Kentucky and Tennessee, to desolate the homes of hundreds and thousands of good people who only asked to live in peace at their old homes, and under the Government of their inheritance. But these comparisons are idle. I want peace, and believe it can only be reached through union and war, and I will ever conduct war with a view to perfect and early success.

But, my dear sirs, when peace does come, you may call on me for any thing. Then will I share with you the last cracker, and watch with you to shield your homes and families against danger from every quarter.

Now you must go, and take with you the old and feeble, feed and nurse them, and build for them, in more quiet places, proper habitations to shield them against the weather until the mad passions of men cool down, and allow the Union and Peace once more to settle over your old homes at Atlanta.

ANNOTATED BIBLIOGRAPHY

No other American war has had more written about it than the Civil War. Like his forefathers in the Revolutionary War, every man who went to war in 1861 realized that he was entering the greatest event of his lifetime. Whether he fought to preserve the Union or to establish a southern Confederacy, each soldier knew that the war would have epic importance. Thousands of men kept journals or diaries and sent millions of letters home. After the war many would write memoirs about their service. Despite thousands of original sources in print, untold numbers wait to be discovered in attics and archives. So many primary sources have been published in the last thirty years that a 350-page book (*Civil War Eyewitnesses: An Annotated Bibliography of Books and Articles, 1955–1986* by Garold L. Cole, 1988) lists almost 1,400 such narratives.

The best military history of the Civil War is Shelby Foote's three-volume series, *The Civil War* (1958–1974). Foote combines a novelist's love for words with a historian's scholarship to write a captivating history of the war. Equally well written, but heavy on anecdotes, is Bruce Catton's centennial trilogy *The Coming Fury* (1961), *Terrible Swift Sword* (1963), and *Never Call Retreat* (1965). Catton's military history of the Union, *This Hallowed Ground* (1956), won a Pulitzer Prize and still ranks as the best one-volume military history of the war. There is no comparable one-volume history of Confederate military operations, but Frank N. Vandiver's *Their Tattered Flags* (1970) is an entertaining and reliable history of the Confederacy that emphasizes military matters.

Possibly the best one-volume history of the era of the Civil War is James McPherson's *Battle Cry of Freedom* (1988), which places battles into the broader perspective of economic, social, and political history. McPherson won a Pulitzer Prize for this work. An important account of military strategy and tactics is Herman Hattaway and Archer Jones's *How the North Won: A Military History of the Civil War* (1983). A useful guide to the most important battles is Craig L. Symonds's *A Battlefield Atlas of the Civil War*, with maps by William J. Clipson (2nd edition, 1983). Three important reference works are Mark Boatner's *Civil War Dictionary* (1959), E. B. Long's *Civil War Day by Day* (1971), and *The Historical Times Illustrated Encyclopedia of the Civil War* (1986), edited by Patricia L. Faust. The Civil War was the first American war to be broadly covered in photographs. A fine collection of them can be found in *The Image of War: 1861–1865* (1981–1984), a six-volume work edited by William C. Davis.

There is no history of the navies to match Catton's or Foote's work, but the most complete, and readable, history is Virgil Carrington Jones's *The Civil War at Sea*, three volumes (1960–62). The best one-volume naval history is Bern Anderson's *By Sea and By River* (1962).

There are more good books about battles, generals, and regiments than can be listed in this entire bibliography. Among the best are George R.

Stewart's *Pickett's Charge* (1959), subtitled "a microhistory of the final attack at Gettysburg, July 3, 1863." John J. Pullen's scholarly and entertaining history of *The Twentieth Maine: A Volunteer Regiment in the Civil War* (1957) is unit history at its best. Soldier life in both armies has been brilliantly reconstructed by Bell Irvin Wiley in *The Life of Johnny Reb* (1943) and *The Life of Billy Yank* (1951). Naval service on the western rivers is well told by John D. Milligan in *Gunboats Down the Mississippi* (1965). Reid Mitchell's *Civil War Soldiers* (1988) is an important, recent work that examines the universal question: Why do men fight in wars?

The best collection of primary sources on the military is a series collectively known as *Battles and Leaders of the Civil War* (1887–1888), which first appeared in the *Century Magazine*. Since then it has been published in many editions. The editors of *Century* prevailed upon leading army and navy officers to write brief memoirs about their military service. Henry Steele Commager's *The Blue and the Gray*, two volumes (1950) is a useful collection of excerpts from letters, diaries, official reports, and memoirs. *The Blue and the Gray* provides entertaining military reading. Richard Wheeler's *Sword Over Richmond: An Eyewitness History of McClellan's Peninsula Campaign* (1986) offers a narrative through primary accounts by participants.

The best biographies are Douglas Southall Freeman's *Lee*, four volumes (1934–1935), and the three-volume biography of Grant begun by Lloyd Lewis in *Captain Sam Grant* (1950) and completed by Bruce Catton in *Grant Moves South* (1960) and *Grant Takes Command* (1969). Freeman supplemented his biography of Lee with *Lee's Lieutenants*, a three-volume tactical study of the Army of Northern Virginia. Other important military biographies are Lloyd Lewis's *Sherman, Fighting Prophet* (1932); G. F. R. Henderson's *Stonewall Jackson and the American Civil War*, two volumes (1898); T. Harry Williams's *P. G. T. Beauregard: Napoleon in Gray* (1955); and Stephen W. Sears's *George B. McClellan: The Young Napoleon* (1988). Ezra J. Warner has written an indispensable reference that provides brief biographies of all Civil War generals in *Generals in Gray* (1959) and *Generals in Blue* (1964).

Many military leaders wrote autobiographies. These include Joseph E. Johnston's *Narrative of Military Operations* (1874); E. Porter Alexander's *Military Memoirs of a Confederate* (1874); William T. Sherman's *Memoirs*, two volumes (1875); George B. McClellan's *McClellan's Own Story* (1887); and Raphael Semmes's *Memoirs of Service Afloat During the War Between the States* (1869). Some of the best memoirs came from men in the ranks. Possibly the most famous is Sam R. Watkins's amusing story of *"Co. Aytch"* [H], *Maury Grays, First Tennessee Regiment; or, A Side Show of the Big Show* (1900). Other good military accounts are John H. Worsham's *One of*

Jackson's Foot Cavalry (1912); J. H. Kidd's *Personal Recollections of a Cavalryman* (1908); Leander Stillwell's *The Story of a Common Soldier* (1920); Stephen F. Blanding's *Recollections of a Sailor Boy* (1886); and *Soldiering: The Civil War Diary of Rice C. Bull* (1977), edited by K. Jack Bauer.

There are several fine novels about the war. The best one written by a participant is John William De Forest's *Miss Ravenel's Conversion from Secession to Loyalty* (1869). Some critics consider Stephen Crane's story of heroism and cowardice, *The Red Badge of Courage* (1895), as one of the best war novels ever written. Three modern works, which have won praise from literary critics and historians, are Joseph Stanley Pennell's *Rome Hanks* (1944), an absorbing story of battle and life in the war, and two tales of battle, *Shiloh: A Novel* (1952) by Shelby Foote, and Michael Shaara's story of Gettysburg, *The Killer Angels* (1974)—both reveal the unfolding of the battle through the eyes of key participants.

THE RISE OF PROFESSIONALISM

Although the Civil War had inspired, or coerced, millions of Americans to join the army and navy, most veterans agreed that a strong armed force was unnecessary in the postwar era. At the end of the war, the United States quickly reduced its military forces and went on a binge of industrial expansion that exploited land, labor, and capital. The last half of the nineteenth century marked the rise of the nation as the world's richest industrial power.

In this race for material prosperity, the military largely had been forgotten. A small American army served in the West chasing Indians, while the navy patrolled remote Pacific atolls. Many officers resented their isolation from the mainstream of American culture. Some tried to explain their profession to the public (while justifying it to themselves) in military periodicals and books. Others warned of the need to prepare for future wars through peacetime training, and argued for larger expenditures for modern arms. Many professional officers disparaged the militia and called for a strengthening of the regular army and navy. They also urged soldiers and sailors to stay out of civilian life, and particularly to avoid politics.

"Scientific" studies in modern disciplines of sociology, anthropology, and history supported the military's arguments, and officers used them to gain a broader sympathy for their profession. Some military men with a scholarly bent looked to discover similarities in past civilizations and other countries. They believed that history could prove that a strong peacetime military force was necessary for a nation's survival in war. Their arguments, combined with the decrepit state of military hardware, brought military reform near the end of the century.

The modernization of the armed forces coincided with the disappearance of the U.S. frontier. Manifest destiny, which two generations before had carried Americans to the Pacific Ocean, now beckoned them overseas. Colonies, raw materials, and large navies appeared as the hallmarks of modern civilization. The United States refused to be left behind. It, too, claimed overseas colonies and began the twentieth century with an empire.

THE FREEDMEN AT WEST POINT

John M. Schofield

The Civil War had not only saved the Union but also had freed black Americans from slavery. Blacks had served with the Union forces, but they were almost always commanded by whites. After the war, the military continued to welcome blacks as enlisted men, but the idea of black officers triggered racial stereotypes and fears. Stumbling blocks were placed in the way of any black man who sought a commission.

A dozen black cadets were appointed to West Point before 1890, but only six remained beyond their first semester. Henry O. Flipper was the first black to graduate from the academy (1877). Two others graduated before 1890. Although the academy's strict regimen was difficult for everyone, white cadets did not have to face the racial epithets and slurs that greeted blacks.

On 6 April 1880, Johnson C. Whittaker, a black cadet from South Carolina, was discovered lying on the floor of his room—bound, cut, and beaten. Whittaker was unable to identify any of his attackers. The academy staff alleged that Whittaker had staged the event himself. Although the deeply religious cadet denied this accusation, and a court of inquiry could never establish how he had managed to tie himself up, the court concluded that Whittaker had feigned the attack. Two years later the judge advocate general overturned the decision. Whittaker had won on appeal, yet he was dismissed from the academy because he had failed a required course.

The following document is a portion of the report to the secretary of war filed by General John M. Schofield (1831–1906), superintendent of West Point. Schofield left no doubts about his racist feelings. With opinions

SOURCE: *Annual Report of the Secretary of War* (1880).

like his so common, it was no wonder that black cadets felt great prejudice. Shortly afterward, President Rutherford B. Hayes replaced Schofield with Oliver Otis Howard, a man whose prior command of the Freedmen's Bureau had made him more sensitive to blacks.

The outrage which was committed at the cadets' barracks on the 6th of last April, and which has occupied so much of the public attention, deserves notice here mainly for the purpose of correcting erroneous impressions which have prevailed respecting the investigation which followed it, and for the important lesson which that investigation teaches. That matter was promptly investigated by the commandant of cadets, under my direction, in the usual way, and in the only way provided by law or regulations. The fraudulent character of the outrage was fully demonstrated within a very few hours of its discovery. Indeed, the fraud was so transparent that it could not possibly have escaped almost immediate detection. The surgeon reported that he had found the cadet in full possession of all his faculties, and yet *feigning* unconsciousness when discovered. His alleged injuries from blows upon the nose and head and in his side had been found utterly fictitious. No such blows and no such injuries had been received. The alleged note of warning was at once discovered to be in the familiar and peculiar hand-writing of the cadet himself. The resemblance in some parts was so striking as to suggest the possibility of skillful imitation. But closer inspection showed the parts bearing such resemblance to have been written in a natural hand, while some other parts were evidently disguised. There was ample ground for the conviction, *produced in the minds of all who saw the note*, that the cadet himself was the author of it. That conviction, added to the glaring falsehoods and attempt at deception, in respect to the alleged blows and feigned condition of unconsciousness, fully justified the commandant's report to me that the cadet was a criminal participant in, if not the sole author of, the fraudulent outrage of which he had pretended to be the victim. . . .

While every lawful right of the colored cadets has been fully secured to them, and their official treatment has been not only just but very kind and indulgent, their social relations to their fellow cadets have not been what they appear to have been led to expect. Military discipline is not an effective method of promoting social intercourse or of overcoming social prejudice. On the contrary the enforced association of the white cadets with their colored companions, to which they had never been accustomed before they came from home, appears to have destroyed any dispositon which before existed to indulge in such association. Doubtless, this was due in part to the bad personal character of some of the young colored men sent to West Point, and in part to the natural reaction against an attempt to govern social intercourse by military regulations. Personal merit may rapidly overcome unjust prejudice when all are free to regulate their own social habits. But when social intercourse is enforced in spite of prejudice on the one side and of personal demerit on the other, the result must be rather an increase than a diminution of the preexisting prejudice. For this reason, the Military Academy cannot be made a favorable place at which to first introduce social intercourse between the white and black man. West Point will, at the most, only be able to follow the example of the country at large in this respect. . . .

The difficulty surrounding this subject is aggravated by the somewhat common error of ascribing it to an unreasonable prejudice against race or color. The prevailing "prejudice" is rather a just aversion to qualities which the people of the United States have long been accustomed to associate with a state of slavery and intercourse without legal marriage, and of which color and its various shades are only the external signs. That feeling could not be removed by the simple act of enfranchising the slave. It can only be done by education and moral elevation of the race. That great work has only been commenced, and it must of necessity require much time. To send to West Point for a four years' competition a young man who was born in slavery is to assume that half a generation has been sufficient to raise a colored man to the social, moral, and intellectual level which the average white man has reached in several hundred years. As well might the common farmhorse be entered in a four-mile race against the best blood inherited from a long line of English racers.

Cavalry officers and Indian scouts near Camp Thomas, Arizona Territory, 25 February 1886 (United States Army Military History Institute). Since colonial times, some Indians had cooperated with whites to fight other Indians. All tribes had a network of allies and enemies. The first reading in this book dealt with the Narragansett Indians, who had aided the New England colonists to find and destroy the Pequots. The formidable terrain in the American West meant that soldiers had to use Indians guides to help them find hidden camps. The Indian scouts were highly effective. When Chalipan, an Apache chief, surrendered his 300 braves at Camp Verde, Arizona Territory (6 April 1873), he told General George Crook that he "had never been afraid of the Americans alone, but now that their own people were fighting against them they did not know what to do; they could not go to sleep at night, because they feared to be surrounded before daybreak; they could not hunt—the noise of the guns would attract the troops; they could not cook mescal or anything else, because the flame and smoke would draw down the soldiers; they could not live in the valley—there were too many soldiers; they had retreated to the mountain tops, thinking to hide in the snow until the soldiers went home, but the scouts found them out and the soldiers followed them."

BATTLE OF BEAR PAW
MOUNTAIN

Edward McClernand

The last quarter of the nineteenth century marked the end of the Indian Wars. By 1900, native Americans either had been forced onto reservations or exterminated. For U.S. soldiers, fighting Indians was a lonely, difficult duty. The soldiers discovered that the best results could be obtained from winter campaigns and surprise attacks on Indian camps at dawn. Both sides commonly committed atrocities.

The following document is part of a letter written by Edward McClernand to Henry Romeyn about the battle of Bear Paw Mountain (30 September 1877). This was the last stand of the Nez Perce Indians on their desperate flight to Canada. Seven hundred hungry Indians (including 250 warriors) had stopped at Bear Paw Mountain, about a day's journey from the border, to hunt buffalo. U.S. soldiers, numbering about six hundred, plus their Indian allies, charged through the Nez Perce camp and then surrounded them. Unable to continue to fight, Chief Joseph surrendered his people to Colonel Nelson Miles. "I am tired of fighting," the Nez Perce chief said. "I want to have time to look for my children and see how many of them I can find. Maybe I shall find them among the dead. Hear me, my chiefs! I am tired: my heart is sick and sad. From where the sun now stands I will fight no more forever."

In 1894, Romeyn was awarded the Congressional Medal of Honor for his bravery in this battle. The citation read, "for most distinct gallant action against hostile Nez Perce Indians at Bear Paw Mountain . . . in leading his command into close range of the enemy there, maintaining his position, and vigorously prosecuting the fight until he was severely wounded."

SOURCE: Letter (11 December 1889) in the Edward McClernand papers, U.S. Army Military History Institute Archives, Carlisle Barracks, Pennsylvania.

*T*he battalion of the Second Cavalry engaged in the action with the Nez Perce Indians at the Bear Paw Mountains in 1877 was composed of troops "F"—"G"—and "H." . . .

If my memory serves me correctly, Troop "G" went into the action fifty-three strong, and the others were about the same strength.

The casualties were few, due principally to the fact that the battalion instead of halting and dismounting under the withering fire from the ravine in which the Indians had taken refuge (as other parts of the command did), continued its charge at a full gallop, sweeping the large pony herd before it, and going within twenty-five or fifty yards of the Indian position to gather a large number of the ponies.

I do not wish to be understood offering a criticism upon the manner in which the battalions were handled, I am aware that rough ground in their front necessarily checked their charge, while on our side of the little creek there was, near the camp, a smooth valley very suitable for charging.

Capt. Tyler saw the importance of making straight for the pony herd as soon as the rough ground, over which we had been galloping for a mile or two, gave way to the little valley and enabled us to see the Indian position and their animals. He promptly gave the necessary directions and in an incredibly short time the greater part of the herd was secured.

A part of the Indians had broken away from the main body in the ravine and were trying to save three or four hundred ponies a half mile still further in our front, down the creek from the main camp, and just as the principal herd was secured an order was received from Genl. Miles to send a troop to capture the other one. . . .

A running fight was kept up for about five miles. The Indians thus pursued were about sixty, many of whom returned under the cover of night to their former camp. They were mostly men and boys, and as men had to be detached from time to time to guard the ponies the Indians were forced to abandon, the enemy finally became stronger than what remained of the troop, and began to work around our flanks and rear.

These facts coupled with the noise of the field guns in the direction where we separated from Genl. Miles, determined the return of the troop to the battle field which the rolling hills completely hid from our sight.

For the purpose of covering our retreat as well as possible, a long and deep ravine leading down to the creek near to the Indian camp was selected, and into this were driven the two-hundred and fifty ponies captured since leaving Tyler. The troop then moved into the ravine and dismounted. At this time the Indians closed in from all sides except immediately in our rear, where they had not yet had time to get. When the troop was dismounted there were not more than thirty men with it, and these divided into two platoons alternately took position in the lateral ravines that put into the main one. The first platoon would hold the enemy in check until the second had taken position several hundred yards to the rear, when the first platoon would fall back and so on.

By this means a disaster, which seemed imminent at the commencement of the retreat, and of which some of the men had began to speak, was averted.

On reaching the immediate vicinity of the main battle field, although an occasional shot was still heard I had, on account of the broken ground, considerable difficulty in finding our line, and posting my troop so as to hold in check the Indians who had been following us, I set off on foot to find Capt. Tyler, thinking I could do so without any trouble. In my wanderings I struck the ravine in which the Indians were, and, near that came upon some of the dead and wounded of the 7th Cavalry. One wounded Sergeant begged me piteously for a drink of water, which I did not have to give. He could not move, or give me any information about our position. I was alone and in full view of the Indians, although I did not realize this at the time. I should judge they were between one-hundred and two-hundred yards away. That evening about dusk Capt. Tyler accompanied by two orderlies and myself went to the same spot to look after the wounded. In this work we were not molested, but in attempting to lead away a cavalry horse which was standing beside a dead trooper whose arm had fallen so that the reins were caught in his elbow, the bullets whizzed about our ears like bees, when we quickly dashed the spurs into our horses and flew over the hill. Had it been perfect daylight, I do not see how we could have escaped. This was the second time during the day that I unconsciously put myself in danger of being shot in this part of the field. On the first occasion I suppose the Indians mistook me for one of the wounded. I am confirmed in this belief by a conversation had with Chief Joseph within the last month. . . .

That evening, several hours after dark, we were ordered to shift our position nearer to the other troops and astride the ravine in which the Indians were. It was very dark and we had great difficulty in getting located, especially as an officer who was to show "F" & "G" troops their position had taken himself off to visit in another part of the command. Here the battalion remained until the next night, when after dark we were shifted back to our former position. . . . On account of the extreme darkness Capt. Tyler got his command nearer to the Indians than was intended; indeed we could distinctly hear their voices in ordinary conversation. The command was dismounted, the horses led a little to the rear, and the men, after being deployed as skirmishers, were directed to lie down. Occasionally some Indians would try to escape when the skirmishers in their front would open fire, directing their fire by the noise made, as it was too dark to see. A few of the Nez Perces succeeded in dashing through between our skirmishers, followed by a perfect volley of wildly directed shots. However, several dead ponies were found in our front next morning. One horse in my troop was killed, and my own horse stampeded and fell into the hands of the Indians. I recovered him after their surrender.

As there were only two officers present we were obliged to pass frequently from one end of the line to the other. Each man was required to call softly to his neighbor at intervals of about five minutes. It was in this way one man was found to be dead, having been shot through the body—probably by the Indians who broke through our lines. Even this frequent calling to each other was not sufficient to prevent some of the men from falling asleep, they were so worn out with fatique and benumbed by cold. It commenced to rain about nine P.M., which rain at midnight became snow. None of the men had their blankets, and for some reason I do not recall I did not have my overcoat. That was certainly the most disagreeable night I ever passed. It was after ten o'clock the next day before anything was had to eat, and several hours later before the much longed for cup of coffee was had.

Either that evening or the next, Capt. Tyler's battalion was moved from the extreme right flank to the left, covering a field gun, pointed so as [to] command the place where the Indians came down in the evening to get water.

U.S.S. Wampanoag, 1868 (National Archives). The Wampanoag was the most successful American steam warship before the twentieth century. It not only surpassed every test that the navy could devise but also was the world's fastest ship, able to cruise at almost 17 knots. Despite the Wampanoag's proven success, senior naval officers (who had been raised in the sailing navy) opposed the introduction of steam-powered vessels. They argued that sailors had always gone to sea under sheets of white canvas and that modern captains had to know how to sail their ships, as well as how to fight them. Steam vessels meant that too many responsibilities were controlled by "engineers" who supervised the steam engines and would be responsible for the ship, except in combat. A compromise was reached when the ships were equipped with both sails and steam engines. Yet even these ugly hybrids met great opposition. A naval board agreed with the senior captains and recommended that the Wampanoag be sold. Their outdated fears were emphasized in their report, which concluded that, "Lounging through the watches of a steamer, or acting as firemen or coal bearers, will not produce in a seaman that combination of boldness, strength and skill which characterized the American sailor of an elder day; and the habitual exercise of an officer of a command, the execution of which is not under his own eye, is a poor substitute for the school of observation, promptness, and command found only on the deck of a sailing vessel."

THE INFLUENCE OF SEA POWER UPON HISTORY

Alfred Thayer Mahan

Alfred Thayer Mahan (1840–1914) was the world's foremost naval strategist at the end of the nineteenth century. Mahan had come by his profession naturally; his father, Dennis Hart Mahan, was Professor of Civil and Military Engineering at West Point, where he had an enormous influence over the officers who would lead the Union and Confederate armies in the Civil War. Young Mahan chose to go to the Naval Academy. Mahan had an undistinguished career until 1885, when he was appointed to the newly established Naval War College. In preparation for his new post, Mahan studied naval history. His research led him to conclude that naval history presented both an example and a moral for all nations to follow.

Captain Mahan's study concentrated on Great Britain, the premier naval power of his day. Not surprisingly, Mahan decided that England's greatness stemmed from the powerful Royal Navy. He extracted naval principles from historical examples, and discussed them in his book, *The Influence of Sea Power Upon History, 1660–1783,* the first of his many works on sea power and naval history.

Mahan's writings soon became required reading for naval officers throughout the world. At home, Mahan's theories were interpreted to justify imperialism, a large navy, and America's predestined role as a great naval power. Mahan's conclusions on the importance of commerce, geography, and national will form the core of modern thought on naval strategy.

SOURCE: Alfred Thayer Mahan, *The Influence of Sea Power Upon History, 1660–1783* (Boston: Little, Brown, 1890).

*I*t is then particularly in the field of naval strategy that the teachings of the past have a value which is in no degree lessened. They are there useful not only as illustrative of principles, but also as precedents, owing to the comparative permanence of the conditions. This is less obviously true as to tactics, when the fleets come into collision at the point to which strategic considerations have brought them. The unresting progress of mankind causes continual change in the weapons; and with that must come a continual change in the manner of fighting,—in the handling and disposition of troops or ships on the battlefield. Hence arises a tendency on the part of many connected with maritime matters to think that no advantage is to be gained from the study of former experiences; that time so used is wasted. This view, though natural, not only leaves wholly out of sight those broad strategic considerations which lead nations to put fleets afloat, which direct the sphere of their action, and so have modified and will continue to modify the history of the world, but is one-sided and narrow even as to tactics. The battles of the past succeeded or failed according as they were fought in conformity with the principles of war; and the seaman who carefully studies the causes of success or failure will not only detect and gradually assimilate these principles, but will also acquire increased aptitude in applying them to the tactical use of the ships and weapons of his own day. He will observe also that changes of tactics have not only taken place *after* changes in weapons, which necessarily is the case, but that the interval between such changes has been unduly long. This doubtless arises from the fact that an improvement of weapons is due to the energy of one or two men, while changes in tactics have to overcome the inertia of a conservative class; but it is a great evil. It can be remedied only by a candid recognition of each change, by careful study of the powers and limitations of the new ship or weapon, and by a consequent adaptation of the method of using it to the qualities it possesses, which will constitute its tactics. History shows that it is vain to hope that military men generally will be at the pains to do this, but that the one who does will go into battle with a great advantage,—a lesson in itself of no mean value. . . .

This study has become more than ever important now to navies, because of the great and steady power of movement possessed by the modern steamer. The best-planned schemes might fail through stress of weather in the days of the galley and the sailing-ship; but this difficulty has almost disappeared. The principles which should direct great naval combinations have been applicable to all ages, and are deducible from history; but the power to carry them out with little regard to the weather is a recent gain. . . .

The first and most obvious light in which the sea presents itself from the political and social point of view is that of a great highway; or better, perhaps, of a wide common, over which men may pass in all directions, but on which some well-worn paths show that controlling reasons have led them to choose certain lines of travel rather than others. These lines of travel are called trade routes; and the reasons which have determined them are to be sought in the history of the world. . . .

Under modern conditions, however, home trade is but a part of the business of a country bordering on the sea. Foreign necessaries or luxuries must be brought to its ports, either in its own or in foreign ships, which will return, bearing in exchange the products of the country, whether they be the fruits of the earth or the works of men's hands; and it is the wish of every nation that this shipping business should be done by its own vessels. The ships that thus sail to and fro must have secure ports to which to return, and must, as far as possible, be followed by the protection of their country throughout the voyage.

The protection in time of war must be extended by armed shipping. The necessity of a navy, in the restricted sense of the word, springs, therefore, from the existence of a peaceful shipping, and disappears with it, except in the case of a nation which has aggressive tendencies, and keeps up a navy merely as a branch of the military establishment. . . .

The needs of commerce, however, were not all provided for when safety had been secured at the far end of the road. The voyages were long and dangerous, the seas often beset with enemies. In the most active days of colonizing there prevailed on the sea a lawlessness the very memory of which is now almost lost, and the days of settled peace between maritime nations were few and far between. Thus arose the demand for stations along the road, like the Cape of Good Hope, St. Helena, and Mauritius, not primarily for trade, but for defence and war; the demand for the possession of posts like Gibraltar, Malta, Louisburg, at the entrance of the Gulf of St. Lawrence,— posts whose value was chiefly strategic, though not necessarily wholly so. Colonies and colonial posts were sometimes commercial, sometimes military in their character; and it was exceptional that the same position was equally important in both points of view, as New York was.

In these three things—production, with the necessity of exchanging products, shipping, whereby the exchange is carried on, and colonies, which facilitate and enlarge the operations of shipping and tend to protect it by multiplying points of safety—is to be found the key to much of the history, as well as of the policy, of nations bordering upon the sea. The policy has varied both with the spirit of the age and with the character and clear-sightedness of the rulers; but the history of the seaboard nations has been less determined by the shrewdness and foresight of governments than by conditions of position, extent, configuration, number and character of their people,—by what are called, in a word, natural conditions. . . .

As the practical object of this inquiry is to draw from the lessons of history inferences applicable to one's own country and service, it is proper now to ask how far the conditions of the United States involve serious danger, and call for action on the part of the government, in order to build again her sea power. It will not be too much to say that the action of the government since the Civil War, and up to this day, has been effectively directed solely to what has been called the first link in the chain which makes sea power. Internal development, great production, with the accompanying aim and boast of self-sufficingness, such has been the object, such to some extent the result. In this the government has faithfully reflected the bent of the controlling elements of the country, though it is not always easy to feel that such controlling elements are truly representative, even in a free country. However that may be, there is no doubt that, besides having no colonies, the intermediate link of a peaceful shipping, and the interests involved in it, are now likewise lacking. In short, the United States has only one link of the three. . . .

What need has the United States of sea power? Her commerce is even now carried on by others; why should her people desire that which, if possessed, must be defended at great cost? So far as this question is economical, it is outside the scope of this work; but conditions which may entail suffering and loss on the country by war are directly pertinent to it. . . .

The question is eminently one in which the influence of the government should make itself felt, to build up for the nation a navy which, if not capable of reaching distant countries, shall at least be able to keep clear the chief approaches to its own. The eyes of the country have for a quarter of a century been turned from the sea; . . . it may safely be said that it is essential to the welfare of the whole country that the conditions of trade and commerce should remain, as far as possible, unaffected by an external war. In order to do this, the enemy must be kept not only out of our ports, but far away from our coasts.

Can this navy be had without restoring the merchant shipping? It is doubtful. . . . in a representative government any military expenditure must have a strongly represented interest behind it, convinced of its necessity. Such an interest in sea power does not exist, cannot exist here without action by the government. How such a merchant shipping should be built up, whether by subsidies or by free trade, by constant administration of tonics or by free movement in the open air, is not a military but an economical question. Even had the United States a great national shipping, it may be doubted whether a sufficient navy would follow; the distance which separates her from other great powers, in one way a protection, is also a snare. The motive, if any there be, which will give the United States a navy, is probably now quickening in the Central American Isthmus. Let us hope it will not come to the birth too late.

THE MILITARY POLICY OF THE UNITED STATES

Emory Upton

The late nineteenth century was the age of industry. Many politicians considered war an aberration of human nature, disruptive to the natural business cycle. The American dream encouraged individuals to use their talents to rise above their fellow citizens. The military, on the other hand, demanded conformity and sublimation of individuality. Some politicians talked of military life as being *un*American and hoped to revive the nation's dependence on the militia.

Emory Upton (1839–1881) had risen to the brevet (or temporary) rank of major general in the Civil War, but returned to his permanent rank of captain following it. Although widely respected as the most brilliant junior officer in the army by his peers, Upton was an introspective and despondent man. His disillusionment with the American way of war began during the Civil War, and his personal despondency was reinforced when his wife died shortly after their marriage. As commandant of cadets at West Point (1870–1875), Upton wondered why he should encourage young men to serve such an ungrateful nation. At the urging of his mentor, William T. Sherman, Upton took a world tour to examine the armies of Europe and Asia. Upton wanted the United States to adopt a military policy like Germany's—a largely autonomous army under limited civilian control.

Using "lessons" that he extracted (and distorted) from his study of history, Upton returned to John C. Calhoun's earlier arguments for an expansible professional army. Upton contended that the militia had always left the United States unprepared to fight. This, according to Upton, was

SOURCE: Emory Upton, *The Military Policy of the United States* (Washington, DC: U.S. Government Printing Office, 1904).

the primary reason for so many casualties in the first months of a war. The best way to ensure future peace, Upton argued, was through a strong, well-trained army. And the best way to obtain that was to initiate an expansible system in which senior officers would be kept on duty and encouraged to pursue their profession.

Upton's polemical manuscript criticized congressmen and presidents, who, in his opinion, had permitted fiscal considerations and outdated traditions to take precedence over human life. He urged the American people to embrace military life as an honorable and necessary profession, the equal of careers in industry or politics. When Upton took a pistol to his head in 1881, he left behind the uncompleted manuscript in which he had developed his arguments for a modern professional army.

The following selection is from the introduction to Upton's book, *The Military Policy of the United States*, which was not published until almost a quarter century after his death. By then Theodore Roosevelt was president. Roosevelt agreed with his Secretary of War, Elihu Root, that Upton's manuscript should be published to back their own arguments for increased spending and military reform.

Our military policy, or, as many would affirm, our want of it, has now been tested during more than a century. It has been tried in foreign, domestic, and Indian wars, and while military men, from painful experience, are united as to its defects and dangers, our final success in each conflict has so blinded the popular mind, as to induce the belief that as a nation we are invincible.

With the greater mass of people, who have neither the time nor the inclination to study the requirements of military science, no error is more common than to mistake military resources for military strength, and particularly is this the case with ourselves.

History records our triumph in the Revolution, in the War of 1812, in the Florida War, in the Mexican War, and in the Great Rebellion [Civil War], and as nearly all of these wars were largely begun by militia and volunteers, the conviction has been produced that with us a regular army is not a necessity.

In relating the events of these wars, the historian has generally limited himself to describing the battles that have been fought, without seeking to investigate the delays and disasters by which they have been prolonged, till, in nearly every instance, the national resources have been exhausted.

The object of this work is to treat historically and statistically, our military policy up to the present time, and to show the enormous and unnecessary sacrifice of life and treasure, which has attended all our armed struggles. . . .

All of our wars have been prolonged for want of judicious and economical preparation, and often when the people have impatiently awaited the tidings of victory, those of humiliating defeat have plunged the nation into mourning.

The cause of all this is obvious to the soldier and should be no less obvious to the statesman. It lies partly in the unfounded jealousy of not a large, but even a small standing army; in the persistent use of raw troops; in the want of an expansive organization, adequate for every prospective emergency; in short and voluntary enlistments, carrying with them large bounties; and in a variety of other defects which need not here be stated. In treating this subject, I am aware that I tread on delicate ground and that every volunteer and militiaman who has patriotically responded to the call of his country, in the hour of danger, may possibly regard himself as unjustly attacked.

To such I can only reply, that where they have enlisted for the period of three months, and, as at Bladensburg and on many other fields, have been hurled against veteran troops, they should not hold me responsible for the facts of history, which I have sought impartially to present. To such volunteers as enlisted for the period of the Mexican War, and particularly for two and three years during the War of the Rebellion, with whom it is my pride to have served and to whom I owe all of my advancement in the service, I but express the opinion of all military men, in testifying that their excellence was due, not to the fact that they were volunteers, but to the more important fact that their long term of service enabled them to become, in the highest sense, regulars in drill, discipline, and courage. . . .

Every battlefield of the war after 1861 gave proof to the world of the valor of the disciplined American soldier; but in achieving this reputation the nation was nearly overwhelmed with debt from which we are still suffering, while nearly every family in the land was plunged in mourning.

Already we are forgetting these costly sacrifices, and unless we now frame and bequeath to the succeeding generation a military system suggested by our past experience and commended by the example of other enlightened nations, our rulers and legislators in the next war will fall into the same errors and involve the country in the same sacrifices as in the past. . . .

Up to this time in our history our military policy has been largely shaped by the Anglo-Saxon prejudice against "standing armies as a dangerous menace to liberty." Assuming that with this as one of his premises the reader has come to the erroneous conclusion that the officers of the army are wholly given over to selfishness and ambition it ought not to be difficult to convince him that no one of their number can suggest any change or modification of our system without being false to his guild.

No one can study the subject without acknowledging that our military policy is weak and that it invites and inevitably produces long wars, and that in the race for military laurels the professional soldier usually distances all competitors.

A century is a short period in the life of a nation, but its history may convey many valuable lessons as the result of the system which we cherish as our own invention; thus, the War of the Revolution lasted seven years, the War of 1812 three years, the Florida War seven years, the Mexican War two years, and the Rebellion four years, not to mention the almost incessant Indian wars of this period. In other words, since the publication of the Declaration of Independence to this time these figures show that for every three years of peace we have had one year of actual war. . . .

In every civilized country success in war depends upon the organization and application of its military resources. The resources themselves consist of men, material, and money. Their organization is wholly within the province of the statesman. Under our Constitution Congress has the power to raise and support armies, and, subject to the supervision of the President, only professional soldiers should command them.

In time of war the civilian as much as the soldier is responsible for defeat and disaster. Battles are not lost alone on the field; they may be lost beneath the Dome of the Capitol, they may be lost in the Cabinet, or they may be lost in the private office of the Secretary of War. Wherever they may be lost, it is the people who suffer and the soldiers who die, with the knowledge and the conviction that our military policy is a crime against life, a crime against property, and a crime against liberty. The author has availed himself of his privileges as a citizen to expose to our people a system which, if not abandoned, may sooner or later prove fatal. The time when some one should do this has arrived. . . .

No longer compelled to doubt the prowess of our armies, the time has come to ask what was the cause of defeats like those of Long Island, Camden, Queenstown, Bladensburg, and Bull Run. The people who, under the war powers of the Constitution, surrender their liberties and give up their lives and their property have a right to know why our wars are unnecessarily prolonged. They have a right to know whether disasters have been brought about through the neglect and ignorance of Congress, which is intrusted with the power to raise and support armies, or through military incompetency. Leaving their representatives free to pay their own salaries, the people have a right to know whether they have devoted their time to studying the art of government.

War, it need scarcely be said, affects the life, liberty, and property of the individual citizen, and beyond that the life of the nation. On its issue necessarily depends the fate of governments and the happiness of millions of human beings, present and future. . . .

In the course of his labors the author has met with many discouragements. As a rule it has only been necessary to mention to his brother officers the words "military policy" to provoke the reply that "We have no military policy"; that everything is left to luck or to chance. While apparently true, this conclusion is nevertheless a mistake.

Laws whose operation have been the same in all our wars constitute a system, wise or unwise, safe or unsafe, according to their fruit. . . . Ultimate success in all our wars has steeped the people in the delusion that our policy is correct and that any departure from it would be no less difficult than dangerous.

Again, our remoteness from powerful nations has led to another delusion—that we shall forever be free from foreign invasion. . . .

As a nation we can afford to imitate the daily example of our citizens. The pioneer who seeks a home in the forest first builds a cabin, then a log house, and next a frame house. He does not accuse himself of extravagance. The cabin answered his purposes when he was poor and without family, but when his children multiplied he tore it down and put such material as was worth saving into the log house. This, too, satisfied his wants, but when he began to have neighbors, when roads were opened and friends and strangers began to visit him, he saw that he lacked room and, having become prosperous, he abandoned the log home and for comfort and appearance built a house and barn which excited the admiration of every passer-by.

Looking at the example of every pioneer, as well as the prosperous man of business, . . . the military policy of an agricultural nation of 3,000,000 people just emerging from the forest, was no policy for a nation extending from ocean to ocean and now numbering more than fifty millions. . . .

It is a popular delusion that armies make wars; the fact is wars inevitably make armies. No matter what the form of government, war, at the discretion of the rulers, means absolute despotism, the danger from which increases as the war is prolonged. Armies in time of peace have seldom if ever overthrown their governments, but in time of anarchy and war the people have often sought to dictate, and purchase peace at the expense of their liberty. If we would escape this danger we should make war with a strong arm. No foreign invader should ever be allowed a foothold on our soil. Recognizing, too, that under popular institutions the majority of the people create the government and that the majority will never revolt, it should be our policy to suppress every riot and stamp out every insurrection before it swells to rebellion. This means a strong government, but shall we find greater safety in one that is weaker?

Battle of Las Guasimas *by Kurg Allison (Library of Congress). By the late nineteenth century, some army regiments were entirely filled with black soldiers commanded by white officers. Most Americans agreed that these "colored" units were every bit as good as white ones. Even Theodore Roosevelt, who had espoused racism in some of his speeches and writings, concurred. In his memoirs of the Spanish-American War, Roosevelt recalled that the battle of Las Guasimas had been fought in "very difficult country, and a force of good soldiers resolutely handled could have held the pass with ease against two or three times their number. As it was, with a force half of regulars, half of volunteers, we drove out a superior number of Spanish regular troops, strongly posted, without suffering a heavy loss. Although the Spanish fire was heavy, it does not seem to me it was very well directed; and though they fired with great spirit while we merely stood at a distance and fired at them they did not show much resolution, and when we advanced, always went back long before there was any chance of our coming into contact with them. Our men behaved very well indeed—white, regulars, colored regulars, and Rough Riders alike."*

THE SPANISH–AMERICAN WAR

Richard Harding Davis

John Hay, an American ambassador to England, called it "a splendid little war." No other war has gained more support from the American people or accomplished as much with so few casualties in such a short time as did the Spanish–American War. A new generation of Americans would show their fathers, the veterans of the Civil War, that they too could defend the flag and achieve military greatness.

Vigorous prewar competition between the Pulitzer and Hearst newspaper chains had helped sensationalize problems in Cuba. When the war began, correspondents accompanied the armed forces into the war zones. Richard Harding Davis (1864–1916) was among this new breed of professional journalists. He and his fellow correspondents brought the war home with their colorful newspaper stories of battles. Their reporting glorified war and emphasized individual heroism. Anyone who read their dispatches could imagine no outcome other than victory for the noble Americans and defeat for the swarthy Spaniards. The tone and temper of their reporting help to explain the naive optimism and enthusiasm in the United States for the Spanish–American War.

The following account of the Battle of Las Guasimas was written by Davis, who was an admirer of Theordore Roosevelt and the Rough Riders. Some critics had accused Colonel Leonard Wood, who commanded the Rough Riders, and Lieutenant-Colonel Roosevelt of failing to protect their front and flanks from a surprise attack, which had caused them to walk into a Spanish ambush. Although Roosevelt was capable of protecting his own self-interest and would do so in his history of the war, this support from a first-hand observer would help his future political career.

SOURCE: Richard Harding Davis, *The Cuban and Porto Rican Campaigns* (New York: Scribner, 1898).

On the afternoon of June 23d [1898] a Cuban officer informed General Wheeler that the enemy were intrenched at Guasimas, blocking the way to Santiago. Guasimas is not a village, nor even a collection of houses; it is the meeting-place of two trails which join at the apex of a V, three miles from the seaport town of Siboney, and continue merged in a single trail to Santiago. General Wheeler, accompanied by Cubans, reconnoitred this trail on the afternoon of the 23d, and with the position of the enemy fully explained to him, returned to Siboney and informed General Young and Colonel Wood that he would attack the place on the following morning. The plan was discussed while I was present, so I know that so far from anyone's running into an ambush unaware, every one of the officers concerned had a full knowledge of where he was to go to find the enemy, and what he was to do when he got there. No one slept that night, for until two o'clock in the morning troops were still being disembarked in the surf, and two ships of war had their search-lights turned on the landing-place, and made Siboney as light as a ball-room. Back of the search-lights was an ocean white with moonlight, and on the shore red camp-fires, at which the half-drowned troops were drying their uniforms, and the Rough Riders, who had just marched in from Baiquiri, were cooking their coffee and bacon. Below the former home of the Spanish commandante, which General Wheeler had made his head-quarters, lay the camp of the Rough Riders, and through it Cuban officers were riding their half-starved ponies, scattering the ashes of the camp-fires, and galloping over the tired bodies of the men with that courtly grace and consideration for Americans which invariably marks the Cuban gentleman. Below them was the beach and the roaring surf, in which a thousand or so naked men were assisting and impeding the progress shoreward of their comrades, in pontoons and shore-boats, which were being hurled at the beach like sleds down a water-chute.

It was one of the most weird and remarkable scenes of the war, probably of any war. An army was being landed on an enemy's coast at the dead of night, but with somewhat more of cheers and shrieks and laughter than rise from the bathers in the surf at Coney Island on a hot Sunday. It was a pandemonium of noises. The men still to be landed from the "prison hulks," as they called the transports, were singing in chorus, the men already on shore were dancing naked around the camp-fires on the beach, or shouting with delight as they plunged into the first bath that had offered in seven days, and those in the launches as they were pitched head-first at the soil of Cuba, signalized their arrival by howls of triumph. On either side rose black overhanging ridges, in the lowland between were white tents and burning fires, and from the ocean came the blazing, dazzling eyes of the search-lights shaming the quiet moonlight.

The Rough Riders left camp after three hours' troubled sleep at five in the morning. With the exception of half a dozen officers they were dismounted, and carried their blanket-rolls, haversacks, ammunition, and carbines. General Young had already started toward Guasimas the First and Tenth dismounted Cavalry, and according to the agreement of the night before had taken the eastern trail to our right, while the Rough Riders climbed the steep ridge above Siboney and started toward the rendezvous along the trail to the west, which was on high ground and a half mile to a mile distant from the trail along which General Young was marching. There was a valley between us, and the bushes were so thick on both sides of our trail that it was not possible at any time, until we met at Guasimas, to distinguish his column.

As soon as the Rough Riders had reached the top of the ridge not twenty minutes after they had left camp, which was the first opportunity that presented itself, Colonel Wood took the precautions he was said to have neglected. He ordered Captain Capron to proceed with his troop in front of the column as an advance guard, and to choose a "point" of five men skilled as scouts and trailers. Still in advance of these he placed two Cuban scouts. The column then continued along the trail in single file. The Cubans were just at a distance of two hundred and fifty yards; the "point" of five picked men under Sergeant Byrne and duty-Sergeant Fish followed them at a distance of a hundred yards, and then came Capron's troop of sixty men strung out in single file. No flankers were placed for the reason that the dense undergrowth and the tangle of vines that stretched from the branches of the trees to the bushes below made it a physical impossibility for man or beast to move forward except along the beaten trail.

Colonel Wood rode at the head of the column, followed by two regular army officers who were members of General Wheeler's staff, a Cuban officer, and Lieutenant-Colonel Roosevelt. They rode slowly in consideration of the troopers on foot, who carried heavy burdens under a cruelly hot sun. To those who did not have to walk it was not unlike a hunting excursion in our West; the scenery was beautiful and the view down the valley one of luxuriant peace. Roosevelt had never been in the tropics and Captain McCormick and I were talking back at him over our shoulders and at each other, pointing out unfamiliar trees and birds. Roosevelt thought it looked like a good deer country, as it once was; it reminded McCormick of southern California; it looked to me like the trail across Honduras. They advanced, talking in that fashion and in high spirits, and congratulating themselves in being shut of the transport and on breathing fine mountain air again, and on the fact that they were on horseback. They agreed it was impossible to appreciate that we were really at war—that we were in the enemy's country. We had been riding in this pleasant fashion for an hour and a half with brief halts for rest, when Wood stopped the head of the column, and rode down the trail to meet Capron, who was coming back. Wood returned immediately, leading his horse, and said to Roosevelt:

"Pass the word back to keep silence in the ranks."

The place at which we had halted was where the trail narrowed, and proceeded sharply downward. There was on one side of it a stout barbed-wire fence of five strands. By some fortunate accident this fence had been cut just where the head of the column halted. On the left of the trail it shut off fields of high grass blocked at every fifty yards with great barricades of undergrowth and tangled trees and chapparal. On the other side of the trail there was not a foot of free ground; the bushes seemed absolutely impenetrable, as indeed they were later found to be.

When we halted the men sat down beside the trail and chewed the long blades of grass, or fanned the air with their hats. They had no knowledge of the situation such as their leaders possessed, and their only emotion was one of satisfaction at the chance the halt gave them to rest and to shift their packs. Wood again walked down the trail with Capron and disappeared and one of the officers informed us that the scouts had seen the outposts of the enemy. It did not seem reasonable that the Spaniards, who had failed to attack us when we landed at Baiquiri, would oppose us until they could do so in force, so, personally, I doubted that there were any Spaniards nearer than Santiago. But we tied our horses to the wire fence, and Capron's troop knelt with carbines at the "ready," peering into the bushes. We must have waited there, while Wood reconnoitred, for over ten minutes. Then he returned, and began deploying his troops out at either side of the trail. Capron he sent on down the trail itself. G Troop was ordered to beat into the bushes on the right, and K and A were sent over the ridge on which we stood down into the hollow to connect with General Young's column on the opposite side of the valley. F and E Troops were deployed out in skirmish-line on the other side of the wire fence. Wood had discovered the enemy a few hundred yards from where he expected to find him, and so far from being "surprised," he had time, as I have just described, to get five of his troops into position before a shot was fired. The firing, when it came, started suddenly on our right. It sounded so close that—still believing we were acting on a false alarm, and that there were no Spaniards ahead of us—I guessed it was Capron's men firing at random to disclose the enemy's position. I ran after G Troop under Captain Llewellyn, and found them breaking their way through the bushes in the direction from which the volleys came. It was like forcing the walls of a maze. If each trooper had not kept in touch with the man on either hand he would have been lost in the thicket. At one moment the underbrush seemed swarming with troopers, and the next, except that you heard the twigs breaking, and the heavy breathing of the men, or a crash as a vine pulled someone down, there was not a sign of a human being anywhere. In a few minutes they all broke through into a little open place in front of a dark curtain of vines, and the men fell on one knee and began returning the fire that came from it.

The enemy's fire was exceedingly heavy, and the aim was low. Whether the Spaniards saw us or not we could not tell; we certainly saw nothing of the Spaniards, except a few on the ridge across the valley. The fire against us was not more than fifty to eighty yards away, and so hot that our men could only lie flat in the grass and fire in that position. . . .

It was an exceedingly hot corner. The whole troop was gathered in the little open place blocked by the network of grape-vines and tangled bushes before it. They could not see twenty feet on three sides of them, but on the right hand lay the valley, and across it came the sound of Young's brigade, who were apparently heavily engaged. The enemy's fire was so close that the men could not hear the word of command, and Captain Llewellyn, by word of voice, and Lieutenant Greenway, unable to get their attention, ran among them, batting them with their sombreros to make them cease firing. Lieutenant-Colonel Roosevelt ran up just then, bringing with him Lieutenant Woodbury Kane and ten troopers from K Troop. Roosevelt lay down in the grass beside Llewellyn and consulted with him eagerly. Kane was smiling with the charming content of a perfectly happy man, exactly as though it were a polo match and his side had scored. When Captain Llewellyn told him his men were not needed, and to rejoin his troop, he led his detail over the edge of the hill on which we lay, although the bullets were passing three feet high. As he disappeared below the crest, walking quite erect, he was still smiling. Roosevelt pointed out that it was impossible to advance farther on account of the network of wild grape-vines that masked the Spaniards from us, and that we must cross the trail and make to the left. The shouts the men had raised to warn Capron had established our position to the enemy, and the firing was now fearfully accurate. Sergeant Russell, who in his day had been a colonel on a governor's staff, was killed, and the other sergeant was shot through the wrist. In the space of three minutes nine men were lying on their backs helpless. The men drew off slowly to the left, dragging the wounded with them. Owing to the low aim of the enemy, they were forced to move on their knees and crawl on their stomachs. Even then they were hit. One man near me was shot through the head. Returning two hours later to locate the body, I found that the buzzards had torn off his lips and his eyes. This mutilation by these hideous birds is, no doubt, what Admiral Sampson mistook for the work of the Spaniards, when the bodies of the marines at Guantanamo were found disfigured in the same fashion. K Troop had meantime deployed into the valley under the fire from the enemy on the ridge. It had been ordered to establish communication with General Young's column, and while advancing and firing on the ridge, Captain Jenkins sent the guidon-bearer back to climb the hill and wave his red and white banner where Young's men could see it. . . .

G Troop meanwhile had hurried over to the left, and passing through the opening in the wire-fence had spread out into open order. It followed down after Captain Luna's troop and D and E Troops, which were well already in advance. Roosevelt ran forward and took command of the extreme left of this line. Wood was walking up and down along it, leading his horse, which he thought might be of use in case he had to move quickly to alter his original formation—at present his plan was to spread out his men so that they would join Young on the right, and on the left swing around until they flanked the enemy. K and A Troops had already succeeded in joining hands with Young's column across the valley, and as they were capable of taking care of themselves, Wood was bending his efforts to keep his remaining four companies in a straight line and revolving them around the enemy's "end." It was in no way an easy thing to do. The men were at times wholly hidden from each other, and from him; probably at no one time did he see more than two of his troops together. It was only by the firing that he could tell where his men lay, and that they were always steadily advancing.

The advances were made in quick, desperate rushes—sometimes the ground gained was no more than a man covers in sliding for a base. At other times half a troop would rise and race forward and then burrow deep in the hot grass and fire. On this side of the line there was an occasional glimpse of the enemy. But for a great part of the time the men shot at the places from where the enemy's fire seemed to come, aiming low and answering in steady volleys. The fire discipline was excellent. The prophets of evil of the Tampa Bay Hotel had foretold that the cowboys would shoot as they chose, and, in the field, would act independently of their officers. As it turned out, the cowboys were the very men who waited most patiently for the officers to give the word of command. At all times the movement was without rest, breathless and fierce, like a cane-rush, or a street-fight. After the first three minutes every man had stripped as though for a wrestling-match, throwing off all his impedimenta [military gear] but his cartridge-belt and canteen. Even then the sun handicapped their strength cruelly. The enemy were hidden in the shade of the jungle, while they had to fight in the open for every thicket they gained, crawling through grass which was as hot as a steam bath, and with their flesh and clothing torn by thorns and the sword-like blade of the Spanish "bayonet." The glare of the sun was full in their eyes and as fierce as a limelight. . . .

The rocks on either side were spattered with blood and the rank grass was matted with it. Blanket-rolls, haversacks, carbines, and canteens had been abandoned all along its length, so that the trail looked as though a retreating army had fled along it, rather than that one company had fought its way through it to the front. Except for the clatter of the land-crabs, those hideous orchid-colored monsters that haunt the places of the dead, and the whistling of the bullets in the trees, the place was as silent as a grave. For the wounded lying along its length were as still as the dead beside them. . . .

The fight had now lasted an hour, and the line had reached a more open country, with a slight incline upward toward a wood, on the edge of which was a ruined house. This house was a former distillery for *aguardiente*, and was now occupied in force by the enemy. Lieutenant-Colonel Roosevelt on the far left was moving up his men with the intention of taking this house on the flank; Wood, who was all over the line, had the same objective point in his mind. The troop commanders had a general idea that the distillery was the key to the enemy's position, and were all working in that direction. It was extremely difficult for Wood and Roosevelt to communicate with the captains, and after the first general orders had been given them they relied upon the latter's intelligence to pull them through. I do not suppose Wood saw more than thirty of his men out of the five hundred engaged at any one time. When he had passed one troop, except for the noise of its volley firing, it was immediately lost to him in the brush, and it was so with the next. Still, so excellent was the intelligence of the officers, and so ready the spirit of the men, that they kept an almost perfect alignment, as was shown when the final order came to charge in the open fields. The advance upon the ruined building was made in stubborn, short rushes, sometimes in silence, and sometimes firing as we ran. The order to fire at will was seldom given, the men waiting patiently for the officers' signal, and then answering in volleys. Some of the men who were twice Day's age begged him to let them take the enemy's impromptu fort on the run, but he answered them tolerantly like spoiled children, and held them down until there was a lull in the enemy's fire, when he would lead them forward, always taking the advance himself. It was easy to tell which men were used to hunting big game in the West and which were not, by the way they made these rushes. The Eastern men broke at the word, and ran for the cover they were directed to take like men trying to get out of the rain, and fell panting on their faces, while the Western trappers and hunters slipped and wriggled through the grass like Indians; dodging from tree-trunk to tree-trunk, and from one bush to another. They always fell into line at the same time with the others, but they had not exposed themselves once while doing so. Some of the escapes were little short of miraculous. The man on my right, Champneys Marshall, of Washington, had one bullet pass through his sleeve, and another pass through his shirt, where it was pulled close to his spine. The holes where the ball entered and went out again were clearly cut. Another man's skin was slightly burned by three bullets in three distinct lines, as though it had been touched for an instant by the lighted end of a cigar. . . .

Toward the last, the firing from the enemy sounded less near, and the bullets passed much higher. Roosevelt, who had picked up a carbine and was firing occasionally to give the direction to the others, determined upon a charge. Wood, at the other end of the line, decided at the same time upon the same manoeuvre. It was called "Wood's bluff" afterward, for he had nothing to back it with; while to the enemy it looked as though his whole force was but the skirmish-line in advance of a regiment. The Spaniards naturally could not believe that this thin line which suddenly broke out of the bushes and from behind trees and came cheering out into the hot sunlight in full view, was the entire fighting force against it. They supposed the regiment was coming close on its heels, and as they hate being rushed as a cat hates water, they fired a few parting volleys and broke and ran. The cheering had the same invigorating effect on our own side as a cold shower; it was what first told half the men where the other half were, and it made every individual man feel better. As we knew it was only a bluff, the first cheer was wavering, but the sound of our own voices was so comforting that the second cheer was a howl of triumph. As it was, the Spaniards thought the Rough Riders had already disregarded all the rules of war.

"When we fired a volley," one of the prisoners said later, "instead of falling back they came forward. That is not the way to fight, to come closer at every volley." And so, when instead of retreating on each volley, the Rough Riders rushed at them, cheering and filling the hot air with wild cowboy yells, the dismayed enemy retreated upon Santiago, where he announced he had been attacked by the entire American Army. One of the residents of Santiago asked one of the soldiers if those Americans fought well.

"Well!" he replied, "they tried to catch us with their hands!" . . .

According to the statement of the enemy, who had every reason not to exaggerate the size of his own force, 4,000 Spaniards were engaged in this action. The Rough Riders numbered 534, of whom 8 were killed and 34 wounded, and General Young's force numbered 464, of which there were 8 killed and 18 wounded. The American troops accordingly attacked a force over four times their own number intrenched behind rifle-pits and bushes in a mountain-pass. In spite of the smokeless powder used by the Spaniards, which hid their position, the Rough Riders routed them out of it, and drove them back from three different barricades until they made their last stand in the ruined distillery, whence they finally drove them by assault. The eager spirit in which all was done is best described in the Spanish soldier's answer to the inquiring civilian, "They tried to catch us with their hands." It should be the Rough Riders' motto.

The army and navy had to play many different roles in the three decades following the Civil War. The army was charged with keeping the peace in the defeated South, policing the rapidly settling West, and quelling occasional disturbances in factories and cities. The navy had a less well defined role and found its chief fight against the parsimonious American public and Congress. The brief war with Spain at the end of the century earned support for the army and navy, which now had to protect America's newly acquired overseas empire. At the same time, officers worked to define a role for the profession of violence, only one of a host of new managerial positions to appear in America's modern industrial economy.

The army's first task was to help restore a South that did not think reconstruction was necessary. James E. Sefton examines the army's limited role in Reconstruction in *The United States Army and Reconstruction, 1865–1877* (1967). In the *Negro Militia and Reconstruction* (1957), Otis A. Singletary discusses the major social change that occurred when blacks were integrated into American society and the military. Civil violence and the army's role in suppressing it is best told by Robert V. Bruce in *1877: Year of Violence* (1959). An unusual and entertaining work on the importance of technology to military policy and civilian life can be found in John Ellis's *The Social History of the Machine Gun* (1975).

The best general history of the Indian wars can be found in Robert Utley's *Frontier Regulars: The U.S. Army and the Indian, 1866–1891* (1974). Dee Brown relates the story of these same wars from the Indians' perspective in *Bury My Heart at Wounded Knee: An Indian History of the American West* (1970). Philip Sheridan's *Personal Memoirs,* two volumes (1902); Nelson A. Miles's *Personal Recollections and Observations* (1896); and George Crook's *General George Crook: His Autobiography,* edited by Martin F. Schmitt (1960), offer views from the army's most famous Indian fighters. The history of the enlisted men on the frontier may be found in Don Rickey's *Forty Miles a Day on Beans and Hay: The Enlisted Soldier Fighting the Indian Wars* (1963). Two excellent accounts of black soldiers on the frontier are William H. Leckie's *The Buffalo Soldiers: A Narrative of the Negro Cavalry in the West* (1967) and Arlen Fowler's *The Black Infantry in the West, 1869–1891* (1971). A different perspective of frontier military life is shown in *An Army Wife on the Frontier: The Memoirs of Alice Blackwood Baldwin* (1975), edited by Robert C. and Eleanor R. Carriker. One of the best biographies to appear in recent times is Evan S. Connell's *Son of the Morning Star* (1984), which tells the tale of Custer, Crazy Horse, and the battle of the Little Big Horn.

Professional problems in the army are discussed in Stephen E. Ambrose's *Upton and the Army* (1964), and naval problems in *The Naval Aristocracy: The Golden Age of Annapolis and the Emergence of Modern American Navalism* (1972) by Peter Karsten and in Walter R. Herrick, Jr.'s, *The American Naval Revolution* (1966). There are several fine biographies of naval leaders of this period. These include Edward William Sloan, III's *Benjamin Franklin Isherwood, Naval Engineer: The Years as Engineer in Chief, 1861–1869* (1965); B. Franklin Cooling's *Benjamin Franklin Tracy: Father of the American Fighting Navy* (1973); and Robert Seager, II's *Alfred Thayer Mahan: The Man and His Letters* (1977). Mahan wrote his memoirs of life in the late-nineteenth-century navy in *From Sail to Steam: Recollections on Naval Life* (1907). The best coverage of the navy's role as protector of American commerce is Kenneth J. Hagan's *American Gunboat Diplomacy and the Old Navy, 1877–1889* (1973).

Possibly the best history of the Spanish-American War appeared shortly after its end in *The Relations of the United States and Spain* (1909–1911), a three-volume work by French E. Chadwick. Modern accounts were written by Walter Millis in *Martial Spirit* (1931) and an illustrated history of the war by Frank Freidel called the *Splendid Little War* (1958). Several naval officers left fine memoirs of the war including George Dewey's *Autobiography* (1913), Winfield Scott Schley's *Forty-Five Years Under the Flag* (1904), and Robert D. Evans's *A Sailor's Log: Recollections of Forty Years of Naval Life* (1903). Ronald Spector has written an excellent biography of Admiral George Dewey in *Admiral of the New Empire: The Life and Career of George Dewey* (1974). The best work on the Philippine insurrection, which followed the war, is John Gates's *Schoolbooks and Krags* (1973).

CHAPTER 6

WORLD WAR I

The Spanish–American War may have been splendid, but it had also revealed serious shortcomings in the American armed forces. Food spoiled, the army fought in the tropics in woolen uniforms, and admirals squabbled over who should get credit for defeating the Spanish fleet off Cuba. Logistical, command, communications, and training problems abounded.

After the war, the United States adopted the Prussian general staff system. This divided military commands into smaller units, and applied the managerial skills of business to military goals. In addition, Theodore Roosevelt's administration sought increased military spending to prepare the armed forces to defend the worldwide interests of the United States. Other Americans hoped to instill the military virtues they thought had existed in the militia by creating a national militia or reserve force, backed by a program of Universal Military Training.

The popular enthusiasm unleashed by the Spanish–American War had offended some, especially the more serious-minded Americans, who feared that military forces around the world had become so powerful that a major war was inevitable. Their fears went unheeded. The United States, like all other major powers, assumed it could meet any military challenge. When war finally broke out in Europe in the fall of 1914, politicians and military men relished the thought of proving their prowess. World War I was the culmination of all the revolutions that had occurred since the end of the eighteenth century: demographic, political, national, industrial, agricultural, technological, and managerial.

In the pursuit of national political goals, both sides expended millions of men, tons of equipment, and billions of dollars in trenches that extended from the Alps to the English Channel. After almost three years of fighting by the world's major powers, the United States entered the war for the self-proclaimed purposes of a "peace without victory," "freedom of the seas," and a "world safe for democracy." U.S. manpower was enough to tip the balance in favor of England, France, and Italy, but American ideals could not change human nature.

Americans who had fought in Europe had tasted war in its most elemental form. Death was everywhere. Commanders seemed to lack any creativity and appeared to demand further bloody sacrifices, while mechanical weapons, armored vehicles, submarines, and airplanes had added new, horrible, and complicated dimensions to the battlefront. War had become more deadly than ever. Tired and disillusioned "Yanks" returned home at the end of the war and swore they would never become involved in European problems again.

THE MORAL EQUIVALENT
OF WAR

William James

The bellicose attitudes that were so widely proclaimed at the turn of the century frightened many pacifists who had hoped humankind could create a modern world without war. Prowar enthusiasts, including Theodore Roosevelt, preached that virility, both personal and national, could best be achieved in war. They worried that the United States had become too effete. Its men, they feared, had lost the hardy virtues of their frontier ancestors. Social Darwinism and racist theories stressed the survival of the fittest; only fighters could survive.

Pacifists, many of them successful businessmen, spoke of a world in which war would be outlawed, people would be more moral, and nations would cooperate to achieve international harmony. They wanted a world of free trade and commerce. America's foremost philosopher, William James (1842–1910), a Harvard professor, physician, and psychologist, challenged these utopian notions. James contended that the virtues of war are real and so inbred in the human species that they could never be removed. Instead of trying to destroy them, James proposed that they be redirected toward more pragmatic, less violent goals.

The war against war is going to be no holiday excursion or camping party. The military feelings are too deeply grounded to abdicate their place among our ideals until better substitutes are offered than the glory and shame that come to nations as well as to individuals from the ups and downs of politics

SOURCE: Reprinted from *Popular Science* with permission. © 1910 Times Mirror Magazines, Inc.

and the vicissitudes of trade. There is something highly paradoxical in the modern man's relation to war. Ask all our millions, north and south, whether they would vote now (were such a thing possible) to have our war for the Union expunged from history, and the record of a peaceful transition to the present time substituted for that of its marches and battles, and probably hardly a handful of eccentrics would say yes. Those ancestors, those efforts, those memories and legends, are the most ideal part of what we now own together, a sacred spiritual possession worth more than all the blood poured out. Yet ask those same people whether they would be willing in cold blood to start another civil war now to gain another similar possession, and not one man or woman would vote for the proposition. In modern eyes, precious though wars may be, they must not be waged solely for the sake of the ideal harvest. Only when forced upon one, only when an enemy's injustice leaves us no alternative, is a war now thought permissible.

It was not thus in ancient times. The earlier men were hunting men, and to hunt a neighboring tribe, kill the males, loot the village and possess the females, was the most profitable, as well as the most exciting, way of living. Thus were the more martial tribes selected, and in chiefs and peoples a pure pugnacity and love of glory came to mingle with the more fundamental appetite for plunder.

Modern war is so expensive that we feel trade to be a better avenue to plunder; but modern man inherits all the innate pugnacity and all the love of glory of his ancestors. Showing war's irrationality and horror is of no effect upon him. The horrors make the fascination. War is the *strong* life; it is life *in extremis*; war-taxes are the only ones men never hesitate to pay; as the budgets of all nations show us.

History is a bath of blood. The Iliad is one long recital of how Diomedes and Ajax, Sarpedon and Hector *killed*. No detail of the wounds they made is spared us, and the Greek mind fed upon the story. Greek history is a panorama of jingoism and imperialism—war for war's sake, all the citizens being warriors. It is horrible reading, because of the irrationality of it all—save for the purpose of making "history"—and the history is that of the utter ruin of a civilization in intellectual respects perhaps the highest the earth has ever seen.

Those wars were purely piratical. Pride, gold, women, slaves, excitement, were their only motives. . . .

Such was the gory nurse that trained societies to cohesiveness. We inherit the warlike type; and for most of the capacities of heroism that the human race is full of we have to thank this cruel history. Dead men tell no tales, and if there were any tribes of other type than this they have left no survivors. Our ancestors have bred pugnacity into our bone and marrow, and thousands of years of peace won't breed it out of us. The popular imagination fairly fattens on the thought of wars. Let public opinion once reach a certain fighting pitch, and no ruler can withstand it. . . . In 1898 our people had read the word WAR in letters three inches high for three months in every newspaper. The pliant politician McKinley was swept away by their eagerness, and our squalid war with Spain became a necessity.

At the present day, civilized opinion is a curious mental mixture. The military instincts and ideals are as strong as ever, but are confronted by reflective criticisms which sorely curb their ancient freedom. Innumerable writers are showing up the bestial side of military service. Pure loot and mastery seem no longer morally avowable motives, and pretexts must be found for attributing them solely to the enemy. England and we, our army and navy authorities repeat without ceasing, arm solely for "peace," Germany and Japan it is who are bent on loot and glory. "Peace" in military mouths to-day is a synonym for "war expected." The word has become a pure provocative, and no government wishing peace sincerely should allow it ever to be printed in a newspaper. Every up-to-date dictionary should say that "peace" and "war" mean the same thing, now *in posse,* now *in actu.* It may even reasonably be said that the intensely sharp competitive *preparation* for war by the nations *is the real war,* permanent, unceasing; and that the battles are only a sort of public verification of the mastery gained during the "peace"-interval. . . .

Reflective apologists for war at the present day all take it religiously. It is a sort of sacrament. Its profits are to the vanquished as well as to the victor; and quite apart from any question of profit, it is an absolute good, we are told, for it is human nature at its highest dynamic. Its "horrors" are a cheap price to pay for rescue from the only alternative supposed, of a world of clerks and teachers, of coeducation and zoophily, of "consumer's leagues" and "associated charities," of industrialism unlimited, and femininism unabashed. No scorn, no hardness, no valor any more! Fie upon such a cattleyard of a planet!

So far as the central essence of this feeling goes, no healthy minded person, it seems to me, can help to some degree partaking of it. Militarism is the great preserver of our ideals of hardihood, and human life with no use for hardihood would be contemptible. Without risks or prizes for the darer, history would be insipid indeed; and there is a type of military character which every one feels that the race should never cease to breed, for every one is sensitive to its superiority. The duty is incumbent on mankind, of keeping military characters in stock—of keeping them, if not for use, then as ends in themselves and as pure pieces of perfection—so that Roosevelt's weaklings and mollycoddles may not end by making everything else disappear from the face of nature.

This natural sort of feeling forms, I think, the innermost soul of army-writings. Without any exception known to me, militarist authors take a highly mystical view of their subject, and regard war as a biological or sociological necessity, uncontrolled by ordinary psychological checks and motives. When the time of development is ripe the war must come, reason or no reason, for the justifications pleaded are invariably fictitious. War is, in short, a permanent human *obligation*. . . .

Turn the fear over as I will in my mind, it all seems to lead back to two unwillingnesses of the imagination, one esthetic, and the other moral: unwillingness, first to envisage a future in which army-life, with its many elements of charm, shall be forever impossible, and in which the destinies of peoples shall nevermore be decided quickly, thrillingly and tragically, by force, but only gradually and insipidly by "evolution"; and, secondly, unwillingness to see the supreme theatre of human strenuousness closed, and the splendid military aptitudes of men doomed to keep always in a state of latency and never show themselves in action. These insistent unwillingnesses, no less than other esthetic and ethical insistencies have, it seems to me, to be listened to and respected. One can not meet them effectively by mere counter-insistency on war's expensiveness and horror. The horror makes the thrill; and when the question is of getting the extremest and supremest out of human nature, talk of expense sounds ignominious. The weakness of so much merely negative criticism is evident—pacifism makes no converts from the military party. The military party denies neither the bestiality nor the horror, not the expense; it only says that these things tell but half the story. It only says that war is *worth* them; that, taking human nature as a whole, its wars are its best protection against its weaker and more cowardly self, and that mankind can not *afford* to adopt a peace-economy.

Pacifists ought to enter more deeply into the esthetical and ethical point of view of their opponents. . . . So long as anti-militarists propose no substitute for war's disciplinary function, no *moral equivalent* of war, analogous, as one might say, to the mechanical equivalent of heat, so long they fail to realize the full inwardness of the situation. And as a rule they do fail. The duties, penalties, and sanctions pictured in the utopias they paint are all too weak and tame to touch the military-minded. . . .

Having said thus much in preparation, I will now confess my own utopia. I devoutly believe in the reign of peace and in the gradual advent of some sort of a socialistic equilibrium. The fatalistic view of the war-function is to me nonsense, for I know that war-making is due to definite motives and subject to prudential checks and reasonable criticisms, just like any other form of enterprise. And when whole nations are the armies, and the science of destruction vies in intellectual refinement with the sciences of production, I see that war becomes absurd and impossible from its own monstrosity. Extravagant ambitions will have to be replaced by reasonable claims, and nations must make common cause against them. I see no reason why all this should not apply to yellow as well as to white countries, and I look forward to a future when acts of war shall be formally outlawed as between civilized peoples.

All these beliefs of mine put me squarely into the anti-militarist party. But I do not believe that peace either ought to be or will be permanent on this globe, unless the states pacifically organized preserve some of the old elements of army-discipline. A permanently successful peace-economy can not be a simple pleasure-economy. In the more or less socialistic future towards which mankind seems drifting we must still subject ourselves collectively to those severities which answer to our real position upon this only partly hospitable globe. We must make new energies and hardihoods continue the manliness to which the military mind so faithfully clings. Martial virtues must be the enduring cement; intrepidity, contempt of softness, surrender of private interest, obedience to command, must still remain the rock upon which states are built—unless, indeed, we wish for dangerous reactions against commonwealths fit only for contempt, and liable to invite attack whenever a centre of crystallization for military-minded enterprise gets formed anywhere in their neighborhood.

The war-party is assuredly right in affirming and reaffirming that the martial virtues, although originally gained by the race through war, are absolute and permanent human goods. Patriotic pride and ambition in their military form are, after all, only specifications of a more general competitive passion. They are its first form, but that is no reason for supposing them to be its last form. . . .

Let me illustrate my idea more concretely. There is nothing to make one indignant in the mere fact that life is hard, that men should toil and suffer pain. . . . But that so many men, by mere accidents of birth and opportunity, should have a life of *nothing else* but toil and pain and hardness and inferiority imposed upon them, should have *no* vacation, while others natively no more deserving never get any taste of this campaigning life at all—*this* is capable of arousing indignation in reflective minds. It may end by seeming shameful to all of us that some of us have nothing but campaigning, and others nothing but unmanly ease. If now—and this is my idea—there were, instead of military conscription a conscription of the whole youthful population to form for a certain number of years a part of the army enlisted against *nature*, the injustice would tend to be evened out, and numerous other goods to the commonwealth would follow. The military ideals of hardihood and discipline would be wrought into the growing fiber of the people; no one would remain blind as the luxurious classes now are blind, to man's real relations to the globe he lives on, and to the permanently sour and hard foundations of his higher life. To coal and iron mines, to freight trains, to fishing fleets in December, to dishwashing, clothes-washing, and window-washing, to road-building and tunnel-making, to foundries and stoke-holes, and to the frames of skyscrapers, would our gilded youths be drafted off, according to their choice, to get the childishness knocked out of them, and to come back into society with healthier sympathies and soberer ideas. They would have paid their blood-tax, done their own part in the immemorial human warfare against nature, they would tread the earth more proudly, the women would value them more highly, they would be better fathers and teachers of the following generation.

Such a conscription, with the state of public opinion that would have required it, and the many moral fruits it would bear, would preserve in the midst of a pacific civilization the manly virtues which the military party is so afraid of seeing disappear in peace. We should get toughness without callousness, authority with as little criminal cruelty as possible, and painful work done cheerily because the duty is temporary, and threatens not, as now, to degrade the whole reminder of one's life. I spoke of the "moral equivalent" of war. So far, war has been the only force that can discipline a whole community, and until an equivalent discipline is organized, I believe that war must have its way. But I have no serious doubt that the ordinary prides and shames of social man, once developed to a certain intensity, are capable of organizing such a moral equivalent as I have sketched, or some other just as effective for preserving manliness of type. It is but a question of time, of skillful propagandism, and of opinion-making men seizing historic opportunities.

The martial type of character can be bred without war. Strenuous honor and disinterestedness abound elsewhere. Priests and medical men are in a fashion educated to it, and we should all feel some degree of it imperative if we were conscious of our work as an obligatory service to the state. We should be *owned*, as soldiers are by the army, and our pride would rise accordingly. We could be poor, then, without humiliation, as army officers now are. The only thing needed henceforward is to inflame the civic temper as past history has inflamed the military temper. . . .

THE RESERVE OFFICERS TRAINING CORPS

Leonard Wood

The end of the nineteenth century had witnessed the close of the frontier, and with it some of the mystique of the "West." Some people worried that American youth, now increasingly born and bred in cities, were losing traditional virtues. These reformers proposed that all American boys should receive Universal Military Training as the best way to preserve these manly traits.

Major General Leonard Wood had become the army's chief-of-staff in 1910. Trained at Harvard to be a physician, Wood had left the medical corps as a captain to lead the Rough Riders in the Spanish–American War. After the war, Wood served in the Philippines before returning to Washington in 1910 when President William Howard Taft named him the army's chief-of-staff. Wood quickly became identified with the military's progressive reformers, who supported the General Staff system, hoped to use military service to teach citizenship, and preached that every American boy should spend some time in the military.

Wood's own proposal called for an annual summer camp where young men could experience military life. The first camp was held at Plattsburgh, New York, which coined for Wood's plan the name the "Plattsburgh idea." Wood also opposed the state militias, now called the National Guard, and challenged Emory Upton's arguments for the increased professionalization of the military. Instead, Wood (who was not a Military Academy graduate) endorsed the idea of a national reserve force of part-time soldiers directly under federal control. The reserves would mark a return to the militia

SOURCE: Leonard Wood, *Our Military History, Its Facts and Fallacies* (Chicago: The Reilly & Britton Co., 1916).

concept, but this time it would be a national militia, not a state one. In place of the state militias, Wood proposed a state police force to handle domestic disturbances.

By 1916, Wood had become a vocal proponent of "preparedness" to ready the United States to fight in World War I. President Woodrow Wilson, running for reelection, opposed Wood's preparedness plans. Still in the army, but no longer chief-of-staff, Wood joined with Wilson's Republican opponents and made countless speeches, penned innumerable articles, and wrote a book to spread his message. In May 1916, Congress passed the National Defense Act. The new law increased the size of the regular army and the National Guard, and, for the first time, established a federal reserve force. As Wood had earlier proposed, officers to command the reserves would come from civilian college campuses, which would host the Reserve Officer Training Corps.

CHAPTER VIII, WHAT WE SHOULD DO

Our past military policy, so far as it concerns the land forces, has been thoroughly unsound and in violation of basic military principles. We have succeeded not because of it, but in spite of it. It has been unnecessarily and brutally costly in human life and recklessly extravagant in the expenditure of treasure. It has tended greatly to prolong our wars and consequently has delayed national development.

Because we have succeeded in spite of an unsound system, those who do not look beneath the surface fail to recognize the numerous shortcomings of that system, or appreciate how dangerous is our further dependence upon it.

The time has come to put our house in order through the establishment of a sound and dependable system, and to make such wise and prudent preparation as will enable us to defend successfully our country and our rights.

No such system can be established which does not rest upon equality of service for all who are physically fit and of proper age. Manhood suffrage means manhood obligation for service in peace or war. This is the basic principle upon which truly representative government, or free democracy, rests and must rest if it is successfully to withstand the shock of modern war.

The acceptance of this fundamental principle will require to a certain extent the moral organization of the people, the building up of that sense of individual obligation for service to the nation which is the basis of true patriotism, the teaching of our people to think in terms of the nation rather than in those of a locality or of personal interest. . . .

Dependence upon militia under state control or partially under state control, spells certain disaster, not because of the quality of the men or officers, but because of the system under which they work.

We must also have a first-class navy, well balanced and thoroughly equipped with all necessary appliances afloat and ashore. It is the first line of defense.

We need a highly efficient regular army, adequate to the peace needs of the nation. By this is meant a regular force, fully equipped, thoroughly trained and properly organized, with adequate reserves of men and material, and a force sufficient to garrison our over-sea possessions. . . .

The regular force must also be adequate to provide sufficient troops for our coast defenses and such garrisons as may be required in Porto Rico and Alaska. The regular force must also be sufficient to provide the necessary mobile force in the United States; by this is meant a force of cavalry, infantry, field artillery, engineers and auxiliary troops sufficient to provide an expeditionary force such as we sent to Cuba in 1898, and at the same time to provide a force sufficient to meet possible conditions of internal disorder. It must also furnish training units for the National Guard, or whatever force the federal government may eventually establish in place of it, and provide sufficient officers for duty under the detail system in the various departments, instructors at the various colleges and schools where military instruction is or may be established, attachés abroad and officers on special missions.

The main reliance in a war with a first-class power will ultimately be the great force of citizen soldiers forming a purely federal force, thoroughly organized and equipped with reserves of men and material. This force must be trained under some system which will permit the instruction to be given in part during the school period or age, thereby greatly reducing the time required for the final intensive period of training, which should be under regular officers and in conjunction with regular troops. . . .

Each year about one million men reach the military age of 18; of this number not more than fifty per cent are fit for military service, this being about the average in other countries. Far less than fifty per cent come up to the standards required for the regular army, but the minor defects rejecting them for the regular army would not reject them for general military service. . . . If the boys were prepared by the state authorities, through training in schools and colleges, and in state training areas—when the boys were not in school . . . it would be possible, when they come up for federal training, to finish their military training—so far as preparing them for the duties of enlisted men is concerned—within a period of approximately three months. We should be able to limit the period of first line obligation to the period from eighteen to twenty-five, inclusive, or seven years, or we could make the period of obligatory service begin two years later and extend it to twenty-seven. This procedure would give in the first line approximately three and one-half millions of men at the age of best physical condition and of minimum dependent and business responsibility. . . . They would be organized and equipped exactly like the regular army and would be held ready for immediate service as our present militia would be were it under federal control.

Men of these organizations would not live in uniform but would go about their regular occupations as do the members of the militia to-day, but they would be equipped, organized and ready for immediate service. If emergency required it, additional organizations could be promptly raised from the men who were within the obligatory period.

There should be no pay in peace time except when the men were on duty and then it should be merely nominal. The duty should be recognized as a part of the man's citizenship obligation to the nation. The organizations to be made up of men within the period of obligatory service, could be filled either by the men who indicated their desire for such training or by drawing them by lot. This is a matter of detail. The regular army as organized would be made up as to-day; it would be a professional army. The men who came into it would be men who had received in youth this citizenship training. They would come into the regular army because they wanted to be professional soldiers. The regular army would be to a certain extent the training nucleus for the citizen soldier organizations and would be the force garrisoning our over-sea possessions. It would be much easier to maintain our regular army in a highly efficient condition, as general military training would have produced a respect for the uniform and an appreciation of the importance of a soldier's duty.

The reserve corps of officers would be composed of men who had had longer and more advanced training, and could be recruited and maintained as indicated below, through further training of men from the military schools and colleges and those from the officers' training corps units of the nonmilitary universities and colleges. There would also be those from the military training camps and other sources, such as men who have served in the army and have the proper qualifications. . . . It would give us a condition of real national preparedness, a much higher type of citizenship, a lower criminal rate and an enormously improved economic efficiency. Pending the establishment of such a system, every effort should be made to transfer the state militia to federal control. By this is meant its complete removal from state control and its establishment as a purely federal force, having no more relation to the states than the regular army has at present. This force under federal control will make a very valuable nucleus for the building up of a federal force of citizen soldiers. Officers and men should be transferred with their present grades and ratings.

The states have full authority to maintain a military force of their own and under their exclusive control, if they desire to do so. Pennsylvania has established a state constabulary and in doing so has taken a long step in the right direction. Pennsylvania has not had to call upon her militia for strike or riot duty for a good many years.

As has been recommended by the General Staff, there should be built up with the least possible delay a corps of at least 50,000 reserve officers, on lines and through means recommended by the General Staff, and by means of a further development of the United States Military Training Camps for college students and older men, which have been in operation for a number of years. These plans include the coordination of the instruction at the various military colleges and schools and the establishment of well-thought-out plans for the nonmilitary colleges at which it may be decided to establish officers' training corps units on lines now under consideration.

This number of officers, fifty thousand, may seem excessive to some, but when it is remembered that there were one hundred and twenty-seven thousand officers in the Northern army during the Civil War, and over sixty thousand in the Southern, fifty thousand will not appear to be excessive. Fifty thousand officers will be barely sufficient properly to officer a million and a half citizen soldiers. . . .

Under legislative provision enacted during the Civil War, commonly known as the Morrill Act, Congress established mechanical and agricultural colleges in each state, among other things prescribing military instruction and providing for this purpose officers of the regular army. There are nearly thirty thousand students at these institutions who receive during their course military instruction for periods of from one to two years. In some cases the instruction is excellent; in others it is very poor.

There are in addition a large number of military colleges and schools; at these there are some ten thousand students, so that there are approximately forty thousand young men receiving military instruction, nearly all of them under officers of the army. This means a graduating class of about eight thousand, of whom not more than forty-five hundred would be fit to undergo military training.

These men should be assembled in United States Military Training Camps for periods of five weeks each for two consecutive years, in order that they may receive that practical and thorough instruction which in the majority of instances is not possible during their college course. With these should be assembled the men who have taken the officers' training course at the various nonmilitary universities. This course, as outlined by the General Staff, will be thorough and conducted, so far as the purely military courses and duties are concerned, under the immediate control of officers of the army.

From all these sources we have practically an inexhaustible supply of material from which excellent reserve officers can be made. From the men assembled in camp each year, fifteen hundred should be selected and commissioned, subject only to a physical examination, as they are all men of college type, for one year as second lieutenants in the line and in the various staff corps and departments of the regular army. They should receive the pay and allowance of second lieutenants, or such pay and allowance as may be deemed to be appropriate.

The men who receive this training would furnish very good material for reserve officers of the grade of captain and major, whereas as a rule the men who have not had this training would qualify only in the grade of lieutenant.

From this group of men could well be selected, subject to the prescribed mental and physical examination, the greater portion of the candidates from civil life for appointment in the army. We have the material and the machinery for turning out an excellent corps of reserve officers. All that is needed is to take hold of it and shape it.

The prompt building up of a reserve corps of officers is one of the most vitally important steps to be taken. It is absolutely essential.

American tanks train for combat in France (United States Army Military History Institute). The most significant change in modern weaponry occurred at the turn of the twentieth century when internal combustion engines were developed. Gasoline or diesel engines were used on land in cars, trucks, and armored vehicles. At sea, they replaced steam power on surface vessels, and permitted practical submarines. They also provided the power for aircraft, and thereby introduced a new dimension to war. This photograph, taken by the army signal corps in France (4 February 1919), shows American Ford tanks bringing 75 mm guns into action. World War I tanks were tiny. They held only two or three men and were vulnerable to the fire of enemy artillery. Yet to soldiers who had never seen "land ships," they appeared formidable. A German infantryman remembered his first encounter with a tank (1916): "Panic spread like an electric current, passing from man to man along the trench. As the churning tracks reared overhead the bravest men clambered above ground to launch suicidal counter-attacks, hurling grenades onto the tanks' roofs or shooting and stabbing at any vision slit within reach. They were shot down or crushed, while others threw up their hands in terrified surrender or bolted down the communication trenches towards the second line."

MARINES IN THE TRENCHES
Clifton B. Cates

Marines have fought in every U.S. war since the corps was founded during the American Revolution. Their service has taken them around the world on ships, on the ground as infantry, or in the air as pilots. The corps' diverse nature, combined with its elitist attitude, has, at times, placed marine units at odds with army or navy commanders under whom they were to serve. Yet it is this same esprit that makes all marines feel special and willing to undertake the most hazardous duties.

The United States declared war on Germany in April 1917, but it took a year for American troops to have any effect in France. American marines and soldiers served alongside each other in the trenches where they participated in the final drive against the German army in the summer and fall of 1918.

The following document is composed of selections from letters sent home to Tennessee by Lieutenant Clifton B. Cates (1893–1970). These letters provide a colorful account of frontline trench warfare and reveal the writer's infectious enthusiasm for the Marine Corps. Cates never lost his zeal. He remained in the corps, which he eventually commanded as commandant (1948–1951).

(*All is well!!*)

June 10th, 1918

U.S.M.C.A.E.F. [U.S. Marine Corps, American Expeditionary Force]
BOURESCHES

SOURCE: Clifton B. Cates Papers, Personal Papers Section, Marine Corps Historical Center, Washington Navy Yard, Washington, DC.

Dear Mother and Sister:

I know that you have read in the last three days what the good old "Marines" have done—I wish I could only describe it, but I cannot describe it like it should be—it was great.

To start with—we left our last rest billet [barracks] about May 27—I believe I wrote you our last day there. We received sudden orders to leave one night. We (the whole division 27,500 men) were jammed into French trucks and started out. We rode all day and all night—it was an awful cold and dirty trip. If you can, imagine about one thousand trucks lined up one behind the other and running as fast as possible. We passed thru the outskirts of gay Paree and on thru numerous towns. The French people would cheer us as we passed thru the towns, and the children would throw us worlds of flowers—it is a sign of good luck.

At dawn we were piled out in a small village and the men all flopped down and got a few hours needed rest. We had gone a long time without much food, so most everyone got something to eat—they had to cook it—chickens, rabbits, potatoes, etc: a lot of wine cellars were located also. The people had all deserted the town. All that day the roads had been full of refugees plodding their way back and old men, women and children: some walking, others on carts trying to carry their valuables back—it was the most pitiful sight I have ever seen, and there is not a man in our bunch that didn't grit his teeth, and say, "Vive la France." "Do or die is our motto"—and the mother that can furnish a boy should say—"America—here's my boy, God grant that he may come back, if not, I am glad he died for a noble cause, and I am willing to give him to you." At 2:30 p.m. we lined up and marched into position. No traffic in N.Y. City can compare with the few miles that we covered that afternoon—truck after truck, automobiles, motorcycles—thousands of troops and lots of airplanes overhead: also lots of artillery and machine guns moving into new positions. At 6 p.m. we occupied our position in line, in the edge of a woods. Of course, we are back of the trenches in open warfare. We immediately started digging in, each man would dig a small hole big enough to get down in, so as to protect him from shrapnel and machine gun bullets. Our position was about a kilometer (5/8 mile) behind the French line—who were out in front. It is the most active front in France today. After two days the French dropped back of us; not driven back, but to occupy a much stronger position: that left us the front line. . . . The entire line was to move forward—the town was my company's objective. We moved across an open field and stopped in a small woods and my platoon was in a wheat field. The Boche [German] machine guns and artillery had opened up on us, and it was some party. At a certain time and signal we got up and swept over a ground literally covered with machine gun bullets—it was my first charge, and Mother it is a wonderful thrill to be out there in front of a bunch of men that will follow you to death. A lot of men went down; most of them only wounded, but a few dead. About three fourths of the way over (600 yds) a bullet hit me solid on the helmet: it knocked me cold, but it did not go thru my helmet. . . . I came to in about a minute or two—just as the men were entering the town—I covered the rest of the distance to the town in less than no time and twenty four of my men drove a company of Boche and five machine guns out of the town. It was a beautiful fight—they ran like rabbits; dropping their equipment as they ran. We only took one prisoner and one machine gun, but lots of ammunition. If we could only have had a few more men we could have taken the whole bunch. We finished a lot of them though—I killed my first German. After we had entered the town a Boche put a bullet thru the brim of my helmet, another bullet entered the shoulder of my coat and came out two inches back—just cutting my O.D. [olive drab—that is, government-issued] shirt and undershirt—it just grazed the skin, so I am safe and sound. . . .

After we had cleared the town, Lt. Robinson went back down a ravine to the rear to get support, so we could hold the town—we were expecting a counterattack and I had only twenty four men to hold it with. I immediately posted my men in the best possible places. Luckily they did not counterattack. . . .

I never worked harder in my life—the artillery had opened up on us and it was some hot all night and the next day—they have kept at us pretty steady since then. They are dropping a shell about every minute into the town just now—they are tearing it down—it's a shame. I am setting here writing on a dining room table and trusting a shell doesn't hit near. I am pretty well worn out, as I have only had four hours sleep the last four days. A man can live on excitement for a long time. . . . All the men should get decorations and the men of my platoon will get more than one. Won't we sport though when we get back. . . . I lost 32 men out of my platoon of fifty-six: only two or three dead—the others wounded—most of them slightly. I am very proud of my men and they deserve a lot of credit. I sure am going to keep my helmet as a souvenir.

BELLEAU WOODS

June 16th

It has been a living hell since I started this. We were shelled all night with shrapnel and gas shells. At times I wished that one would knock me off, but still life is very sweet at its worst. We wore our gas masks for four hours. It was mustard gas and a lot of the men were burned—someday those damn rascals have got to pay for this inhuman warfare. I hope that I can do my part. I finished one a few days ago and another today. I now have two notches cut on my pistol grip, and I hope I can make it fifty. The one I shot today was running . . . across a field about eight hundred yards in front of our lines—my first shot hit right under him—the next one dropped him, and he hasn't moved since then. . . .

The last few days have been the worst of the war. Before daylight on the 13th our battalion was broken out and made a forced march to reinforce the front lines, as a German prisoner captured the night before stated they were to attack in force the next morning. . . . As we had to cross open wheat fields, we realized that the Germans had spotted us as they had observation balloons up at the time. We went into bivouac in a thick woods on the side of a hill near Belleau Woods. Luckily, we had time to dig fox holes before the Germans opened up,—with a heavy barrage and we had intermittent artillery fire all day. Casualties were fairly light. . . .

About dark we received word to make a relief in the woods with the movement to start at midnight. Just a few minutes before, I had put on my equipment and ordered the men to fall out in the wheat fields below the woods, as it was pitch black dark. I had not gone over twenty feet from my fox hole when I heard a salvo of shells heading our way. From the whistle I thought they were gas shells, and when they hit with a thud and no detonation my fears were confirmed. Soon I smelled the gas, and I gave the alarm to the men, and they all put on their masks. By this time there was a steady stream of incoming shells—gas, air bursts, shrapnel, and high explosives. I reached for my gas mask, but it wasn't there. Naturally, I was petrified. I tried to find my hole where I had left it, but I became confused and couldn't locate it. Luckily, I remembered seeing one of my men with a German gas mask which he had picked up as a souvenir. I yelled to him and finally located his hole and jumped in on top of him, and soon had the mask on. Without doubt it saved my life.

The shelling was so heavy we didn't try to move out, which I now realize was a mistake. It kept up for hours, and we suffered rather heavy casualties, both from shell fragments and gas, as many of our masks were defective. Heroes were made that night, as the wounded had to be carried to the dressing station, which was under a stone bridge down the ravine. Many of the stretcher bearers were hit while carrying the wounded. As soon as the Boche artillery fire stopped, we moved out with about half of the company remaining, and went into this hell hole Belleau Woods. Another battalion of our brigade had attacked the night before and had many casualties, so they put my men to work carrying out the wounded. It wasn't over an hour until all of my men became casualties. The mustard gas had saturated their clothing, and when they started sweating it made bad body burns. Also, the fumes caused temporary blindness.

Soon after I arrived in the woods, I stripped completely naked and applied a heavy lather of soap all over my body and let it dry. I also beat the fumes out of my clothing and let them air for a couple of hours. Evidently, that saved me, but I do have bad blisters between my legs, around my neck, and on my forehead where my helmet rubbed. The doctor has tried his best to evacuate me, but I am not going unless I get worse. . . .

June 17

We were relieved from the front line last night by an Army unit. It is the first time they have been in action, and it's a tough spot to put them in for their first baptism of fire. I felt sorry for them last night when they came in. They had just arrived and were starting the relief when all hell broke loose. The Boche in our rear started firing, . . . then our men returned it, the Germans to our front started firing, we answered, then both their artillery and ours opened up. We thought they were attacking, and they probably thought we were. It kept up for over thirty minutes, and it was a madhouse. Imagine the poor Army boys that have not been under fire before.

When the fracas started, I was at the Company C.P. [command post] (right in the front Line) arranging the relief. As we thought the Germans were attacking, we sent up one flare after another until we ran out. As I had more at my hole, I ran up to it. Just as I arrived I heard a salvo of incoming shells, and I made a jump for it. As I did, a bayonet went right up between my legs almost ripping my trousers off. I landed on a man in the hole, and, at first, I thought he was a Dutchman, but it turned out to be an Army boy, and he had been shot thru the hand. He had set his rifle down in the hole with the bayonet pointing upward. It was a close call, as I could have received a nasty wound. . . .

BORIS GROS JEAN on the PARIS-METZ HIGHWAY

June 18th

We are now a few miles back of the lines in support, and we have been resting very well as we have not been shelled here. It sure is good to get back where we can get hot food and a little sleep. Can you imagine men nibbling old hard bread and enjoying it—for many days we didn't get that in the front lines—really, we lived on excitement. I didn't average one hours sleep a day. The strain has been terrible, but the few that have come thru will soon recuperate back here. Honest, when I look out at the few men left I really cry—I am the only officer out of two companies and I am in charge of the remains of both companies—one good platoon. I didn't realize how I loved the old bunch until it had been broken up—only a few have been killed but a lot wounded and gassed—I am hoping that we can get a lot of them back in a few weeks.

The last night of our tour in the trenches, the Boche tried to take our woods twice—each time we met them with the hottest fire imaginable—you cannot possibly imagine the roar that our rifles, machine guns and artillery made. They never reached our lines at all—they fell back with considerable losses while we didn't lose a man. They kept a constant stream of bullets cutting over our heads—you should hear them whiz over and cut out thru the woods. That is, what used to be—a few trees are still standing, but our artillery cut it to pieces before we drove the Boche out. Today the bodies of Boche are laying all over the woods—it's suicide to get out to try and bury them, so we let them stay.

June 26th, 1918

Woods Northwest of Lucy

Last night I took fifty-two men out to put some barb wire—the Boche spotted us about midnight and began shelling us—I withdrew my men and waited until they had stopped and then started back to work; just as we renewed work they started again, so I brought my men in—no one was hurt. We found coffee, ham, steak, bread, and potatoes waiting for us—we get one hot meal a day here. They bring it in in big thermos cans on a Ford truck. They also bring canned meat, bread, bacon, sugar, candles, and solidified alcohol. During the day we take either the alcohol or candles and cook the bacon in our mess gears; then we fry the bread in the bacon fat, and put sugar on it—it's a swell dish. We either heat the canned meat or eat it cold. The water is brought in in large water carts. Of course, we are not so lucky while we are in the front line—the "chow" gets shot up real often, and we have to go without. . . .

I wish you could see your son with his equipment on—dirty, torn, ragged suit; wrapped puttees [leggings], shoes, that used to be boots, but are now cut off; steel helmet, with a hole thru it and a big dent; pistol belt and suspenders; first aid package and cover; pistol and holster; canteen, cup and cover; knapsack, which holds toilet articles, maps, message books, extra cartridges, etc; field glasses and case, two extra postal clips and cases; German gas mask (which saved my life); French gas mask; big German luger pistol and holster; big musette bag with cigarettes, chocolate bars, magazine, writing paper, condiment can, malted milk tablets, comb, little clothes brush, alkaline tablets (for gas) and other junk; a blanket roll which contains a poncho, blanket, air pillow, handkerchiefs, socks, underwear, etc; and a German raincoat slung over my arm. A nice load, but I need every bit of it. . . .

(July 15th)

(will now try and finish this letter)

The morning of the 4th, we got up early and cleaned up and tried to look half way decent, but we still looked like a bunch of bums. At eight we left our camp and marched to where the parade formed. Mother, you cannot imagine the cheer that would go up as the French people would recognize the Marine flag—it was one continual shout—Viva la Marines—la Marines, etc. They literally covered us with roses—I would carry each bouquet a piece and then drop it—then another girl would load me down with more flowers. It was truly wonderful and it made us Marines feel very good as they give us all of the credit. . . . We have certainly made a name in France—Gee! I am glad that I joined the Marines.

August 1st, 1918

Chavigny, France

It was about the 17th July that we received rush orders to go to a certain place. We were then back in support in a pretty small village on the Marne River. We broke the men out in a big hurry and marched a short piece down the river where we waited for the French trucks that were to carry us. There we had to wait about four hours until about dark. Just as we commenced loading into the trucks, the Boche commenced shelling the railroad directly under this bridge, so everyone was a bit nervous until we had passed. A shell did get one truck; killing two and wounding five others. You cannot imagine what a dirty tiresome trip we had that night and the next day. . . .

While we were there a daring German aviator swept down on us and fired at us with his machine gun, but he didn't do any damage. The French were soon after him and we had the satisfaction of seeing him take a nice tumble to the ground. His plane made a pretty nose dive and he could not right it, so it hit the ground and burst into flames. . . .

Then we received orders to move to a certain place and attack at seven-fifteen. We were soon under way and it was a happy bunch even if a lot of them would never see the sun rise again. We filed down the hill into a big ravine in single file at a good fast pace, and then up on the railroad track. There we saw a lot of German heavy artillery that they had deserted in their hasty retreat the day before. There was a lot of ammunition and all kind of supplies. You know they ran fast when they ran off and left their big guns which they keep well back of the lines at all times. We marched up thru a small French village that had canteens full of water. We formed our waves just outside of the town. Just as I was getting my men into position, a machine gun bullet cut thru in my shoulder. I thought that someone had hit me with a rock at first, so I had a man to look at it, and he pulled a bullet out. It had just broken the skin and had caught in my coat. In a few minutes the big tanks that were to follow lumbered out into position. At a given signal we moved forward. It was a pretty sight to look out at that bunch of men in eight waves moving across the open wheat fields. The big tanks were in the front wave, so we had to walk very slowly. The Boche had turned their artillery on us and were cutting at us with about fifty machine guns. As fast as they would cut our men down, the waves would close up and take up a perfect formation again. Big shells would hit and tear big holes in the lines, but still the men never wavered nor lost their formation. . . . In the meantime, a shell hit right at me and cut a slit in my breeches about four inches across the knee. It gave me a slight wound. Soon we were up to the Boche trenches and they jumped out and ran like wild deer. Up to that time the men had kept perfect formation, but when the Boche commenced running the men swarmed after them shooting as they ran. The men yelled like a bunch of cowboys as they chased them. It was too funny for words. We ran off and left the tanks far in the rear. They saw that they were not needed, so they beat it back slowly. I do not like to advance with them, as they go too slow. They are very good when it comes to breaking down barbed wire or destroying a machine gun nest, but otherwise I had rather advance with the infantry alone. We chased the Boche back about two kilometers and then I organized what men were left and had them to occupy some old abandoned Boche trenches. They were shelling the devil out of us by that time, and I thought sure that they were going to counterattack, but they didn't. The planes were also flying very low over us shooting at us with the explosive machine gun bullets. They would sweep down on us and shoot to beat the devil, but they did very little damage. We soon had the satisfaction of seeing a machine gunner of ours bring one down. That was the finish of him, as he burned up the minute he hit the ground. We stayed in the trenches all day waiting for their counterattack. It was a very hot day, and we were dying for water, but none was to be had. The men did wonderful work in getting the wounded off of the field. Every time a man would start in with a wounded man, the damn Boche would cut at him with a machine gun or a one pounder. Some day those damn rascals have got to pay for such things. Not satisfied with that dirty work, they shelled the dressing station with gas. . . .

We went about nine kilometers in our drive. That is, the Marine

Brigade went that far. We slaughtered a lot of them and captured many prisoners. They left all kind of guns, ammunition, and equipment in their hasty retreat. This drive of ours has put new energy in the allied troops. It is wonderful to see the men marching to the front; they go with quick step, heads up, and lots of singing. You would never realize that some were marching to their own funeral. We had about a dozen different kind of troops in our sector; Marines, American artillery, Algerians, French, English, Scotch Highlanders in their kilts (the Boche call them "the ladies from hell"), and Moroccans.

This warfare is the worst kind of warfare. It is not open warfare, nor is it trench warfare. It is a mixture. After we gain our objective, we always dig small holes to get into so as to be protected from artillery fire, but they are not connected up, and a person cannot move about unless he gets out and lets them pop at him. That is what I had to do the day of our attack. I had to get the men grouped and organized, so I had to run all over the field getting them into shape. The damn Boche shot at me every time I would get out, but luckily, none of them hit. They had me dancing many times, as they seemed to cut right at my feet with the machine guns. Every time they would shoot at me with the artillery, I would hear them coming and would hit the dirt. Some of them came very close, but none hit, although one did blow a shovel, that I was carrying, out of my hand; it left me holding part of the handle.

August 12th

I saw something last night that I have never seen before. That is, the bombing of a large town by aeroplanes. I was making my rounds over the posts when I heard a bunch of planes going over. In a few minutes I saw some gigantic search lights flash on from this town. The next thing I saw was a lot of archies (anti-aircraft shell) bursting in the air. It was so far away that I could not hear the report of the guns. They looked like a lot of stars twinkling. In a few seconds I saw an enormous flash, and then a deafening roar as the big aeroplane bombs exploded. All at once about fifty big search lights were switched on and all of the archies opened up on the Boche planes. They continued to drop bombs that made large flashes and big roars. In a few minutes I heard them come back over us headed for Germany. . . .

I also saw an incident up near Soissons just after our last attack that is very interesting. We had just come out of the line after our attack and were resting in the woods well back of the line. There was a large French observation balloon up just to our right. It was an awful windy day and a lot of dust was flying. All at once, a Boche plane swept down on him and shot at him so as to set his balloon on fire. The Frenchman in the balloon had to make a quick daring drop in his parachute to save himself. The wind caught the thin silk parachute and drove it straight into the woods that we were in. It was about a forty mile gale, so you see he was going very fast when he hit the woods. Just as he hit the first tree, he cut himself away from the parachute and clung to the tree like a flying squirrel. It certainly did slam him up against the tree, and I do not see how he kept from falling, as it hurt him real badly. However, he managed to hold on and then he took a cord out of his pocket and lowered it down. Some of the men had gotten a large rope and had tied knots in it, and they tied it to the string and he pulled it up; tying it firmly, he then slid down. Just before he got to the ground, he fainted, but the men had gotten a blanket and were holding it under him, so they caught him as he fell the remaining few feet. The damn German failed to accomplish what he set out to do as the balloon did not burn, and he payed the supreme penalty, as he was shot down as he tried to bet back to his own lines.

October 13th, 1918

Nantivet Bks., Champagne Sector

I have forgotten when I last wrote to you, but I know that it has been a long time, so I will begin about September 30th. That day at 6 p.m. we all loaded into French trucks and proceeded towards the front. I had over 250 men in my company and nine second lieutenants, so you see that I had some large company to handle. We rode about half of the night and then unloaded and marched about three hours. We could tell that the Boche were very nervous, as he kept the sky blazing with lights. There was moderate artillery fire. We marched to a big deep ditch where we bivouacked for that night, the next day, the next night and the next day. That day we received our maps and attack plan. At eight that night we hiked up the road where we drew hand grenades, ammunition, and . . . flares. We then marched on until we met some French guides that were to guide us into the trenches; merely ditches. The regiment that we were relieving had attacked and taken the Boche front line trenches. It was as dark as pitch and the ditches were full of dead Boche and Frenchmen. We had a lot of trouble getting into our right position, but finally did get into our right place just before daylight; luckily, the Boche artillery was not working very much, but the machine guns and flares did worry us a lot, as we had to walk over open territory within fifty yards of their lines. Every time that they would shoot up a flare, we would hit the dirt; then they would cut loose with their machine guns, but they did not damage us much. We finally did take up our position in a communication trench that ran perpendicular to the Boche line, and of course, it was a bum place. They slipped down the other end of it and bombed us with potato masher grenades, but our men gave them just as much as we received. We stayed cramped up here all of the next day. At 6 p.m. I received orders to take two platoons of my company and to take Trench d'Essen. I lined the men up the best that I could and instructed the two remaining platoons to get superiority of fire on the Boche machine gunners which were very thick on my left. At a given time, or zero hour, I went over with my first wave. The second wave was to follow at thirty paces. The men went over with a whoop and a hollow. It was a regular Indian war hoop and it sure put the fear of God into the Boche. They opened up with a few machine guns, and I saw about twelve grenades come flying over, but that was all; they ran like sheep. My men went at it on the dead run, as the trench was only three hundred yards away. In less than two minutes we had gained our objective, so I sent up a flare signaling to that effect. We had lost only about ten men wounded, and we soon had them cleared off of the field.

We stayed in this trench all night and at 5:45 the next morning our artillery put on the fiercest barrage that I have ever heard. At 5:55 a.m. we went over the top again. This time we had to go in four wave formation and had to go very slow, as we were following our creeping barrage which only moved forward at the rate of one hundred yards every four minutes. The regiment was in columns of battalions and our battalion was the leading battalion, with my company the company in front. We moved forward in perfect formation, although they were cutting us with machine guns real heavily. On we went; we followed our barrage as close as possible without getting into it.

After the first 600 yards the opposition was not so great. Naturally, the heinies [Germans] did not like that heavy barrage, so they would go into their dugouts, and as we were real close up to our barrage, we would be on top of them before they could get out and get into position. A few showed fight, but they were soon shot down; some ran and they all shared the same fate. If we failed getting them, then our barrage caught them, as they had to pass back thru it. Most of them threw up their hands and yelled, "kamerad." We would send them running to the rear with very light guards or none at all. They were only too glad to be alive. . . .

On we went; the artillery was putting over a smoke screen by this time and what few showed fight could not see us until we were on top of them. The men were taking lots of prisoners and we were going fine when we came to our objective. What we had taken had cost the French 175,000 men since the beginning of the war, and they claimed that it could not be taken. We had gained over four kilometers in all. We immediately commenced digging in and reorganizing for a counter attack which we knew was bound to come, but when it did come, we slaughtered them and they did not gain an inch. . . .

Wednesday, 27th of November 1918

Beigleback, Luxemburg

It was the eleventh hour of the eleventh day of the eleventh month that the last Boche shell came whistling into our lines and exploded with a terrific crash. Luckily, it did not get anyone. Then there was a death like stillness along the whole front. Could it be that it was all over? We could not believe it possible. Each man would look at the others in doubt. Finally, word came that the armistice had been signed. Not a cheer did I hear, but there was not a man in the regiment that did not thank God that rainy, muddy, cold morning that it was all over and that he was safe. It didn't seem possible that it was all over, and could stop so suddenly. We had been in the thick of it the night before, and a few had paid that supreme penalty. It was a shame that any man had to be killed at the last moment. Although there was no outburst of joy at the good news, there was that feeling way down in every heart of thankfulness; and only a man that has been thru such hell, as we have had for the last two months, can realize how happy we all were.

We had gone thru the worst fight of our lives. It was not the fighting, but it was the cold, rainy, muddy weather. It rained every day and was bitter cold. We were drenched to the skin and our blankets were soaked. A lot of the men threw them away. We went for hours and hours without food. No shelter of any kind and we couldn't have fires at night, as they would show and in the day time, the smoke would show, so we did without. God only knows how we existed. It was truly hell on earth. I went in with a company of 250 and I came out with less than 50. Only one killed and twenty-eight wounded; the others were sent back sick. All of my lieutenants got sick and I was never as near dead in my life, but I couldn't leave, as someone had to take care of the company.

The night of the eleventh was spent in thawing out and getting dry; there must have been a million bon fires along the front. It was a beautiful sight to look at. The woods on both sides looked as if they were all afire. This was one time that a person could light an open fire and not get shelled, and the men sure made good use of that privilege. We bivouacked in this woods for about a week. We were issued new underwear, socks, etc., and got cleaned up a bit.

American airplane practices bombing run (United States Army Military History Institute). This photograph shows a Curtis-Jenning plane making a practice bombing run over Ellington Field, Texas (17 October 1918). In World War I, most airplanes were used as "spotters" to observe enemy action. However, it soon became apparent that they could aid the ground troops by dropping bombs on enemy positions. World War I bombers had no sights to ensure accuracy. In some cases, the bombs were simply dropped by hand over the side of the plane. Combining tactical air power with armor produced dramatic results. These tactics removed the advantages enjoyed by the defense for more than a century and restored mobility to the battlefield. At the beginning of World War II, this combination produced the "blitzkrieg" (lightning war) tactics that were so effectively used by the Germans in Poland, Holland, and France.

AN AERIAL BATTLE

E. C. Leonard

*T*he introduction of the airplane to war meant that battle lines were no longer held captive to terrain. A third dimension—height—was added. At first, planes were used as spotters for ground forces. When enemy planes tried to stop them, "dogfights" occurred. Eventually airplanes flew behind the enemy's line and bombed civilian resources. This became known as "strategic air power."

The following selection is a brief memoir written by an observer and "bomber." It describes the airplane's tactical and strategic use in the First World War, and also reveals the unique camaraderie that existed among World War I air crews. The airplane was the modern equivalent of a medieval knight's steed, and a chivalric code quickly appeared among pilots. When captured, World War I air crews were often treated with respect, and even admiration. These courtesies only lasted for that one war. Once strategic airpower had brought terror bombing home to enemy cities, pilots would sometimes be condemned as war criminals.

On the morning of September 26, 1918, we had orders to be ready to leave the ground at eight o'clock on a bombing raid, two from our squadron and one from each of the other two squadrons. We were sure this time that a new drive was to start, for we could hear the steady rumble of artillery. Consequently, at the appointed hour, we were ready. Four bombs were on each plane, the machine guns and motors tested out. It was a mean morning for a flight. A thick fog covered everything, making it impossible to see any

SOURCE: Guy B. Wiser papers, U.S. Army Military History Institute Archives, Carlisle Barracks, Pennsylvania.

distance along the ground. It looked foolish to attempt leaving the ground at all, but we knew weather would not stop flying on the first day of an offensive. After half an hour's wait, the fog did not lift, but we had a good smoke standing by the machines in our goggles and flying clothes. At last the planes began to take off, but our turn did not come at first. As some of the planes left the ground from farther down the field, they flew directly over us. We could hear the heavier sound of a motor coming nearer, but we could see nothing, until suddenly the machine burst into view through the fog and flew directly overhead, only thirty or forty feet up. It was a moment of excitement. One could see the fastenings of the bombs hanging underneath the wings. The plane passed on and was swallowed up in the fog, with a diminishing roar of the engine.

Soon our turn came. How high did the fog go? We didn't know, but it was important, for over thirty machines were already in the air, and the danger of a collision in the air was great.

Our wheels left the ground at nine o'clock and we rose into the fog, straining our eyes for the sight of another plane above, below, on all sides. Our own motor made so much noise that we could hear nothing else. Consequently our eyes were the only guard against collision. The ground faded out of sight and we were swallowed up in the mist. It was like another world. It lasted but for a minute, thank goodness. The sun began to grow brighter and suddenly we burst into daylight and blue sky. A mile ahead was the rest of our flight, climbing and slowly climbing and slowly closing into a V formation. Below the fog appeared as a tremendous snow field and as we gained altitude, we could see a larger expanse of country and that the fog hung only along the river valleys and lowlands. It was a beautiful sight; it was a long climb with the load of bombs and once when we climbed a little too steeply, our plane started down sideways, but only for an instant. The higher we climbed, the colder it got, and I began to wish for the sheepskin flying boots and face mask left at the airdome. There arose visions of a frozen nose and feet.

We had been up nearly an hour and were at a height of two miles and a half. Perhaps fifteen miles away we could see the lines of trenches and smoke puffs of artillery and breaking shells. Our formation of eight machines was pretty well closed up by now and we were slowly circling over the point agreed upon for the several flights to meet, but no other flights were to be seen. Consequently we started over alone. The Germans must have been watching us before we headed for the lines, for we were barely above the trenches when their anti-aircraft batteries began shelling us. I did not see the first shell break, but I heard it—a short sharp sound, as of a muffled piece of linen ripping. My first thought was that an engine part had been thrown back into the plane, tearing the fabric, but I could not locate the tear and the engine sounded all right. Soon the "woof" came again and this time I woke up and saw that the noise was caused by shrapnel breaking close by. The engine made so much noise that the explosions were considerably deadened, but we could see the explosions, lots of them, black and yellow blots in the atmosphere, now a little higher, now in the middle of our V formation. It was thrilling. There was nothing to do but to fly straight along and anyway "Archie" [antiaircraft shells] seldom made a hit. One hit in 30,000 shots was considered good shooting. Then there was the comforting thought that we would never know what hit us if we did get hit, so it was good sport, all right; but the fellow on the ground had all the sport about it.

At our altitude of thirteen thousand feet, we could not see much on the ground, but roads, rivers, villages, and here and there the tiny pin point of white smoke which showed a battery in action now and then. I let them have a few shots from my machine guns just to keep the oil from freezing and gumming up the guns.

We were nearing the objective now, and the machines were flying closer together, getting ready to drop the bombs. I could see a brother observer in the next plane grin as we clasped our hands and shook them to one another; the observer in the leading machine fired a very light signal telling us to prepare to drop our bombs. I leaned over the side with my hand on the release, watching for the bombs to drop from the plane ahead. In a few moments, I saw them fall from the next plane and pulled the lever and marked up 448 pounds more of TNT for the Germans. At the release of weight, our plane gave a jump forward as if glad of the chance to hit the Hun [German].

I was glad I was not on the ground at that particular point, with thirty-two hundred and twelve pound bombs [sic] coming down. We watched the bombs as far as we could see them and a few seconds later saw a number of black puffs and then a fire start in the town.

At once we began turning back toward home. I began to get cold again with nothing to do but watch the sky for Boche and swing the guns every three or four minutes for a few shots at the prettiest village in sight.

It looked as though we were going home with no more excitement than a few anti-[air]craft shells. I was beginning to think that it was only a joy ride after all, when I saw the Boche. There they were, tiny specks in the distance and yet, almost before we could think they were on us, five life size Fokkers, painted yellow and black. They slid around our heavier machines like yellow jackets, swerving up for an instant to let a stream of bullets go at us. I couldn't shoot at him without shooting away part of our own machine. The tremendous noise from the engine and wind from the propeller made it impossible for me to tell the pilot, so I wiggled the controls from my seat to attract his attention and pointed out Mr. Boche to him. Promptly he turned, first to the right a little, then a little to the left. At every turn the Fokker under our tail came into plain view about seventy-five yards away. Each time we swung, I was waiting and let him have both guns. I could see the tracer bullets going right into his cockpit, and knew that one bullet at least must find the mark. And it did. At the third burst, my bullets reached home and Mr. Boche started down in a nose spin, out of control, dead, wounded or disabled.

The Fokkers remaining then left us, evidently deciding that the odds were too much in our favor, there being still eight of us. I felt pretty fine at having shot down a Boche and also glad to have a breathing spell with time to put some fresh magazines on the guns. But the breathing spell didn't last very long, for in front and above, strung out across the sky, I counted twelve more little specks. In less time than it takes to read it, they had grown from specks to fire spitting Fokkers—Another nest of angry hornets, they came diving right through the middle of our formation, shooting a steady stream of fire. The tracer bullets made it look as though it really was fire. It was like a dream. I was so busy that three pairs of hands wouldn't have been enough.

We were perhaps fifty yards below the rest of the formation, having come down to help a brother plane, which had gotten below in the first scrap. Naturally we offered a very good target for the Fokkers. The guns wouldn't swing fast enough—There were too many Huns, they were all around, above and below. It was a beautiful sight. Eight of our two seated machines and twelve of the single seated German Fokkers. Each of us shooting at the Germans with two guns, each gun sending six hundred bullets a minute and each of the German planes shooting at us from three guns. The air was one huge network of fire from the tracer bullets. It looked impossible for any one to escape from the storm of bullets going both ways. It was magnificent. Something had to happen—it couldn't last.

One of our planes rose suddenly higher than the rest and gradually turned nose down toward the ground, leaving a trail of flame and smoke behind it. It was beautiful and yet terrible, for two of our friends and pals were in that plane, burning up. I redoubled my efforts to shoot more Huns and took great care in aiming.

We were still below the rest of our formation and it seemed as though all the lines of tracer bullets were coming in our direction. I worked faster and faster but had not time to tell whether a Hun that slid away from my bullets was hit or not, for as fast as one moved away, a second took his place for a shot. I knew that couldn't last forever and was beginning to wonder how long it could last, when "blam" I got it in the neck. The shot knocked me down on the seat with the sudden force of a pile driver. I thought my end had come, but it hadn't. The Fokker who had shot me, and seen my guns stop shooting, was coming up close behind us. I got on my feet, took good aim, shot at him with both guns from about fifty yards. The tracer bullets went right into his cockpit and he slid out of sight, [I told my pilot] "Coop" [Marion C. Cooper] that he went down in flames. Probably he did. I was too busy to watch him the instant his bullets stopped coming. I was conscious of only one thing—to get rid of three other Fokkers which had begun to close in on us from the other sides.

Suddenly our plane dropped into a nose spin. My first thought was that "Coop" had been shot and that in a very few seconds we would hit the ground and be through with everything. I slipped down on the seat unconscious, but only for an instant. When I regained my senses, we were still falling in a spin, but "Coop" had unfastened his safety belt and was standing up with one foot over the side in the act of jumping overboard. And no wonder, for his cockpit was a mass of flames from the motor which was on fire. It was a question of dying an easy death by jumping overboard, or of burning to death. His first thought was to escape the terrible agony of the flames. He did not know whether I was dead or alive, but when he saw me open my eyes, he did not hesitate. Rather than desert a wounded and helpless comrade, he stepped back into what seemed, at the time, the certainty of burning to death.

We came out of the spin upside down and went into a side slip in a fruitless endeavor to extinguish the flames. By this time his hands were so badly burned that the stick slipped from his fingers and he had to use knees and elbows to work the controls. Finally by diving straight down with the motor turned on as much as it would go, the almost impossible was accomplished, and the flames put out.

I could do nothing as we came down, but sit in the back seat and wonder when the flames would reach the gas tank. I could look up and see the fight still going on, farther and farther away as we got closer to the ground, until the planes looked like large and small gnats.

We were still over German territory, but with the flames out, there seemed to be a chance of getting back home, but the motor would barely turn over. There was nothing for it, but to land, and all we could do was smile at one another when the engine sounded so like a couple of tin cans rattling together.

We landed in a large field, barely missing some telephone wires as we came into the field. "Coop" landed the machine with the control stick between his knees and elbows. Although we hit the ground with force enough to send the plane up on its nose and break the wings, neither of us was thrown out. The machine was pretty well shot up. The motor was a wreck. There were bullet holes all over the plane, sixty or more of them; little round ones and long gashes in the fabric. Surely a Divine providence must have guided the bullets from the vital parts.

Before we could climb out, a Fokker which had followed us down from the flight flew past about fifty feet up, turned and flew back and forth, motioning us away from our plane with his arm. There was only one thing to do and we climbed out and walked a little distance away, whereupon the Fokker landed and the pilot walked over to meet us.

He was a good clean looking fellow with a first class iron cross pinned on his coat together with a number of other medals. We had heard many stories of the cruel treatment given prisoners by the Germans, and we did not know what to expect. Imagine our surprise when he saluted just as though he was a brother officer in our own army. Each of us had a pistol and we surrendered them to him, handle first, when he asked in English if we were wounded. By this time a crowd of German soldiers had collected around us, and an automobile had arrived from the nearby village. A man in the automobile had some bandages, and proceeded to tie them around my wound and stop the flow of blood which had pretty well soaked my clothes, but he could do nothing for burns. I had to take all my flying suit off and left it on the field when we came away. That, in itself, was unimportant, but I left my pipe in the pocket, which was very important.

The bullet entered the right side of my neck at the height of the collar and went out my back between the spine and shoulder blade. Luckily it missed all veins, windpipe and bones, although a quarter of an inch variation would have meant death.

While my wound was being tied up, the German Fokker pilot looked the plane over pretty thoroughly. He found a picture which "Coop" had fastened on the instrument board and very graciously took it out and gave it to the pilot asking him if he did not wish to keep it, which made [us] think that we had human beings to deal with, after all. We were then taken in the automobile to a hospital in the village, where we had to wait half an hour for a surgeon to come. It was an agonizing wait for "Coop" whose hands and face grew more painful each minute. The suspense was terrible and still we were not sure that the evidence of good treatment we had experienced might not prove to be a trick. Neither one of us could understand a word of German, which did not help matters any. However, the attendants were kind enough and did all they could to help, by getting some chairs and a drink of water for us.

When the surgeon did get there, it was agony to see him cut away the burned skin from "Coop's" hands. Yet he worked as fast as he could, and seemed to do a good job. When he finished my comrade's hands looked like two huge white boxing gloves, but the powder and salve which had been applied, eased the pain somewhat. After the surgeon had looked at my bullet hole and tied it up again, we were conducted to a room in the hospital and put to bed. . . .

We had not been long in the room, when an attendant came in with a cup of "coffee" (made from acorns, we later learned) and some black bread sandwiches, which tasted fine, and helped our talk along in great shape. Of course we regretted the fact that we were out of action, and prisoners, but it had to be, and anyway we had accounted for one German plane, certainly, and possibly two, for my pilot stoutly claimed that I shot down one after being wounded. Be that as it may, it was the splendid heroism and nerve of "Coop" that got us on the ground with our lives. We felt that a miracle had happened that day for us. It seems more a miracle than ever, to look back upon.

THE BODY OF AN AMERICAN

John Dos Passos

The Great War had shattered America's illusions. Some of its young men had joined the Canadian, British, French, or Italian army before the United States entered the war in 1917. Their idealism had arisen out of the Progressive movement at home. Progressives accepted the idea that dedicated work in pursuit of high motives could make the world a better place. Major social, economic, and political reforms had changed American life in the first two decades of the twentieth century. The Progressives believed that these same values could transform the rest of the world.

But the sheer magnitude of the wartime horror quickly destroyed their belief in progress. It seemed as if the tens of millions of dead had achieved nothing. One character in Ernest Hemingway's A Farewell to Arms (1929) remarked that their "sacrifices" were meaningless; they were "like the stockyards at Chicago if nothing was done with the meat except to bury it." Reform no longer mattered. Americans in the 1920s were concerned with personal pleasure: bathtub gin, speakeasies, flappers, and gangsters had replaced traditional values. A few felt so violated by the war that they refused to return home. Instead, they joined other American expatriates on the Left Bank of the Seine River in Paris, where they sought answers to fundamental questions about the meaning of life.

John Dos Passos (1896–1970) was the son of a wealthy Chicago attorney (whose own father had come to America from Portugal with nothing but the clothes on his back). Young Dos Passos earned a degree from Harvard before volunteering to drive ambulances in France and Italy. The war transformed him into a radical Marxist. In 1936, Dos Passos completed his greatest work, the U.S.A. trilogy. He used his own journalistic style,

SOURCE: John Dos Passos, 1919 (New York: Houghton Mifflin, 1932). Reprinted by permission of Elizabeth H. Dos Passos.

which combined fiction with news reports and stream-of-consciousness with impressionistic word pictures. By the time he had completed the third novel of his trilogy, Dos Passos already had begun to move away from Marxism toward capitalism. By the end of his life, Dos Passos, who once had written for the communist journal *New Masses,* was supporting conservative political causes and American involvement in Vietnam. Yet in all his writings, Dos Passos remained a champion of the underdog, the person who struggled against the impersonalness of modern life.

The following reading is from Dos Passos's novel *1919* (1932), the second part of the *U.S.A.* trilogy. This reading deals with the selection of the remains of America's "unknown soldier." The ceremony Dos Passos describes took place on 11 November 1921, the third anniversary of the armistice that had ended World War I. Dos Passos uses words spoken by the common people of his time. Thus "dinge," "guinea," and "kike" are derogatory slang for black, Italian–, and Jewish–Americans. "OD" is an abbreviation for olive-drab, the color of the American military uniforms. "Slum" is a shortened form of "slumgullion" or stew; "forty men and eight horses" describes the capacity of French railroad cars, often called "40 and 8's"; a "shortarm inspection" is a genital inspection for venereal diseases; "cooties" are lice, which infested the trenches; "Ish gebibbel" is Yiddish for "What a mess!"; and "the propho station" refers to the prophylactic station where venereal diseases were treated. Dos Passos's colorful language, combined with the prejudice he describes, removes the bombastic patriotism of the ceremony, forcing readers to concentrate on the dignity of every American who had died for his country in the war.

Whereasthe Congressoftheunitedstates byaconcurrentresolutionadop- tedon the4thdayofmarch lastauthorizedthe Secretaryofwar to cause to be brought to theunitedstatesthe body of an American whowasamem- beroftheamericanexpeditionaryforcesineurope   wholosthislifeduring- theworldwarandwhoseidentityhasnotbeenestablished for burial in- thememorialamphitheatreofthe nationalcemeteryatarlingtonvirginia

In the tarpaper morgue at Chalons-sur-Marne in the reek of chloride of lime and the dead, they picked out the pine box that held all that was left of
enie menie minie moe plenty other pine boxes stacked up there containing what they'd scraped up of Richard Roe
and other person or persons unknown. Only one can go. How did they pick John Doe?
Make sure he aint a dinge, boys,
make sure he aint a guinea or a kike,

how can you tell a guy's a hunredpercent when all you've got's a gunnysack full of bones, bronze buttons stamped with the screaming eagle and a pair of roll puttees?

. . . and the gagging chloride and the puky dirt-stench of the yearold dead . . .

The day withal was too meaningful and tragic for applause. Silence, tears, songs and prayer, muffled drums and soft music were the instrumentalities today of national approbation.

John Doe was born (thudding din of blood in love into the shuddering soar of a man and a woman alone indeed together lurching into

and ninemonths sick drowse waking into scared agony and the pain and blood and mess of birth). John Doe was born

and raised in Brooklyn, in Memphis, near the lakefront in Cleveland, Ohio, in the stench of the stockyards in Chi, on Beacon Hill, in an old brick house in Alexandria Virginia, on Telegraph Hill, in a halftimbered Tudor cottage in Portland the city of roses,

in the Lying-In Hospital old Morgan endowed on Stuyvesant Square,

across the railroad tracks, out near the country club, in a shack cabin tenement apartmenthouse exclusive residential suburb;

scion of one of the best families in the social register, won first prize in the baby parade at Coronado Beach, was marbles champion of the Little Rock grammarschools, crack basketballplayer at the Booneville High, quarterback at the State Reformatory, having saved the sheriff's kid from drowning in the Little Missouri River was invited to Washington to be photographed shaking hands with the President on the White House steps;—

though this was a time of mourning, such an assemblage necessarily has about it a touch of color. In the boxes are seen the court uniforms of foreign diplomats, the gold braid of our own and foreign fleets and armies, the black of the conventional morning dress of American statesmen, the varicolored furs and outdoor wrapping garments of mothers and sisters come to mourn, the drab and blue of soldiers and sailors, the glitter of musical instruments and the white and black of a vested choir

—busboy harveststiff hogcaller boyscout champeen cornshucker of Western Kansas bellhop at the United States Hotel at Saratoga Springs office boy callboy fruiter telephone lineman longshoreman lumberjack plumber's helper.

worked for an exterminating company in Union City, filled pipes in an opium joint in Trenton, N. J.

Y.M.C.A. secretary, express agent, truckdriver, fordmechanic, sold books in Denver Colorado: Madam would you be willing to help a young man work his way through college?

President Harding, with a reverence seemingly more significant because of his high temporal station, concluded his speech:

We are met today to pay the impersonal tribute;
the name of him whose body lies before us took flight with his imperishable soul . . .
as a typical soldier of this representative democracy he fought and died believing in the indisputable justice of his country's cause . . .

by raising his right hand and asking the thousands within the sound of his voice to join in the prayer:

Our Father which art in heaven hallowed be thy name . . .

Naked he went into the army;
they weighed you, measured you, looked for flat feet, squeezed your penis to see if you had clap, looked up your anus to see if you had piles, counted your teeth, made you cough, listened to your heart and lungs, made you read the letters on the card, charted your urine and your intelligence,
gave you a service record for a future (imperishable soul)
and an identification tag stamped with your serial number to hang around your neck, issued O D regulation equipment, a condiment can and a copy of the articles of war.
Atten'SHUN suck in your gut you c——r wipe that smile off your face eyes right wattja tink dis is a choirch-social? For-war-D'ARCH.

John Doe
and Richard Roe and other person or persons unknown
drilled hiked, manual of arms, ate slum, learned to salute, to soldier, to loaf in the latrines, forbidden to smoke on deck, overseas guard duty, forty men and eight horses, shortarm inspection and the ping of shrapnel and the shrill bullets combing the air and the sorehead woodpeckers the machineguns mud cooties gasmasks and the itch.
Say feller tell me how I can get back to my outfit.

John Doe had a head
for twentyodd years intensely the nerves of the eyes the ears the palate the tongue the fingers the toes the armpits, the nerves warmfeeling under the skin charged the coiled brain with hurt sweet warm cold mine must dont sayings print headlines:

Thou shalt not the multiplication table long division, Now is the time for all good men knocks but once at a young man's door, It's a great life if Ish gebibbel, The first five years'll be the Safety First, Suppose a hun tried to rape your my country right or wrong, Catch 'em young, What he dont know wont treat 'em rough, Tell'em nothin, He got what was coming to him he got his, This is a white man's country, Kick the bucket, Gone west, If you dont like it you can croaked him

Say buddy cant you tell me how I can get back to my outfit?

Cant help jumpin when them things go off, give me the trots them things do. I lost my identification tag swimmin in the Marne, roughhousin with a guy while we was waitin to be deloused, in bed with a girl named Jeanne (Love moving picture wet French postcard dream began with saltpeter in the coffee and ended at the propho station);—

Say soldier for chrissake cant you tell me how I can get back to my outfit?

John Doe's
heart pumped blood:
alive thudding silence of blood in your ears
down in the clearing in the Oregon forest where the punkins were punkincolor pouring into the blood through the eyes and the fallcolored trees and the bronze hoopers were hopping through the dry grass, where tiny striped snails hung on the underside of the blades and the flies hummed, wasps droned, bumblebees buzzed, and the woods smelt of wine and mushrooms and apples, homey smell of fall pouring into the blood,
and I dropped the tin hat and the sweaty pack and lay flat with the dogday sun licking my throat and adamsapple and the tight skin over the breastbone.

The shell had his number on it.

The blood ran into the ground.

The service record dropped out of the filing cabinet when the quartermaster sergeant got blotto that time they had to pack up and leave the billets in a hurry.
The identification tag was in the bottom of the Marne.

The blood ran into the ground, the brains oozed out of the cracked skull and were licked up by the trenchrats, the belly swelled and raised a generation of bluebottle flies,
and the incorruptible skeleton,
and the scraps of dried viscera and skin bundled in khaki

they took to Chalons-sur-Marne
and laid it out neat in a pine coffin
and took it home to God's Country on a battleship
and buried it in a sarcophagus in the Memorial Amphitheatre in the Arlington National Cemetery
and draped the Old Glory over it
and the bugler played taps
and Mr. Harding prayed to God and the diplomats and the generals and the admirals and the brasshats and the politicians and the handsomely dressed ladies out of the society column of the *Washington Post* stood up solemn
and thought how beautiful sad Old Glory God's Country it was to have the bugler play taps and the three volleys made their ears ring.

Where his chest ought to have been they pinned
the Congressional Medal, the D.S.C., the Medaille Militaire, the Belgian Croix de Guerre, the Italian gold medal, the Vitutea Militara sent by Queen Marie of Rumania, the Czechoslovak war cross, the Virtuti Militari of the Poles, a wreath sent by Hamilton Fish, Jr., of New York, and a little wampum presented by a deputation of Arizona redskins in warpaint and feathers. All the Washingtonians brought flowers.

Woodrow Wilson brought a bouquet of poppies.

In the twentieth century the American army and navy focused on the Philippines, China, the Pacific Ocean, Latin America, and Europe. Modern technology replaced wind as the chief propellant of ships, and internal combustion engines meant that future wars could be fought in the air and under the seas. The great diversity of American military interests in the first decades of the century precludes any single volume from tracing the entire history.

Naval sources for the first years of the twentieth century are both more abundant and better than works about the army. Particularly valuable is William R. Braisted's *The United States Navy in the Pacific*, two volumes (1958–1971), which does devote some coverage to the Atlantic fleet. Also useful is Robert A. Hart's *The Great White Fleet: Its Voyage Around the World, 1907–1909* (1965). Elting E. Morison has written a fine biography of Admiral William S. Sims in *Admiral Sims and the Modern American Navy* (1942). United States involvement in the Caribbean is discussed in David Healy's *Gunboat Diplomacy in the Wilson Era: The U.S. Navy in Haiti, 1915–1916* (1976).

The history of the army in this era is fragmented by many small campaigns in remote areas of the world. The Boxer Uprising in China is the subject of Chester Tan's *The Boxer Catastrophe* (1955) and Victor Purcell's *The Boxer Uprising: A Background Study* (1963). There are three good works on problems along the Mexican border: Herbert M. Mason's *The Great Pursuit* (1970) and two works by Clarence C. Clendenen, *The United States and Pancho Villa* (1961) and *Blood on the Border: The United States Army and the Mexican Irregulars* (1969). Other good works about U.S. incursions include Allan Millet's *The Politics of Intervention: Military Occupation of Cuba, 1906–1909* (1968); Dana Munro's *Intervention and Dollar Diplomacy in the Caribbean, 1900–1921* (1964); Jack Sweetman's *The Landing at Vera Cruz: 1914* (1968); and Robert Quirk's *Affair of Honor: Woodrow Wilson and the Occupation of Vera Cruz* (1967).

The peacetime history of the army in the early twentieth century is told in Hermann Hagedorn's two-volume biography, *Leonard Wood: A Biography* (1931); Jack C. Lane's *Armed Progressive: General Leonard Wood* (1978); John G. Clifford's *The Citizen Soldiers: The Plattsburg Training Camp Movement, 1913–1920* (1972); and Marvin Fletcher's *The Black Soldier and Officer in the United States Army, 1891–1917* (1974). An additional source on army policy in the early twentieth century is Richard Leopold's interpretative biography of *Elihu Root and the Conservative Tradition* (1954)

There are two good military histories of the First World War: S. L. A. Marshall's *The American Heritage History of World War I* (1964), which has more text and fewer illustrations than one might expect from this publisher, and Edward M. Coffman's *The War to End All Wars* (1968). Laurence Stallings served with the American Expeditionary Force in France and later wrote *The Doughboys: The Story of the AEF, 1917–1918* (1963). The history of the air war is well told by James J. Hudson in *Hostile Skies: A Combat History of the American Air Service in World War I* (1968). Three good memoirs of the war are *Over the Top* by Arthur Guy Empey, an American who served with the British army; John W. Thomason, Jr.'s, *Fix Bayonets!* (1926), an American marine's account of trench warfare; and Joseph Douglas Lawrence's *Fighting Soldier: The AEF in 1918* (1985), edited by Robert H. Ferrell. An autobiographical novel, *Through the Wheat* (1923), describes Thomas A. Boyd's life as an infantryman.

Many military leaders wrote memoirs after the war. John J. Pershing entitled his, *My Experiences in the World War* (1931), and Army Chief of Staff Peyton C. March wrote *The Nation at War* (1932). Both were so self-serving that George C. Marshall kept his own from appearing until after his death when it was published under the title *Memoirs of My Service in the World War, 1917–1918* (1976). Each of these men has found a biographer worthy of the subject. Pershing's life was undertaken by Donald Smythe in *Guerrilla Warrior: The Early Life of John J. Pershing* (1973) and *Pershing: General of the Armies* (1986). These volumes are joined by Edward M. Coffman's *The Hilt of the Sword: The Career of Peyton C. March* (1966) and Forrest C. Pogue's *George C. Marshall: The Education of a General, 1880–1939* (1963). Other important biographies are the first volume of D. Clayton James's *The Years of MacArthur, 1880–1941* (1970) and Alfred T. Hurley's *Billy Mitchell: Crusader for Air Power* (1964).

Following the war, American troops were sent to Siberia in a futile effort to aid Russian moderates. This controversial action is told in Betty Miller Unterberger's *American Siberian Expedition, 1918–1920* (1956) and a history by the commander of the American troops in Russia, William Sidney Graves, in his book, *America's Siberian Adventure, 1918–1920* (1931). Peacetime enlisted life is described in *Army Brat, a Memoir* (1980) by William J. Smith.

WORLD WAR II

World War I had left Europe with the new challenges of fascism and communism. Adolph Hitler rebuilt Germany's economy and military might after its humiliation in World War I. Hitler wanted to control the heartland of Europe, and he challenged the Soviet Union, under Joseph Stalin, who feared German hegemony. The United States' first response to fascism's growing truculence was a foreign policy of isolation, at least until President Franklin D. Roosevelt could convince Congress and the public that the United States had to actively support the Western democracies against the Nazi menace.

By 1939, Europe was again at war. Two years later, Hitler controlled most of the European continent. Only Great Britain and the Soviet Union remained to fight German military might. Roosevelt gradually had prepared the United States to fight the war he knew was inevitable. Democracy, he believed, could not survive in a world dominated by dictators. The United States first aided England and then the Soviet Union. American ships, supplies, and monies were sent to help defeat fascism. At home, Roosevelt ordered critical materials stockpiled, persuaded Congress to approve a peacetime draft, and encouraged factories to fill Britain's orders for military hardware.

Meanwhile in Asia, a militaristic Japan seized extensive territory and soon dominated much of China. The United States had received early warnings that Japan would strike U.S. territories and bases in the Pacific, but most American strategists assumed the attack would come in the Philippines. By the time Japanese planes bombed Pearl Harbor in Hawaii on 7 December 1941, President Roosevelt's preparedness plans had made the

United States better prepared to fight a war than at any other time in its history.

Unlike World War I, the United States entered the Second World War as the richest and strongest economic power in the world. Twenty million Americans went to war. American sailors and soldiers steadfastly approved of the war's goals. And after fascism's defeat, they were assured, peace would be guaranteed by the active participation of the United States in a postwar United Nations.

Following the examples set by the German and Japanese military forces, the U.S. Army, Navy, and Marine Corps, accompanied by a powerful air force, reintroduced mobility to the battlefield. Air strikes could reach German and Japanese cities, and the rapidity of troop movement on battlefields in Africa, Europe, and the Pacific were incredible. Between the wars the Marine Corps had developed the doctrine of amphibious landings; these soon became "triphibious" with the addition of air support. After four years, the United States and its allies, having successfully fought in every conceivable type of terrain, had conquered Germany and turned their attention to Japan. The war ended dramatically when atomic bombs were dropped on Hiroshima and Nagasaki. The destruction of these Japanese cities was proof to all the world that humankind had harnessed one of the mysteries of science.

THE GOD-DAMNED INFANTRY

Ernie Pyle

No wartime correspondent's writings ever meant more to the American people than Ernie Pyle's (1900–1945) stories of World War II. Pyle lived with the men he wrote about; he told of their hopes, fears, sufferings, and small joys. To him, every soldier was a hero, a man with dignity. And he died with them, killed by a Japanese sniper late in the war.

Collectively, Pyle's columns are among the finest pieces of descriptive war literature ever written. Individually, they opened America's heart to its fighting sons. Pyle's stories were like soldiers' letters home. He never discussed the movement of armies, international strategy, or politics. Instead, he wrote about the commonplace G.I.,* a man who seemed every bit as important to Pyle as he was to his family back home. Pyle made "G.I. Joe" the central figure in the terrible madness of the war. The following selection is typical of Pyle's wartime columns.

IN THE FRONT LINES BEFORE MATEUR, NORTHERN TUNISIA, MAY 2, 1943

—We're now with an infantry outfit that has battled ceaselessly for four days and nights.

This northern warfare has been in the mountains. You don't ride much anymore. It is walking and climbing and crawling country. The mountains aren't big, but they are constant. They are largely treeless. They are easy to defend and bitter to take. But we are taking them.

SOURCE: Scripps-Howard newspapers; copyright, Scripps-Howard Foundation. Used by permission.

* The term "G.I." came from the initials in "government issue," which was a standard description for all equipment and materials issued to military personnel—and ultimately, for the soldiers themselves.

The Germans lie on the back slope of every ridge, deeply dug into foxholes. In front of them the fields and pastures are hideous with thousands of hidden mines. The forward slopes are left open, untenanted, and if the Americans tried to scale these slopes they would be murdered wholesale in an inferno of machine-gun crossfire plus mortars and grenades.

Consequently we don't do it that way. We have fallen back to the old warfare of first pulverizing the enemy with artillery, then sweeping around the ends of the hill with infantry and taking them from the sides and behind.

I've written before how the big guns crack and roar almost constantly throughout the day and night. They lay a screen ahead of our troops. By magnificent shooting they drop shells on the back slopes. By means of shells timed to burst in the air a few feet from the ground, they get the Germans even in their foxholes. Our troops have found that the Germans dig foxholes down and then under, trying to get cover from the shell bursts that shower death from above.

Our artillery has really been sensational. For once we have enough of something and at the right time. Officers tell me they actually have more guns then they know what to do with.

All the guns in any one sector can be centered to shoot at one spot. And when we lay the whole business on a German hill the whole slope seems to erupt. It becomes an unbelievable cauldron of fire and smoke and dirt. Veteran German soldiers say they have never been through anything like it.

Now to the infantry—the God-damned infantry, as they like to call themselves.

I love the infantry because they are the underdogs. They are the mud-rain-frost-and-wind boys. They have no comforts, and they even learn to live without the necessities. And in the end they are the guys that wars can't be won without.

I wish you could see just one of the ineradicable pictures I have in my mind today. In this particular picture I am sitting among clumps of sword-grass on a steep and rocky hillside that we have just taken. We are looking out over a vast rolling country to the rear.

A narrow path comes like a ribbon over a hill miles away, down a long slope, across a creek, up a slope and over another hill.

All along the length of this ribbon there is now a thin line of men. For four days and nights they have fought hard, eaten little, washed none, and slept hardly at all. Their nights have been violent with attack, fright, butchery, and their days sleepless and miserable with the crash of artillery.

The men are walking. They are fifty feet apart, for dispersal. Their walk is slow, for they are dead weary, as you can tell even when looking at them from behind. Every line and sag of their bodies speaks their inhuman exhaustion.

On their shoulders and backs they carry heavy steel tripods, machine-gun barrels, leaden boxes of ammunition. Their feet seem to sink into the ground from the overload they are bearing.

They don't slouch. It is the terrible deliberation of each step that spells out their appalling tiredness. Their faces are black and unshaven. They are young men, but the grime and whiskers and exhaustion make them look middle-aged.

In their eyes as they pass is not hatred, not excitement, not despair, not the tonic of their victory—there is just the simple expression of being here as though they had been here doing this forever, and nothing else.

The line moves on, but it never ends. All afternoon men keep coming round the hill and vanishing eventually over the horizon. It is one long tired line of antlike men.

There is an agony in your heart and you almost feel ashamed to look at them. They are just guys from Broadway and Main Street, but you wouldn't remember them. They are too far away now. They are too tired. Their world can never be known to you, but if you could see them just once, just for an instant, you would know that no matter how hard people work back home they are not keeping pace with these infantrymen in Tunisia.

American bombers over Japan (Smithsonian Institution Photo No. 3340). By World War II, the doctrine of strategic airpower had been well developed. This required that enemy cities be bombed to destroy the industrial base that supported Germany and Japan. Shown in this photograph are B-29 Superfortresses (from the 58th Bombardment Wing) over a Japanese city. Two of their two-ton bombs are visible beneath the upper plane and a third can be seen under the wing of the lower plane. The results of the strategic bombing of Japan were so dramatic that General Henry "Hap" Arnold, commander of the Army Air Corps, told President Harry Truman that an atomic bomb was unnecessary because Japan was "already on the verge of collapse." After the war, survey teams were sent to Germany and Japan to assess the damage. Their conclusions were not as sanguine as General Arnold's. The Strategic Bombing Survey (1946) concluded that "cities had a surprising and extraordinary ability to recover from the effects of numerous attacks. The raids on Hamburg in July–August 1943 were among the most devastating of the war. Yet, despite the deaths of over 60,000 people, the total destruction of one-third of all houses in the city and the disruption of normal processes of living, Hamburg as an economic unit was not destroyed. It never fully recovered from the bombing, but in five months it had regained 80 per cent of its former productivity, despite the fact that great areas of the city lay . . . in dust and rubble. As in the case of industrial plants, when it was found much easier to destroy the buildings than the machines in them, so also it is much easier to destroy the physical structure of a city than to wipe out the economic life."

A BOMBING RUN

"An Officer"

Few World War II assignments were as dangerous as flying bombing missions over Germany. Strategic bombing had brought the war to the enemy's homeland, often at a costly price to Allied air crews. Although the American B-17 bombers were reliable, they were slow and lumbering when compared to the sporty German fighters. The B-17s' altitude and direction indicated their most likely targets, and once they crossed the German border, they faced the Luftwaffe (the German Air Force) in the air and antiaircraft flak from guns on the ground.

England and the United States had agreed to open a "second front" against Germany to relieve the pressure on the eastern front, where German troops were deep in Russian territory. When the Allied leaders did not open a "second front" with land forces on the European continent, they made do with an "air front" using round-the-clock bombing. The British found that daylight bombing missions brought high losses to their bombers and aircrews. Nevertheless, the United States chose to use its better bombsights for daytime precision bombing, while British planes shifted to night missions. Daytime bombing did offer some protection to German civilians living near munitions plants, railroad yards, and gasoline tanks, but it also made German defense easier.

The following document is an after-action report by a member of a bomber squadron who had asked that his name not be released. It demonstrates the difficulties that all air crews found in locating and destroying targets.

SOURCE: The National Archives, Record Group No. 319; Records of the Army Staff; CCSGLM Copy.

CONFIDENTIAL
HEADQUARTERS, 100TH BOMBARDMENT GROUP (H)

25 August 1943.

SUBJECT: Personnel report on the REGENSBURG Mission, 17 August, 1943.

When the 100th Group crossed the coast of Holland south of the Hague at 1008 hours at our base altitude of 17,000 feet, I was well situated to watch the proceedings, being co-pilot in the lead ship of the last element of the high squadron. The Group had all of its 21 B-17s tucked in tightly and was within handy supporting distance of the 95th Group, ahead of us at 18,000 feet. We were the last and lowest of the seven groups of the 4th Air Division that were visible ahead on a southeast course, forming a long, loose-linked chain in the bright sunlight, too long, it seemed. Wide gaps separated the three combat wings. As I sat there in the tail-end element of that many miles long procession, gauging the distance to the lead group, I had the lonesome foreboding that might come to the last man about to run a gauntlet lined with spiked clubs. The premonition was well founded.

At 1017 hours, near Woensdrecht, I saw the first flak [antiaircraft rounds] blossom out in our vicinity, light and inaccurate. A few minutes later, approximately 1025 hours, two FW-190's [German fighters] appeared at 1 o'clock level and whizzed through the formation ahead of us in a frontal attack, nicking two B-17's of the 95th Group in the wings and breaking away beneath us in half-rolls. Smoke immediately trailed from both B-17's, but they held their stations. As the fighters passed us at high rate of closure, the guns of our group went into action. The pungent smell of burnt powder filled our cockpit, and the B-17 trembled to the recoil of nose and ball turret guns. I saw pieces fly off the wing of one of the fighters before they passed from view. . . .

It was 1041 hours, over Eupen, that I looked out my co-pilot's window after a short lull and saw two whole squadrons, 12 Me-109's and 11 FW-190's climbing parallel to us. The first squadron had reached our level and was pulling ahead to turn into us and the second was not far behind. Several thousand feet below us were many more fighters with their noses cocked at maximum climb. Over the interphone came reports of an equal number of enemy aircraft deploying on the other side. For the first time, I noticed an Me-110 sitting out of range on our right. He was to stay with us all the way to the target, apparently reporting our position to fresh squadrons waiting for us down the road. At the sight of all these fighters, I had the distinct feeling of being trapped—that the Hun was tipped off, or at least had guessed our destination and was waiting for us. No P-47's [American fighters] were visible. The life expectancy of the 100th Group suddenly seemed very short, since it had already appeared that the fighters were passing up the preceding groups, with the exception of the 95th, in order to take a cut at us.

Swinging their yellow noses around in a wide U-turn, the 12-ship squadron of Me-109's came in from 12 to 2 o'clock in pairs and in fours, and the main event was on.

A shining silver object sailed past over our right wing. I recognized it as a main exit door. Seconds later, a dark object came hurtling through the formation, barely missing several props. It was a man, clasping his knees to his head, revolving like a diver in a triple somersault. I didn't see his 'chute open.

A B-17 turned gradually out of the formation to the right, maintaining altitude. In a split second, the B-17 completely disappeared in a brilliant explosion, from which the only remains were four balls of fire, the fuel tanks, which were quickly consumed as they fell earthward.

Our airplane was endangered by various debris. Emergency hatches, exit doors, prematurely opened parachutes, bodies, and assorted fragments of B-17's and Hun fighters breezed past us in the slip-stream.

I watched two fighters explode not far beneath, disappearing in sheets of orange flame, B-17's dropping out in every state of distress, from engines on fire to control surfaces shot away, friendly and enemy parachutes floating down, and, on the green carpet far behind us numerous funeral pyres of smoke from fallen fighters, marking our trail.

On we flew through the strewn wake of a desperate air battle, where disintegrating aircraft were commonplace and 60 'chutes in the air at one time were hardly worth a second look.

I watched a B-17 turn slowly out to the right with its cockpit a mass of flames. The co-pilot crawled out of his window, held on with one hand, reached back for his 'chute, buckled it on, let go and was whisked back into the horizontal stabilizer. I believe the impact killed him. His 'chute didn't open.

Ten minutes, twenty minutes, thirty minutes, and still no let-up in the attacks. The fighters queued up like a breadline and let us have it. Each second of time had a cannon shell in it. The strain of being a clay duck in the wrong end of that aerial shooting gallery became almost intolerable as the minutes accumulated towards the first hour.

Our B-17 shook steadily with the fire of its .50's [.50 calibre machine guns] and the air inside was heavy with smoke. It was cold in the cockpit, but when I looked across at Lt. Thomas Murphy, the pilot, and a good one, sweat was pouring off his forehead and over his oxygen mask. He turned the controls over to me for a while. It was a blessed relief to concentrate on holding station in formation instead of watching those everlasting fighters boring in. It was possible to forget the fighters. Then the top-turret gunner's twin muzzles would pound away a foot above my head, giving a realistic imitation of cannon shells exploding in the cockpit, while I gave an even better imitation of a man jumping six inches out of his seat.

A B-17 of the 95th Group, with its right Tokyo tanks [auxiliary fuel tanks] on fire, dropped back to about 200 feet above our right wing and stayed there while 7 of the crew successively baled out. Four went out the bomb-bay and executed delayed jumps, one baled from the nose, opened his 'chute prematurely and nearly fouled the tail. Another went out the left waist gun opening, delaying his 'chute opening for safe interval. The tail gunner dropped out of his hatch, apparently pulling the ripcord before he was clear of the ship. His 'chute opened instantaneously, barely missing the tail, and jerked him so hard that both his shoes came off. He hung limp in the harness, whereas the others had shown immediate signs of life after their 'chutes opened, shifting around in the harness. The B-17 then dropped back in a medium spiral, and I did not see the pilots leave. I saw it just before it passed from view, several thousand feet below us, with its right wing a solid sheet of yellow flame.

After we had been under constant attack for a solid hour, it appeared certain that the 100th Group was faced with annihilation. Seven of our group had been shot down, the sky was still mottled with rising fighters and it was only 1120 hours, with target-time still 35 minutes away. I doubt if a man in the Group visualized the possibility of our getting much further without 100% loss. I know that I had long since mentally accepted the fact of death, and that it was simply a question of the next second or the next minute. I learned first-hand that a man can resign himself to the certainty of death without becoming panicky. Our group fire power was reduced 33%, ammunition was running low. Our tail-guns had to be replenished from another gun station. Gunners were becoming exhausted and nerve-tortured from the prolonged strain, and there was an awareness on everybody's part that something must have gone wrong. We had been aiming point for what seemed like most of the Luftwaffe and we fully expected to find the rest of it primed for us at the target. . . .

Near the I.P. [initial point of the bombing run], at 1150 hours, one hour and a half after the first of at least 200 individual fighter attacks, the pressure eased off, although hostilities were still in the vicinity. We turned at the I.P. at 1154 hours with 14 B-17's left in the group, two of which were badly crippled. They dropped out soon after bombing the target and headed for Switzerland. . . .

Weather over the target, as on the entire trip, was ideal. Flak was negligible. The group got its bombs away promptly on the leader. As we turned and headed for the Alps, I got a grim satisfaction out of seeing a rectangular column of smoke rising straight up from the Me-109 shops, with only one burst over in the town of Regensburg.

The rest of the trip was a marked anti-climax. A few more fighters pecked at us on the way to the Alps. A town in the Brenner Pass tossed up a lone burst of futile flak. Col. LeMay, who had taken excellent care of us all the way, circled the Air Division over Lake Garda long enough to give the cripples a chance to join the family, and we were on our way toward the Mediterranean in a gradual descent. The prospect of ditching as we approached Bone, short of fuel, and the sight of other B-17's falling into the drink, seemed trivial matters after the vicious nightmare of the long trip across Southern Germany. We felt the reaction of men who had not expected to see another sunset.

At 1815 hours, with red lights showing on all our fuel tanks in my ship, the seven B-17's of the group who were still in formation circled over Bertoux and landed in the dust. Our crew was unscratched. Sole damage to the airplane: a bit of ventilation around the tail from flak and 20 mm. shells. We slept on the hard ground under the wings of our B-17, but the good earth felt softer than a silk pillow.

SUBMARINE WARFARE

D. H. McClintock

*L*ike airplane crews, submariners lived in constant danger. Unlike most airmen, who can return to a safe haven after their mission, submariners must stay in enemy waters for weeks, lurking there to torpedo unsuspecting ships. By the end of the war, the American blockade of Japan was as tight as any ever attempted—the U.S. Navy had achieved a mortal stranglehold on Japanese commerce.

The following document is a transcript of an interview with Commander D. H. McClintock conducted by the U.S. Navy on 9 March 1945, near the end of World War II. Submarine captains and other commanders were surveyed to evaluate their experiences in order to gain insight for future naval strategy and tactics. Officers were given time to prepare their statements. There was no cross-examination and few probing questions, but, as a group, these interviews are an important resource of firsthand accounts about American naval activity in the Second World War. This type of primary source is an example of "oral history."

My World War II experience began on December 7, 1941. I was 4th officer and Officer of the Deck of the submarine PLUNGER returning to Pearl Harbor from San Francisco. The PLUNGER was in company with, and leading two other units of Submarine Division 43, the POLLACK and POMPANO. The Division Commander was embarked in the PLUNGER. We were due to arrive off the Pearl Harbor entrance at eight a.m. on the 7th. Bad weather had delayed us so that at eight we were about 100 miles northeast of Pearl Harbor. . . .

SOURCE: Bureau of Personal Interviews, World War II. Naval Historical Center, Operational Archives Branch, Washington Navy Yard, D.C.

At approximately 0840 a radioman stuck his head up the conning tower hatch and said, "We just received a message. 'Air raid on Pearl Harbor—no drill!' " I told him to report it to the Captain, Lt. Comdr. White, and the Division Commander, and then to find out what the message *really* said. Two minutes later he was back with the radio log which showed the same wording. We then rigged ship for dive, and ordered the POLLACK and POMPANO to do likewise, reporting the contents of the message to them.

I warned the lookouts that we were probably at war with Japan and to be especially "on the ball." By 0900 the PLUNGER was ready to dive. Shortly thereafter the forward lookout sighted a plane which looked to me like a Jap scout. The skipper was on the bridge at this time. The PLUNGER submerged, as did the other ships in the division. The Division Commander was not convinced that the plane was a Jap, and he gave the order to surface. As soon as we got to the bridge, a plane flew over at about 200 feet making a strafing run. The plane then proceeded on a northerly and very steady course, and was in sight for about 10 minutes, on the same bearing. When informed of the strafing, the Division Commander had been below, the Division Commander remarked, "That was probably just one of our planes trying to signal us." The commanding officer, Dave White, then asked and later begged the Division Commander permission to send in a contact report of the planes and the fact that they had disappeared on a steady northerly course, perhaps indicating the location of the carriers. As it happened, this would have given Pearl Harbor a report which probably would have meant locating the Jap Force. However, the Division Commander refused permission, since he said it would just clutter up the air, when probably the Japs were already being annihilated. Further, he was not convinced that the planes were enemy.

Later that morning a message (probably Jap) was received, "Enemy transports off Barber's Point, U.S. Fleet attack." We were already engaged in fitting the exploders in the warheads of the reload torpedoes. The tubes had been carried full of ready war shots since September, 1941. We worked to get the reload torpedoes ready before arriving off the Pearl entrance, envisioning Japs pouring ashore near Barber's Point and wondering if the Army coastal guns would leave us any targets.

Shortly after noon, we were ordered to Lahaina to wait orders. There we steamed in circles, submerging during daylight of the 8th. On the 9th we entered Pearl. We had heard a San Francisco broadcast reporting a battleship sunk. That's all we knew. Many of the crew had big bets that it was all a drill.

The PLUNGER stood up the channel first. The Division Commander was on the bridge. The channel was choked with fuel oil. The NEVADA, partially sunk, came into view just short of the turn near Ford Island. The Division Commander said, "Well, guess they had to get one." Next the ruins of Ford Island hanger were sighted. Then around the turn—no one said anything for at least a minute, gazing with awe at the sunken battleships. Then from the Division Commander, *"The whole damn battle line! They got the whole damn battle line!"* The ARIZONA was still smoldering. We could hardly believe our eyes.

Upon mooring at the Sub Base, we found ourselves dazed. We asked anybody in sight on the docks how it happened. When told it was torpedoes, we felt *somewhat* better. Not bombs, but torpedoes had done it. Torpedoes—that was our weapon. We could hit back!

From then on, we busied ourselves with war patrol preparations. It was up to us, the small ships. The big ones were gone.

Before we left, there were several false air raid alarms. On one of these we were ordered to moor near the ARIZONA. The VESTAL was sitting on the bottom nearby. As we lay there waiting for the raid, which never came, we noted hundreds of boxes piled on the beach near the Aiea landing. What were they? Then we began to see 50 foot motor launches go by—loaded to the gunnels [tops of the sides]—at first we could not see what the cargo was, then suddenly we knew! Oil soaked bodies from the battle wagons— hundreds of them! The boxes on the beach were rough caskets!

We sailed on the 13th of December. . . .

I think none of us expected to come back. On the way west "Tokyo Rose" sent greetings. She said she knew that American subs were headed west from Pearl Harbor. She said that "If American submariners are wise, you will turn back. Certain death awaits you over here." The PLUNGER was the second American sub to sight Japan in this war. We arrived off the Kobe entrance to the Inland Sea on January 2. We were promptly depth charged on the 4th by a destroyer which beat us to the draw. We wondered if there wasn't something in what Tokyo Rose said. Eventually we sank a ship and returned safely, to spread a little news on what a war patrol was like.

Then came more war patrols on the PLUNGER and later on the CERO. I had command of the submarine DARTER on her third, and later on her fourth and last patrol. We sailed from Brisbane on September 1, 1944. . . .

On October 2nd, after we turned west, we contacted the submarine SEAWOLF, proceeding westward, in the safety lane, on schedule. She was well astern. By late afternoon she had passed us and was out of sight ahead. The next day, early in the afternoon, DARTER came upon what appeared to be a U.S. hunter-killer group working in the safety lane. We had great difficulty in convincing the group that we were friendly. We were afraid to dive because they might gain the impression we were enemy. After shaking this group of planes and DE's [destroyer escorts], we speeded up to get well clear. We should have overtaken the SEAWOLF in the lane very shortly, but didn't. She was never seen again as far as I know, and there is a possibility that she was lost on the 2nd or 3rd of October. I have heard it rumored that a hunter-killer group depth charged a submarine in the safety lane that day. . . .

At midnight on the 20th, we picked up a news broadcast on the beginning of the Leyte landings. This was the first we knew of the Philippine Invasion. We immediately headed for Balabac Strait, since the shortest route for the Jap Fleet from Singapore to Leyte is via Balabac Strait. . . .

DARTER and DACE were steaming at 5 knots, 50 yards apart, on battery. Two convoy reports had been received. The DACE was to take one before leaving for base, DARTER the other. This had been decided and we were about ready to part company, when 16 minutes after midnight from our conning tower came the report, "Radar contact, 131° T, 30,000 yards—contact doubtful—probably rain."

"*The Jap Fleet*" was what flashed through my mind. Almost immediately the radar operator stated that the contact was ships. The DACE was given the range and bearing by megaphone. The answer came back "Let's go get them." By twenty minutes after midnight (it was now October 23rd) both DARTER and DACE were chasing the contact at full power. The ships were in Palawan Passage, headed north. We were on the left flank. DARTER soon drew ahead of DACE, DACE trailing temporarily when her radar went out of commission.

It was now apparent that we had not a convoy, but a large task force, which we assumed was headed for Leyte to interfere with our landing. Three contact reports were sent—the final one estimating that the force included at least eleven heavy ships, the main body of the Jap Fleet, we hoped! I decided that we should not attack before dawn, considering it vital to see and identify the force.

Our initial speed estimate of 22 knots had soon dropped to 15; the targets were not zigging; we could detect their radars sweeping. With this 15 knot speed we could easily gain position ahead.

The left flank column, nearest us, consisted of 5 heavy ships, of which the last ship in column gave by far the largest radar pip. Probably a battleship. There may have been more ships in this column, but at the long range at which we were tracking and the probable close formation, this is all that showed up on the radar screen. I picked this column for DARTER's target, hoping for a crack at what we hoped was a battleship. The DACE, trailing us very closely, was assigned to the starboard column. We planned to make a periscope attack at dawn.

At 0425, DARTER was 10 miles ahead of the left flank (western) column. We slowed to target speed, waiting for the dawn. By 0500 DACE had passed to port, then crossed our bow, headed for a position ahead of the eastern column.

I went down below to see where radio had delivered our contact reports. I looked in the mess room; it was filled with a large part of the mid-watch. After the previous night's fruitless chase, the crew was not very hopeful of gaining position for an attack. When I told them we would probably be attacking the Jap Fleet in about an hour, they were obviously skeptical. But I didn't blame them; I wasn't absolutely sure myself. I had a small fear that the ships might be high speed transports, and *not* the Fleet.

At about 0430 all hands were called for coffee before the expected attack. At about 10 minutes before five we manned battle stations. Ten minutes after five we reversed course, heading down the throat of the western column. It was getting to be faintly light in the east. There wasn't a cloud in the sky. In 20 minutes we wanted to shoot. We submerged to 300 feet to get the depth of density layer, then returned to periscope depth.

The first periscope look showed a huge gray shape. It was the whole column seen bows on. Was it cruisers or battleships? A look to the southeast, where the light was better, showed battleships, cruisers, and destroyers. That column would pass about three miles to the east of us. Two destroyers could be seen part way between the columns. Our sound gear was silent. Weren't they echo ranging at all? As I swung the periscope around to the east I would give something not recordable, an exclamation at every point I stopped the periscope. The Exec [executive officer] would say, "What's there?" and I would say "battleships." "What's there?" "Cruisers." "What's there?" "Cruisers." "What's there?" "Battleships." Now back to our own column.

The gray ships kept getting larger. We were a little to the east of the column's track. We would pass on almost parallel courses. At 5:25 the first ships in column could be identified as heavy cruisers, with huge bow waves. There were sighs of disappointment throughout the conning tower that the targets weren't all battleships. A beautiful sight, anyway. They were in close column. We could imagine the Japs at general quarters, water-tight doors closed, the officers in white service pacing the bridge. I hoped the lead ship would be the flag ship. It was! At 5:27 the range to the leading cruiser was under 3,000 yards. All tubes were ready.

Then the column zigged west to give a perfect torpedo range of just under one thousand yards. Their profiles could be seen clearly. ATAGO cruisers! The fifth ship in column was observed as she started the turn, and seemed to be a battleship. Where were the rest of the destroyers? I got a setup on the new target course. TDC [target direction center] reported ready. I had the 'scope up for what seemed like several minutes, watching. The leading cruiser looked huge now. She had a bone in her teeth [the ship was steaming at full speed ahead]. The forward slant of her bridge seemed to accentuate her speed. The ATAGO, my favorite target on the attack teacher! Estimating the angles on the bow off her flat bridge face was easy; I had done that many times before on models. Angle on the bow was getting bigger now, 55, 60, 65. Range under a thousand . . . "shooting bearing" . . . "mark" . . . "FIRE ONE!"

As the next five forward fish [torpedoes] left us, from the bridge of the target came signals from a searchlight pointed to the east. Did she see our torpedoes? She was going by now. No, she wasn't zigging!

"Shift targets to second cruiser" . . . "bearing mark." "Give me a *range* . . . give me a range . . . give me a range," sang out Dennis Wilkinson, the TDC operator. "I want you to shoot." "You can't shoot without a range!" He finally got it. 1500 yards to the next ATAGO. They were in line of bearing now. "TDC Ready"—"Bearing Mark"—"Fire Seven." The first stern torpedo was on its way. As this torpedo left, heavy explosions started. "Depth Charges!" said Schwab, the Exec. "Depth Charges hell . . . torpedoes!" said I. "Christ, we're hitting 'em, we're hitting 'em!," from Walter Price, who was punching the torpedo firing keys, and jumping up and down as each torpedo hit.

After the tenth torpedo was on its way, six at the leader and four at the second in column, I swung the periscope back to the first target, which had been hit with five of the bow torpedoes. I will never forget what I saw. She was belching flame from the base of the forward turret to the stern; the dense black smoke of burning oil covered her from forward turret to stern. She was still plowing ahead, but she was also going down by the bow. Number One Turret was cutting the water. She was finished.

As we started deep four more torpedoes hits were heard, the fourth being about 30 seconds late for the 1500 yard torpedo run to the second target. This may have been a hit in the third cruiser, since they were in line of bearing. On the way down we knew we had sunk one, thought probably the second would sink.

The depth charging was sketchy, the destroyers which stopped with the targets apparently searching only in the vicinity of the targets.

At about six o'clock the DACE attacked and more explosions were heard. (She sank a battleship or a heavy cruiser.) We now tried to reconstruct the picture of the Force. I had seen three battleships, at least one of which was YAMATO class, eight cruisers, and three destroyers. There may well have been more ships astern, since I concentrated only on the western column during the last ten minutes of the approach. . . .

After two approaches on the cruiser were thwarted by the destroyers, we decided to await night-fall and rest the crew. We had been in contact with the enemy for two nights, and the crew was almost exhausted. . . .

We passed through a sea of fuel oil. This must have extended for miles, as I believe we were in it for over an hour. The cruiser seemed to be steering a very erratic course as though she had no rudder. Her slow speed and her varying speed, sometimes it would vary as much as four knots, indicated she was in great difficulty.

At about midnight we had about an hour to go to gain position for attack ahead of the cruiser. . . . The night was pitch black. Every now and then we could catch a glimpse of the cruiser appearing merely as a black shape to the southeast.

At about five minutes after midnight we were making over 17 knots, trying to attack before the cruiser could pick up more speed. The navigator was plotting in the conning tower, all officers were at their battle stations, most of the crew, except for the watch and the plotting party, was asleep.

At about five minutes after midnight, it was now the 24th, we hit a shoal, rode up over it, taking a large up angle. The officer of the deck and myself thought we were gone. I thought we'd been torpedoed. I watched the stern go under water, went under water as far as the engine room hatch. We seemed to be going down quite rapidly. Then all of a sudden the stern rode on up, and after several seconds we came to rest high and dry. Still we couldn't see the reef. After two or three minutes we were able to make out that the water was very light colored around us. . . .

At this time the destroyer screen of the cruiser apparently had heard us hit because now the destroyer started closing in. He got closer and closer and closer until finally the range got in to 12,000 yards. That may not sound close now, but it sounded close then to us sitting there on the reef with no arms but one four-inch gun and a couple of smaller guns.

As soon as we ran aground I had a peculiar feeling, I thought we'd probably get off, but there were so many other pessimists on board that we wouldn't, that we immediately commenced burning the confidential publications. Finally at about one o'clock we lost the destroyer on the radar and could breathe a little easier. The tide was still coming in and about 0140 was high tide. We knew it was then or never as far as getting off was concerned.

Down on the main deck there was great activity. The gunner's mates, with some help from the rest of the crew, were throwing all the ammunition overboard, except for about 20 rounds which we were saving for the destroyer at daylight if he should come back. The commissary officer, Don Miller, was busy with part of the crew throwing overboard all of the commissary provisions. The engineer was having all fuel oil and all fresh water blown over the side. The torpedo officer was trying to get rid of our torpedoes up forward, but we were afraid to fire them in that position for fear they would explode as they hit the reef, as they dropped from the tubes, and our efforts to get off would have been to no avail. We were not able to get the six torpedoes left out of the tubes.

However, by about 0140 we had done everything that was humanly possible in that time to lighten the ship. At this time we tried to back off. The engines would start but the sea suctions were plugged, with coral apparently. We were afraid to run them. There wouldn't be any use of getting off if we had no engines to run on. So we tried backing with the battery. This had no effect. The compass never moved more than a half degree.

To augment the effect of the propellers we tried sallying ship. The crew was assembled first aft, where they would run forward, then aft. Then in conjunction with this we had another part of the crew who would assemble on one side and run from side to side in conjunction with the backing. This didn't do any good either. Several times the white water rushing forward from the propellers would make it look as though we were coming off, and there would be cheers from down on deck, but then looking farther we could see that the water was still and that we weren't moving. . . .

Down below activities of another nature were going on. All equipment down below was being destroyed. In the conning tower the TDC was being wrecked with a sledge hammer, also the radars. In the forward battery, particularly in the officers' shower, fires were burning where all registered publications were being destroyed.

After I gave up trying to get her off I had little to do except walk around down below to see what was going on. The air down below was so full of smoke that, in fact, it was all I could do to stay down there more than five or ten minutes at a time. I remember seeing one mess attendant, a six footer named Lewis, who was having the time of his life. He had a sledge hammer and he was destroying things, and he really was enjoying it.

There were other fires burning in the radio shack and more fires burning back aft in the engine room.

It was certainly a different looking submarine down below and the worse mess I have ever seen, as far as an orderly state is concerned.

At about 0300, I'm only guessing at the times now, we commenced abandoning ship in rubber boats to the DACE, who had just showed up. Captain Claggett on the DACE brought the DACE right up the edge of the shoal. I think he touched with his bow several times. I kept telling him though the megaphone to get well clear or else we'd both be up there, but he was so anxious to get us off that he held the ship right up close to the reef. He sent us a line from his bow to our stern and by twisting with his screws he managed to stay about 50 yards off our stern for the whole time the abandoning ship was taking place. . . .

By this time the tide was so low that it was about a 20-foot drop from the fantail to the life rafts which were rising and falling with the waves. The waves weren't so bad at that. If it had been at all rough that morning we never would have made it.

Finally, there was no one left on the DARTER but the gunnery officer, the executive officer, myself, the chief of the boat and one other gunner's mate. The gunner's mates being busy rigging the demolition outfit. . . .

After witnessing the demolition time clock set in the control room, we went topside and went over the side into the life raft. I was the last one to leave.

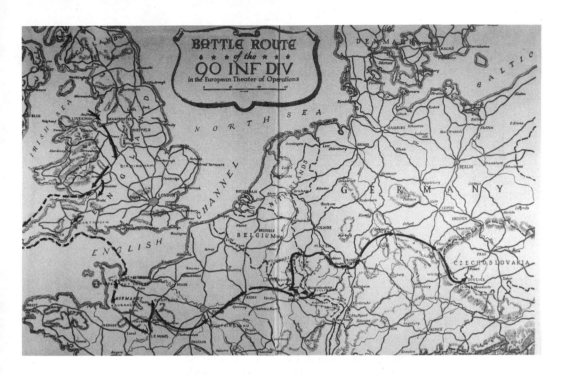

Battle route of the 90th Infantry Division (United States Army Military History Institute). This map was printed inside the covers of the History of the 90th Division in World War II *(1946). Like most unit histories published at the end of the war, it was written to be a souvenir of the soldiers' wartime experiences. This drawing takes a modern road map and adds a dark line (with arrows) to trace the movement of the 90th division. Although it is not a topographical or military map, it does show enough detail so that a competent commander, or tourist, could find his way across Europe. Modern military maps have become so detailed that they are difficult for an untrained person to read. Today, the army requires "map reading" as part of its basic training for all officers and enlisted men.*

THE BEACHES AND THE HEDGEROWS

*E*veryone eventually recognized that the only way to defeat Hitler was to invade the German homeland via the English Channel into France. American strategists had argued for a cross-channel invasion since the United States had first entered the war, although the British, at various times, advocated other uses of Allied resources in Italy or Greece or southern France. The landing would be a problem of enormous magnitude: Thousands of men, ships, and planes would have to be readied in England. Russian leaders told President Roosevelt that they could not wait indefinitely for a second front to open against Germany. Roosevelt overruled his generals and ordered them to join the peripheral war by landing in North Africa in November 1942. Six months later, the Allies invaded Sicily and Italy. Rome fell two days before the long-awaited invasion of France began.

On D-Day (6 June 1944), a combined Allied army surprised Hitler by landing at Normandy, rather than at the expected invasion point of Calais. Allied strategists knew that an amphibious landing's success depended upon rapid movement inland, supported by additional manpower and supplies. By the end of the first day, the beachhead had been secured. Artificial harbors had permitted the landing of necessary equipment. The breakout from the Normandy beaches and the Cotentin peninsula was difficult because of well-defended hedgerows. By July, the Allies had put ashore almost a million men, 177,000 vehicles, and more than a half-million tons of supplies. Armor, artillery, and tactical air support returned mobility to the battlefield. By August, the Allies had penetrated the German defenses and were on their way to liberate Paris (25 August).

The movement had been so rapid that the invaders were running out

SOURCE: United States Army, 90th Infantry Division, *A History of the 90th Division in World War II, 6 June 1944 to 9 May 1945* (Baton Rouge, LA: Army & Navy Publishing Co., 1946).

of supplies, especially fuel. A keen competition developed between British General Bernard Montgomery in the north and George Patton, the American commander of the Third Army in the south. Although the supreme Allied commander, Dwight D. Eisenhower, preferred a balanced movement along the entire front, he permitted Montgomery to attempt a quick thrust into Holland. Montgomery's operation, "Market Garden," was too ambitious and failed.

By November, enough supplies had reached the frontlines to permit the Allies to launch an attack at the Rhine River. But unseasonably cold and wet weather, combined with the rugged defense of their homeland by the German army, slowed the attack. By year's end, the Allies had penetrated only thirty miles into Germany, but not before a massive German counterattack had broken through the Allied lines in the Ardennes Forest. The Battle of the Bulge (16 December 1944–31 January 1945) was Germany's last offensive gasp. The German government surrendered unconditionally on 7 May 1945.

The Allied armies were divided into corps, divisions, regiments, and battalions. Many units had personnel, some of them historians, record their wartime experiences in an official history. These unit histories were written, and sometimes distributed, to the soldiers before they returned home. The results were uneven and frequently uncritical. Yet, except for primary sources (diaries, letters, and official reports), they are often the only firsthand accounts available. Collectively, unit histories are an indispensable reference on the military campaigns of the Second World War. The following selection is taken from the history of the 90th Infantry Division. This division went ashore at Normandy late on D-Day, where it met little resistance. Then, as part of the First Army, it fought its way into the heart of France, driving back the German army, hedgerow by hedgerow. After the liberation of Paris, the 90th Division moved to the southern flank as part of Patton's Third Army, where it participated in the offensive along the Rhine.

THE BEACHES AND THE HEDGEROWS

"Blossomtime in Normandy" came to the staccato accompaniment of whistling artillery rounds, whining rifle bullets, the sharp crack of mortars on the beaches, and the angry stuttering voices of a thousand emplaced guns. Overhead, fighters and bombers roared to their targets, while offshore, warships of the Navy pounded enemy defenses with devastating fire. . . .

As the boats approached the shore the troops leaped into the hip-deep water with weapons held high overhead, raced across the artillery-churned sands of Utah Beach, past the burning vehicles caught in previous barrages, and found momentary protection at a seawall 400 yards distant. The beach was constantly shelled, and inevitable casualties were suffered. . . .

This was what the long months of training were for, the marching and crawling and the endless, repetitious harping on details. Schooldays had ended, and now began the final examinations. No more after-problem critiques, except where mistakes were written in blood, and errors in judgment were entered on the casualty lists.

As part of the First Army, VII Corps, the Division laid its plans. Orders called for the 90th to cross the Merderet river and proceed westward, seizing high ground east of the Douve river, thirteen kilometers distant, in an effort to deepen the Corps beachhead. Reconnaissance parties from the Infantry and the Engineers reconnoitered possible crossing sites. All necessary equipment and supplies were put ashore. Troops were shifted to their jump-off positions, and all was in readiness for the arrival of H-Hour.

At four o'clock in the morning of June 10th the 90th Division moved forward, a movement that was to honor no obstacles, acknowledge no hindrance until it reached the hills of Bohemia eleven months away.

Thrusting forward quickly, the 357th and the 358th Regiments forced their crossings of the Merderet with the towns of Amfreville and Pont L'Abbe the immediate objectives. But the enemy was prepared. For four years they had anticipated landings in France, and for four years they had perfected their defenses, building a wall of steel to repel the might of the invaders. This, then was the test . . . an irresistible force versus an immovable object.

The hedgerows of Normandy were designed by the French to conserve the soil and to prevent erosion. But the Germans utilized them for other purposes. The hedgerows of France made ideal lines of defense. You could place a strong force of Wehrmacht [German army] defenders behind one row and cover the approaches with murderous fire from small arms. At each end of the row properly emplaced machine guns could sweep the fields before them with deadly crossfire.

And suppose, somehow, the Americans succeeded in neutralizing the defenses of row number 1. In that case row number 2 would go into action with mortars zeroed in on the fields, mortars that burst without warning, spreading fragments and death like a scythe. And to round it off neatly, row number 3 was well defended with 88's and other artillery of assorted calibres with all possible targets within range duly noted and accurately plotted.

It was an ingenious plan of defense, simple and effective. If the attacking troops succeeded in taking one row of hedges, there were miles of addition[al] rows upon which the Germans could fall back. Advances, if they were made at all, would be costly; so costly, in fact, that the Americans would lose heart and eventually retire to the shores of England smarting under the bloodiest defeat in military history.

The German plan was a good one. The men of the 90th Division, pushing forward inch by inch and yard by yard, clinging desperately to whatever gains they could win, lashing at their enemy with guns and knives and stones and fists and sheer unadulterated guts, can testify to that. The German plan was a good one, but it had one flaw. It didn't work.

The Americans had no intention of returning to England. Their course led straight through the hedgerows, out across the plains of France, across the Rhineland and to a meeting with the Russians in Hitler's own backyard. . . .

The hedgerows slowed the 90th's attack, but each day saw new gains scored. Slowly but surely, from row to row, the veteran units of the mighty Wehrmacht fell back before the inexperienced troops . . . Pont L'Abbe fell on the third day, and three days later Amfreville and Gourbesville, slightly to the north, were securely in the 90th's hands. Weary, mud begrimed and bloody, the Division was able to report . . . "Mission accomplished." . . .

Immediately, a new mission was assigned to Division. Elements of the VII Corps were working northward in an attempt to take the port of Cherbourg, vitally necessary for the landing of the huge quantities of supplies and reinforcements required to maintain a fighting army. The 90th was to advance to the northwest, seize and hold a line running east-west approximately seven kilometers south of the hub city of Valognes, located in the central portion of the Cotentin peninsula, and there to prevent enemy movements northward or southward.

Faced with heartbreaking marshy terrain and endless rows of hedges, the troops pushed toward their objective against fierce enemy resistance. They waded through swamps and stormed the hedgerows, walking, running, sliding through the mud of France. And always under enemy observation.

At no time since the landings on Utah Beach had the invaders been free of the watchful eye of the enemy, an enemy [who] observed their movements and positions and delivered deadly accurate artillery fire from his vantage points. Eighteen kilometers to the south was Hill 122, Mont Castre. From this observation post the Germans were able to observe almost at will with practically unlimited visibility. Until it was taken every move made by the American divisions was subject to the closest enemy scrutiny. Until it was taken tactics must necessarily consist of the strong-arm variety . . . outfire, outfight, outnerve and outlast the Germans, who were sitting pretty on Hill 122.

But the hill would come later. For the present it sufficed that enemy observation and enemy fire were costing the lives of thousands of American troops. Nevertheless, the 90th moved forward. Artillery pulverized the contested areas; the infantry moved forward a few more yards; the engineers cleared the roads of mines and booby-traps. Again the artillery, again the infantry, again the engineers, again and again, and slowly the gains were made, slowly and with tragic losses.

Two days after the jump-off the objective was reached. The VII Corps had its necessary protection. The 90th Division halted briefly, counted heads, drew a deep but hasty breath, and licked its wounds. The following day, June 18th, the Division was placed under VIII Corps control.

The 357th Regiment was now assigned a defensive mission in the western portion of the Cotentin peninsula and repelled constant and successive attempts by enemy armored and infantry elements to break out of the narrow neck into which they were sealed.

The succeeding days were used to improve positions, to train replacements, and to receive instruction in enemy mines, tank-infantry tactics and rehabilitation. Aggressive patrolling was conducted at all times within the defensive sector, and the enemy was cleared from the area south to the Douve river. German patrols were also active during this period.

And so the month of June came to an end. The Cotentin peninsula had been secured, Cherbourg had fallen, and the only minor mopping-up operations were in progress. The peninsula had fallen but across its base Field Marshal Rommel had drawn a line of fire and steel and planned to contain the Allies within their small area until he could draw upon reserves. When those reserves became available, then a counter-offensive would be launched to drive the Americans back to and hurl them into the sea. In the meantime, the line across the base of the peninsula had to be held at all costs.

That was the plan of the enemy. But the American plans were radically different. Theirs called for the liberation of the soil of France.

And so, with the arrival of July, new orders had arrived. They read with a familiar ring . . . "The 90th Division will attack. . . ."

HELL AND HIGH WATER

The 5th Infantry Division on the Corps right, south of Metz, was to break out of its small bridgehead across the Moselle and attack in a northeasterly direction. . . .

H-hour was scheduled for sometime between November 6th and November 9th. And so the plans were made for the offensive which was to rip the province of Lorraine from the grasp of Germany and to expose the Siegfried Line to immediate assault.

Two crossing sites were selected, one at Malling, and another upstream at Cattenom. All preliminary moves had to be made under the cloak of darkest secrecy. The Foret de Cattenom, west of the selected bridge sites, provided the required defilade and concealment for the necessary preparations. All troops and supplies were moved into the Foret during hours of darkness, and enemy patrols were sealed tightly from the area.

But now a new enemy struck at the 90th Division, an enemy dangerous and resourceful and treacherous . . . the weather. Rain, cold and penetrating, soaked the troops to the bone, transformed foxholes into deep pools of icy water, altered dirt roads into quagmires impossible to negotiate. Day after day the rain poured down. Trucks, bringing vital supplies into the assembly area by night, were sunk to the axles in a clutching sea of mud. Miserable and saturated, the troops awaited H-hour.

The initial crossings were to be made in assault boats, and after the bridgehead had been established the Engineers were to build their bridges in order to allow armor and vehicles to cross to the support of the infantry. The Engineers watched the rain and studied the river carefully. Normally, the bridging of a river 350 feet in width would have offered no insuperable problems. They watched the current flowing northward, and they grew concerned as they noted how the waters now began to race between Moselle's banks. The river, never mild at its best, sounded in an angry roar, foamed and swirled and eddied and flung itself against its shores. And still the rain poured down, feeding the wild Moselle.

H-hour was 0330 on November 9th. . . . The Engineers manning the assault boats performed herculean labors guiding the craft to the proper point, discharging their cargo of men and guns and returning to the starting point to begin the adventure anew. The raging Moselle contested every inch. It surged above its banks in uncontrollable fury and tossed the laden boats in its crazy currents like a juggler tossing eggs.

The other enemy, the opposing troops, were momentarily stunned by the sheer insolence of the attack. Lulled into a sense of security by weeks of relative inactivity and by the added assurance that the flooded Moselle would surely deny a crossing to the Americans, the German outposts were quickly overrun and the immediate objectives wrested from their control. But the surprise was only momentary. Enemy reaction, when it came, was violent and deadly. German artillery and mortars, aided by excellent observation posts across the river, proceeded to shell the crossing sites with costly accuracy. Fort Koenigsmacker in particular enjoyed a panorama view of American activities. . . . Fort Koenigsmacker perched smugly on a hill whose interior was honey-combed with tunnels immune to artillery and bombs.

And still the rain continued, and the Moselle rose with a vengeance. Bursting from its narrow confines it stretched out 400, 600, 800 yards, eight times its normal span. Against hopeless odds the Engineers fought back in an attempt to bridge the river. Working knee deep, waist deep, chest deep in the ever-rising waters, they secured the pontoons to the banks of the river and extended the construction toward the opposite shores. And each time the Moselle defiantly ripped the bridge from its moorings.

Each hour the gravity of the situation increased immeasurably. The infantry across the river faced armor with only small arms and courage. Desperately needed support was denied them. Only limited supplies such as could be ferried across the river in small motor launches reached the frozen, thoroughly soaked infantrymen, who nevertheless slugged their way through mud and swamps, overcoming obstacles with such valor and perseverance that even the enemy testified its grudging admiration. . . .

At the [next] day's end [November 10th] the Division's situation was critical. The river had broadened its channel to a width of one and a half miles. The eight infantry battalions were still unsupported by armor, and a major enemy counter-attack could be expected momentarily. The infantry had fought steadily for two days and two nights; they were numbed with cold and utterly exhausted. No blankets were available, rations were insufficient, ammunition was running dangerously low. It was difficult to say which was the more formidable foe, the Germans to the front, or the river to the rear.

In spite of the incessant shelling to which they were exposed, in spite of casualties suffered in the river itself as boats capsized and sank, the valiant attempt to supply the troops continued. Somehow a few motor launches managed to get through, somehow the wounded were evacuated. On November 11th the bridge at Malling was completed, but the water on the causeway approach was so deep [that] the vehicles were unable to reach the bridge. . . .

The inviolable Fort Koenigsmacker, defended by an entire battalion of the enemy fell. In what was possibly the most dramatic episode of the 90th Division's career, the Fort, symbol to the Nazi of solid impregnability, to the American a most painful stiletto thrust in the 90th's back, succumbed to the decimated elements of the 1st Battalion. For 72 hours the doughs [doughboys, that is, the infantrymen] on the top of the Fort had fought without respite, for three days and three nights they had accepted heavy casualties and still fought on. . . .

The attackers poured gallons of gasoline into the ventilators, ignited the gasoline with white phosphorus grenades, touched off the hellish ingredients with a satchel charge. More charges were dropped through other ventilator shafts, the steel doors were blown from their hinges. The enemy, blackened by smoke and flame, raced desperately from the man-made holocaust. In the meantime, another company had gained access to another section of tunnels in the rear of the Fort. The frantically fleeing Germans found themselves cut off from all avenues of escape. At the day's end the 90th Division could truthfully say, "This fort is ours."

And so, without a bridge, without adequate supplies, without armor, without rest, warmth or sufficient food, the Division doubled the area of its penetration in a single day [November 11th]. At six in the evening, the

Moselle, too, surrendered. The crest of the flood had been reached and now the waters began to subside reluctantly and sullenly at the rate of 3/4 of an inch per hour. Soon the bridge would be secured and adequate support would reach the other side.

The enemy, knowing of this, perceived that no time could be lost if the 90th's bridgehead was to be destroyed. Early in the morning of November 12th the Germans struck and struck hard. In Regimental strength, supported by tanks and self-propelled artillery, they smashed from the direction of Kerling toward the village of Petite Hettange, aiming at the Moselle River and also at cutting the bridgehead in two. The 359th Regiment, outnumbered and outarmed, fell back before the initial on-slaught. Some elements, completely encircled, contemptuously refused all surrender demands and fought on. . . . .

In the early morning hours two tank destroyers succeeded in crossing the turbulent Moselle and waded directly into battle. Troops of the 359th, unaccustomed to the sight of friendly armor for the past three days, assumed the TDs were hostile. A bazooka man offered battle only to be tackled immediately by another soldier who had fortunately recognized the painted white star on the vehicle. The football tackle just in time prevented the destruction of the destroyers. The TDs entered the fray at once and knocked out two self-propelled guns, and immobilized a third.

But the two TDs were not the vanguard of the stream of armor for which the infantry was praying. The Moselle, as if in a final gesture of defiance, hurled its weight against the bridge, snapped it once more and swept its remnants 800 yards downstream. Nevertheless, in spite of the lack of armor, in spite of the cold and the rain, despite innumerable cases of "trench foot," the 359th held. One battalion launched a flanking attack from the south, routing the enemy regiment and driving it back in confusion. This was accomplished by utterly fatigued troops who had little more than spirit and a high disregard for hazards.

On the fifth day a ferry service had been installed and a new bridge had been constructed at Cattenom. The armor and artillery began rolling now in earnest. This was added punch needed to continue the drive. The bridgehead was secure, and the Division, though six of its infantry battalions were operating at only 50% strength, aimed its next blow toward the objective, contact with the 5th Division.

The sixth day saw new advances made in the face of stiff resistance. But on the sixth day the infantry was finally supplied with several luxuries to which they had grown unaccustomed in the preceding days of privation . . . luxuries in the form of blankets, overcoats, clean socks and, for some, a hot meal.

November 15th, and the Germans launched a still fiercer counterattack in an attempt to retake the town of Distroff in which elements of the 358th were positioned. Preceded by a heavy artillery preparation, the armored attack succeeded initially in splitting the defending garrison. Accurate artillery fire and the refusal of the out-numbered defenders to be moved from their positions drove the attacking regiment back.

Over toward the east the 357th Regiment was experiencing some of the most intense enemy artillery fire in its history in the vicinity of the village of Budling. It was determined that the devastating fire was coming from the Hackenberg fortifications on the left front. Tank destroyers attempted to blast the enemy guns, but their rounds merely glanced off the concrete and steel emplacements. Eight inch and 240 mm howitzers tried their hand at reducing the gun positions, but the fire continued to halt the forward motion of the regiment. Thereupon the high velocity self-propelled Long Toms were called into action. Firing at a range of 2,000 yards they blasted the guns of Hackenberg with murderous fire. Subsequent inspection revealed that the protecting cover had been blown to shreds, the enemy guns uprooted from their mounts, and all personnel killed at the gun positions by the fierce effective fire of the Long Toms and the eight inch howitzers.

Evidence was gathered that the garrison in Metz, sensing the imminent closing of the trap, was preparing to evacuate the city. The 90th sent its troops racing southward toward a junction with the 5th Division to close the jaws of the pincers. One after another the escape highways leading out of the doomed city of Metz were cut. Enemy convoys, desperately attempting to squeeze through the ever narrowing gamut, were met by concentrated artillery fire, small arms and mortar. Now there was no stopping the 90th. With the objective in sight the Division smashed forward, brushing obstacles aside with confidence and assurance born of success.

On November 19th the 90th Reconnaissance Troop, driving south on the Division's right, established contact with elements of the 5th Infantry Division. The operation begun eleven days before, had succeeded. The men of the 90th had once more defeated Germany's finest. They had waged battle with torrential rains, with mud and cold and hunger. They had violated the impregnability of Fort Koenigsmacker, reduced the guns at Hackenberg, broken through the Maginot line, and defeated on its own terms the rampaging, berserk Moselle.

Said the Army Commander, "The greatest military achievement of the war!"

ARTICLE 42

PRISON MEMOIRS
Lewis C. Beebe

*I*nternational conventions dealing with prisoners of war are clear about the humane treatment that captors must provide. Although there is no excuse for the brutal treatment most Americans received in Japanese prison camps or Eastern Europeans in German ones, cultural differences and history offer some explanation for the severity of the treatment. American soldiers believed that when there was no other possible alternative than death, surrender was permissible. Surrender, in Japanese eyes, was disgraceful; Japanese soldiers were expected to die for their emperor. The Japanese captors believed that their prisoners of war had disgraced themselves, and so they showed the Allied prisoners little respect and even less mercy.

Colonel Lewis C. Beebe was captured on Corregidor in 1942 and spent the rest of the war in Japanese prison camps in the Philippines, Formosa, Japan, and Manchuria. His brief memoirs, written in 1945, recount the harsh conditions in the camps. Despite his bitter memories, Colonel Beebe's memoirs display surprisingly little animosity toward his captors. The following selection is a portion of his prison memoirs.

Thus at Karenko, began the worst period of starvation we were to endure as prisoners of war. I believe it to be a fact that few people in the United States know what it is like to be really hungry—hungry to the point of starvation. I had been hungry before, after a fashion. I had been without food for forty-eight hours or more during the last world war, but I didn't know what it was like to be really hungry. To be really hungry one must be starved to the

SOURCE: Lewis C. Beebe papers, U.S. Army Military History Institute Archives, Carlisle Barracks, Pennsylvania.

point where the body subsists in part on itself. That is the way one of our doctors explained it to me. In other words, if you don't get enough to eat to maintain your body, you begin to consume the fatty tissue in your system. You burn up a certain number of calories every day, and if you don't eat that much you take it from your own system. After you have consumed all the fat in your system you begin to consume your own muscular tissue and, if the process continues long enough, you will have nothing left of your body but your skin stretched over your skeleton. That is the ultimate. We didn't go that far, but we went quite far enough along the road to starvation to satisfy all of us.

During the starving process one is *always* hungry. The first thought on waking in the morning is food. The last thought at night, or the last sensation, is one of hunger. A bowl of soup and a cup of rice, such as we received, appeared only to intensify the craving for more food. Long since I had learned to like rice—I loved it, in fact, I felt that I could eat my weight in plain boiled rice.

And don't let anyone tell you that he (or she) can't reduce. I have heard many people make that statement and, at the time, I thought there might be something to it. I know better now. We had some men in our camp who could have qualified for the championship fight in a fat mans' competition. But they soon lost the excess weight. And some of them lost their good disposition as well. . . .

For the first month no mention was made of work. Then, in keeping with his pronouncement when we arrived, the camp commander asked us all to volunteer to work in a garden. We were to have the produce—so he said. Since work for officer and non-commissioned officer prisoners of war is not in accord with the rules of war, we refused. He insisted and we continued to refuse. Then he put on the pressure by further restricting our already scanty diet. The soup became even more watery, and we received slightly less than a level cupful of rice for each meal.

After a month of this treatment, when certain death by starvation appeared to be just around the corner for many prisoners, the camp commander reopened the question and generously permitted us to "volunteer" to work. On his part, he was supposed to increase the rice issue by about one additional cupful for each day we worked—a one third increase.

By this time many of the prisoners were so weak that they could barely stagger out to the plot which had been set aside for our garden. However, we were all turned out at nine o'clock each morning, and at one o'clock each afternoon, and were marched under guard to our work. Each officer was given a chunkle or coowa—I am not sure about the spelling so I have spelled the words phonetically. This implement has the appearance of an adz, except that the head is broader and heavier. The Japs use it instead of a hoe.

Like most of the Jap products, it was poorly constructed, and the prisoners broke them faster than they could be procured.

With this implement we had to clear the ground of grass, brush and small trees, dig it up to a depth of five or six inches, and prepare it for planting. Many of the prisoners were not physically able to work but a Jap guard watched us all the time and pounced on anyone who, in his opinion, was slacking. At that, he had his hands full, for most of the officers became experts at going through the motions without really doing any work.

As I stated before, the Japs had promised to give us additional rice if we worked, but they were blessed with conveniently short memories. More than half the time they "forgot" to issue the rice, and when they did make the issue it amounted to no more than about one third of a cup.

As a result we all continued to lose weight. I was more fortunate than most of the prisoners, for I had weighed only one hundred and fifty three pounds at the beginning of the war, I weighed one hundred and forty five as a result of the short diet on Corregidor. Solid meat does not wear off as rapidly as fat, and I had little of that to lose. At my lowest point, which I reached in December, 1942, I weighed one hundred and twenty three pounds. Some officers, during this same period, had lost in the neighborhood of one hundred pounds. Others were able to keep in fair condition due to a difference in the ability of different individuals to assimilate such a starchy diet. . . .

It was interesting, at this time, to note the reaction of different individuals. Some stated very frankly that they thought we were going to be starved to death, but I don't believe the majority of the prisoners held such an opinion. Almost everyone was what we called "food conscious." That is, the thought of food was uppermost in everyone's mind. Almost everyone became extremely short tempered and irritable. With some people it was almost impossible to make any kind of an innocent statement without starting an argument. For example, one night after the lights were out two of the officers were discussing the difference in time between Formosa and Washington. One officer made a statement. The other contradicted it. The discussion became heated at once and one of them told the other to shut his blank blank mouth. The officer who had been cussed didn't propose to take such talk. He jumped out of bed, switched on the lights, and was going to fight right then and there. The matter was amicably settled the following morning when each one apologized. Both officers were middle aged men and, under ordinary conditions, neither would think of becoming involved in such a situation. Exhibitions of temper were not confined to the officers of one nationality. We had members of the English and Dutch armies in our group and I saw a nice set-to one day between two senior officers of another nationality.

The first law of nature—the law of self preservation—begins to assert itself under such conditions and most of the prisoners hoarded everything they could find. Many of them would part with nothing—except at a price, which was usually food. On the other hand, generosity under such conditions is, indeed, a virtue and I knew that some of my friends among the prisoners would literally give me the shirts off their backs if I really wanted one. Such a donor might be shirtless, but he exemplifies the old adage that a friend in need is a friend indeed!

Some prisoners carried their hoarding to the point of folly. One man was admitted to the hospital, later in another camp, and the doctors diagnosed his case as ordinary malnutrition. He had saved his individual Red Cross packages and stored them away, thinking that he might be starved by the Japs and the food would come in handy at that time. He weighed less than one hundred pounds at the time.

All the time we were prisoners there was a lively traffic in foodstuffs of all kinds, in tobacco, clothing, or anything which might be useful. Most of the officers and men had some money, and those who didn't have money were able to produce blank checks. A can of corned beef was always worth twenty five dollars. A pound can of powdered milk brought between twenty and thirty dollars. American cigarettes sold as high as one dollar each, but, ordinarily, they were five or six dollars per package. Everything was governed by the old law of supply and demand.

Some time in January we began to notice that there was a slight increase in the food—not enough for us to gain weight, but enough for us to hold our own. The Japs must have figured that we were all so weak that we were harmless and they would keep us in that condition. In February and March there was another slight increase when we began to get some Irish potatoes in our soup. Those potatoes were really wonderful. We hadn't had any since the beginning of the war. Then the magnanimous Japs gave us what we called the "edible offal" from some cattle which were being butchered for their soldiers. They took the parts which are really edible and gave us the intestines, stomach and lungs. But we were glad to get anything in the form of animal proteins. Our diet had contained none.

While we were on a restricted diet of rice many of us began to show signs of beri-beri which is a well known disease in Asia where the people subsist largely on this grain. I noticed in my own case that I had developed what we called "foot slap" which comes from inability to control the muscles which govern the raising and lowering of the toes. In walking, instead of lowering the toes to the floor, which is the ordinary procedure, mine fell of their own weight, resulting in a distinct slapping sound when the sole of the shoe struck the floor.

There was nothing to be done about it. Beri-beri results from a lack of vitamin B1 which is contained in the germ of rice. During the polishing process this germ is removed, and since the natives prefer the polished rice we had to eat it also. The disease can be cured very easily by taking a concentrated vitamin B1 but we had no such medicine and couldn't obtain it.

I had what is called dry beri-beri but there is also a wet type which causes the ankles to swell, and, if remedial action is not taken, the swelling extends to the entire body and the patient dies. Many of our officers had the wet type and some were very seriously ill. . . .

When Christmas of 1942 arrived we were all at low ebb, physically and mentally, but we did our best to create a holiday atmosphere. Most of the prisoners made some attempt to decorate their rooms although few materials were available. But it is surprising what one can do with what appears to be nothing. Using the colored wrappers of cigarette packages and cartons, and the paper from other containers, the prisoners cut out letters to make the words "Merry Christmas and Happy New Year." With tin foil from packages of tea they made glittering stars. They improvised candles and cut from wood a small image of Santa Claus. They made wreaths from the boughs of evergreen trees, and long chains of colored paper were strung across the halls and in some of the rooms. Before Christmas arrived, the inside of the building presented quite a festive appearance.

Several days before Christmas a group of choral singers was organized under the direction of Colonel "Bill" Braly, of the Coast Artillery. Bill had managed to bring his violin with him—and he could make that violin turn handsprings. I mean he could play the violin. On Christmas Eve we had old, familiar carols sung by a male chorus of about twenty voices and my thoughts turned back again to the stockings of my small son which used to hang over the fireplace in Minnesota; to thoughts of my family and friends who were living in a snow blanketed land on the other side of the globe. What a contrast between the life I was then leading and the life I had lived in the land of ten thousand lakes!

American marines land on Saipan, June 1944 (United States Army Military History Institute). By 1944, the Marine Corps had perfected the tactics of amphibious landings. Between the First and Second World Wars, Marine Corps officers had studied the best way to land troops in enemy-controlled areas. They determined that the landing force was most vulnerable on the beaches. To succeed, the invaders had to move inland as quickly as possible, taking as much land as necessary. The marines designed special landing craft for men and equipment, determined the best way to pack supplies so that the most critical ones would be landed first, and organized a system to transfer command from the ships to shore. Tactical air power made the Pacific landings "triphibious" and gave the Americans an advantage over the enemy defenders. But many Japanese refused to accept the inevitable. On Saipan, General Yoshitsugu Saito wrote an apology to the emperor and then ordered every Japanese soldier to take seven American lives with his own. General Saito committed ritual suicide while waves of his soldiers, many armed only with sticks or swords, hurled themselves at the marines. American cooks, typists, and headquarters personnel helped man the defenses as machine-gun fire mowed down more than 4,000 enemy soldiers. Shortly after, another mass suicide occurred when Japanese mothers (with their children in their arms) jumped off 800-foot cliffs into the rocky waters below. The remaining Japanese committed suicide with knives or hand grenades. The Saipan campaign had cost the Americans 3,000 lives, and the Japanese more than 45,000.

ON BOARD A FIGHTING SHIP
Ernie Pyle

*E*rnie Pyle's wartime dispatches won him a Pulitzer Prize in 1943, bringing fame, fortune, and love. Pyle feared that he had gotten too close to the men he was covering in Europe and Africa. He admired the American fighting man but hated war. A man with many personal problems (both physical and emotional), Pyle did not want to return to the front after he came home from the European Theater in September 1944. His stories, however, had made him a national hero. Pyle bowed to the government's request that he spend some time in the Pacific, especially with the navy. Despite evil premonitions, Pyle traveled to the Pacific Theater in January 1945. Three months later, he was cut down by Japanese machine-gun fire on the island of Ie Shima.

Ernie Pyle's account of life on board an aircraft carrier contrasts sharply with the story of the sleek, spartan submarine in a previous reading. The aircraft carrier was visible proof of the skill, power, and wealth of American culture. Carriers could transport an entire city across 6,000 miles of ocean to the enemy's homeland. Pyle, and most of his countrymen, admired the technology that had made this possible.

In the Western Pacific, *March 15, 1945*

—An aircraft carrier is a noble thing. It lacks almost everything that seems to denote nobility, yet deep nobility is there.

A carrier has no poise. It has no grace. It is top-heavy and lopsided. It has the lines of a well-fed cow.

SOURCE: Scripps-Howard newspapers; copyright, Scripps-Howard Foundation. Used by permission.

It doesn't cut through the water like a cruiser, knifing romantically along. It doesn't dance and cavort like a destroyer. It just plows. You feel it should be carrying a hod, rather than wearing a red sash.

Yet a carrier is a ferocious thing, and out of its heritage of action has grown its nobility. I believe that today every Navy in the world has as its No. 1 priority the destruction of enemy carriers. That's a precarious honor, but it's a proud one.

My carrier is a proud one. She's small, and you have never heard of her unless you have a son or husband on her, but still she's proud, and deservedly so.

She has been at sea, without returning home, longer than any other carrier in the Pacific, with one exception. She left home in November 1943.

She is a little thing, yet her planes have shot two hundred thirty-eight of the enemy out of the sky in air battles, and her guns have knocked down five Jap planes in defending herself.

She is too proud to keep track of little ships she destroys, but she has sent to the bottom twenty-nine big Japanese ships. Her bombs and aerial torpedoes have smashed into everything from the greatest Jap battleships to the tiniest coastal schooners.

She has weathered five typhoons. Her men have not set foot on any soil bigger than a farm-sized uninhabited atoll for a solid year. They have not seen a woman, white or otherwise, for nearly ten months. In a year and a quarter out of America, she has steamed a total of one hundred forty-nine thousand miles!

Four different air squadrons have used her as their flying field, flown their allotted missions, and returned to America. But the ship's crew stays on—and on, and on.

She is known in the fleet as "The Iron Woman," because she has fought in every battle in the Pacific in the years 1944 and 1945.

Her battle record sounds like a train-caller on the Lackawanna Railroad. Listen—Kwajalein, Eniwetok, Truk, Palau, Hollandia, Saipan, Chichi Jima, Mindanao, Luzon, Formosa, Nansei Shoto, Hong Kong, Iwo Jima, Tokyo . . . and many others.

She has known disaster. Her fliers who have perished could not be counted on both hands, yet the ratio is about as it always is—about one American lost for every ten of the Exalted Race sent to the Exalted Heaven.

She has been hit twice by Jap bombs. She has had mass burials at sea . . . with her dry-eyed crew sewing 40-mm shells to the corpses of their friends, as weights to take them to the bottom of the sea.

Yet she had never even returned to Pearl Harbor to patch her wounds. She slaps on some patches on the run, and is ready for the next battle. The crew in semi-jocularity cuss her chief engineer for keeping her in such good shape they have no excuse to go back to Honolulu or America for over-haul.

My carrier, even though classed as "light," is still a very large ship. More than a thousand men dwell upon her. She is more than seven hundred feet long.

She has all the facilities of a small city. And all the gossip and small talk too. Latest news and rumors have reached the farthest cranny of the ship a few minutes after the captain himself knows about them. All she lacks is a hitching rack and a town pump with a handle.

She has five barbers, a laundry, a general store. Deep in her belly she carries tons of bombs. She has a daily newspaper. She carries fire-fighting equipment that a city of fifty thousand back in America would be proud of.

She has a preacher, she has three doctors and two dentists, she has two libraries, and movies every night, except when they're in battle. And still she is a tiny thing, as the big carriers go. She is a "baby flat-top." She is little. And she is proud.

She has been out so long that her men put their ship above their captain. They have seen captains come and go, but they and the ship stay on forever.

They aren't romantic about their long stay out here. They hate it, and their gripes are long and loud. They yearn pathetically to go home. But down beneath, they are proud—proud of their ship and proud of themselves. And you would be too.

March 16, 1945

Living was very comfortable aboard our carrier. I shared a cabin with Lt. Comdr. Al Masters from Terre Haute, Indiana, just a few miles from where I was born and raised.

In our cabin we had metal closets and writing desks and a lavatory with hot and cold water. We had a telephone, and a colored boy to clean up the room. Our bunks were double-decked, with good mattresses. I was in the upper one.

Our food was wonderful, and you could buy a whole carton of cigarets a day if you wanted to (doesn't that make you jealous?). We saw a movie every night except when in battle. The first four nights our movies were *New York Town, The Major and the Minor, Swing Fever,* and *Claudia.* I don't know enough about movies to know whether they were old or not, but it doesn't make any difference to a sailor who hasn't been home.

I came aboard with a lot of dirty clothes, for I'd had nothing washed since leaving San Francisco about a month before.

Our cabin boy took my clothes to the laundry about nine-thirty one morning. When I came back to the cabin about an hour and a half later, here was my washing all clean and dry and ironed, lying on the bed. What a ship!

March 17, 1945

—It's easy to get acquainted aboard a Naval vessel.

The sailors are just as friendly as the soldiers I'd known on the other side. Furthermore, they're so delighted to see a stranger and to have somebody new to talk to that they aren't a bit standoffish.

They're all sick to death of the isolation and monotony of the vast Pacific. I believe they talk more about wanting to go home than even the soldiers in Europe.

Their lives really are empty lives. They have their work, and their movies, and their mail, and that's just about all they do have. And nothing to look forward to.

They never see anybody but themselves, and that gets mighty old. They sail and sail, and never arrive anywhere. They've not even seen a native village for a year.

Three times they've been to remote, lifeless sandbars in the Pacific, and have been allowed to go ashore for a few hours and sit under palm trees and drink three cans of beer. That's all.

Yet they do live well. Their food is the best I've run onto in this war. They take baths daily, and the laundry washes their clothes. Their quarters are crowded, but each man has a bunk with a mattress and sheets, and a private locker to keep his stuff in. They work hard, but their hours are regular.

The boys ask you a thousand times how this compares with the other side. I can only answer that this is much better. They seem to expect you to say that, but they are a little disappointed too.

They say, "But it's tough to be away from home for more than a year, and never see anything but water and an occasional atoll." And I say yes, I know it is, but there are boys who have been in Europe more than three years, and have slept on the ground a good part of that time. And they say yes, they guess in contrast their lives are pretty good.

Seaman Paul Begley looks at his wartime life philosophically. He is a farm boy from Rogersville, Tennessee. He talks a lot in a soft voice that is Southern clear through. He's one of the plane pushers on the flight deck.

"I can stand this monotony all right," he says. "The point with us is that we've got a pretty good chance of living through this. Think of the Marines who have to take the beaches, and the infantry in Germany. I can stand a lot of monotony if I know my chances are pretty good for coming out of it alive."

But others yell their heads off about their lot, and feel they're being persecuted by being kept out of America a year. I've heard some boys say, "I'd trade this for a foxhole any day." You just have to keep your mouth shut to a remark like that. . . .

Very few of the boys have developed any real love for the sea—the kind that will draw them back to it for a lifetime. Some of course will come back if things get tough after the war. But mostly they are temporary sailors, and the sea is not in their blood.

Taking it all in all, they're good boys who do what is asked of them, and do it well. They are very sincere and genuine, and they are almost unanimously proud of their ship.

TODAY'S TARGET: NAGASAKI

William L. Laurence

No other war ended as dramatically as World War II. Fascism had been destroyed in Europe by May 1945, and the United States turned its attention to Japan. Allied scientists had been working on harnessing atomic energy to make weapons since the early days of the war. They succeeded and presented their results to Harry S. Truman, who had become president in April upon Franklin D. Roosevelt's death. President Truman consulted a board of prominent civilians—they recommended that the atomic bombs be dropped on Japanese cities without warning. The first bomb destroyed Hiroshima on 6 August 1945. Three days later a second bomb leveled Nagasaki. Japan surrendered the following day.

  Somehow, *New York Times* science writer and Pulitzer Prize–winning correspondent William Laurence (1888–1977) found the right words to describe the awesome power of an atomic blast—the U.S. government had invited him to fly on the mission to bomb Nagasaki. Laurence's dispatch was published a month after the event and won him a second Pulitzer Prize. Laurence's account displays his intense intellectual curiosity and his admiration for the weapon's power. To him, the horrible beauty of the explosion symbolized that human beings had discovered the key to the universe.

With the atomic-bomb mission to Japan, August 9 (Delayed)—We are on our way to bomb the mainland of Japan. Our flying contingent consists of three specially designed B-29 Superforts, and two of these carry no bombs. But our lead plane is on its way with another atomic bomb, the second in

---

three days, concentrating in its active substance an explosive energy equivalent to twenty thousand and, under favorable conditions, forty thousand tons of TNT.

We have several chosen targets. One of these is the great industrial and shipping center of Nagasaki, on the western shore of Kyushu, one of the main islands of the Japanese homeland.

I watched the assembly of this man-made meteor during the past two days and was among the small group of scientists and Army and Navy representatives privileged to be present at the ritual of its loading in the Superfort last night, against a background of threatening black skies torn open at intervals by great lightning flashes.

It is a thing of beauty to behold, this "gadget." Into its design went millions of man-hours of what is without doubt the most concentrated intellectual effort in history. Never before had so much brain power been focused on a single problem.

This atomic bomb is different from the bomb used three days ago with such devastating results on Hiroshima.

I saw the atomic substance before it was placed inside the bomb. By itself it is not at all dangerous to handle. It is only under certain conditions, produced in the bomb assembly, that it can be made to yield up its energy, and even then it gives only a small fraction of its total contents—a fraction, however, large enough to produce the greatest explosion on earth.

The briefing at midnight revealed the extreme care and the tremendous amount of preparation that had been made to take care of every detail of the mission, to make certain that the atomic bomb fully served the purpose for which it was intended. Each target in turn was shown in detailed maps and in aerial photographs. Every detail of the course was rehearsed—navigation, altitude, weather, where to land in emergencies. It came out that the Navy had submarines and rescue craft, known as Dumbos and Superdumbos, stationed at various strategic points in the vicinity of the targets, ready to rescue the fliers in case they were forced to bail out.

The briefing period ended with a moving prayer by the chaplain. We then proceeded to the mess hall for the traditional early-morning breakfast before departure on a bombing mission.

A convoy of trucks took us to the supply building for the special equipment carried on combat missions. This included the Mae West [life jacket], a parachute, a lifeboat, an oxygen mask, a flak suit, and a survival vest. We still had a few hours before take-off time, but we all went to the flying field and stood around in little groups or sat in jeeps talking rather casually about our mission to the Empire, as the Japanese home islands are known hereabouts.

In command of our mission is Major Charles W. Sweeney, twenty-five, of 124 Hamilton Avenue, North Quincy, Massachusetts. His flagship, carrying the atomic bomb, is named *The Great Artiste,* but the name does not appear on the body of the great silver ship, with its unusually long, four-bladed, orange-tipped propellers. Instead, it carries the number 77, and someone remarks that it was "Red" Grange's winning number on the grid-iron.

We took off at 3:50 this morning and headed northwest on a straight line for the Empire. The night was cloudy and threatening, with only a few stars here and there breaking through the overcast. The weather report had predicted storms ahead part of the way but clear sailing for the final and climactic stages of our odyssey.

We were about an hour away from our base when the storm broke. Our great ship took some heavy dips through the abysmal darkness around us, but it took these dips much more gracefully than a large commercial air liner, producing a sensation more in the nature of a glide than a "bump," like a great ocean liner riding the waves except that in this case the air waves were much higher and the rhythmic tempo of the glide was much faster.

I noticed a strange eerie light coming through the window high above the navigator's cabin, and as I peered through the dark all around us I saw a startling phenomenon. The whirling giant propellers had somehow become great luminous disks of blue flame. The same luminous blue flame appeared on the plexiglas windows in the nose of the ship, and on the tips of the giant wings. It looked as though we were riding the whirlwind through space on a chariot of blue fire.

It was, I surmised, a surcharge of static electricity that had accumulated on the tips of the propellers and on the di-electric material of the plastic windows. One's thoughts dwelt anxiously on the precious cargo in the invisible ship ahead of us. Was there any likelihood of danger that this heavy electric tension in the atmosphere all about us might set it off?

I expressed my fears to Captain Bock, who seemed nonchalant and unperturbed at the controls. He quickly reassured me.

"It is a familiar phenomenon seen often on ships. I have seen it many times on bombing missions. It is known as St. Elmo's fire."

On we went through the night. We soon rode out the storm and our ship was once again sailing on a smooth course straight ahead, on a direct line to the Empire.

Our altimeter showed that we were traveling through space at a height of seventeen thousand feet. The thermometer registered an outside temperature of thirty-three degrees below zero Centigrade, about thirty [twenty] below Fahrenheit. Inside our pressurized cabin the temperature was that of a comfortable air-conditioned room and a pressure corresponding to an altitude of eight thousand feet. Captain Bock cautioned me, however, to keep my oxygen mask handy in case of emergency. This, he explained, might mean either something going wrong with the pressure equipment inside the ship or a hole through the cabin by flak.

The first signs of dawn came shortly after five o'clock. Sergeant Curry, of Hoopeston, Illinois, who had been listening steadily on his earphones for radio reports, while maintaining a strict radio silence himself, greeted it by rising to his feet and gazing out the window.

"It's good to see the day," he told me. "I get a feeling of claustrophobia hemmed in in this cabin at night."

He was a typical American youth, looking even younger than his twenty years. It took no mind reader to read his thoughts.

"It's a long way from Hoopeston," I found myself remarking.

"Yep," he replied, as he busies himself decoding a message from outer space.

"Think this atomic bomb will end the war?" he asked hopefully.

"There is a very good chance that this one may do the trick," I assured him, "but if not, then the next one or two surely will. Its power is such that no nation can stand up against it very long." This was not my own view. I had heard it expressed all around a few hours earlier, before we took off. To anyone who had seen this man-made fireball in action, as I had less than a month ago in the desert of New Mexico, this view did not sound overoptimistic.

By 5:50 it was really light outside. We had lost our lead ship, but Lieutenant Godfrey, our navigator, informed me that we had arranged for that contingency. We have an assembly point in the sky above the little island of Yakushima, south-east of Kyushu, at 9:10. We are to circle there and wait for the rest of our formation.

Our genial bombardier, Lieutenant Levy, comes over to invite me to take his front-row seat in the transport nose of the ship, and I accept eagerly. From that vantage point in space, seventeen thousand feet above the Pacific, one gets a view of hundreds of miles on all sides, horizontally and vertically. At that height the vast ocean below and the sky above seem to merge into one great sphere.

I was on the inside of that firmament, riding above the giant mountains of white cumulus clouds, letting myself be suspended in infinite space. One hears the whirl of the motors behind one, but it soon becomes insignificant against the immensity all around and is before long swallowed by it. There comes a point where space also swallows time and one lives through eternal moments filled with an oppressive loneliness, as though all life had suddenly vanished from the earth and you are the only one left, a lone survivor traveling endlessly through interplanetary space.

My mind soon returns to the mission I am on. Somewhere beyond these vast mountains of white clouds ahead of me there lies Japan, the land of our enemy. In about four hours from now one of its cities, making weapons of war for use against us, will be wiped off the map by the greatest weapon ever made by man: In one tenth of a millionth of a second, a fraction of time immeasurable by any clock, a whirlwind from the skies will pulverize thousands of its buildings and tens of thousands of its inhabitants.

But at this moment no one yet knows which one of the several cities chosen as targets is to be annihilated. The final choice lies with destiny. The winds over Japan will make the decision. If they carry heavy clouds over our primary target, that city will be saved, at least for the time being. None of its inhabitants will ever know that the wind of a benevolent destiny had passed over their heads. But that same wind will doom another city.

Our weather planes ahead of us are on their way to find out where the wind blows. Half an hour before target time we will know what the winds have decided.

Does one feel any pity or compassion for the poor devils about to die? Not when one thinks of Pearl Harbor and of the Death March on Bataan.

Captain Bock informs me that we are about to start our climb to bombing altitude.

He manipulates a few knobs on his control panel to the right of him, and I alternately watch the white clouds and ocean below me and the altimeter on the bombardier's panel. We reached our altitude at nine o'clock. We were then over Japanese waters, close to their mainland. Lieutenant Godfrey motioned to me to look through his radar scope. Before me was the outline of our assembly point. We shall soon meet our lead ship and proceed to the final stage of our journey.

We reached Yakushima at 9:12 and there, about four thousand feet ahead of us, was *The Great Artiste* with its precious load. I saw Lieutenant Godfrey and Sergeant Curry strap on their parachutes and I decided to do likewise.

We started circling. We saw little towns on the coastline, heedless of our presence. We kept on circling, waiting for the third ship in our formation.

It was 9:56 when we began heading for the coastline. Our weather scouts had sent us code messages, deciphered by Sergeant Curry, informing us that both the primary target as well as the secondary were clearly visible.

The winds of destiny seemed to favor certain Japanese cities that must remain nameless. We circled about them again and again and found no opening in the thick umbrella of clouds that covered them. Destiny chose Nagasaki as the ultimate target.

We had been circling for some time when we noticed black puffs of smoke coming through the white clouds directly at us. There were fifteen bursts of flak in rapid succession, all too low. Captain Bock changed his course. There soon followed eight more bursts of flak, right up to our altitude, but by this time were too far to the left.

We flew southward down the channel and at 11:33 crossed the coastline and headed straight for Nagasaki, about one hundred miles to the west. Here again we circled until we found an opening in the clouds. It was 12:01 and the goal of our mission had arrived.

We heard the prearranged signal on our radio, put on our arc welder's glasses, and watched tensely the maneuverings of the strike ship about half a mile in front of us.

"There she goes!" someone said.

Out of the belly of *The Great Artiste* what looked like a black object went downward.

Captain Bock swung around to get out of range; but even though we were turning away in the opposite direction, and despite the fact that it was broad daylight in our cabin, all of us became aware of a giant flash that broke through the dark barrier of our arc welder's lenses and flooded our cabin with intense light.

We removed our glasses after the first flash, but the light still lingered on, a bluish-green light that illuminated the entire sky all around. A tremendous blast wave struck our ship and made it tremble from nose to tail. This was followed by four more blasts in rapid succession, each resounding like the boom of cannon fire hitting our plane from all directions.

Observers in the tail of our ship saw a giant ball of fire rise as though from the bowels of the earth, belching forth enormous white smoke rings. Next they saw a giant pillar of purple fire, ten thousand feet high, shooting skyward with enormous speed.

By the time our ship had made another turn in the direction of the atomic explosion the pillar of purple fire had reached the level of our altitude. Only about forty-five seconds had passed. Awe-struck, we watched it shoot upward like a meteor coming from the earth instead of from outer space, becoming ever more alive as it climbed skyward through the white clouds. It was no longer smoke, or dust, or even a cloud of fire. It was a living thing, a new species of being, born right before our incredulous eyes.

At one stage of its evolution, covering millions of years in terms of seconds, the entity assumed the form of a giant square totem pole, with its base about three miles long, tapering off to about a mile at the top. Its bottom was brown, its center was amber, its top white. But it was a living totem pole, carved with many grotesque masks grimacing at the earth.

Then, just when it appeared as though the thing had settled down into a state of permanence, there came shooting out of the top a giant mushroom that increased the height of the pillar to a total of forty-five thousand feet.

The mushroom top was even more alive than the pillar, seething and boiling in a white fury of creamy foam, sizzling upward and then descending earthward, a thousand Old Faithful geysers rolled into one.

It kept struggling in an elemental fury, like a creature in the act of breaking the bonds that held it down. In a few seconds it had freed itself from its gigantic stem and floated upward with tremendous speed, its momentum carrying it into the stratosphere to a height of about sixty thousand feet.

But no sooner did this happen when another mushroom, smaller in size than the first one, began emerging out of the pillar. It was as though the decapitated monster was growing a new head.

As the first mushroom floated off into the blue it changed its shape into a flowerlike form, its giant petals curving downward, creamy white outside, rose-colored inside. It still retained that shape when we last gazed at it from a distance of about two hundred miles. The boiling pillar of many colors could also be seen at that distance, a giant mountain of jumbled rainbows, in travail. Much living substance had gone into those rainbows. The quivering top of the pillar was protruding to a great height through the white clouds, giving the appearance of a monstrous prehistoric creature with a ruff around its neck, a fleecy ruff extending in all directions, as far as the eye could see.

We Can Do It! (National Archives). American women had always supported the wars as enthusiastically as their men. During World War II, some women joined the military as nurses or enlisted in a special corps to work as military clerks, thereby freeing men to fight. Most women, however, served their country by replacing men in factories or on farms. This poster depicts the strong, but feminine, arm of one such worker. She is the epitome of "Rosie the Riveter": capable, confident, and dedicated. It also illustrates what General Sherman had told the citizens of Atlanta about modern war (see Article 27). Civilians on the home front are every bit as important to the war effort as the soldiers on the front line, and,

therefore, every bit as legitimate as targets. This poster was one of hundreds that were produced by the government during the war. Although World War II placed many women in jobs their mothers never held, this social revolution was only temporary. Most Americans (both men and women) still agreed that the women should work only until their men returned home. Then everything was supposed to return to "normal": the men would return to the factories and the women to their homes to raise families.

THE ONES THAT STINK THE WORST

T/Sgt. Donald Haguall as told to Sgt. Ralph G. Martin

Some writing stands on its own. The following selection, an article from *Yank* magazine, was published by the U.S. government during World War II. It eloquently sums up all the horrors of war.

"Sure, there were lots of bodies that we never identified," said T/Sgt. Donald Haguall of the 48th Quartermaster Graves Registration. "You know what a direct hit by a shell does to a guy. Or a mine, or a solid hit with a grenade, even. Sometimes all we have is a leg or a hunk of arm.

"The ones that stink the worst are the guys who got internal wounds and are dead about three weeks with the blood staying inside and rotting, and when you move the body the blood comes out of the nose and mouth. Then some of them bloat up in the sun, they bloat up so big that they bust the buttons and then they get blue and the skin peels. They don't all get blue, some of them get black.

"But they all stink. There's only one stink and that's it. You never get used to it, either. As long as you live, you never get used to it. And after a while, the stink gets in your clothes and you can taste it in your mouth.

"You know what I think? I think maybe if every civilian in the world could smell that stink, then maybe we wouldn't have any more wars."

SOURCE: *Yank Magazine.*

Like the Civil War, there are many good histories, biographies, and memoirs about World War II. All the armed services have published multivolume official histories of the war. The navy, air force, and marine histories are chronological and generally better at specific campaigns than general issues. The army's "Green Book" series is the most ambitious military history project ever attempted. In more than eighty volumes, professional historians tell the story of the war from global strategy to individual campaigns, from the role of the technical and service branches (chemical, ordnance, and signal) to the conscription of men and the employment of blacks and women. The series, *The United States Army in World War II*, is still not complete, after nearly a half-century. Kent Roberts Greenfield, one of the series' main editors, compiled a valuable summary of the major issues entitled *Command Decisions* (1959). Greenfield offered his own conclusions of wartime strategy in *American Strategy in World War II: A Reconsideration* (1963). Students interested in global strategy should also consult Forrest C. Pogue's volumes on *George C. Marshall: Ordeal and Hope, 1939–1942* (1966) and *George C. Marshall: Organizer of Victory, 1943–1945* (1973).

The best analysis of what happened at Pearl Harbor is Gordon W. Prange's *At Dawn We Slept: The Untold Story of Pearl Harbor* (1981). For background information from the Japanese perspective, readers should consult *The Rising Sun: The Decline and Fall of the Japanese Empire, 1936–1945* (1970) and *But Not in Shame: The Six Months After Pearl Harbor* (1961), both by John Toland. Walter Lord's *Day of Infamy* (1957) is a very readable account of the Japanese attack on Pearl Harbor. Lord's *Incredible Victory* (1967) is an excellent history of the naval battle at Midway. The best single-volume narrative of World War II in the Pacific is John Costello's *The Pacific War, 1941–1945* (1981). Readers should also consult Douglas MacArthur's memoirs, *Reminiscences* (1964) and two biographies: D. Clayton James's *The Years of MacArthur* (1975) and William Manchester's *American Caesar: Douglas MacArthur, 1880–1964* (1978). Other good studies of American leaders in the Pacific War include William F. Halsey and J. Bryan III's *Admiral Halsey's Story* (1947), Robert B. Asprey and Alexander Archer Vandergrift's *Once a Marine: The Memoirs of General A. A. Vandergrift, USMC* (1964), E. B. Potter's *Nimitz* (1976), and George Dyer's *The Amphibians Came to Conquer: The Story of Admiral Richmond Kelly Turner* (1972).

The best single-volume history of the Second World War is Kenneth S. Davis's *The Experience of War: The United States in World War II* (1965). Also useful are Peter Calvocoressi and Guy Wint's *Total War: Causes and Courses of the Second World War* (1972), James L. Stokesbury's *A Short History of World War II* (1980), Winston Churchill's six-volume history of *The Second World War* (1948–1953), and B. H. Liddell-Hart's *History of the Second World War* (1971).

Memoirs and biographies of the European commanders include Dwight D. Eisenhower's memoirs, *Crusade in Europe* (1948), and two biographies of Eisenhower, Kenneth S. Davis's *Eisenhower: American Hero* (1969) and Stephen Ambrose's *The Supreme Commander: The War Years of General Dwight D. Eisenhower* (1970). Other important studies include Omar N. Bradley's candid memoirs, *A Soldier's Story* (1951), Martin Blumenson's *The Patton Papers: 1940–1945* (1974), Henry H. Semmes's *Portrait of Patton* (1955), and Ladislas Farago's *Patton: Ordeal and Triumph* (1964). Good popular accounts of the European war include Cornelius Ryan's anecdotal history of the Normandy Invasion, *The Longest Day* (1959), S. L. A. Marshall's *Night Drop* (1962), which describes the confusion behind the lines on D-Day, Larry Collin's *Is Paris Burning?* (1965), and Cornelius Ryan's *A Bridge Too Far* (1974) about the failed attempt to take a bridge in Holland. John Dugan and Carroll Stewart's *Ploesti* (1962) narrates the story of one of the greatest air battles of the war.

In addition are several good works about junior officers and enlisted men. Studs Terkel's *The Good War: An Oral History of World War II* (1984) probes many people's recollections, in the military and on the homefront, for reminiscences about the war. Possibly the most popular memoir to come from any war is cartoonist Bill Mauldin's *Up Front* (1945), an irreverent look at the army and its senior officers by two G.I.'s named "Willie" and "Joe." Also worth reading are two collections of Ernie Pyle's war stories, *Brave Men* (1943) and *Here Is Your War* (1943). Among the best soldiers' memoirs are Audie Murphy's *To Hell and Back* (1949), Charles B. MacDonald's *Company Commander*, revised edition (1961), and Paul Boesch's *Road to Huertgen— Forest in Hell* (1962). For the marines in the Pacific see William Manchester's *Goodbye Darkness: A Memoir of the Pacific War* (1979). There are two fine accounts by pilots of their wartime experiences: Bert Stiles's *Serenade to the Big Bird* (1952) and Philip Ardey's *Bomber Pilot: A Memoir of World War II* (1978). Two excellent memoirs by submariners are Paul Schratz's *Submarine Commander: A Story of World War II and Korea* (1989) and the autobiographical German novel *Das Boot* [*The Boat*] by Lothar G. Buchheim (1974), possibly the best submarine book ever written.

The war in China, and its future implications on world peace, is discussed in Barbara W. Tuchman's *Stilwell and the American Experience in China, 1911–45* (1971). The best history of the development of the atomic bomb can be found in Peter Wyden's *Day One: Before Hiroshima and After* (1984). Lastly, many critics contend that Norman Mailer's *The Naked and the Dead* (1948) is one of the best war novels in literature.

KOREA AND THE
COLD WAR

The United States emerged from the Second World War as the most powerful nation in history. The war had ended the Great Depression, crushed the military power of Germany and Japan, and seriously damaged the economies of England, France, and the Soviet Union. The United States hoped that the United Nations would ensure future peace, and so prepared to back the U.N. with American economic resources and military might.

Much to its chagrin, the United States soon discovered that it did not have exclusive control of atomic weapons. An elaborate spy network had managed to give information about the Anglo–American atomic experiments to the Soviet Union, which had long feared hostile nations on its western borders. At the end of the war, the Soviet Union brought Eastern Europe under its hegemony. Within a few years, the world was once again divided into two hostile camps. This time, however, each side had enough weapons to destroy human civilization.

The Cold War caused fundamental changes in American attitudes. The United States turned to spying, peacetime conscription, and a huge military budget. A key change came when the Departments of War and the Navy were combined into the Department of Defense. Everyone had known what the war and navy departments were supposed to do. The defense department took on those responsibilities and added many more. Military expenditures grew. Now money was spent on deterring war; humanity prayed that the new weapons would never be used. Much of the antagonism between the superpowers was verbal, but occasionally the two sides clashed indirectly, often using client nations to do the fighting.

Communist North Korea challenged American prestige in 1950 when its army invaded South Korea. The United Nations asked its member states to aid South Korea. The United States led the effort to turn back the "red horde." The initial U.N. effort was such a success that the United States found that it had not only freed South Korea but also occupied most of North Korea. Some Americans wanted to go further and destroy the new communist regime in China, but President Truman, under increasing pressure from European allies, refused to permit direct attacks on China. After a determined assault by the Chinese to push the U.N. forces back to South Korea, the two sides settled into a prolonged stalemate along the 38th parallel that divided the Korean peninsula.

Meanwhile, life in the United States had begun to change. The armed forces were integrated. As blacks moved into more important positions, the military found itself at the forefront of domestic social change. At the same time, military spending increased and civil defense measures were begun to prepare the American population for an atomic war with the Soviet Union, which seemed inevitable.

BLACKS IN THE MILITARY

World War II had marked the beginning of the end of racial segregation in the United States. During the war, most blacks served in menial jobs, such as mess stewards in the navy or truck drivers in the army. Black soldiers soon discovered that European society was more liberal than their own. Their experiences in Europe convinced blacks that segregation could be overthrown at home, and so after the war, civil rights organizations began a campaign to end all racial discrimination in the United States. Successful revolutions in Africa and Asia destroyed racist myths by proving that nowhites could govern themselves; these also aided the movement in the United States to end discrimination. But the most compelling argument against segregation was that World War II had shown that discrimination was fundamentally unjust. The United States could not in good conscience conscript minorities into the armed forces, send them overseas to fight racism, and then bring them back home to an equally racist society.

President Truman also had appointed a civil rights committee to study discrimination in the armed forces. Its members concluded that racial discrimination did exist, and recommended that all segregation in the military be ended. In July 1948, the president, motivated by a sense of justice as much as the realization that he needed the minority vote in the upcoming presidential election, ordered the armed forces to integrate "as rapidly as possible." The process would take decades, and subtle forms of racism persist now in the late twentieth century. Yet Truman's order had placed the military at the forefront of the fight for racial equality and integration in the United States.

SOURCE: *To Secure These Rights: The Report of the President's Committee on Civil Rights* (Washington, DC: The Library of Congress, 1947).

All of the armed forces have recently adopted policies which set as explicit objectives the achievement of equality of opportunity. The War Department has declared that it "intends to continue its efforts to make the best possible use of available personnel resources in the postwar army and in any future emergency, without distinction as to race, religion, color or other non-military considerations." The Navy Department, speaking for both the Navy and Marine Corps, has stated that:

> No distinction is made between individuals wearing a naval uniform because of race or color. The navy accepts no theory of racial differences in inborn ability, but expects that every man wearing its uniform be trained and used in accordance with his maximum individual capacity determined on the basis of individual performance.

The Coast Guard has stressed "the importance of selecting men for what they are, for what they are capable of doing, and insisting on good conduct, good behavior, and good qualities of leadership for all hands. . . . As a matter of policy Negro recruits receive the same consideration as all others."

However, despite the lessons of the war and the recent announcement of these policies, the records of the military forces disclose many areas in which there is a great need for further remedial action. Although generally speaking, the basis of recruitment has been somewhat broadened, Negroes, for example, are faced by an absolute bar against enlistment in any branch of the Marine Corps other than the steward's branch, and the army cleaves to a ceiling for Negro personnel of about 10 percent of the total strength of the service. . . .

Within the services, studies made within the last year disclose that actual experience has been out of keeping with the declarations of policy on discrimination. In the army, less than one Negro in seventy is commissioned, while there is one white officer for approximately every seven white enlisted men. In the navy, there are only 2 Negro officers in a ratio of less than 1 : 10,000 Negro enlisted men; there are 58,571 white officers, or 1 for every 7 enlisted whites. The Marine Corps has 7,798 officers, none of whom is a Negro, though there are 2,190 Negro enlisted men. Out of 2,981 Coast Guard officers, 1 is a Negro; there are 910 Negro enlisted men. The ratio of white Coast Guard commissioned to enlisted personnel is approximately 1 : 6.

Similarly, in the enlisted grades, there is an exceedingly high concentration of Negroes in the lowest ratings, particularly in the navy, Marine Corps, and Coast Guard. Almost 80 percent of the Negro sailors are serving as cooks, stewards, and steward's mates; less than 2 percent of the whites are assigned to duty in the same capacity. Almost 15 percent of all white enlisted marines are in the three highest grades; less than 2½ percent of the Negro marines fall in the same category. The disparities in the Coast Guard are similarly great. The difference in the army is somewhat smaller, but still significant: Less than 9 percent of the Negro personnel are in the first three grades, while almost 16 percent of the whites hold these ranks.

Many factors other than discrimination contribute to this result. However, it is clear that discrimination is one of the major elements which keeps the services from attaining the objectives which they have set for themselves.

The admission of minorities to the service academies and other service schools is another area in which the armed forces have enjoyed relatively little success in their efforts to eliminate discrimination. With regard to schools within the services, the disparities indicate that selection for advanced training is doubtless often made on a color basis. As for the service academies, in the course of the last seventy-five years the Military Academy at West Point admitted a total of only thirty-seven Negro cadets, while the Naval Academy at Annapolis admitted only six. The Coast Guard Academy, while it selects applicants on the basis of open, competitive examinations without regard to color, has no knowledge of any Negro ever having been accepted. The absence of Negroes from the service academies is unfortunate because it means that our officers are trained in an undemocratic environment and are denied the opportunity to learn at an early stage in their service careers that men of different races can work and fight together harmoniously. . . .

The record is not without its brighter side. A start has been made toward eliminating differentials in opportunity and treatment of minorities in the armed forces. The army is making experimental use of small all-Negro units as organic parts of large white organizations. Significantly, of the thirty-seven Negroes admitted to the Academy at West Point since 1870, twenty-one were accepted in the last ten years. In 1947, five Negroes were accepted, the largest enrollment of Negro cadets for a single year in the last seventy-five years. The navy had adopted a policy of nonsegregation and has officially opened all branches to all personnel. The Coast Guard had abandoned, as a matter of policy, the restriction of Negro guardsmen to duty as cooks, stewards, and bakers. Training courses, indoctrination programs, pamphlets, and films have been provided for officers and enlisted men in the army and navy to promote understanding between groups and to facilitate the use of minority personnel.

But the evidence leaves no doubt that we have a long way to go. The armed forces, in actual practice, still maintain many barriers to equal treatment for all their members. In many cases, state and local agencies and private persons disregard the dignity of the uniform. There is much that remains to be done, much that can be done at once. Morally, the failure to act is indefensible. Practically, it costs lives and money in the inefficient use of human resources. Perhaps most important of all, we are not making use of one of the most effective techniques for educating the public to the practicability of American ideals as a way of life. During the last war we and our allies, with varying but undeniable success, found that the military services can be used to educate citizens on a broad range of social and political problems. The war experience brought to our attention a laboratory in which we may prove that the majority and minorities of our population can train and work and fight side by side in cooperation and harmony. We should not hesitate to take full advantage of this opportunity.

"*Spring cleaning in Korea*" (*United States Army Military History Institute*). War is not all battle. Much of the time a soldier spends in war is routine and boring. Despite the nearby enemy, all soldiers try to be as comfortable as possible. Good commanders recognize the need to rotate their men from the frontline to the rear to give them enough time to feel like human beings again. This army sergeant obtained a portable tub from a mail order catalog so that he can bathe while reading a popular American magazine. As he relaxes in the tub, other soldiers wash the tank. This human element is sometimes ignored by motion pictures, which often portray war as constant tension and combat.

TROUBLE IN THE PASS
S. L. A. Marshall

On 25 June 1950, the North Korean army unexpectedly invaded South Korea. Within weeks, the invaders had driven the South Koreans into a defensive perimeter around the port of Pusan. The invasion was the first real test for the United Nations. The Soviet delegation had refused to attend U.N. meetings because the communist Chinese were not represented, so the Western democracies were able to pass a resolution condemning the North Korean attack, and then to ask the U.N.'s member nations to help South Korea.

General Douglas MacArthur was the American proconsul in postwar Japan. He was appointed head of the U.N. forces, which were confined to a tiny toehold at the southeastern corner of the Korean penisula. MacArthur gambled by directing a brilliant amphibious landing at Inchon on the west coast near Seoul (15 September 1950). The North Korean army crumbled. By Thanksgiving, U.N. forces were on the Yalu River, the border between North Korea and communist China. True to its repeated warnings, communist China entered the war and just as rapidly drove MacArthur's U.N. troops back into South Korea. The war seesawed back and forth across the 38th parallel for another two-and-one-half years until an armistice was signed.

The following selection describes the confusion that occurred during the retreat of the Eighth Army from the Chongchon River, near the Chinese border, in November 1950. To get to the coast and safety, a portion of the army had to run the gauntlet of a narrow pass through the mountains. Along with Bruce Catton, who wrote about the Civil War, and Walter

---

SOURCE: S. L. A. Marshall, *The River and the Gauntlet* (New York: William Morrow & Co., 1953). Copyright held by the University of Texas at El Paso. Permission granted by the University Library, S. L. A. Marshall Military History Collection.

Lord, who wrote of World War II, S. L. A. Marshall is one of the best writers of "anecdotal" military history. Marshall takes the reader to the battlefield, where he concentrates on small-unit action and individual emotions, leaving the reader with a clear impression of the utter confusion that infests all battle.

Once troops entered the gauntlet, they had to keep straining forward. The alternative was to abandon hope and forsake any useful part in the salvage operation. Merely to keep moving required greater resolution than to take cover and await what developed. The strong made that choice; some of the weak rejected it, waited overlong for help which did not come, and paid the price of death or capture. The reader must judge whether, in what was done, American honor was sustained by the action of the majority.

In the memories of those who made the journey, there are many vivid pictures, instinct with courage. They recall seeing Colonel Chung and his Koren staff officers jogging past the blocked vehicles toward "The Pass," running as calmly as their own countrymen in a Boston Marathon. They remember that their own division staff walked the route heads up. . . . Their own generals came out in open jeeps so that their closed vans could be used for ambulances.

The giving of praise or blame is always easy but the understanding of anything is difficult; it is a truth which applies to this story. Under the most normal conditions, there are limits to what the mind may perceive and require of the will. The stress imposed on 2nd Division during the withdrawal was abnormal even by the standards of the battlefield. Its numbing effect upon action and reaction cannot be ignored by those who would judge fairly of the event.

In the anxieties which attended the urge to stay mobile, other values were slighted. The leader of a small group or the driver of a vehicle was absorbed in his task of getting just a few people through to safety. The column became a train of small rescue parties, each operating in relative detachment from all others. The local problem blanked out everything on the horizon. There wasn't time for any man to think acutely of what possibly might happen to the people who came along later, or to govern his action according to their need.

Of these things came in part the extra ordeal in "The Pass" above the village of Karhyon during the late afternoon. The potential threat in this manmade terrain feature was clear from the beginning. . . .

Still, there had been no action to prevent the door's swinging shut. The Division Command, not yet on the road, had no knowledge of its menace. The junior commanders, though sensing the danger as they rode

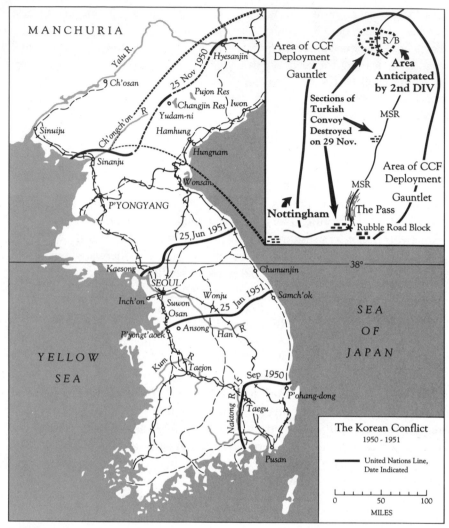

SOURCE: Inset map from S. L. A. Marshall, *The River and the Gauntlet*. Larger map from
Maurice Matloff (ed.), *American Military History* (Washington, D.C.: Office of the Chief of
Military History, U.S. Army, 1969).

through "The Pass," were weighted with other burdens. On reaching
sanctuary, they had to find and regroup their shattered units.

Furthermore, doubling back was for them out of the question. The
British brigade, driving north along the Sunchon road, had fought hard
through the day, attempting to gain "The Pass" from the south end, and had
been stopped by strong mortar and machine-gun fire from the ridges directly
west of it. . . .

There were no engineers and no heavy machinery to keep the passage
clear of rubble and wrecked transport. Whatever was dropped there by any

part of the column further constricted "The Pass" against the elements which followed. A jeep crushed at the wrong point or a truck deserted and not ditched were like self-inflicted wounds in the side of the division.

In midafternoon, the Chinese coil of automatic fire tightened around this situation. All along, the enemy had been doing a little random skirmishing with small arms around the exits. Now a circle of machine guns closed around the ramparts.

In the next sequence, a few vehicles left standing at the wrong point became the cork in the bottle. This was the day's most savage irony—that by making too much haste, the Americans built a better roadblock against themselves at the top of "The Pass" in late afternoon through sheer accident than the enemy had been able to engineer at its southern foot in early morning with malice aforethought.

So the enemy worked his design, abetted by the errors of those whom he sought to entoil. But of their mistakes—if that be a fair word—it needs be said that they were not mean or craven, and whether they could have been avoided is a great question. Men rushed not because they were thoughtless of the distant comrade back along the road, but because they were conscious of the anguish of the comrade right at hand. Not all judgments were clear, nor could they be. For this was a host which had for five days survived massacre without sleep and, unrested, unfed, and freezing, was now being extended to the limit of human endurance.

Yet it is wonderful what just a little rest will do for a man. Consider again the strange case of Sergeant McGregor of Fox Company. He was completely spent when . . . he fell across Captain Benton's lap and started his truck ride to "The Pass." . . .

"The Pass" was almost empty of moving vehicles when the truck entered the cut, and the Chinese had at last completed their fire encirclement of its heights. Along the cap of both embankments and at both ends of the slot, enemy machine guns were firing down onto the roadway. There were perhaps twenty to thirty knocked-out vehicles cluttering its surface; one of them . . . now prevented Benton's passage. Dodging or hiding among these wrecked vehicles were about a score of American riflemen and a few ROKs [South Korean troops]. They had tried several times, they told McGregor, to break out of "The Pass," and, at both ends of it, had been turned back by a sheet of machine-gun fire, losing several of their number. But there was no refuge within it. Chinese snipers were working down the slate slopes. The wrecked trucks were being subjected to a well-aimed bullet fire. Hand grenades were exploding in the alley.

With McGregor in the truck were Benton, Captain Miller, First Battalion's surgeon, Captain Caley, regimental dental officer, and M/S [master sergeant] Holt from Item Company. They held a council of war and decided the best course was to round up the men and try to break out by climbing the right-hand embankment. The start was good. Twenty-three men started. McGregor found a brush-covered slot in the face of the cliff which shielded them from easy view and, climbing hand over foot, they made it to the top of the wall without a shot being fired on them. That put them on a lower fold of a quite formidable ridge. McGregor decided to keep climbing. The party had progressed perhaps another 200 yards when McGregor spied a knob ringed with empty foxholes. He yelled "Let's get in there and hold them off!"

The Chinese must have heard that cry. Immediately, from somewhere upslope, a machine gun cracked down on them. In the duck-away the party split into three or four groups. McGregor now had only seven followers. He led them downhill along the south slope of the ridge, doing no fighting whatever and going to ground whenever they sighted any enemy skirmishers. At last they found themselves moving through a maze of quite low hills. A platoon of Chinese came toward them. McGregor countermarched his group for about 600 yards; this time he was stopped by a Chinese company coming from the opposite direction.

He took a third tack. Experience had taught him caution. This time, after proceeding for only a short distance, he called for a volunteer to go to the next rise and see what lay ahead. A Negro private responded but he was weaponless. McGregor gave him his own carbine and field glasses. He made it to the ridge top, and the others saw him train the glasses forward. At that moment a strafing A-26 let go at the hill with several rockets, and one of them missed the boy by a whisper. He tore back through McGregor's party like a man gone mad. They heard him shriek something about "Chinks" and "strafing" as he went past. He was still carrying McGregor's gun and glasses when they saw him for the last time bounding over the hill toward the point where they had seen the Chinese company. For another hour, McGregor kept steering this little band through the wilderness. . . .

In such an operation, men do not actually observe the battlefield. They see the world as a rabbit sees it, crouching to earth, with an eye on one little patch. On broken ground, like that of Korea, men under fire may witness nothing except possibly the lip of a bank 10 feet away, with the dust kicking up all around it as the bullets hit.

There were exceptions. Sometimes a man walks upright because he must. It happened to one individual on this day. General Keiser had been phenomenally lucky in his jeep run through the greater part of the gauntlet. After leaving his command post in the bivouac area at about 1330, he doubled along the stalled parts of the column almost without stopping and got to the final ridge at about 1515. This placed him in "The Pass" approximately twenty minutes after the column had wedged there. He personally witnessed the atrophy of the troops who had closed in just prior to his arrival. The dead lay in the ditches and sprawled across the roadway. Most of the living—even those still unwounded—were in such a state of shock that they responded to nothing, saw nothing, and seemingly heard nothing. The Chinese fire beat like hail among the rocks and next the vehicles where they stood or reclined. But they neither cried out nor sought better cover. Their facial expressions remained set, appearing almost masklike because of the heavy coating of dust and the distortion from the dropping of the jaw. An occasional one whispered, "Water! Water!" as if he had been saying it over and over and could not stop, but there was little else which was intelligible. They were saying nothing and doing nothing except that a few shuffled about aimlessly, seeming to reel in their tracks. The division commander walked among them, moving from group to group to group, barking questions, trying to startle them back to consciousness. "Who's in command here?" "Who *are* you?" "Can any of you do anything?" He got not a single response. The Americans remained as mute as did the ROKs and Turks, who probably didn't understand his words.

Keiser decided to walk to the south end of "The Pass." He wanted to see if the Chinese had effectively blocked the exit with fire, and he was still looking for men who might be rallied. It was an incredible reconnaissance for the top man. The Air Force was now working back and forth along the embankments on both sides, and the bullet stream was chipping the rocks less than 75 yards above the floor of the cut. Napalm spilled down onto the road, as it bounced off the cliffs, and set several of the vehicles afire. Clips from the .50 caliber guns were flying about everywhere. The din was terrific.

One thing made his heart leap up. A sergeant from the 9th Infantry had taken an 81-mm mortar from a ¼-ton truck, set it up in the middle of the roadway, and was now singlehandedly firing the piece on line of sight against the Chinese positions atop the south exit. It was the only fire Keiser saw being delivered by an American. But he noted a few other self-possessed individuals, most of whom were trying to help the wounded. One man sat on the hood of a jeep trying to bandage the wound of a second man braced up against the windshield. Keiser saw that the man's foot had been shot away clean at the ankle. He passed another badly wounded man who was lying in a ditch. A second soldier, himself wounded, was trying to drag him to a better cover behind a jeep, but was having a hard tussle. So he was helping with his voice. Keiser heard him say: "Now get your Goddamned leg around the corner of that jeep. Do it, I say! That's the way. Goddamn it, I knew you could make it." Keiser wanted to stay and help but couldn't. There were too many wounded for any one man to be able to do much. He was looking for officers; he felt if he could find just one or two officers, he could start a recovery. So he continued on to the south exit, and when he got there, he found that the Chinese guns were bearing on the road from both embankments.

The pile-up of American, Turk, and ROK dead in the ditches and along the roadside was mute proof that the enemy gunners were on their mark. Keiser started back toward the top of "The Pass," convinced that until the air strikes, coupled with infantry parties attacking up the embankment, succeeded in neutralizing the Chinese machine guns, the clearing away of the wrecked vehicles still would not free the column.

As he trudged uphill, he found that his feet were leaden. His journey along this terrible ambush was sapping his physical energy at an excessive rate, even as it drained the last reserve of the private soldier. Never had his shoe pacs weighed so heavy! Directly in his path, crosswise of the road, lay the body of one of his men. He tried to step across it, but failing to lift his foot high enough, struck his toe against the figure's midriff. Thereupon the supposed corpse sat bolt upright and said: "You damned son-of-a-bitch." Keiser was so astonished that he replied only: "My friend, I'm sorry," and continued on his way. . . .

Still far back in the column, a tall, spare man of about forty was carrying along with the main rescue mission. Capt. William O. Burla, photo intelligence officer of the Division G2 Section, had been told that morning that, on the move south, it would be his task to collect the wounded. There were no doctors to help him; he was given a staff of four drivers and two first-aid men. Together they organized a train which included the three generals' vans, two ambulances from the Engineer Battalion, two 2½-ton trucks from the 38th Infantry, and one small truck from the Division Aviation Section.

There was hard common sense in Burla. Before ever hitting the road or lifting a casualty, he had his men load the trucks with all the bedrolls and blankets which were to be found in the command post area. The convoy started forward in midafternoon. By then the ambulances were already filled, as were the vans, with litter cases, and at least twenty more lightly wounded were riding on the trucks.

They proceeded very slowly along the road, checking the ditches and scanning the nearby paddies in search for any American, ROK, or Turk who still moved. It was not a perfect job; frequently the fields aflank were hidden by ruined portions of the column or vehicles temporarily stalled. Also, before the party was far along, it became obvious that the train would be overloaded long before the run was done. So Burla gave his helpers a rule of thumb: If a body lay perfectly still, they should not check it for a heartbeat, but to save time and help those with the best chance to live, would regard it as dead. In clearing wounded to the vehicles, the sweep also cleared the dead from the road to the ditches. Burla continued to collect bedding wherever it had been abandoned. . . .

When the shock cases whimpered from the cold, they were tucked in with bedrolls and blankets. There were enough ampules of morphine at hand to take care of the chest- and belly-wound patients. This was about all the care that could be given. Perhaps it was enough. Burla said in his matter-of-fact way, "They asked only for water, and of that we were not short."

But two men of the 140 died on the ride out, both from stomach wounds. Only twice did the train come under Chinese fire, and luck was with it each time. One of the ambulances had its radiator shot away by a machine-gun burst; a 2½ took it in tow immediately. One wounded man laying in the bed of a truck was hit by a second bullet; he managed to survive. . . .

When the column became wedged in "The Pass," just after General Keiser's arrival, these elements became long stalled in the median ground one to two miles short of the final ridge. There they were taken under mortar and machine-gun fire from the flanking high ground. The road became littered with knocked-out vehicles. Quad-50s and 155-mm howitzers were deployed to the paddy fields to provide protective fires. As the day wore on toward sunset, with still no sign of a break-up ahead, anticipating that they might be held for the night, he began to consider how they would defend if this was to be the final stand.

Meantime, the lavishing of rockets, napalm, and .50 machine-gun fire in repeated air strikes against the embankment tops and the ridge extensions was the only consistent counter against the Chinese effort to keep the trap closed at "The Pass." For the planes which participated, it was a race not less with the setting sun than with the enemy reserves boring down from the hills to keep possession of the heights, despite the knocking out of gun after gun. To win it, the pilots risked to the limit, coming in so low against the ridges that it many times seemed to the men in "The Pass" that a crash was certain. . . .

Not far away Keiser was coping with this same problem. The stalled vehicles were still drawing rifle and tommy gun fire from the heights. But the cry was going up from many parts of the column: "Cease fire! Cease fire! Cease fire!" Keiser is an old China hand and he sensed a trick. He moved down the line shouting: "Stop this 'cease fire' talk! These Commies know English. They're yelling that from the ridges and you're echoing it. We're just beginning to get them on the run."

Two light tanks from the Reconnaissance Company had just pulled up to within a few hundred yards of the north exit and were shelling the ridges.

Bradley went to Keiser with the suggestion that they might be more useful within the cut. A captain from the 38th Infantry said to Keiser, "If I can have the tanks, I can use them to bulldoze the wrecked vehicles aside and open up the way again." Keiser told him to collect the tanks and go at the job. This was soon done, with Bradley and the unnamed captain directing the operation. Coupled with the final air strikes, the restoration of movement within "The Pass" was what mainly shook loose the Chinese still trying to hold the south exit. . . .

By then first light was breaking. The Chinese saw the movement and converged . . . from north, northeast and east. Six air strikes were ordered up in a vain endeavor to hold back this tide. The surge continued unabated. The formation simply fell apart, and it became every man for himself. Some of the Americans ran until they collapsed from exhaustion. Others held their ground and fought back. Those who stayed were butchered. The others who had run themselves into the ground were picked up bodily by the Chinese, supported until their legs were again working, and then pushed on their way back to the American lines.

This war is a succession of enigmas. None is less scrutable than the nature of the Chinese enemy.

Paratroopers jump into combat in Korea, October 1950 (Smithsonian Institution Photo No. 37850). Air assaults by combat paratroopers had been used in World War II. Although they were successful in a few places such as Crete, more often they left soldiers vulnerable behind enemy lines. Despite its limited combat success, paratrooper training has become symbolic of individual bravery in the modern army. Today, airborne school is almost a requirement for a successful career as an army officer. Airborne units encourage this esprit by wearing a distinctive uniform. This photograph "over enemy territory in Korea" shows paratroopers from the army's 187th Regimental Combat Team jumping out of air force C-46 "commandos." This airborne assault at Sukchon-Sunchon (October 1950) was the first of two used in the Korean War. Once on the ground, the paratroopers had to be supplied from the air, until the ground forces could link-up with them.

A KOREAN WAR DIARY

Robert A. Howes

T he Korean War proved to be one of the most frustrating wars ever fought by Americans. For two-and-one-half years, communist and U.N. forces fought over small areas of the peninsula. Soon after the successful communist drive in November 1950, the U.N. allies were ready to sign an armistice dividing the peninsula at the 38th parallel. The communists, however, hoped to gain more. It was not until Dwight D. Eisenhower, who was elected president in 1952, made a surprise visit to Korea and threatened the enemy with atomic weapons that the leaders of North Korea and China changed their minds. Yet even after the armistice was signed the following year, fire fights were common along the border.

The following selection is part of a journal written by Second Lieutenant Robert A. Howes, a West Point graduate (class of 1951) and artilleryman. He accompanied infantry patrols as a "forward observer," directing artillery fire on enemy positions. Howes's journal graphically describes his initiation into Asian culture, the emotions he felt before his first battle, the exhilaration of combat, and its bittersweet afterglow. Like soldiers in every war, Howes frequently uses epithets to refer to the enemy. In World War I, Americans had fought the "Huns"; in World War II, it was the "Krauts" and "Japs." Korean War soldiers called the Chinese communists "chinks" and their sons in Vietnam would frequently refer to their enemies as "gooks."

4 April [1952].   This was the day of my first night patrol, or any type of patrol. All last night I was nervous and jumpy. I have never quite felt that way before. I guess I was just plain scared. . . .

SOURCE: Robert Arthur Howes papers, U.S. Army Military History Institute Archives, Carlisle Barracks, Pennsylvania. Courtesy of Lt. Col. Robert A. Howes, U.S. Army (Ret).

Captain Green gave the overall plan and mission of the Patrol. Baker Company was to take three platoons and sweep the hill mass in no-mans-land known as Pokkae. The mission of the patrol was to deny the enemy the use of no-mans-land, locate enemy positions and capture a prisoner. If the patrol could capture a prisoner at the base of Pokkae the mission would be accomplished and the patrol could return. . . . The 3rd platoon would set up an ambush at the base of Pokkae to protect our rear and as a base of operations. The first platoon followed by the second was to continue along up the right or East side to a point just short of the northern tip. Then the first platoon would move up onto the high ground to establish an O.P. [observation post] and base of fire. When the first platoon was in position the second would sweep around the northern tip through the town of Samii. . . . The radio signal to come home was "Scrambled Eggs." The plan was all set and understood by all, and was a good one. I explained the artillery concentrations to the Infantrymen and told them how to call for them, also that I would be along with them to adjust the fire.

After the briefing I came back to the battery and wrote a last letter to Dottie in case anything should happen to me. I have left it in my personal belongings in case anything should happen in the future. . . .

When 8:15 came around . . . we started off in the first Platoon. . . . The Second Platoon was about 20 to 30 yards behind us when we started out. As we walked over the M.L.R. [main line of resistance—that is, the frontline] we crouched down so as not to be outlined on the ridge. The moon was quite bright and about 3/4 full. We walked along in front of our lines for a ways and then cut out into no-man's-land. As we walked along I picked up some enemy communist propaganda and some that we had shot out into no-mans-land for the commies. Oh yes just as we were starting out to cross the M.L.R. two men came up to Lt Tom Ralston and asked if they could come along. One was a doctor, Captain Philpot who had no weapon. The other was a 2nd Lt. Medic a man named ———. He had on a bullet proof vest and carried a carbine. As we walked through no-man's-land picking up some of the propaganda we would stop every now and then to let the scouts look over an area we were going to pass through. . . . When we would stop, Powers, Watkins and I would talk in whispers. Before we went out on the patrol I had told them not to call me Sir or Lt., to use either my first or last name. Just a precaution so the chinks [Chinese communists] wouldn't know who the officers were. I carried no identification but my dog tags and wore only my wedding ring and watch. Another precaution was not to tell the chinks that you had had any schooling or did anything more than a common laborer or owned much of anything—never a house or a car. That is what Tom Ralston had told me and I passed it on to the men. None of us wanted to be a capitalist if captured—just poor workers and friends of the communists. The commies hate the artillery and F.O.'s [forward observers] so I took off my bar and cross cannons and would say I was an infantryman if captured. . . .

We got to the base of Pokkae about 9:30 or at least the 1st squad did. The scouts were around the side clearing the ruins of a small village. The second platoon now was about 30 to 40 yards behind us. As our squad started around to the side of Pokkae we heard a chink call out something that must have been a warning to his buddys. When we heard that we knew there were chinks around and were a lot more cautious. We moved out about 50 more yards from the bottom of the hill.

All was quiet from the time we heard the chinks until we were about three quarters of the way up the east side of Pokkae. Evidently the chinks didn't see our second and third platoons for they hit us from both sides and the rear. One second it was quiet as church and the next minute all hell broke loose. The chinks came in shooting and throwing grenades. They came from the left side, Pokkae, and others were already on our right in ambush. The ones that came from the Pokkae side came through between the second and third squads and the First and Second Platoons. That cut our squad off completely from our other platoon and the rest of our platoon. . . . They must have thought that the litter bearers at the end of our squad were carrying recoilless rifles for they hit three, killing one medic and wounding two, and ran off with the litters. Another medic who wasn't hurt hit the ground and played dead. The chinks took his carbine right off of his back. Another one, 5 chinks started to carry off bodily as a prisoner.

Right after they hit us I called for the artillery concentrations on top of Pokkae and when they hit it was one of the sweetest sounds I have ever heard, our own artillery screaming over our heads and landing on the enemy. . . . About that time the chinks on our right started coming in on us from the other edge of that rice paddy. I saw one duck down behind the bank of this terraced rice paddy so I threw the first grenade I had ever thrown and didn't know for sure if I had hit him with it. After we got back Captain Philpot said, "You sure did get him, the grenade landed right on top of him." There was another one that Tom saw so I gave him my other grenade. He got the chink.

Mortars and machine guns were opening up on us from Pokkae on the side of the hill so I started to turn toward the hill to adjust the artillery down the side of the hill close to us. As I turned around to see, I saw two chinks running toward us from our left or the rear from where we were first shooting. The moon made the straw in the rice paddy above us bright and I could see the two of them plain as day against the straw in the paddy. I pulled the trigger on my carbine as I just aimed along the barrel as you would with a shotgun. I fired six shots and cut him down. Then I realized my M-2 carbine was on semiautomatic. I quickly put it on full automatic and blasted the other chink with a spray of about eight rounds. Then I finished calling the artillery down the side of the hill 50 yards at a time till it was about 75 to 100 yards from us. One round went off so close that the fragments buzzed right over our heads, another raised us up off of the ground. I told Tom Ralston it was in quite close and asked him if he wanted it moved out a little. His answer was an emphatic, "Hell no—keep it coming." I turned around to our right flank again and saw a guy named Rogers operating a light 30 caliber machine gun cutting the chinks down like cord wood. I found out later that when the chinks first hit us one came running at Rogers and his assistant gunner, thinking they were chinks. Rogers didn't have the machine gun loaded yet so his assistant gunner fired at the chink with a .45 pistol and missed. At that time the chink realized his mistake, put on the brakes and put it into reverse. It was too late! Rogers had the machine gun loaded by then and was holding it in his hands shooting the chink to ribbons.

When I turned around and saw Rogers shooting a number of chinks with his gun on the low mount a G.I. named Bennett, the one the chinks were carrying off bodily, stood up about 15 feet left from where Rogers was shooting. The chinks stood up to drag him down behind the paddy bank, and Bennett yelled, "get those over there." Most of us thought it was an English speaking chink, and were ready to cut him down. He yelled, "For Christ's sake Rogers don't shoot," then Rogers recognized him and told the rest of us not to shoot. Two more chinks got up to drag Bennett down again when he socked one in the head with his fist, yelled, "Get those two," and dove toward us. Ray Powers got one of those two and someone the other. Bennett just got in to us and was hit in the left shoulder by a chink. Captain Philpot did a wonderful job there, he took out the slug and dressed the wound by moonlight. . . .

When we took stock after the enemy broke contact, we had one dead and six wounded and no litters to carry them in. We waited about 10 minutes or more for the litters from the other platoons, but it seemed like an eternity almost as long as the 5 minutes seem when you're waiting for your fire mission to go through the mill and the rounds to get to the target. The litters, a few, finally came and they made others out of jackets and rifles. We were ordered at first to go on with the mission, but when the Lt. Colonel with the Third Platoon heard of the dead and wounded and the trouble we were going to have getting them out, he gave us "Scrambled Eggs." It was still some time before we could get the dead and wounded out. We cut down on the artillery and moved the fire out from us as we started to move back.

I'll never forget the boy who lay there dead in the moonlight with his guts blown out and a river of blood about 3 feet long flowing about 6 inches wide from his belly. When the chinks first hit he had hit the ground and landed right on a chink grenade with his belly. They had no litter to carry him on so they put his body over some logs and carried him that way till the medics behind the M.L.R. could get out to us with more litters and litter bearers.

As we moved back Sgt. Morrison went around feeling pulses trying to get a live prisoner. No Soap! When we fell back I called the artillery down 50 yards at a time to cover our retreat. I kept up the artillery on our flanks and I think that is the only reason we didn't get any mortar fire coming home. The trip home was fairly quiet. We made the only noise, but the enemy didn't fire a shot. Tom and I waited at the M.L.R. till all the boys were home and then walked slowly and tired back to the Company with the Lt. Colonel.

We sat around the C.P. [command post] and discussed the evenings events from about 2:30 A.M. to 3:30 A.M. It wasn't until this time that I realized what had happened and I started to be a little scared. I wasn't scared since we left the company area to go on patrol. I guess you don't get scared while you're actually doing it, but only when you stop and think about what you are going to do or what you have done. . . .

14 April.   We were relieved from the hill today, but not until we had gotten up at 8:30 to go out and make a few crater analyses and get some shell fragments [to determine if they had been fired by U.S. artillery]. We didn't go out and in front of our lines as most of the shells there had landed beyond or in the barbed wire. We started down the back of the hill and analyzed the sixth shell to hit; azimuth 5500 m̊. The azimuth of all the craters was about 5560 m̊ and we found ample shell fragments that confirmed our belief that the rounds were 155 mm [U.S. howitzers]. We finally got down to where the first round had landed but we found no crater. Several men we talked to said it had gone off on a pile of rock and so left no crater. I at first thought it had been a tree burst but as we looked around for freshly cut wood or trees we found a large rock just above where the men were sitting where the shell had hit, knocked a large piece out of the rock and traveled another fifteen feet and gone off in the air just above and to the east of the men. That is why it had done so much damage. As we looked around for shell fragments we found a chunk of a man's leg, and part of a hand with the stubs of two fingers on it. One of the men buried them. The thing that hurt the most about this tragedy was the picture I found laying in the rubble left by the explosion. It was a picture of a blonde curly headed boy about 2 years old, just as cute as a bug's ear. Who knows what happened to his Daddy? Was he looking at the picture or was it blown or ripped out of his pocket by fragments? Will that cute little kid ever see his father again to smile at as he was in the picture? God only knows!

B-26s Wipe Out Red Stronghold

T/Sgt. Dick Bartlett

Although North Korea was a backward agrarian country with a modest industrial output and primitive transportation lines, the United States used strategic bombing to try to destroy its tiny industrial and agricultural base. Many critics questioned bombing targets with such limited military value. In *This Kind of War* (1963), a widely acclaimed history of the Korean War, T. R. Fehrenbach contended that "you may bomb [a nation], atomize it, pulverize it and wipe it clean of life—but if you desire to defend it, protect it, and keep it for civilization, you must do this on the ground, the way the Roman legions did, by putting your young men into the mud" (p. 427).

The following story was written by Tech Sergeant Dick Bartlett, a reporter for the military newspaper *Stars and Stripes*. His account offers a vivid taste of the thrill of flying high-speed aircraft over enemy targets. Modern technology had not only made war more lethal but also more exhilarating.

HQ, 452D BOMB WING   I visited an age-old town in North Korea. I traveled in a B-26. That town no longer exists!

It took just 22 minutes, by the clock on the instrument panel, for four 452d Bomb Wing B-26s to wipe out Pungha-dong.

Let's get it into the record right away that the B-26 is the answer to the foot-soldier's prayer. Air–ground support means just that: the Air Force eradicates certain ground-troop obstacles. With rockets, fragmentation

---

SOURCE: *Stars and Stripes* (Pacific ed.), 3 December 1950.

bombs, napalm and .50-caliber machineguns these B-26s can eradicate without mercy.

Have you ever seen a 5-inch rocket zip into an ammo dump? We did, this morning!

Briefing officer, Lt. L. F. Levy of Los Angeles told us the target had been "requested" by the infantry. "Flak," he said, "is negligible in the area." Sound like good news? Any flak at all can mean the worst kind of news. "You're carrying the maximum load," he said. "Rockets, napalms, frags and full fifties. Put that load where it'll do the most good!"

We were given "last resort" targets to hit in case Pungha-dong was weathered-in, and in the event the "last resorts" were unavailable, were reminded that, "north of the battleline anything that moves lends itself to eradication."

The weather would be cold, we were told. About 35 degrees below. I found a friend in Sgt. Floyd Spangler of Santa Ana, Calif., who wasn't flying this day and who lent me his warm flight clothing. No heated suit, however, because there are only two outlets in the cockpit.

Fine! Well at least I would be sitting where I could see the action, even if I did freeze. Sitting, did I say? I spent five and a half hours squirming around on a "jump seat!" That's a small, metal torture instrument in the general shape of a seat invented by a Communist-inspired American tricycle manufacturer.

An hour or so after take-off a certain anatomical area of mine was absolutely numb, the effects no longer felt. The "seat" was now just something that held up me and about 80 pounds of parachute and heavy winter flying clothing.

We were passing Taegu and from 6000 feet the jagged winter-hued hills appeared freckled with old mortar bursts.

Our navigator, 1st Lt. Dennis O. Boyle, of Pasadena, Calif., twisted around easily in his comfortable seat, "Navigation is pretty rugged in North Korea," he said. "Too damn many small hamlets and groups of farm buildings. They all look alike."

I thought of the stories I'd heard of planes bombing their own troops and supplies and wondered if Boyle would find his target. He did. Right on the nose!

Below us was a small peaceful appearing valley, complete with farmhouses and a few haystacks. From out of somewhere appeared a small L-5 "Mosquito" plane, directing two F-80s out harvesting a few fields. You know, there just aren't any more haystacks left in North Korea!

Our pilot, Lt. Col. Claude J. Norton of Santa Ana was talking to ground control. He turned around, "We are to take the assigned target. Jello hasn't got anything special this morning." He reached up and for the sixth time checked his gun switches.

We were over the target now. A typical, small, thatched roof village laying at the apex of three valleys. Rough, tree-covered ridges rimmed the target. A horse stood patiently tied to a post near one of the outlying buildings. His owner had evidently left hurriedly.

Our flight of four B-26s was strung-out in a "follow-the-leader" formation and we went in for the first pass. Boyle swung the bullet-proof glass shield around in front of Norton. If the windshield got it, our pilot would be protected. That's good procedure! You only have one pilot and one set of controls in these B-26s. And you're a long way from home!

"Bombs away!" Boyle hollered.

Behind us, Cpl. Ernest D. Sowerds of Santa Ana, our turret gunner, was leaning out into the bomb bay. Over the inter-phone his "They walked right through the town," brought a smile to Colonel Norton's face. He pulled the plane up sharply to miss a ridge by only a couple of feet and I thought of the briefing officers warning that the North Koreans were setting off land mines on ridge tops as low-flying planes passed over. Nothing happened!

We went around for another pass. Rockets this time. Norton put the plane on a wing tip and brought it around carefully. The rockets swooshed earthward. It was easy to follow the smoking trail of one into a small building. This was the ammo dump. Flames and smoke and bits of building shot upward for 600 feet. Another hit!

Around again for another pass. This time the napalms, like dropping fused 50-gallon tanks of 100 octane gasoline. They speak horribly for themselves. As we pulled up through the boiling smoke from the ammo dump, something seemed to float lazily up then suddenly whiz pass the right wing. We learned later that it was enemy automatic weapons fire.

A large building to one side of the target was still virtually untouched. A burst from the nose guns tracked along the ground and into a nearby building. Norton banked a little and cut his wing guns in with the nose bursts and that building began to disintegrate. The incendiaries soon had it afire. Up the valley to the north now and some extra strafing for good measure on several likely looking farm type buildings and it was over.

Multiply those passes by four and you'll have a new meaning of the word "eradication." The conservative report will list 75 percent of target destroyed. But we were there. We saw the explosions, watched the buildings crumple, saw the smoke and fire belch skyward while Pungha-dong died.

The horse? I looked through my binoculars. There he was still tied to the post, apparently unhurt and only slightly excited by the entire proceedings.

OLD SOLDIERS NEVER DIE, THEY JUST FADE AWAY

Douglas MacArthur

On 11 April 1951, President Harry Truman dramatically removed General Douglas MacArthur (1880–1964) from command of the U.N. troops in Korea. For some time, MacArthur had publicly opposed the Truman administration's limited military strategy in Korea. The surprise communist Chinese attack across the Yalu River in November 1950 had humiliated MacArthur. He demanded that U.S. planes bomb the Chinese bases and that Chiang Kai Shek, the leader of the Nationalist Chinese on Taiwan, be allowed to invade mainland China. Truman and the U.N. allies refused to expand the war. MacArthur sought support from the Republican opposition in Congress. On 5 April 1951, House Minority Leader Joseph W. Martin, Jr., released a letter he had received from MacArthur criticizing the Truman administration's policy in Korea. Six days later, Truman fired MacArthur.

The general returned to the United States, where he was greeted as a hero. On 19 April, Congress received him at a special combined session. In possibly the most famous speech by any American general, MacArthur summed up his world strategy and left the door open for the Republican Party to nominate him for president in 1952. Although the American public admired MacArthur as a general, it feared him as a president. MacArthur and his supporters were stunned to learn that his closing words had correctly predicted that he would "just fade away."

SOURCE: *Congressional Record*, 82nd Congress, 1st Session, Vol. 97, Part 3.

Mr. President, Mr. Speaker, and distinguished Members of the Congress, I stand on this rostrum with a sense of deep humility and great pride— humility in the wake of those great American architects of our history who have stood here before me, pride in the reflection that this forum of legislative debate represents human liberty in the purest form yet devised. Here are centered the hopes, and aspirations, and faith of the entire human race.

I do not stand here as an advocate of any partisan cause, for the issues are fundamental and reach quite beyond the realm of partisan consideration. They must be resolved on the highest plane of national interest if our course is to prove sound and our future protected. I trust, therefore, that you will do me the justice of receiving that which I have to say as solely expressing the considered viewpoint of a fellow American. I address you with neither rancor nor bitterness in the fading twilight of life with but one purpose in mind—to serve my country.

The issues are global and so interlocked that to consider the problems of one sector, oblivious to those of another, is but to court disaster for the whole.

While Asia is commonly referred to as the gateway of Europe, it is no less true that Europe is the gateway to Asia, and the broad influence of the one cannot fail to have its impact on the other.

There are those who claim our strength is inadequate to protect on both fronts—that we cannot divide our effort. I can think of no greater expression of defeatism. If a potential enemy can divide his strength on two fronts, it is for us to counter his effort.

The Communist threat is a global one. Its successful advance in one sector threatens the destruction of every other sector. You cannot appease or otherwise surrender to communism in Asia without simultaneously under-mining our efforts to halt its advance in Europe. . . .

I now turn to the Korean conflict. While I was not consulted prior to the President's decision to intervene in support of the Republic of Korea, that decision, from a military standpoint, proved a sound one as we hurled back the invaders and decimated his forces. Our victory was complete and our objectives within reach when Red China intervened with numerically superior ground forces. This created a new war and an entirely new situation—a situation not contemplated when our forces were committed against the North Korean invaders—a situation which called for new decisions in the diplomatic sphere to permit the realistic adjustment of military strategy. Such decisions have not been forthcoming.

While no man in his right mind would advocate sending our ground forces into continental China and such was never given a thought, the new situation did urgently demand a drastic revision of strategic planning if our political aim was to defeat this new enemy as we had defeated the old.

Apart from the military need as I saw it to neutralize the sanctuary protection given the enemy north of the Yalu, I felt that military necessity in the conduct of the war made mandatory:

1. The intensification of our economic blockage against China;

2. The imposition of a naval blockade against the China coast;

3. Removal of restrictions on air reconnaissance of China's coastal area and of Manchuria;

4. Removal of restrictions on the forces of the Republic of China on Formosa with logistic support to contribute to their effective operations against the common enemy. . . .

I called for reinforcements, but was informed that reinforcements were not available. I made clear that if not permitted to destroy the build-up bases north of the Yalu; if not permitted to utilize the friendly Chinese force of some 600,000 men on Formosa; if not permitted to blockade the China coast to prevent the Chinese Reds from getting succor from without; and if there were to be no hope of major reinforcements, the position of the command from the military standpoint forbade victory. We could hold in Korea by constant maneuver and at an approximate area where our supply line advantages were in balance with the supply line disadvantages of the enemy, but we could hope at best for only an indecisive campaign, with its terrible and constant attrition upon our forces if the enemy utilized his full military potential. I have constantly called for the new political decisions essential to a solution. Efforts have been made to distort my position. It has been said, in effect that I am a war monger. Nothing could be further from the truth. I know war as few other men now living know it, and nothing to me is more revolting. I have long advocated its complete abolition as its very destructiveness on both friend and foe has rendered it useless as a means of settling international disputes. . . .

But once war is forced upon us, there is no other alternative than to apply every available means to bring it to a swift end. War's very object is victory—not prolonged indecision. In war, indeed, there can be no substitute for victory.

There are some who for varying reasons would appease Red China. They are blind to history's clear lesson. For history teaches with unmistakable emphasis that appeasement but begets new and bloodier war. It points to no single instance where the end has justified that means—where appeasement has led to more than a sham peace. Like blackmail, it lays the basis for new and successively greater demands, until, as in blackmail, violence becomes the only alternative. Why, my soldiers asked of me, surrender military advantages to an enemy in the field? I could not answer. Some may say to avoid spread of the conflict into an all-out war with China; others, to avoid Soviet intervention. Neither explanation seems valid. For China is already engaging with the maximum power it can commit and the Soviet will not necessarily mesh its actions with our moves. Like a cobra, any new enemy will more likely strike whenever it feels that the relativity in military or other potential is in its favor on a world-wide basis.

The tragedy of Korea is further heightened by the fact that as military action is confined to its territorial limits, it condemns that nation, which it is our purpose to save, to suffer the devastating impact of full naval and air bombardment, while the enemy's sanctuaries are fully protected from such attack and devastation. Of the nations of the world, Korea alone, up to now, is the sole one which has risked its all against Communism. The magnificence of the courage and fortitude of the Korean people defies description. They have chosen to risk death rather than slavery. Their last words to me were, "Don't scuttle the Pacific."

I have just left your fighting sons in Korea. They have met all tests there and I can report to you without reservation they are splendid in every way. It was my constant effort to preserve them and end this savage conflict honorably and with the least loss of time and minimum sacrifice of life. Its growing bloodshed has caused me the deepest anguish and anxiety. Those gallant men will remain often in my thoughts and in my prayers always.

I am closing my 52 years of military service. When I joined the Army even before the turn of the century, it was the fulfillment of all my boyish hopes and dreams. The world has turned over many times since I took the oath on the plain at West Point, and the hopes and dreams have long since vanished. But I still remember the refrain of one of the most popular barrack ballads of that day which proclaimed most proudly that—

"Old soldiers never die; they just fade away."

And like the old soldier of that ballad, I now close my military career and just fade away—an old soldier who tried to do his duty as God gave him the light to see that duty.

Good-by.

THE MILITARY-INDUSTRIAL COMPLEX

Dwight D. Eisenhower

In 1961, Dwight D. Eisenhower (1890–1969) completed eight successful years as president of the United States. During his administration, he had brought inflation under control and had shown American strength and determination around the world. The United States appeared to be on the road to unknown heights of prosperity and power. Eisenhower recognized, however, that the country he had known as a child growing up in late nineteenth-century Kansas was no more. The pressures of being a world power had changed American culture. Eisenhower feared that too many American liberties already had been sacrificed in the name of national defense.

Nuclear disarmament was one area where he knew his administration had failed. Instead of forging treaties to end the arms race with the Soviet Union, he and Secretary of State John Foster Dulles had devised a strategy to place most of the defense budget into long-range bombers and nuclear missiles. Eisenhower feared that the military budget was becoming so large that it would soon place an enormous debt on future generations of Americans. Yet, although he recognized the problem, Eisenhower knew that he had failed to find a solution to stem the growing cost of military armament. Shortly before leaving office, Eisenhower addressed the American people on television. He warned them of the high economic and social costs they would have to bear to remain a superpower in a hostile world.

SOURCE: *Public Papers of the Presidents of the United States: Dwight David Eisenhower, 1960–1961* (Washington, DC: Government Printing Office, 1961).

*T*hree days from now, after a half century in the service of our country, I shall lay down the responsibilities of office as, in traditional and solemn ceremony, the authority of the Presidency is vested in my successor.

This evening I come to you with a message of leave-taking and farewell, and to share a few final thoughts with you, my countrymen.

Like every other citizen, I wish the new President, and all who will labor with him, Godspeed. I pray that the coming years will be blessed with peace and prosperity for all.

Our people expect the President and the Congress to find essential agreement on issues of great moment, the wise resolution of which will better shape the future of the Nation. . . .

We now stand ten years past the midpoint of a century that has witnessed four major wars among great nations. Three of these involved our own country. Despite these holocausts America is today the strongest, the most influential and most productive nation in the world. Understandably proud of this preeminence, we yet realize that America's leadership and prestige depend, not merely upon our unmatched material progress, riches and military strength, but on how we use our power in the interests of world peace and human betterment.

Throughout America's adventures in free government, our basic purposes have been to keep the peace; to foster progress in human achievement, and to enhance liberty, dignity and integrity among people and among nations. To strive for less would be unworthy of a free and religious people. Any failure traceable to arrogance, or our lack of comprehension or readiness to sacrifice would inflict upon us grievous hurt both at home and abroad.

Progress toward these noble goals is persistently threatened by the conflict now engulfing the world. It commands our whole attention, absorbs our very beings. We face a hostile ideology—global in scope, atheistic in character, ruthless in purpose, and insidious in method. Unhappily the danger it poses promises to be of indefinite duration. To meet it successfully, there is called for, not so much the emotional and transitory sacrifices of crisis, but rather those which enable us to carry forward steadily, surely, and without complaint the burdens of a prolonged and complex struggle—with liberty the stake. Only thus shall we remain, despite every provocation, on our charted course toward permanent peace and human betterment.

Crises there will continue to be. In meeting them, whether foreign or domestic, great or small, there is a recurring temptation to feel that some spectacular and costly action could become the miraculous solution to all current difficulties. A huge increase in newer elements of our defense; development of unrealistic programs to cure every ill in agriculture; a dramatic expansion in basic and applied research—these and many other possibilities, each possibly promising in itself, may be suggested as the only way to the road we wish to travel.

But each proposal must be weighed in the light of a broader consideration: the need to maintain balance in and among national programs—balance between the private and public economy, balance between cost and hoped for advantage—balance between the clearly necessary and the comfortably desirable; balance between our essential requirements as a nation and the duties imposed by the nation upon the individual; balance between actions of the moment and the national welfare of the future. Good judgment seeks balance and progress; lack of it eventually finds imbalance and frustration.

The record of many decades stands as proof that our people and their government have, in the main, understood these truths and have responded to them well, in the face of stress and threat. But threats, new in kind or degree, constantly arise. I mention two only.

A vital element in keeping the peace is our military establishment. Our arms must be mighty, ready for instant action, so that no potential aggressor may be tempted to risk his own destruction.

Our military organization today bears little relation to that known by any of my predecessors in peacetime, or indeed by the fighting men of World War II or Korea.

Until the latest of our world conflicts, the United States had no armaments industry. American makers of plowshares could, with time and as required, make swords as well. But now we can no longer risk emergency improvisation of national defense; we have been compelled to create a permanent armaments industry of vast proportions. Added to this, three and a half million men and women are directly engaged in the defense establishment. We annually spend on military security more than the net income of all United States corporations.

The conjunction of an immense military establishment and a large arms industry is new in the American experience. The total influence— economic, political, even spiritual—is felt in every city, every State house, every office of the Federal government. We recognize the imperative need for this development. Yet we must not fail to comprehend its grave implications. Our toil, resources and livelihood are all involved; so is the very structure of our society.

In the councils of government, we must guard against the acquisition of unwarranted influence, whether sought or unsought, by the military-industrial complex. The potential for the disastrous rise of misplaced power exists and will persist.

We must never let the weight of this combination endanger our liberties or democratic processes. We should take nothing for granted. Only an alert and knowledgeable citizenry can compel the proper meshing of the huge industrial and military machinery of defense with our peaceful methods and goals, so that security and liberty may prosper together.

Akin to, and largely responsible for the sweeping changes in our industrial-military posture, has been the technological revolution during recent decades.

In this revolution, research has become central; it also becomes more formalized, complex, and costly. A steadily increasing share is conducted for, by, or at the direction of, the Federal government.

Today, the solitary inventor, tinkering in his shop, has been overshadowed by task forces of scientists in laboratories and testing fields. In the same fashion, the free university, historically the fountainhead of free ideas and scientific discovery, has experienced a revolution in the conduct of research. Partly because of the huge costs involved, a government contract becomes virtually a substitute for intellectual curiosity. For every old blackboard there are hundreds of new electronic computers.

The prospect of domination of the nation's scholars by Federal employment, project allocations, and the power of money is ever present— and is gravely to be regarded.

Yet, in holding scientific research and discovery in respect, as we should, we must also be alert to the equal and opposite danger that public policy could itself become the captive of a scientific-technological elite.

It is the task of statesmanship to mold, to balance, and to integrate these and other forces, new and old, within the principles of our democratic system—ever aiming toward the supreme goals of our free society.

Another factor in maintaining balance involves the element of time. As we peer into society's future, we—you and I, and our government—must avoid the impulse to live only for today, plundering, for our own ease and convenience, the precious resources of tomorrow. We cannot mortgage the material assets of our grandchildren without risking the loss also of their political and spiritual heritage. We want democracy to survive for all generations to come, not to become the insolvent phantom of tomorrow.

Down the long lane of history yet to be written America knows that this world of ours, ever growing smaller, must avoid becoming a community of dreadful fear and hate, and be, instead, a proud confederation of mutual trust and respect.

Such a confederation must be one of equals. The weakest must come to the conference table with the same confidence as do we, protected as we are by our moral, economic, and military strength. That table, though scarred by many past frustrations, cannot be abandoned for the certain agony of the battlefield.

Disarmament, with mutual honor and confidence, is a continuing imperative. Together we must learn how to compose differences, not with arms, but with intellect and decent purpose. Because this need is so sharp and apparent I confess that I lay down my official responsibilities in this field with a definite sense of disappointment. As one who has witnessed the horror and the lingering sadness of war—as one who knows that another war could utterly destroy this civilization which has been so slowly and painfully built over thousands of years—I wish I could say tonight that a lasting peace is in sight.

Happily, I can say that war has been avoided. Steady progress toward our ultimate goal has been made. But, so much remains to be done. As a private citizen, I shall never cease to do what little I can to help the world advance along that road.

So—in this my last good night to you as your President—I thank you for the many opportunities you have given me for public service in war and peace. I trust that in that service you will find some things worthy; as for the rest of it, I know you will find ways to improve performance in the future.

You and I—my fellow citizens—need to be strong in our faith that all nations, under God, will reach the goal of peace with justice. May we ever be unswerving in devotion to principle, confident but humble with power, diligent in pursuit of the Nation's great goals.

To all the peoples of the world, I once more give expression to America's prayerful and continuing aspiration:

We pray that peoples of all faiths, all races, all nations, may have their great human needs satisfied; that those now denied opportunity shall come to enjoy it to the full; that all who yearn for freedom may experience its spiritual blessings; that those who have freedom will understand, also, its heavy responsibilities; that all who are insensitive to the needs of others will learn charity; that the scourges of poverty, disease and ignorance will be made to disappear from the earth, and that, in the goodness of time, all peoples will come to live together in a peace guaranteed by the binding force of mutual respect and love.

An air raid warden directs fire fighters (National Archives). Although the United States stood ready to meet any Soviet threat during the 1950s, many civil defense measures were silly. One plan designated the major highways out of New York City as emergency routes to be used during an air attack. This not only called attention to the obvious but also it ensured that no thoughtful person would risk his life on the overcrowded highways. Meanwhile, school children practiced crouching in hallways to protect themselves from a nuclear attack and some citizens built fallout shelters in their yards. Common sense returned when people began to wonder how the survivors would be able to cope with the millions of dead around them and the lingering effects of radiation. Many concluded that it would be better to die in the first blast than to survive and suffer. This photograph shows another impractical but well-intentioned measure to reassure the public. A New York City air raid warden directs two fire fighters, who are shown using specially designed fire trucks that are small enough to be carried in an elevator. Each cart could be handled by one man and carried axes, helmets, firecoats, boots, lanterns, rakes, rope, fire extinguishers, and buckets of sand. They were photographed during a mock air raid drill at the Port Authority Building (1951). To appreciate their impracticality, one only needs to recall the signs in most public buildings that advise people never to use an elevator in case of fire (let alone during an air raid).

ETHICS AT THE SHELTER DOORWAY

L. C. McHugh, S.J.

During the first quarter century after World War II, many Americans accepted that a nuclear war between the United States and the Soviet Union was probable. Cities adopted civil defense measures to prepare for the anticipated Russian attack. Children were taught to crouch in school hallways away from glass. Automobile owners were told to keep a half-tank of gasoline in their cars at all times so they could flee the cities to the supposedly safer suburbs. Some American families built fallout shelters in their backyards to protect themselves from the dangers of nuclear war.

The following article was written by the Reverend L. C. McHugh, a Jesuit priest who had taught ethics at Georgetown University. Father McHugh's article shows the mind-set of the American public, which had accepted the inevitability of nuclear war and had begun "thinking about the unthinkable." McHugh also presents some of the moral problems that relate to nuclear war. He based his conclusions on traditional Judaeo-Christian principles that, he said, could be applied in all situations where violence, even nuclear war, might be an option.

The American people are burrowing underground in a grassroots movement for survival; the shelter business is booming. Civil defense officials have already noted that many citizens are very furtive about building a modest haven in the cellar or yard. The more secret the nuclear hideaway, the less

SOURCE: *America* (30 September 1961). Reprinted with permission of America Press, Inc., 106 West 56th Street, New York, NY 10019. © 1961. All rights reserved.

likely they are to be troubled by panicky neighbors at the shelter door when the bombs start falling.

Some rugged householders are not banking on mere secrecy to insure their families a fair chance of survival. *Time*, on August 18, [1961] cited a Chicago suburbanite who intended to mount a machine gun at his shelter in order to keep unwelcome strangers out, and it also quoted a Texas businessman who was ready to evict unbidden guests with tear gas if any such occupied his shelter before his family did. Inevitably, *Time* raised the question: what do the guardians of the Christian ethic have to say about the pros and cons of gunning one's neighbor at the shelter door? *Time* got some strange answers in its brief clerical poll, and one was rather remarkable:

> *If someone wanted to use the shelter, then you yourself should get out and let him use it. That's not what would happen, but that's the strict Christian application.*

I cannot accept that statement as it stands. It argues that we must love our neighbor, not as ourselves, but more than ourselves. It implies that the Christian law runs counter to the instinct of self-preservation that is written in the human frame. If I am right, then the American people need more than blueprints for shelter construction. They also need a little instruction in the grim guidelines of essential morality at the shelter hatchway. Are there any moral constants that apply when unprepared or merely luckless neighbors and strangers start milling around the sanctuary where you and your family have built a refuge against atomic fire, blast and fallout? . . .

Each of us has a natural right to life and the essential goods, such as liberty and food, without which life is brutish—or impossible.

The right to life and its equivalent goods is a curtain of inviolability drawn around the human personality. But if that curtain is torn aside by unreasonable interference with one's freedom, nature still provides a second line of defense against injustice. This is the right to use violence as a last resort or emergency measure for securing the just needs of the human person. This right to employ violence, which the moralists call "co-activity," is a *limited* grant of power, just like the rights for whose protection it is given. Nobody enjoys unlimited rights, simply because no human being can have unlimited needs.

Working from this basis, Catholic moralists teach that the use of violence to defend life and its equivalent goods is justifiable, when certain conditions are met, even if the violent defense entails the death of the aggressor. It will be very enlightening to reflect on what these conditions are.

1.   The situation is such that violence is the last available recourse of

the aggrieved party. Either you take desperate action now or, in your best judgment, you are going to be done in.

2.   The violence used is employed at the time of assault. It is not vengeance for a deed already done, neither is it a preventive against a merely projected assault. The violence is leveled against an attack which, in the prudent estimation of the victim, has been actually initiated. . . .

3.   The third condition is that the violence is employed against an attack that is unjust. In other words, the violence is used to ward off an unwarranted invasion of one's undoubted rights. In the technical vocabulary of moralists, the assailant is called an unjust aggressor, but the term refers to an objective situation, not to a state of soul. The delirious madman who thrusts at me with a rapier may be incapable of moral guilt at the moment, but his invasion of my basic immunities is as objectively unjust as if he were a paid emissary of Murder, Inc.

4.   Finally, when one uses violence to defend his essential rights, he may employ no more violence than is needed to protect himself. Coactivity is thus a marginal grant, strictly tailored to the end it serves. Moralists have argued for centuries whether this grant ever allows one to intend the death of his adversary. We do not need to resolve this scholastic dispute here. What moralists agree on is that a man under grave attack may take those emergency measures which will effectively terminate the assault, even if they include the death of the assailant. Moreover, common sense tells us that men under attack seldom have a nice discrimination of weapons to employ in self-defense. They must use the means at hand, rough and ready as they are. Unless they use them in the surest way, they are likely to come out on the worse end of an unequal contest.

So much for the general conditions that cover the use of violence in defense of life. Two more observations are very much in order before the picture is complete.

To say that one has the right to employ violence in defense of life is not to say that one has the duty to do so. Indeed, in the Christian view, there is great merit in turning the other cheek and bearing evils patiently out of the love of God. But it should be noted that people who consistently manifest this exalted brand of supernatural motivation are deservedly called heroic Christians. Their conduct reveals a dedication to the full Christian ethic that is far above what God requires under pain of eternal loss in the way of the Ten Commandments. Nowhere in traditional Catholic morality does one read that Christ, in counseling nonresistence to evil, rescinded the right of self-defense which is granted by nature and recognized in the legal system of all nations.

Again, we must observe that because of special responsibilities the individual bears to other members of society, circumstances may easily arise in which it is positively immoral to turn the other cheek: one may have a positive duty to employ violence in his own behalf and/or for the sake of others. Secret Service agents are bound in justice not to bear ills patiently when the President is set upon by assassins. So, too, a well-armed hunter who surprises three hoodlums attacking a lonely woman in the forest cannot absolve his grave and obvious duty in charity with a shocked "tsk-tsk" and a resolution to inform the State police when he gets to the nearest telephone. . . . More relevant to our immediate interest, we ought to note that the father of a family is tied to his wife and children by bonds of both love and justice. His every normal instinct prompts him to nourish and protect his dependents. He cannot carelessly squander their essential welfare for the needy stranger and call this irresponsibility an act of charity. He may not idly stand by while his brood is robbed of what is necessary for life and then explain that his cowardice is actually a wholehearted obedience to the Biblical injunction to overcome evil by good.

I think that this review of some constants in the general morality of human survival has an obvious relevance to the questions that are raised in the mind of the cautious householder when he thinks about building a family shelter, and wonders how he can insure its availability, in the moment of greatest need, for those in whose behalf it was intended. . . .

What is your family shelter? It is more than a piece of property that should be secure against trespass. It is a property of a most vital kind. When the bombs start falling, it is likely to be the one material good in your family's environment which is equivalent to life itself. The shelter is your ultimate line of defense against fire, blast, radiation and residual fallout. Moreover, because of its strictly limited resources (space, food, medical supplies, etc.), its use must be carefully regulated if it is to guarantee even marginal opportunity for survival over a protracted period. If you go underground with just one occupant above the maximum number for which the shelter was designed, the survival value of the shelter diminishes for all that take refuge in it.

If a man builds a shelter for his family, then it is the family that has the first right to use it. The right becomes empty if a misguided charity prompts a pitying householder to crowd his haven to the hatch in the hour of peril; for this conduct makes sure that no one will survive. And I consider it the height of nonsense to say that the Christian ethic demands or even permits a man to thrust his family into the rain of fallout when unsheltered neighbors plead for entrance. On the other hand, I doubt that any Catholic moralist would condemn the man who used available violence to repel panicky aggressors plying crowbars at the shelter door, or who took strong measures to evict trespassers who locked themselves in the family shelter before his own family had a chance to find sanctuary therein. . . .

ANNOTATED BIBLIOGRAPHY

The Korean War has not attracted the same number of memoirs, novels, or histories as earlier wars or the later one in Vietnam. After the Second World War, the United States worried about global strategy and its role in ensuring international peace. Many histories of this era substitute passion for objectivity. Paul Y. Hammond has written two objective works on the era, *The Cold War Years* (1969) and *Cold War and Detente* (1975). Among the proponents in favor of the option of having tactical and strategic nuclear weapons, no author is better known than Henry Kissinger who offered his arguments in *Nuclear Weapons and Foreign Policy* (1957) and *The Necessity for Choice* (1961). James M. Gavin's *War and Peace in the Space Age* (1958) and Maxwell D. Taylor's *The Uncertain Trumpet* (1959) present the views of two senior generals, who argue that the Cold War requires choice and a strategy of flexible response.

Four authors have written good single-volume histories of the Korean War: Robert Leckie's *Conflict: The History of the Korean War, 1950–53* (1962) is both readable and reliable, T. R. Fehrenbach's *This Kind of War* (1963) relies on personal interviews to relate the war from the enlisted man's perspective, David Rees's *Korea: The Limited War* (1964) is the best treatment of high-level policy and its effect on fighting the war, and Harry J. Middleton's *The Compact History of the Korean War* (1965) is a brief, but dependable history. The best account of the feud between General Mac-Arthur and President Harry S Truman can be found in John W. Spanier's *The Truman-MacArthur Controversy and the Korean War* (1959).

In addition to the biographies and memoirs of MacArthur cited in the chapter on the Second World War are the memoirs of Matthew B. Ridgway, *The Korean War* (1967), who commanded the Eighth Army in Korea before replacing MacArthur. S. L. A. Marshall not only wrote *The River and the Gauntlet* (1953), a portion of which is included in this anthology, but he also wrote *Pork Chop Hill* (1956) about the later stages of the Korean War when both sides fought for limited terrain in the middle of the peninsula. The landings at Inchon and the capture of the Korean capital from the North Koreans is well chronicled in Robert D. Heinl's *Victory at High Tide: The Inchon-Seoul Campaign* (1968).

The armed services did produce official histories of the Korean War, but these lack the breadth and depth of the earlier volumes on the Second World War. The army's official history includes four chronological volumes on military campaigns, plus a fifth on logistics. The navy and the air force published a one-volume history of the war: James A. Field, Jr.'s *History of the United States Naval Operations, Korea* (1962) and Frank B. Futrell's *The United States Air Force in Korea, 1950–1953* (1961). The Marine Corps's history is told in five volumes, each describing a different campaign.

C H A P T E R   9

THE VIETNAM WAR

Neither the United States nor the Soviet Union wanted a face-to-face confrontation during the Cold War years. Instead, each preferred to use client states to do its fighting. In Southeast Asia, first France and then South Vietnam, supported by U.S. money, equipment, and military advisers, fought Soviet-equipped guerrilla (Vietcong) forces and North Vietnamese regulars. The Vietnamese people have a long history of subjugation by the Chinese, French, and Japanese. American aid during the Second World War had encouraged Vietnamese communists and nationalists to work together to defeat Japan. After the war, France, supported by Britain, attempted to recolonize Vietnam. Vietnamese communists resisted with a strategy of guerrilla warfare. The French managed to regain control over the cities, but they could not deny Ho Chi Minh and his followers the countryside. In 1954, France ended its frustrating war and agreed to allow communist control in the north and noncommunist rule in the south.

The new president of South Vietnam was Ngo Dinh Diem, an upper-class Roman Catholic. Diem claimed to represent the interests of democracy and freedom in Southeast Asia, but his government never gained the support of the Buddhist and peasant majority of South Vietnam. In 1963, the United States approved a military coup to overthrow Diem. Two years later, the United States found itself in an undeclared war against communist South Vietnamese guerrillas and North Vietnamese regulars.

Instead of declaring war to defeat the communist forces, President Lyndon B. Johnson relied on a more limited commitment. The United States employed sophisticated military technology and financial resources in a futile attempt to avoid all-out war. Furthermore, the Johnson administration tried to conceal the extent of its commitment in Vietnam from the

American people. When the public discovered this deceit and American casualties continued to grow, widespread opposition to the war grew at home.

Many Americans became convinced that the war could not be won; some concluded that the United States probably had supported the wrong side all along. Unable to win a clear victory, President Richard M. Nixon muddied the goals by redefining the original strategy of destroying the communist insurgents to the more nebulous one of winning a "peace with honor." In 1972, Nixon forced the South Vietnamese government to agree to allow U.S. forces to abandon the country, leaving money, weapons, and broken promises behind. Nixon's domestic problems over the Watergate break-in and cover-up soon removed him from the presidency and destroyed what little support was left for his policy of "Vietnamization."

Marines in Vietnam, 1966 (National Archives). This photograph illustrates the cultural shock that many American "grunts" experienced in Vietnam. Shown here is a marine patrol on a search and destroy mission passing a Montagnard tribesman and his elephant. Unable to establish static lines, American troops went out on patrols to find the Vietcong. Because the enemy could easily blend into the civilian population, it was usually the Vietcong who found the Americans. The Americans rarely held onto a position; instead, they counted their success by the number of enemy killed. These "body counts" were often inflated to please commanders whose future careers would be determined by their unit's "kill ratio." Victories were kept on a gruesome score sheet (rather than measured by the amount of ground captured and occupied). This strategy, called attrition, is usually used by a weaker power against a stronger one. Colonel Dave R. Palmer, who later rose to be a general and the superintendent of West Point, criticized this strategy in his military history of the war, Summons of the Trumpet *(1978). Palmer contends, "Attrition is not a strategy. It is, in fact, irrefutable proof of the absence of any strategy. A commander who resorts to attrition admits his failure to conceive of an alternative. He rejects warfare as an art and accepts it on the most non-professional terms imaginable. He uses blood in lieu of brains. To be sure, political considerations left military commanders no choice other than attrition warfare, but that does not alter the hard truth that the United States was strategically bankrupt in Vietnam in 1966."*

A VIETNAM WAR JOURNAL

King J. Coffman

The following selection is part of a daily journal kept by Lieutenant-Colonel King J. Coffman during his year-long tour in Vietnam. Coffman wanted to have a record of what might be the most important year of his life. He also knew that he might never return home alive from Vietnam. His journal then would be his way of sharing the last days of his life with his family. It is against army regulations to keep a diary in a war zone. Therefore, each day he was in Vietnam Coffman wrote his narrative on standard notebook paper and mailed it home to his wife. She then placed the pages in a looseleaf binder.

Coffman firmly believed in the legitimacy of the American role in Southeast Asia. He was a deeply religious man who was convinced that the United States had to protect the people of South Vietnam—and the rest of the free world—from communism.

Lt. Col. Coffman's tour in Vietnam was a mixture of successes and failures. Like most officers, his time "in-country" was divided into six months of staff work and six months in command of a frontline unit. Coffman chafed at the restraints of the former and welcomed the opportunity to lead a mechanized infantry battalion. At times, Coffman was frustrated by the corruption he found among many South Vietnamese officers, but he continued to focus on the righteousness of the American goals. He was elated when he succeeded in convincing some captives to leave the Vietcong and join the South Vietnamese government. More sensitive and articulate than most of his peers, Coffman's entries offer important insights into the nature of the war in Vietnam, and war in general.

SOURCE: King J. Coffman papers, U.S. Army Military History Institute Archives, Carlisle Barracks, Pennsylvania. Courtesy of Col. King J. Coffman, U.S. Army (Ret).

6 Sep '67.   Overslept 'til 0545—Had to rush to make breakfast. Read some stuff and got ready for the flight to the 1st Cavalry Division to the *North.* . . .

I looked to our front . . . and down—and at my feet lay 8 Viet Cong soldiers, in grotesque positions, some horribly mutilated by weapons fire, all very dead. Thus my initiation to the brutal realities of war. Their weapons were lined up neatly behind them; 4 were U.S.: 2 automatic M-16 rifles, an M-14 rifle, and an M-79 grenade launcher. The latter caused several US casualties (wounded) in this company. They lost one soldier, shot through the head. These VC [Vietcong] had been hiding in the village. (Capt. Mallony, the C.O. [commanding officer] gave us an after-action briefing an hour or so before.) His company had come in on a routine "cordon & search" operation where we suddenly pounce from the air on a village, without warning, surround it, send in a small combat unit to see if any *organized* enemy unit is there; and if not, send in a strong contingent of VN National Police (who travel with the US unit) to search the village yard by yard to root out VC stragglers, sympathizers, weapons, rice, etc. . . . by interrogating *every* man, woman, & child there. THIS HAS BEEN EXTREMELY EFFECTIVE. This was a small village, so the encircling cordon was quickly thrown around. It was so sudden that the VC panicked. Some climbed the palm trees to see what we were doing. They made the fatal mistake of firing from the tree tops—because, as the C.O. put it, "we simply hosed the tree tops down [with bullets] and they fell out like coconuts." Others made a break for the river, but our men were down *in* the river, and as they reached the bank, they were mowed down like dogs. In this VC controlled area, the villagers who get in the way often get it, too, although not deliberately. This was the case today. I did not see them, however. I saw these VC because they had been dragged over to one point *to be counted.* Our authorities accept only actual "body counts," so they go through this routine, often at a hazard! Next, a bull-dozer comes through and levels the village completely, destroying bunkers, tunnels, houses & everything. The VC bodies are left right there. Any VC sympathizers coming through see the destroyed village & the VC remains. Maybe they'll get the message that supporting the VC is an unhealthy way to make a living. (In practice, however, the VC will sneak in & carry away the bodies later, to avoid that very thing.) That grisly scene still haunts me—those eyes, open but unseeing; a soul for whom Christ died gone to meet his Maker, forever without hope. I thought to myself, "what a dirty business this is—is *this* where I belong?" Then I thought of the *thousands* of defenseless village elders, school teachers, and administrators that have been murdered by these fiends—their tongues cut out, stomachs ripped open, while their families were forced to watch—and I thought that why should the protection of the innocents of South Vietnam be left to those whose hardened hearts perhaps enjoy killing people, even if they are enemy? No, perhaps God's people by being here, by exercising effective control of our troops, can *limit* this awful bloodshed to only that actually necessary to destroy this red menace.

I *am* in the right place though I miss my family so. Maybe my small part, added to that of others, can prevent this demonic scourge from reaching our beloved shores. . . .

7 Mar '68. Mortared & rocketed last night & early this morning—no [casualties] in 2/22 [Coffman's unit].

Ground fog kept me out of the air for an agonizing 2 hours while the battalion moved into position. They managed to thread their way through the rubber plantation and stretches of jungle by map and compass, arriving just at 0900, while I stewed & fretted. . . . Our mission was to push into the jungle 200–300 meters to see what damage had been done by artillery & air since the day before. By noon, we had begun to find bunker and trench systems in our sector, relatively still intact. Then B Co's lead element came under machine gun and rocket fire, wounding the Squad Leader, who was out in front: took rocket frags [shrapnel] in the arm and 3 submachine bullets struck him in the chest and were *deflected away* by a belt of machine gun ammo that he was wearing across his chest! The others returned fire and pulled the squad leader back. I pulled the company back while we ordered an artillery bombardment—but this was held up because we couldn't get clearance to fire from the Medevac ships—I was furious. The war can't stop because one helicopter might be in the way (it *wasn't*—I took care of that). In addition I ordered in an air strike—which always takes an inordinate amount of time. The total elapsed bombardment time took *two hours.* . . . In all I was in that cramped little chopper [helicopter] for *7 hours* today & I'm bushed. . . .

My first attack didn't turn out to be much of a fight, but my knowledge of how to handle the complexities of a battalion in the attack jumped substantially. I've worked out a scheme for supporting fires that I shall apply to future attacks—hoping to speed up the support *and* to make it operate more closely to the troops so they can come in right behind it while the enemy still has his head down. . . .

10 Mar '68. Had an uneventful day. No [armored personnel] carriers blown up by mines PTL [Praise the Lord]. One of my sweeper teams found one in the road, close to where the other one was yesterday! That's finding them the *easy* way! . . .

Am planning to start airmobile [helicopter assault] operations with the battalion to cover *deep* objectives. We're too restricted here by roads, rivers, etc. We need to stretch our wings.

Reliable intelligence predicts a large mortar and *ground* attack early next morning. I have the only ground counterattack force available. I have called in my commanders, discussed C-ATK [counterattack] plans, told them how and in what order I plan to commit them. One company is deployed off the base in NDP (Night Defensive Position). There are advantages and disadvantages to this. But his position is good, so the former outweigh the latter. All is in readiness.

11 Mar '68.   Hit medium hard with a rocket attack at about 0700. Being forewarned, however, the—disregard! Even as I write this, my people tell me the attack was a big *hoax*. One of our *own* heavy mortars firing on a suspected target dropped it short into my B Co's area! This was followed by several more erratic rounds and the "fight" was on! After it was over, everyone was patting the others on the back for being so "ready" that the VC had to break off the attack. Many red faces around here—and some of them mine.

I launched the entire battalion into the Michelin [rubber plantation] today. Co B made early contact, encountering 2 VC, who fled. They hit one and seized him. They captured a pistol and documents also. I ordered careful treatment and a medevac helicopter. Military Intelligence (MI) was alerted and we converged on the hospital. He was brought in in bad shape, with a terrible wound in his forehead. I almost had to order the doctor to work on him. (He had been working hard on a *little boy*, son of one of the VN orderlies, hit & badly wounded (lost one eye) by a VC mortar round—so his hatred of the VC was obvious). I carefully explained that we don't get prisoners from the Michelin very often, and that with kind treatment we might get valuable information from him. Soon a team of about 8 medics were in "full swing" while our MI began to draw info out of him. He "sang" like a canary, as terribly wounded as he was. His name is Hung, a member of the D71 Company of a Recon Services Bn [battalion] that had entered the Michelin at 0700 hrs this morning. He was one of 100 men. They had split up and he didn't know where the others were. He also gave us the location of his base camp to the North!

I looked through his wallet and saw what appeared to be pictures of his wife & little girl. He's just another guy like me. There was no animosity in me whatsoever, just pity. Laying down his life for Communism. What a waste. How I wish I could capture all of them and not have to kill them—and then reason with them. My instructions to my men are clear, however. Every effort will be made to capture, *provided* no additional risk is involved. I was appalled by the later remark by an officer senior to me who said, "I hope he dies, so we could have a 'body count.' " The statistics game that has been imposed upon us is turning men into monsters. If only I can instill (or restore) some sense of values in my people here. Hung was farther evacuated to Long Binh and the MI team went right with him. He is not expected to live.

We swept the area further and poured artillery and napalm into the Base Camp area given us by Hung. As I was checking out another area west of Co B, I spotted my first VC on the hoof and loose! Two dashed through a clearing and into the jungle. We worked that area over with artillery, bombs, napalm, 20 mm cannon, and helicopter gunships. About 1600 hrs we headed for Base camp. My stomach was really hurting—from the messy POW and from a 3 hr air ride in an O-2 observation plane which turns on a dime and leaves my stomach hanging in mid-air. . . .

12 Mar '68.   Woke up feeling queasy and uneasy—I suppose it was because of our switch to airmobile operations, scheduled for tomorrow, and we're *totally* inexperienced at it. We're so married to our carriers that people don't think that way in this battalion. It's been a one man battle to shift gears and I'm gaining. The staff is *beginning* to get interested—and produced an imaginative draft plan. As the day wore on, and convoy and sweep operations were going well, my uneasiness went away, PTL. Later we were notified that choppers were not available, so the operation is temporarily postponed. Meanwhile our intell[igence] reports movement of an enemy battalion to the west & I'm going to get my A Co back (for a day). I also got hold of a VC deserter . . . who came out of the very area the *night before last* and reports 500 VC in hiding in about a 4–6 square km [kilometer] area. I don't believe it of course, but it's worth checking out. You must check *everything*—and have patience. We quickly drew up new plans, sufficiently flexible to react to any intell that comes in tonight. I prayed much today, and at supper, "in support of our arms and our just cause."

The VC deserter was probably not much over 14 yrs old and he said there were many in his age group. I asked him how he got mixed up in this dirty business. "He and many others were forced into it." If so, I persisted, why do they fight so hard? He replied that they were young and not afraid to die! He himself has lost his family—and apparently has nothing to live for. . . .

13, 14 Mar.   What started out as a routine sweep operation turned out to be the most harrowing experience of my life. We found little except empty bunkers on the north side of the river. Then as we began (with Co C) [to enter] the south side into a heavy patch of jungle, Co C began to receive murderous fire from devilishly concealed bunkers only 10–15 feet away. 2 men were killed almost instantly and 5 wounded. Most of the leaders of the 2d Plat were casualties and many of the men headed for the rear, with 3 of the 4 tracks [armored personnel carriers] (one later returned). They pulled back too fast and *couldn't get the 1st two casualties out,* so therefore I could not bring in artillery, air, or gunships to support them lest I hit my own men (Bde Cdr [brigade commander] wouldn't let me run *any* risk whatsoever. I disagree with this strict caution because other lives are at stake also) & then committed C.O. Co B (with only 1 plat) to take control of the situation, which he did. But he couldn't get the 2 men out either. But at least no one ran. Then I moved Co A around the right "flank" (we found out later: enemy position was *circular*—no flanks)—and they ran into heavy fire. A VN unit attached to them got scattered and 4 US came up missing. What a mess! And worse, darkness began to fall in the deep jungle. My little helicopter doesn't fly at night so I had to set down on the ground where I had the rear elements & remainder of C Co formed into a wagon train in a clearing. I made the agonizing decision to pull back and leave the missing in there, in order to get reorganized, and perhaps to go back. I know that if any wounded remained alive, they would be almost impossible to retrieve since they were hit almost on top of the bunkers. So I decided to fire artillery cover to the north and to shoot flares every 30 min all night. 4 men came in guided by the flares (1 US, 3 ARVN) [Army of the Republic of Vietnam—that is, South Vietnamese]. Now, 5 US were missing. I again agonized over the situation—what next? By 0200 I formulated a plan to send A Co back over the same ground at dawn—mounted [riding in armored personnel carriers], so they'll have their heavy firepower with them. The other companies would be prepared to attack from the south. If Co A received heavy fire on their probe, I would again withdraw them and pour in air strikes and artillery. And then go in the 3d time. Co A swept in (*after* the Bde Cdr insisted I put in the air strike) and found a perfectly organized perimeter with 19 fighting bunkers all with 3' of overhead cover. But no VC (Thank the Lord— because I *still* didn't know where the missing were, and would have been restricted on the use of heavy fires), they found the 5 men, one of them alive. He was scared to death by the air strike but otherwise unharmed from the bombardment. From there we swept the entire jungle patch (about 1 km square), found a lot of documents, destroyed bunkers, etc. . . .

15 Mar '68.   Total casualties for this fiasco (yesterday) was 4 US killed, 10 wounded against only 2 VC killed and 3 possibles. Our greatest victories by far over the VC come when they attack us on *our* ground, and not the reverse. I felt terrible about our first big bn fight. It was all so inconclusive.

A medic aids a lieutenant (National Archives). War can bring out the best in men. Shown here is a young, white lieutenant who had just triggered a booby trap mine that seriously burned his leg. The black medic immediately came to the officer's aid, and a marine corps photographer (sent to take pictures of enemy positions) snapped this poignant photograph. It is sometimes said that there is no racial problem on the frontline. Male bonding is greatest in wartime when men can openly show their emotions and join together in close camaraderie. Although moments like this one were repeated many times in Vietnam, once the men returned to their base camp, they often split into racial or ethnic groups. Toward the end of the war, racial problems became more acute as antiwar protestors at home drew attention to the disproportionately large percentage of minorities serving in combat in Vietnam.

THE GRUNTS' WAR

Arthur E. Woodley, Jr., as told to Wallace Terry

The Vietnam War was largely fought by the poor, the undereducated, the minorities, and the young. Deferments could be obtained by students and fathers, and bright and wealthy Americans could usually find some medical reason to stay out of the war. There was a degree of altruism in the young men who first went to Southeast Asia to stem the flow of communism. News reports, however, quickly showed the venality of the South Vietnamese government, and Americans began to question the Johnson administration's commitment to it. When the Vietcong and North Vietnamese forces attacked hundreds of South Vietnamese hamlets and cities during the 1968 Tet offensive, it confirmed what many Americans had feared: There was no way to *win* the war. The election of Richard M. Nixon that same year brought his promise to remove all U.S. forces from Vietnam. Everyone knew then that the American commitment to the government and people of South Vietnam had been compromised. No one wanted to be the last man to die in Vietnam.

Nixon's policy, which he called Vietnamization, caused tragic disruption in the morale of the American fighting men in Vietnam. They knew the war could not be won. Vietnam became a nightmare where men spent "365 days and a wake-up," until they could board a "freedom bird" to return them to "the World." The "grunts," as infantrymen called themselves, wanted as little hassle as possible from career officers and sergeants whom they called "lifers." Overzealous lieutenants and noncommissioned officers might find themselves with a warning tied around a hand grenade to curtail their enthusiasm.

The following reading is from Wallace Terry's oral history of the black man's wartime experiences in Vietnam. Specialist 4 "Gene" Woodley came from an impoverished neighborhood in Baltimore. He enlisted for the best of reasons: patriotism and a chance to test his manhood. In the army, he was taught how to lead long-range patrols (LURPs) behind the enemy lines, where he and his men remained for days at a time. Because their work was secret and dangerous, these patrols rarely took prisoners. Woodley soon went "native," imitating by his dress and nonconformist attitude the primitive mountain people of Vietnam (the Montagnards). When Woodley returned to the United States he, like so many other Vietnam War veterans, found that his military experiences had not prepared him for civilian life. His wartime memories continue to haunt him.

I went to Vietnam as a basic naïve young man of eighteen. Before I reached my nineteenth birthday, I was a animal. When I went home three months later, even my mother was scared of me. . . .

We was in very thick elephant grass. We had sat down for a ten-minute break. And we heard the Vietn'ese talking, coming through the elephant grass. So we all sat ready for bein' attacked.

I heard this individual walking. He came through the elephant grass, and I let loose on my M-16 and hit him directly in his face. Sixteen rounds. The whole clip. And his face disappeared. From the chin up. Nothing left. And his body stood there for 'proximately somewhere around ten, fifteen seconds. And it shivers. And it scared me beyond anyone's imagination.

Then it was chaos from then on. Shooting all over. We had a approximate body count of five VC. Then we broke camp and head for safer ground.

After thinkin' about that guy with no face, I broke into a cold sweat. I knew it could've been me that was in his place instead of me in my place. But it changed me. Back home I had to defend myself in the streets, with my fist, with bottles, or whatever. But you don't go around shooting people. As physical as I had been as a teenager, there were never life-threatening situations. I had never experienced anything quite as horrible as seeing a human being with his face blown apart. I cried. I cried because I killed somebody.

You had to fight to survive where I grew up. Lower east Baltimore. What they call the Bottom. I lived basically three blocks from the waterfront. It was very difficult for us to go from one neighborhood to another without trying to prove your manhood. . . .

Being from a hard-core neighborhood, I decided I was gonna volunteer for the toughest combat training they had. I went to jump school, Ranger school, and Special Forces training. I figured I was just what my country needed. A black patriot who could do any physical job they could come up with. Six feet, one hundred and ninety pounds, and healthy.

They prepared us for Vietnam as a group of individuals who worked together as a unit to annihilate whatever enemy we came upon. They taught us karate, jumping out of airplanes, of course, and, not with any exaggeration, a thousand and one ways to destroy a human being, even decapitation with a piece of wire and two pieces of wood. But the basic thing is that we are the world's greatest fighting unit, and nothing will stand in the way.

In basic I noticed something funny. We Bloods slept on separate sides of the barracks. And it seemed like the dark-skinned brothers got most of the dirty details, like sweepin' up underneath the barracks or KP, while the light-skinned brothers and Europeans got the easy chores. But I didn't think too much about it.

We got to Cam Ranh in November 1968. And I got the biggest surprise of my life. There was water surfing. There was big cars being driven. There was women with fashionable clothes and men with suits on. It was not like being in a war zone. I said, Hey, what's this? Better than being home. . . .

I didn't ask no questions about the war. I thought communism was spreading, and as an American citizen, it was my part to do as much as I could to defeat the Communist from coming here. Whatever America states is correct was the tradition that I was brought up in. And I, through the only way I could possibly make it out of the ghetto, was to be the best soldier I possibly could. . . .

We were assigned to First Field Force, which hired our unit out as a recon unit to anyone who needed our services. Sort of modern-day gunfighters. Or low-priced mercenaries. We was stationed near An Khe. We lived rough. We only got hot meals maybe once or twice a week. We ate mostly little dry-good foods that were in plastic bags. You add hot water and spices, let it sit for five minutes, and you got a perfect meal. A lotta things we had to steal from other units—refrigerators, jeeps, or whatever. We were the type of unit that had no basic supplies. An' no rear area either. The only rear we had was a ass.

I was still a cherry boy—and that's what you stay until you get 90 days in country—when we had been dropped in a area s'spose to've been classified as a friendly area. We was goin' 'cross some water. I'm the point man. I'm on the other side of the stream, and now the team's comin' 'cross. All of a sudden, the whole world start to explode. People start to screamin' and hollerin' and runnin' around. . . .

Then came the second week of February of '69.

This was like three days after we had a helicopter go down in some very heavy foliage where they couldn't find no survivors from the air. We were at LZ [landing zone] Oasis. We were directed to find the wreckage, report back. They see if we can find any enemy movement and find any prisoners.

We're headin' north. It took us ten hours to get to the location. The helicopter, it was stripped. All the weaponry was gone. There was no bodies. It looked like the helicopter had been shot out of the air. It had numerous bullet holes in it. But it hadn't exploded. The major frame was still intact.

The next thing we do is to stake out the observers to make sure that we were not being observed, that the area is safe.

We recon this area, and we came across this fella, a white guy, who was staked to the ground. His arms and legs tied down to stakes. And he had a leather band around his neck that's staked in the ground so he couldn't move his head to the left or right.

He had numerous scars on his face where he might have been beaten and mutilated. And he had been peeled from his upper part of chest to down to his waist. Skinned. Like they slit your skin with a knife. And they take a pair of pliers or a instrument similar, and they just peel the skin off your body and expose it to the elements.

I came to the conclusion that he had maybe no significant value to them. So they tortured him and just left him out to die.

The man was within a couple of hours of dying on his own.

And we didn't know what to do, because we couldn't move him. There was no means. We had no stretcher. There was only six of us. And we went out with the basic idea that it was no survivors. We was even afraid to unstake him from the stakes, because the maggots and flies were eating at the exposed flesh so much.

The man had maggots in his armpits and maggots in his throat and maggots in his stomach. You can actually see in the open wounds parts of his intestines and parts of his inner workings bein' exposed to the weather. You can see the flesh holes that the animals—wild dogs, rats, field mice, anything—and insects had eaten through his body. With the blood loss that he had, it was a miracle that the man was still alive. The man was just a shell of a person.

The things that he went through for those three days. In all that humidity, too. I wouldn't want another human being to have to go through that.

I was a heavy shock on all of us to find that guy staked out still alive.

With an open belly wound, we could not give him water. And we didn't have morphine.

And he start to cryin', beggin' to die.

He said, "I can't go back like this. I can't live like this. I'm dying. You can't leave me here like this dying."

It was a situation where it had to be remove him from his bondage or remove him from his suffering. Movin' him from this bondage was unfeasible. It would have put him in more pain than he had ever endured. There wasn't even no use talkin' 'bout tryin' and takin' him back, because there was nothing left of him. It was that or kill the brother, and I use the term "brother" because in a war circumstance, we all brothers.

The man pleaded not only to myself but to other members of my team to end his suffering. He made the plea for about half an hour, because we couldn't decide what to do.

He kept saying, "The motherfuckers did this to me. Please kill me. I'm in pain. I'm in agony. Kill me. You got to find 'em. You got to find 'em. Kill them sorry bastards. Kill them motherfuckers."

I called headquarters and told them basically the condition of the man, the pleas that the man was giving me, and our situation at that time. We had no way of bringin' him back. They couldn't get to us fast enough. We had another mission to go on.

Headquarters stated it was up to me what had to be done because I was in charge. They just said, "It's your responsibility."

I asked the team to leave.

It took me somewhere close to 20 minutes to get my mind together. Not because I was squeamish about killing someone, because I had at that time numerous body counts. Killing someone wasn't the issue. It was killing another American citizen, another GI.

I tried my best not to.

I tried to find a thousand and one reasons why I shouldn't do this.

I watched the bugs and the stench that was coming from his body. I heard his crying and his pleading.

I put myself in his situation. In his place. I had to be as strong as he was, because he was askin' me to kill him, to wipe out his life. He had to be a hell of a man to do that. I don't think I would be a hell of a man enough to be able to do that. I said to myself, I couldn't show him my weakness, because he was showin' me his strength.

The only thing that I could see that had to be done is that the man's sufferin' had to be ended.

I put my M-16 next to his head. Next to his temple.

I said, "You sure you want me to do this?"

He said, "Man, kill me. Thank you."

I stopped thinking. I just pulled the trigger. I cancelled his suffering.

When the team came back, we talked nothing about it.

We buried him. We buried him. Very deep.

Then I cried. . . .

Now it begins to seem like on every mission we come across dead

American bodies, black and white. I'm seeing atrocities that's been done on them. Markings have been cut on them. Some has been castrated, with their penises sewed up in their mouth with bamboo.

I couldn't isolate myself from all this. I had gotten to the conclusion today or tomorrow I'll be dead. So it wasn't anything I couldn't do or wouldn't do.

There was this saying: "Yeah though I walk through the valley of death, I shall fear no evil, 'cause I'm the baddest motherfucker in the valley."

I figured if I'm gonna be a bad motherfucker, I might as well be the baddest motherfucker in the valley. . . .

But the Vietn'ese, they called me Montagnard, because I would dress like a Montagnard. I wouldn't wear conventional camouflage fatigues in the field. I wore a dark-green loincloth, a dark-green bandana to blend in with the foliage, and a little camouflage paint on my face. And Ho Chi Minh sandals. And my grenades and ammunition. That's the way I went to the field.

I dressed like that specifically as the point man, because if the enemy saw anyone first, they saw myself. They would just figure I was just another jungle guy that was walking around in the woods. And I would catch 'em off guard.

When we first started going into the fields, I would not wear a finger, ear, or mutilate another person's body. Until I had the misfortune to come upon those American soldiers who were castrated. Then it got to be a game between the Communists and ourselves to see how many fingers and ears that we could capture from each other. After a kill we would cut his finger or ear off as a trophy, stuff our unit patch in his mouth, and let him die.

I collected about 14 ears and fingers. With them strung on a piece of leather around my neck, I would go downtown, and you would get free drugs, free booze, free pussy because they wouldn't wanna bother with you 'cause this man's a killer. It symbolized that I'm a killer. And it was, so to speak, a symbol of combat-type manhood. . . .

Some days when we came back on a POW snatch we played this game called Vietn'ese Roulette on the helicopter. We wouldn't be told how many to capture. Maybe they only wanted one. But we would get two or three to find out which one is gonna talk. You would pull the trigger on one. Throw the body out. Or you throw one without shooting 'im. You place fear into the other Vietn'ese mind. This is you. This is next if you don't talk.

It was never a regular means of deciding this one or that one. You never know their rank or anything until you start to eliminate them one by one. You would sit them down with the ARVN or *chieu hoi* who has come over to your side. So he's translating the conversation back and forth. If one talk too much, you might get rid of him. He has no basic information to give you. He just gonna talk to try to save his life. Or you just might say from the start, "Throw this motherfucker out." The other one will get to talkin'. And then you get that one word of intelligence, one piece of pertinent information.

One particular day we went out of LZ Oasis and captured three prisoners. We on the helicopter coming back, and we radio headquarters we got three bodies. They said, "We only want one." You had to determine which one of these guys you gonna keep and which ones you don't. We tied one by the foot to this rappeling rope, and he's danglin' on the rope. We even dragged him through the trees. He wasn't gonna say anything. The other two wasn't either. So we tied one more the same way, then the other one got to talkin'. We just cut the rope and let the others go. You have to eliminate the others. This was a war-type situation. These two soldiers might go kill two of your soldiers if you turn them loose.

I guess my team got rid of about eight guys out of the chopper one way or another, but I only remember pushing two out myself.

One night we were out in the field on maneuvers, and we seen some lights. We were investigating the lights, and we found out it was a Vietn'ese girl going from one location to another. We caught her and did what they call gang-rape her. She submitted freely because she felt if she had submitted freely that she wouldn't have got killed. We couldn't do anything else but kill her because we couldn't jeopardize the mission. It was either kill her or be killed yourself the next day. If you let her go, then she's gonna warn someone that you in the area, and then your cover is blown, your mission is blown. Nothin' comes before this mission. Nothin'. You could kill thousand folks, but you still had to complete your mission. The mission is your ultimate goal, and if you failed in that mission, then you failed as a soldier. And we were told there would be no prisoners. So we eliminated her. Cut her throat so you wouldn't be heard. So the enemy wouldn't know that you was in the area.

This other time we were in a ambush site. This young lady came past. She spotted us. It was too late. We had to keep her quiet. We ran after her. We captured her. We gagged her.

We thought, Why kill a woman and you had no play in a couple weeks? We didn't tie her up, because you can't seduce a woman too well when she tied up. So we held her down. They didn't wear what we call underclothes. So there wasn't nothing when you tear off her pajama pants. She was totally nude 'cept for the top part of her body. But you wasn't after the top part of the body anyway. We found out she was pregnant. Then we raped her.

We still had five days to be out there without any radio contact. So we wouldn't let her go. We didn't want the enemy to know that we were there. She had to die. But I don't think we murdered her out of malice. I think we murdered her because we didn't want to be captured.

After a while, it really bothered me. I started saying to myself, What would I do if someone would do something like this to my child? To my mother? I would kill 'im. Or I would say, Why in the hell did I take this? Why in the hell did I do that? Because I basically became a animal. Not to say that I was involved in both incidents, but I had turned my back, which made me just as guilty as everybody else. "Cause I was in charge. I was in charge of a group of animals, and I had to be the biggest animal there. I allowed things to happen. I had learned not to care. And I didn't care.

When I seen women put to torture as having Coca-Cola bottles run up into their womb, I did nothing. When I heard this other team raped a woman and then rammed a M-16 in her vagina and pulled the trigger, I said nothing. And when I seen this GI stomp on this fetus after this pregnant woman got killed in a ambush, I did nothin'. What could I do? I was some gross animal.

One time we went to a village to watch for VC, and this young lady spotted us out in the field. We signaled her not to run, but I guess she didn't understand. We ran behind her to try to snatch her and keep her from notifying other people we were in the area. By the time she got in the center of the village, everybody start to runnin' out. Automatically in a combat-like situation you feel that your life is threatened, so you open fire on anything and everything that moves. It was like instantaneous. You couldn't stop it. That's how you're trained. We killed everything that moved. Dogs. Chickens. Approximately 20 some people, mostly women and children. No young men at all. Couple old men. We checked the huts, the bodies. Two was wounded, and we killed them. We was told not to leave anybody alive that would be able to tell. . . .

With 89 days left in country, I came out of the field.

At the time you are in the field you don't feel anything about what you are doin'. It's the time that you have to yourself that you sit back and you sort and ponder.

What I now felt was emptiness.

Here I am. I'm still eighteen years old, a young man with basically everything in his life to look forward to over here in a foreign country with people who have everything that I think I should have. They have the right to fight. I've learned in this country that you don't have the right to gather forces and fight back the so-called oppressor. You have the right to complain. They had the right. They fought for what they thought was right.

I started to recapture some of my old values. I was a passionate young man before I came into the Army. I believed that you respect other peoples' lives just as much as I respect my own. I got to thinkin' that I done killed around 40 people personally and maybe some others I haven't seen in the fire fights. I was really thinkin' that there are people who won't ever see their children, their grandchildren.

I started seeing the atrocities that we caused each other as human beings. I came to the realization that I was committing crimes against humanity and myself. That I really didn't believe in these things I was doin'. I changed. . . .

I left Vietnam the end of '69. I flew from An Khe to Cam Ranh Bay, still in my jungle fatigues. I hadn't bathed in six months. I had a full-grown beard. My hair was so matted against my head I couldn't pull my fingers through it. I smelled like a cockroach on Christmas. Like Mount Rushmore in the springtime. I was funky. I was really funky.

Then they put me in this big fabulous airplane. I'm sittin' there with filth all over me. From my head to my toe. I felt like I was in the Twilight Zone.

We landed in California when it was dark. We were taken to some barracks. We took a shower, and they gave us some new clothes and a steak dinner. Then I got on another plane.

The same day I left Vietnam, I was standin' back on the corner in Baltimore. Back in the States. A animal. And nobody could deal with me. . . .

Me and some vet'rans started what we call Base Camp One. We met at this church. It's to bring the comradeship that we had in the service into civilian life. To get a positive foundation to grow on. Because we feel that we are still in a combat situation.

We talk about the old enemy. The war. Our lives. The ghosts. The nightmares.

We didn't gain no respect for the Viet Cong until after we got into combat and found out that we had millions of dollars worth of equipment which s'posed to be advanced and so technical, and they were fighting us with whatever was available or whatever they could steal. I don't think we were well trained enough for that type of guerrilla warfare. But we were better soldiers, better equipped. And we had the technology.

In fact, we had the war beat until they started this pacification program. Don't shoot, unless shot upon. The government kept handicapping us one or 'nother. I don't think America lost. I think they gave up. They surrendered.

And this country befell upon us one big atrocity. It lied. They had us naïve, young, dumb-ass niggers believin' that this war was for democracy and independence. It was fought for money. All those big corporations made billions on the war, and then America left.

I can't speak for other minorities, but living in America in the eighties is a war for survival among black folks. And black vet'rans are being overlooked more than everybody. We can't find jobs, because nobody trusts us. Because we killers. We crazy. We went away intelligent young men to do the job of American citizens. And once we did, we came back victims.

Sometimes I'm walkin' on the street. I see Kenneth McKnight. I see Cook, James Cook. Brothers I knew in west Baltimore, in D.C.

One time I saw Kenneth on this corner. When I got there, he had turned down the street and was not there.

Another time I saw James on the other side of the street.

I called 'im, "James. Wait for me, man."

When I got over there, he was gone.

I ask this guy, "Did you see a brother standing right here?"

"No, man."

I still cry.

I still cry for the white brother that was staked out.

I still cry because I'm destined to suffer the knowledge that I have taken someone else's life not in a combat situation.

I think I suffered just as much as he did. And still do. I think at times that he's the winner, not the loser.

I still have the nightmare twelve years later. And I will have the nightmare twelve years from now. Because I don't wanna forget. I don't think I should. I think that I made it back here and am able to sit here and talk because he died for me. And I'm living' for him.

I still have the nightmare. I still cry.

I see me in the nightmare. I see me staked out. I see me in the circumstances where I have to be man enough to ask someone to end my suffering as he did.

I can't see the face of the person pointing the gun.

I ask him to pull the trigger. I ask him over and over.

He won't pull the trigger.

I wake up.

Every time.

Marines help a buddy to the medevac (Marine Corps photo). Marines have an admirable tradition: They never leave a fellow marine behind. This photograph shows "leathernecks" from the Seventh Marine Regiment carrying a wounded comrade to a medevac helicopter (1967). Medevac pilots often had to bring their "birds" into hot areas, sometimes dropping stretchers on cables through the jungle canopy to pull out the wounded. Their heroic flying gained them the utmost respect of the grunts on the ground. Helicopters had changed the face of war in Vietnam. They permitted American commanders to insert military units deep into enemy territory, bring supplies under enemy fire, evacuate the wounded and swiftly fly them to modern hospitals, and extricate troops from a battlefield. The army's air cavalry was able to go into almost impenetrable areas with helicopters. Helicopter assaults replaced the paratrooper in the Vietnam War, but not every commander used his helicopters well. Some senior officers liked to fly over their platoons and companies, trying to direct fire fights on the ground—much to the regret of the lieutenants who had to fight them.

WAR IS HELL

James Brady

The following selection contains excerpts from the letters of an army enlisted man in Vietnam, who was writing to his fiancee. Like most American soldiers serving in Southeast Asia, James Brady was young. To him, the Vietnam War was a great adventure. Assigned to the 134th Assault Helicopter Company, he helped retrieve and repair wrecked helicopters. High-level policy decisions formed before the war made helicopter assaults an intrinsic part of American tactics. In Vietnam, helicopters brought in troops and supplies, and took out the wounded and the dead.

Brady's letters were sensitive. They mirrored his emotions during his Vietnam tour: the fear he felt before his first battle, his elation at having successfully met the test of combat, and his sorrow over the death of a friend. Brady realized that he would never again experience the intensity of these feelings. He gave them a transcendent value when he requested his fiancee to save them so that some day his child would know what the war was really like.

March 24, 1968, 0330. I started a letter about 01:00 A.M. but I didn't get far. I'm down on the flite line and I was waiting for engine shop to finish so I could do my work. I heard some explosions I think I'll go see if it's us shooting out, or Charlie [Vietcong] shooting in —!! I put the dashes because I had planned on coming back. I did come back but just to kill the light and grab the letter. I was trying to answer yours but Charlie kind of messed me up. I went out and saw all hell breaking loose, so I figured the best thing was to run like hell. This time we didn't lose a ship [helicopter], but they sure perforated the company area.

SOURCE: James Brady papers, U.S. Army Military History Institute Archives, Carlisle Barracks, Pennsylvania. Courtesy of James Brady.

I jumped in the truck and took off but I saw the mortar landing near the orderly room, which was where I was going. The damn things were walking right down the street. The nearest one to us was about 25 yards, the canvas on the truck got torn and one of my buddies, Gray, got a small cut from a fragment. But he's O.K. We cut across the flite line and came in the back way, where the shells already fell. Then we got our weapons and came back to the hanger. There was a fire fight about a mile away and we sat around and watched the tracers go out. The chopper pilots were really great. While the shells were still falling, they were out firing up the ships. I don't know if they killed any V.C. but they did sink two sampans.

I can't remember being afraid, but I guess I was, all I remember is being fascinated with the whole thing while I was running and believe me, running and finding a bunker was the first and foremost thing on my mind. I'm not trying to sound like a hero. And I'm not trying to be one. I want to write these things down while they're still fresh in my mind. . . . Don't worry too much dear I'm learning to run very fast. You wouldn't believe how it felt, you'd have to experience it to believe the sensation.

March 27, 1968.   About V.C. I got arguing with a hootch maid today. I came in and found her in my locker. So I gave her hell, and she started giving me hell in Vietnamese. She started telling all of us in English how her brother was V.C. and tonite we all die, so I slapped the strait poop out of her and drug her down to the Major. I told him what she said and what I did, and he said, O.K., then called intelligence. I had to talk to them for awhile and they arrested her. You can't trust any of them over here.

April 22, 1968.   I'm sorry I haven't written in a couple of days but I've been working pretty late. The other day we had a 40 ship combat assault and needed gunners. So I flew along. We took some 173rd Airborne Bde troops in. We never touched ground. Just came in low & slow and they hopped out at about 5 feet. All the time we kept up a pretty good chatter with the M-60's [machine guns]. You could see where the tracers were coming from and all you did was shoot back. I was getting pretty good after a while. I started putting them right on target. I'm kind of proud because I returned fire on one target and stopped his. I claimed one kill and Hernandez who was in the ship behind us confirmed it. No emotion. Just a job. It was exciting but it's not something I'd like to do every day. It gets hairy.

April 19, 1968.   I had guard last nite. Nothing real exciting. But once we heard a shot and then a scream. We watched the Koreans ambush a V.C. patrol later on, that really makes me mad. Sometimes we can see people moving around out there, and it's an easy grenade throw from the village to our bunker, but we can't shoot up a flare or fire until we get permission which we almost never get. Even if you get a sniper you're supposed to call and tell the Koreans, and they'll send a patrol out. The guys on Post 1 heard somebody on the wire so they just shot up a flare and opened up when they saw two guys with rifles out in front, the O.D. [officer of the day] raised all kind of hell about it, but we kept saying how good it was to have two dead V.C. instead of 4 dead G.I.'s. But regulations are regulations.

Aug. 5, 1968.   Well, we took it through the nose last nite. They clobbered the whole battalion with 44 rounds of 51 mm mortar. I was in bed asleep. The first one was real close and woke me up right away. I made it to the bunker before the second one hit. And old Papa-San [Vietcong] was really humping. They were coming in about 2–3 every 5 seconds. They started in our company area and worked through to headquarters company, and then the 203rd. We haven't had a working over like that since I've been here. They didn't hit anything of importance in our area, but headquarters and 203rd got it bad. . . . In one hooch a couple of guys took some shrapnel. In the other, the round hit the roof, top bunk, bottom bunk, and blew up on the floor. The guy who lived in the area slept on the top. Only God, Lady Luck, and the First Sgt saved his life. He had guard and was out on the perimeter. The medics weren't so lucky. They heard its [f]lite and started for the bunkers. Just as they opened the doors of the dispensary a round hit about 10 feet away. It blew the legs out from under one guy and caught the others in the face, neck, and chest. They'll both be O.K. Two guys from the 203rd weren't that lucky. The aircraft they were working on took a direct hit. That didn't get them, but the rockets the ship carried (14 of them) went off. It's now 10:45 PM, they haven't even been dead for a full day yet.

All told, the battalion lost 18 wounded, and two killed.

Jan. 4, 1969.   I guess you can understand the tension we have. . . . The tension is getting worse with Tet [the lunar New Year, and chief holiday in Vietnam] coming. The uncertainty is stronger now than ever. But soon I'll be home. Time is starting to drag by. Things are slowing down, except the work. We have more of that than ever. Charlie is getting pretty good at hitting our ships. We're getting quite a lot of combat damage. I really enjoyed that recovery [of a downed helicopter] the other nite. Especially when the shooting started. The Chinook [helicopter] lifted out our ship that was shot down, and it was 5–10 minutes before anybody came for us. We were having a good old lay in the mud shoot out. The tracers really made it exciting because you could see where you were shooting and you could see Charlie's rounds coming. He uses green tracers, ours are red. The [helicopter] gunships were putting cover out too. The rockets were hitting so close that we had to get down when they were coming in. I liked it, after we were out of there and back in Phu Hiep. I'm proud of myself and the people out with me. Everything was done professional.

We got a big well done from everybody all the way up. That's the kind of experiences I secretly hoped for when I came over here. A taste of combat, it has a taste all its own. Kind of bitter-sweet. It wasn't much compared to what the grunts live with but it was the real thing and I'm glad I had the chance. You probably think I'm nutty or the place is getting to me but I got to shoot back for a change.

Jan. 21, 1969.   SHORT! 44 days [left in Vietnam]. Sorry I haven't written but in the last 3 days (for example) we have worked all day and all nite catching sleep when possible. Its getting rough around here and its going to get worse. Ever since [helicopter] 295 went down & I hurt my leg and we had to go after [helicopter] 150 it hasn't let up. We're working longer and harder than ever.

My leg healed up pretty good (finally) but its still a little sore and gets bad every now and then.

I'm so happy I'm getting short. Pretty soon I'll be home and we'll be together again. I'll probably be all confused and goofed up in the head and run around like I'm out of my environment. The heat, rain, dirt, having to keep your ear tuned for the siren or the blast of a mortar and the sound I love, the screaming engine and popping blades of my aircraft.

Feb. 6, 1969.   I should be happy on my birthday, but I can't. Today I had one of my good buddies die as we were trying to get him out of the ship and into an ambulance. His name was Ogden and he was from South Philly [Philadelphia]. There was a C.A. [combat assault] today south of Cam Ranh near an air base called Phan Rang. We were on a recovery standby at Phan Rang when they called in aircraft 319 (Philly Dog) was coming in with a wounded gunner. When they landed me and Cook ran over and started unbuckling him. Then Webb, the crew chief (North Philly) got out and came over, the three of us got him out and I had him around the shoulders when he came to. He looked at Webb and said "Hey Pee Wee, Philly Dog." That was all he said then he died. We laid him on the ground and took his armor plate off. He got hit in the back and it went up by his heart. He was a real good guy we were always arguing about me being from North Philly and him being from South Philly. It really shook me up. Me and Pee Wee just knelt there beside him and looked at each other. We couldn't believe it. All I could say for a half hour was, "No, not Ogden." It really tore me up.

Later we got a call that [helicopter] 326 ("the 11th Commandment") had crashed and burned at Phan Rang when we flew out to it. The fire was out and all that was left was cinders. A medevac had already been there and got the wounded out. Baxter, who used to be on the Line Crew was the crew chief, his leg was burned so bad they amputated it as soon as he got to the hospital. The pilot was O.K. and the gunner got tore up pretty bad. And they took out a burned body. They thought it was W.O. [Warrant Officer] Harrison but it turned out to be a Korean. We came and started going over the wreckage for weapons and radios. I turned over what was left of a seat and there it was. His legs were still burning. I almost gagged it was so horrible, and the smell was overpowering. Here he was, only 3 hours before we were bullshitting in the revetments before take-off, and now I was looking at him. I'll never forget it. Mr. Harrison was a good officer. He came over on the same plane with me. I met him at Nha Trang and we got to know each other pretty good. He got married 4 months before he came in the army and has 2 kids. We put the remains in a poncho, and put it on our ship. As we were leaving the L.Z. [landing zone], Chuck [Vietcong] came back and started tearing the place apart. I saw about 5 Koreans go down and for a minute I thought we were going to wind up staying there. But Lt. Doyle did a nose dive over the cliff and we got out of the line of fire. Not before I burned up damn near all the ammo I had. Chuck and his buddies just hopped over these rocks which surround the L.Z. and opened up. They were right in plain sight. I blew 3 of them clean away with the door gun. I actually saw them go down. I hope one of them was the one that got Ogden, kind of settle the score.

When we got back to Phan Rang and shut down, we were waiting for the ambulance to come, a bunch of Air Force lifers and officers crowded around and wanted to know what happened. We were telling them when I saw a captain lifting up the poncho to see what was in or just to get a look at the body. That did it, it was [the last] straw on the camel and all that. I pinned his hand to the floor with my rifle butt. He started hollerin' and saying about how many witnesses he had, and I told him to leave him alone; couldn't a man even have privacy when he's dead? Without some morbid sonofabitch staring at him? Our C.O. Major Chancellor showed up with Col. Gonzales our Battalion C.O. and wanted to know what was going on. He just told them about me and my rifle butt. Lt. Doyle saw the whole thing and got into it too. The maj and the col marched the A.F. clod away. I wouldn've done it, except after all I had seen and been through, I was tired, scared, shook-up and felt like crying and my nerves had had it. So now I'm back at Phu Hiep and the day's over. All in all my birthday 1969 made me a man both in age and experience. It's one I'll never forget, I'll never be able to. I came over here looking for war and I found it. Now I just want to come home and leave it behind. I want to come home to you and lose myself in your love. I'm getting scared now. I've only got 27 days left and all I want is out of the army. It kills your friends and drains you dry. I love you hon.

Save this letter so I can show it to my son when he thinks that war is a game. Gen. Sherman was right. I never knew exactly what he meant when he said "Now it looks like all glory boys, but believe me war is Hell." Now I do, it is hell. The excitement is gone, so is the adventure. Now its just hell.

A marine burns a Vietcong memorial (Marine Corps photo). Although the Marine Corps clearly labeled this photograph to explain that the marine was burning an enemy memorial honoring Vietcong dead, its image is startling and largely negative. The marine brandishing the flamethrower in Operation New Castle (1967) appears almost larger than life, using a frightening weapon to destroy a simple, and seemingly innocuous, grass hut. Because most Americans did not understand Asian culture, which focuses on ancestor worship, they often violated graves and thereby alienated all Vietnamese. Almost every American was contemptuous of the culture he found in Vietnam. Not only did it appear to be primitive but also the American presence had transformed South Vietnam into a brazen, brassy imitation of the worst part of American life. The easy availability of prostitutes, alcohol, and drugs only increased American contempt for Vietnam.

AN UNJUST AND IMMORAL WAR

Dale Noyd

The Vietnam War stirred up more protest than any other war in American history. Young men burned their draft cards or fled to Canada, Vietnam veterans threw their medals onto the steps of the U.S. Capitol, bloody riots occurred in the streets of Chicago during the 1968 Democratic Party convention, and some protestors chose jail rather than fight a war they considered unjust and immoral. These acts prompted other Americans, whom President Nixon called "the silent majority," to rally around U.S. policy in South Vietnam and to label the antiwar protestors as "traitors."

The following document is a letter of resignation from Air Force Captain Dale Noyd. Noyd's letter is unusual because he was a pilot and a psychology instructor at the Air Force Academy. Noyd challenged the war on humanitarian grounds. Since colonial times, some Americans have been excused from military service if their religious beliefs opposed all war. Noyd, however, was neither a religious man nor a pacifist. He opposed the Vietnam War, but not all wars, on secular, humanitarian grounds. Although Noyd was denied conscientious objector status, his letter of resignation eloquently states the essential arguments against the Vietnam War.

1. I, Dale Edwin Noyd, Captain, . . . hereby voluntarily tender my resignation from all appointments in the USAF. . . .

2c. Increasingly I find myself in the position of being highly involved and *caring* about many moral, political, and social issues—of which the war

---

SOURCE: U.S. District Court, Denver, Colorado, *Noyd v. McNamara, Secretary of Defense et al.*, 1967. Records and briefs.

in Vietnam is the most important—and yet I cannot protest and work to effect some change. Not only may my convictions remain unexpressed and the concomitant responsibilities unfulfilled, but I am possibly confronted with fighting in a war that I believe to be unjust, immoral, and which makes a mockery of both our constitution and the charter of the United Nations—and the human values which they represent. Apart from the moral and ethical issues, and speaking only from the point of view of the super-patriot, it is a stupid war and pernicious to the self-interest of the United States. . . .

   2d. . . . . This country has made it abundantly clear in the last twenty years, on several continents, that the political freedoms and social aspirations of other peoples are not the principal considerations in the determination of our foreign policy. We have been opposed to any social change that carried the taint of the political left, especially any change that could be labeled "communistic." We have supported fascists, dictators, and military juntas—anyone who professes "anti-communism"—no matter how oppressive and reactionary, no matter how they retard the legitimate aspirations of the people, as long as they served the perceived temporary self-interests of the United States. We have become the caretakers of the status quo. Anti-communism is an inadequate substitute for a rational and humanitarian foreign policy; we should express a concern for people and not only their ideology. Our policies have been inimical to the quest for peace and human welfare. . . .

   2g. It is an immoral war for several sets of reasons. It is not only because our presence is unjustified and for what we are doing to the Vietnamese . . . but also because of our "sins" of omission. This country is capable of achieving for its people, and encouraging in other nations, enormous social advancement, but we are now throwing our riches—both of material and of purpose—into the utter waste of the maelstrom of increasing military involvement. If we as a nation really care about people, then we had best make concepts like freedom and equality *real* to all our citizens—and not just political sham—before we play policeman to the world. Our righteousness is often misplaced. Our behavior in Vietnam is immoral for another set of reasons which concern our conduct of that war. As many newsmen have witnessed, time and again we have bombed, shelled, or attacked a "VC village" or "VC structures" and when we later appraise the results, we label dead adult males as "VC" and add them to the tally—and fail to count the women and children. Our frequent indiscriminate destruction is killing the innocent as well as the "guilty." In addition, our left-handed morality in the treatment of prisoners is odious—we turn them over to the ARVN for possible torture or execution with the excuse that we are not in command but are only supporting the South Vietnam government. Again, this hypocrisy needs no explication. Also frighteningly new in American morality is the pragmatic justification that we must retaliate against the terrorist tactics of the VC. Perhaps most devastatingly immoral about the war in Vietnam are the risks we are assuming for the rest of the world. Each new step and escalation appears unplanned and is an attempt to rectify previous blunders by more military action. The consequences of our course appear too predictable, and although we as a people may elect "better dead than red," do we have the right to make this choice for the rest of mankind?

2h. I am not a pacifist; I believe that there are times when it is right and necessary that a nation or a community of nations employ force to deter or repel totalitarian aggression. My three-year assignment in an operational fighter squadron—with the attendant capacity for inflicting terrible killing and destruction—was based on the personal premise that I was serving a useful deterrent purpose and that I would never be used as an instrument of aggression. This, of course, raises the important and pervasive question for me: What is my duty when I am faced with a conflict between my conscience and the commands of my government? What is my responsibility when there is an irreparable division between my beliefs in the ideals of this nation and the conduct of my political and military leaders? The problem of ultimate loyalty is not one for which there is an easy solution. And, unfortunately, the issues are most often obscured by those who would undermine the very freedoms they are ostensibly defending—by invoking "loyalty" and "patriotism" to enforce conformity, silence dissent, and protect themselves from criticism. May a government or nation be in error? Who is to judge? . . . The individual *must* judge. We as a nation expect and demand this—we have prosecuted and condemned those who forfeited their personal sense of justice to an immoral authoritarian system. We have despised those who have pleaded that they were only doing their job. If we are to survive as individuals in this age of acquiescence, and as nations in this time of international anarchy, we must resist total enculturation so that we may stand aside to question and evaluate—not as an Air Force officer or as an American, but as a member of the human species. This resistance and autonomy is difficult to acquire and precarious to maintain, which perhaps explains its rarity. . . . We must not confuse dissent with disloyalty and we must recognize that consensus is no substitute for conscience. . . .

2i. . . . I find that I am incapable of acquiescing and living within that system as it exists—that if I attempt to do so, I cannot live with myself. When confronted with the ubiquitous injustices of this world, the only possible individual morality is activism.

2j. I have attempted to sincerely state the values and beliefs that are both most meaningful in my life and relevant to my present dilemma. It would appear that I am no longer a loyal Air Force officer if this loyalty requires unquestioning obedience to the policies of this nation in Vietnam. I cannot honestly wear the uniform of this country and support unjust and puerile military involvement. Although it may be inconsistent, I have been able to justify (or rationalize) my position here at the Academy by my belief that my contribution in the classroom has had more effect in encouraging rationalism, a sense of humanism, and the development of social conscious-ness than it has had in the inculcation of militarism. My system of ethics is humanistic—simply a respect and love for man and confidence in his capability to improve his condition. This is my ultimate loyalty. And, as a man trying to be free, my first obligation is to my own integrity and conscience, and this is of course not mitigated by my government's permission or command to engage in immoral acts. I am many things before I am a citizen of this country or an Air Force officer; and included among these things is simply that I am a man with a set of human values which I will not abrogate. I must stand on what I am and what I believe. The war in Vietnam is unjust and immoral, and if ordered to do so, I shall refuse to fight in that war. I should prefer, and respectfully request, that this resignation be accepted.

ANNOTATED BIBLIOGRAPHY

The Vietnam War has produced a remarkable number of excellent histories and memoirs. There are several good general chronicles of the war. The best is Stanley Karnow's *Vietnam: A History* (1983), which offers a clear history of the war from the French colonial period to the fall of Saigon. Other useful histories include Michael Maclear's *The Ten Thousand Day War, 1945–1975* (1981), which emphasizes the confusion of American decisions, and George C. Herring's *America's Longest War: The United States in Vietnam, 1950–1975* (1979), the most objective of them. Two books concentrate on the military history of the war, Dave R. Palmer's *Summons of the Trumpet: US-Vietnam in Perspective* (1978) and Bruce Palmer's *The 25-Year War: America's Military Role in Vietnam* (1974). Since both men are former generals, it is no surprise that they focus their criticism on civilian policymakers for asking the military to do the impossible.

The most remarkable aspect of the literature on the Vietnam War is the quantity and quality of memoirs by lower-ranking officers and enlisted men. One of the best memoirs from any war is Philip Caputo's *A Rumor of War* (1977), which tells of one young marine's change from a gung-ho supporter of the war to a reflective, antiwar veteran. Equally sensitive are Tim O'Brien's *If I Die in a Combat Zone, Box Me Up and Ship Me Home* (1973) and Lynda Van Devanter's *Home Before Morning: The Story of an Army Nurse in Vietnam* (1983). Two particularly devastating stories about the war are Ron Kovic's *Born on the Fourth of July* (1976), which describes the experiences of a grunt crippled for life by his war wounds and C. D. B. Bryan's *Friendly Fire* (1976), which tells a family's search for the transcendent meaning of their son's death from American artillery fire in Vietnam. The best prisoner-of-war memoir is James N. Rowe's gripping tale of his captivity in a Vietcong jungle prison entitled *Five Years to Freedom* (1971). Robert Mason's *Chickenhawk* (1983) describes a helicopter pilot's life in Vietnam. Mark Baker's *Nam: The Vietnam War in the Words of the Men and Women Who Fought There* (1981) and Al Santoli's *Everything We Had* (1981) are oral histories mostly told by grunts about their combat experiences in Vietnam.

There are also many excellent histories of small unit actions or battles. Don Oberdorfer's *Tet* (1971) details the most important battle of the war and Francis J. West's *The Village* (1972) tells how the war affected one small, Vietnamese village in northern South Vietnam. S. L. A. Marshall has written two excellent accounts of battle, *Bird: The Christmastide Battle* (1968) and *Battles in the Monsoon: Campaigning in the Central Highlands, Vietnam, Summer, 1966* (1967). Two *Newsweek* reporters, Peter Goldman and Tony Fuller, told what happened to one group of men, from basic training to their return to the United States, in *Charlie Company: What Vietnam Did to Us* (1983).

William C. Westmoreland, the overall commander of the American forces in Vietnam, has written his memoirs of the war in *A Soldier Reports* (1976). The best biography of any major military figure in the Vietnam War is Neil Sheehan's Pulitzer prize-winning life story of John Paul Vann, *A Bright Shining Lie: John Paul Vann and America in Vietnam* (1988), which not only relates the entire history of the war through one man's eyes, but, more important, describes how the military was blinded by its own mystique and failed to confront the reality of the war in Vietnam.

Many excellent novels have been written by veterans of the Vietnam War. Before reading any of them, students should familiarize themselves with Graham Greene's *The Quiet American* (1982), which describes the arrogance of America's Cold War policy. The best war novels are John Del Vecchio's *The 13th Valley: A Novel* (1982), which relates the frustrations of men in a patrol behind enemy lines who must continuously search for an unseen, deadly foe, and James Webb's *Fields of Fire: A Novel* (1978), which builds on the ethnic diversity of American marines and their need for camaraderie on the battlefield. Although there is argument over whether Michael Herr's *Dispatches* (1977) is fact or fiction, there is no disagreement that it is one of the best portrayals of men in battle during the Vietnam War. Most literary critics consider Tim O'Brien's *Going After Cacciato: A Novel* (1978) to be the most creative work to come from the war. Questions of good and evil raised by the war are reflected in this surrealistic novel of a squad of grunts who walk to Paris to get away from the battlefield.

C H A P T E R   10

CONTEMPORARY ISSUES

The controversy over U.S. involvement in Vietnam provoked widespread opposition to the military at home. ROTC units were driven off college campuses and morale plunged in the armed forces. Although some Americans might have preferred a retreat to isolationism, the power and wealth of the United States made it impossible to hide from international problems.

On the 200th anniversary of the United States Constitution, it appeared that many of the dreams of the Founders had been fulfilled. The nation they had created still retained its unity and independence, and had become the richest and most powerful nation in history. Yet, it also had realized their primary fear that an excessive fondness for military power could lead to a curtailment of liberty.

Military power and great power status came to the United States with many costs. Spending for military defense and social concerns had forced the nation to accumulate the largest debt ever owed by any country. The national deficit was bankrupting the federal government, forcing it to reach further into private life for revenues. In addition, the exceptional wartime powers of the presidency were now ordinary: The mushrooming power of the executive branch threatened traditional American liberties and freedom. Only a long period of sustained peace with a curtailment of military spending might correct these imbalances.

M-16: A BUREAUCRATIC HORROR STORY

James Fallows

By the end of the Vietnam War, the U.S. defense industry had become gigantic and amorphous, a semipublic, quasi-private business, controlled by neither the Pentagon nor the marketplace. The armed services clamored for the fastest, most powerful, complex, and expensive weapons ever produced. While some inventors and military leaders worked to design better weapons, a counterforce in the defense department bureaucracy often frustrated their best efforts.

In the following reading, James Fallows, editor of *The Atlantic Monthly*, shows how the stubbornness and hardheadedness of some members of the army ordnance corps destroyed the proven success of a new rifle. Unfortunately, his expose neither solved this problem nor prevented later ones.

Between 1965 and 1969 more than a million American soldiers served in combat in Vietnam. One can argue that they should never have been sent there, but no one would argue that, once committed to battle, they should have been given inferior equipment. Yet that is what happened. During those years, in which more than 40,000 American soldiers were killed by hostile fire and more than 250,000 wounded, American troops in Vietnam were equipped with a rifle that their superiors knew would fail when put to the test.

The rifle was known as the M-16; it was a replacement for the M-14, a heavier weapon, which was the previous standard. The M-16 was a brilliant

---

SOURCE: From *National Defense* by James Fallows. Copyright © 1981 by James Fallows. Reprinted by permission of Random House, Inc.

technical success in its early models, but was perverted by bureaucratic pressures into a weapon that betrayed its users in Vietnam. By the middle of 1967, when the M-16 had been in combat for about a year and a half, a sufficient number of soldiers had written to their parents about their unreliable equipment and a sufficient number of parents had sent those letters to their congressmen to attract the attention of the House Armed Services Committee, which formed an investigating subcommittee. The subcommittee, headed by Representative Richard Ichord, a Democrat from Missouri, conducted a lengthy inquiry into the origins of the M-16 problem. Much of the credit for the hearings belongs to the committee's counsel, Earl J. Morgan. The hearing record, nearly 600 pages long, is a forgotten document, which received modest press attention at the time and calls up only dim recollections now. Yet it is a pure portrayal of the banality of evil.

Nearly a century before American troops were ordered into Vietnam, weapons designers had made a discovery in the science of "wound ballistics." The discovery was that a small, fast-traveling bullet often did a great deal more damage than a larger round when fired into human or (for the experiments) animal flesh. A large artillery round might pass straight through a human body, but a small bullet could act like a gouge. During the early stages of the congressional hearings, Ichord asked Eugene Stoner, the designer of the original version of the M-16, to explain the apparent paradox of a small bullet's destructive power. The answer emerged in the following grisly exchange.

> ICHORD: *One Army boy told me that he had shot a Vietcong near the eye with an M-14 [which uses a substantially heavier bullet] and the bullet did not make too large a hole on exit, but he shot a Vietcong under similar circumstances in the same place with an M-16 and his whole head was reduced to pulp. This would not appear to make sense. You have greater velocity but the bullet is lighter.*
>
> STONER: *There is the advantage that a small or light bullet has over a heavy one when it comes to wound ballistics. . . . What it amounts to is the fact that bullets are stabilized to fly through the air, and not through water, or a body, which is approximately the same density as the water. And they are stable as long as they are in the air. When they hit something, they immediately go unstable. . . . If you are talking about .30-caliber [like the bullet used in the M-14], this might remain stable through a human body. . . . While a little bullet, being it has a low mass, it senses an instability situation faster and reacts much faster. . . . [T]his is what makes a little bullet pay off so much in wound ballistics.*

The farsighted Willard G. Wyman, the commanding general of the Continental Army Command, had asked Stoner to design a rifle precisely to take advantage of the "payoff" of smaller bullets. The AR-15, the precursor of the M-16, used .22-caliber bullets instead of the .30-caliber that had long been standard for the Army. As early as 1928, an Army "Caliber Board" had conducted firing experiments in Aberdeen, Maryland, and had then recommended a move toward smaller ammunition, perhaps of the .27-caliber range; but the Army, for reasons that were partly technical but largely traditional, refused then and for the next thirty-five years to change from the .30-caliber bullet, which it chose to describe as "full-sized."

A second discovery about weaponry lay behind the design of Eugene Stoner's AR-15. In studies of combat units during World War II, S. L. A. Marshall found that nearly four fifths of combat soldiers never fired their weapons during battle. The finding prompted the Army to take a closer look at the weapons the soldiers used. It turned out that one group of soldiers was an exception to this rule: those who carried the Browning automatic rifles (BARs). These were essentially portable machine guns, which could spray out bursts of continuous fire. (The rifles that the other soldiers carried, M-1s, were "semiautomatic," requiring a separate trigger squeeze for each round.) Within a combat group, firing would begin with the BAR man and spread out from him. The nearer a soldier with an M-1 stood to the BAR man, the more likely he was to fire. The explanation most often suggested was that the infantryman carrying a normal rifle felt that his actions were ultimately futile. John Keegan said in *The Face of Battle*, "Infantrymen, however well-trained and well-armed, however resolute, however ready to kill, remain erratic agents of death. Unless centrally directed, they will choose, perhaps badly, their own targets, will open and cease fire individually, will be put off their aim by the enemy's return of fire, will be distracted by the wounding of those near them, will yield to fear or excitement, will fire high, low, or wide." The normal infantryman could not see the enemy clearly or have any sense of whether he had made a hit. The BAR man, by contrast, had the sense that he could dominate a certain area—"hose it down," in the military slang—and destroy anyone who happened to be there.

After World War II, there was a demand from some officers for a new infantry weapon that would be light, reasonably accurate, and capable of fully automatic fire. The Army's response was to build the M-14, adopted in 1957. This was basically an automatically firing, less solidly made version of the Army's previous standard, the M-1. Like the M-1, it used a large .30-caliber round. Its disadvantage was that it was virtually uncontrollable when on fully automatic fire. The explosive charge needed to propel the heavy bullets was so great, and the rifle itself so flimsily built (in an effort to make it lightweight), that the kick was ferocious. A soldier who used it on automatic fire was likely to get a nosebleed, in addition to being unable to control the weapon's aim. It was with this rifle that American troops trained in the early and middle sixties, and it was the weapon they took to Vietnam in the first years of the war.

The M-14 was a product of the Army's own arsenal system—an informal congeries of weapons laboratories, private contractors, and Army officials which is often collectively known as the "ordnance corps." At various times in their history, the Army bureaus responsible for small-arms development have gone by different names, including, in the period relevant to this story, the Army Materiel Command and the Ordnance Department. The ordnance corps had been in charge of small-arms design for the Army for more than a hundred years. In questions of technology, it emphasized the outlook of the "gravel-bellies"—the sharp-shooters and marksmen who measured a weapon by how well it helped them hit a target 400, 500, 600 yards away in peacetime rifle competition. "The M-14 had been developed on the premise that aimed fire, the fire of the marksman, was of the utmost importance in combat," a Rand employee named Thomas McNaugher wrote in a study of the M-16. "To the U.S. Army, it was more than a premise, it was a creed that had evolved over nearly a century since the service adopted its first rifle in 1855." Giving generous credit to the element of rationality in the ordnance corps' practices, McNaugher says that the marksman's philosophy was appealing because the "Ordnance Department, the agency that developed and produced the services' rifles and ammunition, preferred tactics that stressed slow and deliberate fire because it meant less waste of ammunition and hence less strain on the Department's supply lines and production facilities."

For the marksman's purposes, a large, heavy round was preferable, since it remained steady in flight and was less sensitive to the wind. Hand in hand with this marksman's outlook went an insistence on rigid technical specifications. If a round didn't leave the muzzle at 3,250 feet per second, it was no good; if it couldn't be fired in the Arctic and the Sahara and perform just as well in either place, it was not fit for Army duty. These emphases had little to do with the experience of jungle combat, in which most fire fights took place at ranges of no more than thirty to fifty yards, and in which speed and surprise were so important that it might often cost a soldier his life to take the time to aim his rifle instead of simply pointing it in the right direction and opening up on automatic.

The ordnance corps was small-time, insular, old-fashioned. Its technical experts were divided into a number of subspecialties: internal ballistics (which concerns the bullet's behavior before it leaves the weapon), external ballistics (the bullet in flight), wound ballistics, and other areas. Its organization was further fragmented among technicians at the arsenals and the research center and the military bureaucrats at the Pentagon. Historically, its first instinct, when presented with a new technical possibility, had been to reject it and to stick to traditional solutions. Twice since the Civil War, American Presidents had had to force the ordnance corps to adopt new rifles that had come from outside its own shop.

There was also an air of coziness in relations between the ordnance corps and the rifle- and ammunition-makers who supplied it. "Sole-source" contracts, which gave one company a monopoly on the Army's business, were not unusual. One of the most important of these, which would prove to have an especially crucial effect on the development of the M-16, was with the Olin-Mathieson Corporation, which since the end of World War II had been the Army's supplier of a kind of gunpowder known as "ball powder."

The ordnance corps had every reason to dislike the AR-15. It came from an outside inventor, and threatened to replace the M-14, a product of the corps' own arsenal system. It was not a gravel-belly's or a technician's rifle. And it used what was, by the standards of the corps, a laughably small round—a .22-caliber bullet, the kind kids used to shoot at squirrels. In the early fifties, the U.S. ordnance corps had fought a grueling battle against European governments in NATO, which wanted to have a small bullet adopted as the NATO standard. The ordnance corps' struggle to impose the .30-caliber bullet as NATO standard had been successful, but it had left much ill will in its wake. Having won that struggle, the Army was not likely to surrender meekly on the same point in its own home territory.

At about the time the M-14 was adopted as the Army's standard, Eugene Stoner was completing his work on the AR-15. Stoner was known as one of the great figures in the special calling of small-arms design. Like some of the other outstanding American rifle designers—including John Browning, inventor of the Browning automatic rifle, who had to sell his weapon to foreign governments after rejection by the American ordnance corps—Stoner had never seen his models win easy acceptance by the Army. He was working for the Armalite Corporation when he finished developing the AR-15.

The rifle combined several advantages. One was the lethal "payoff" that came with its .22-caliber bullets. The smaller, lighter ammunition meant that the rifle could be controlled on automatic fire by the average soldier, because its kick was so much less than the M-14's. The rifle itself was also lighter than the M-14. These savings in weight meant that a soldier using the AR-15 could carry almost three times as many rounds as one with the M-14. This promised to eliminate one of the soldier's fundamental problems in combat: running out of ammunition during a fire fight. The rifle had two other, technical advantages. One was the marvelous reliability of its moving parts, which could feed, fire, extract, and eject 600 or 700 cartridges a minute and practically never jam. The other was a manufacturing innovation that drastically cut the cost of the weapon. The parts were stamped out—not hand-machined, as in previous rifles—and they could be truly mass-produced. The stock was made of plastic, which further cut the cost, and to traditionalists, this was one more indication that the AR-15 was not a real weapon. They said that you couldn't use a plastic rifle as a club. Stoner's reply, in effect, was that with the AR-15's reliability and destructive power you wouldn't need to.

The AR-15 was tested in 1958 at three military bases. The reports were favorable, but there were reservations from the ordnance establishment about the propriety of using such small-caliber ammunition. To reconcile the differences in opinion, the Army commissioned an extensive series of tests at its Combat Developments Experimentation Command, known as CDEC, at Fort Ord, California. These tests ran from the fall of 1958 until the spring of 1959, and were designed not to follow the usual marksman's pattern but to simulate the conditions of small squads in combat. In the tests, the AR-15 was matched against the M-14 and another lightweight rifle, made by Winchester. The results, released in May of 1959, included these findings:

> *a.   With a total combat weight per man equivalent to that planned for riflemen armed with the M-14, a squad consisting of from 5–7 men armed with the [AR-15] would have better hit distribution and greater hit capability than the present eleven-man M-14 squad. . . .*
>
> *b.   By opinion poll, the experimentation troops favor the [AR-15] because of its demonstrated characteristics of lightness in weight, reliability, balance and grip, and freedom from recoil and climb on full automatic. . . .*
>
> *h.   The attributes demonstrated by the prototype weapons of the lightweight high-velocity category indicate an overall combat potential superior to that of the M-14. Such advantages include . . . lightness in weight of arms and ammunition, ease of handling, superior full automatic firing capability, accuracy of the Winchester and functional reliability of the Armalite [AR-15].*

The report's conclusion was that the Army should develop a lightweight rifle "with the reliability characteristics of the Armalite" to replace the M-14. "Concurrent with the adoption of a lightweight high-velocity rifle," the report said, "serious consideration [should] be given to reduction in the size of the present squad," in light of the increased firepower of the new weapons. The repeated references to the "reliability" of the AR-15 bear emphasis, in view of the weapon's unreliability after it had been transformed into the M-16 and sent to war.

After the CDEC tests, the Army admitted the theoretical "promise" of the lightweight system but rejected it as a practical proposition. Emphasizing the importance of having all rifles and machine guns use the same ammunition, the Army ordered full production of the .30-caliber M-14.

However, advocates of the AR-15 enlisted the support of a redoubtable gun enthusiast, General Curtis Lemay, then the Air Force's Chief of Staff. Based on his interest, the Air Force conducted further tests and inspections and declared the AR-15 its "standard" model in January of 1962. The Air Force then took a step that later had enormous significance. On the advice of the Armalite Corporation, which owned the design of the rifle, and of Colt, which had the contract to manufacture it, the Air Force tested the ammunition that the Remington Arms Company had developed for the AR-15. After the tests, the Air Force declared the ammunition suitable for its purposes. In May of 1962, it ordered 8,500 rifles from Colt and 8.5 million rounds of ammunition from Remington.

At this point, decisions about the rifle moved from the world of tests and paper specifications to that of actual combat. In 1962, the Defense Department's Advanced Research Projects Agency, prompted by staff members who were advocates of the AR-15, managed to get 1,000 AR-15s shipped to Vietnam for tests by soldiers of the Army of the Republic of Vietnam (ARVN). The rationale was that Vietnamese soldiers were too short and slight to handle rifles with full-sized ammunition. The reports were glowing, especially about the phenomenal reliability of the weapon. There were no broken parts reported in the firing of 80,000 rounds during one stage of the tests. In the whole period, only two replacement parts were issued for all 1,000 rifles. The report recommended that the AR-15 be shipped in bulk to South Vietnam as standard equipment for the ARVN soldier. But Admiral Harry Felt, then the Commander in Chief, Pacific Forces, rejected the recommendation, based on Army advice, saying that it would create a complicated logistics problem to have different rifles using different rounds in the war zone. The Joint Chiefs of Staff supported his decision.

Through 1962 and 1963, there followed a series of tests, evaluations, and counter-evaluations by the American military, the repeated theme of which was the lightness, "lethality," and the reliability of the AR-15. The results of one test, conducted by the Defense Department's Advanced Research Projects Agency, were summed up in September of 1962 by the Comptroller of the department:

> Taking into account the greater lethality of the Ar-15 rifle and improvements in accuracy and rate of fire in this weapon since 1959, in overall squad kill potential the AR-15 rifle is up to 5 times as effective as the M-14 rifle. . . .
>
> The AR-15 rifle can be produced with less difficulty, to a higher quality, and at a lower cost than the M-14 rifle.

In reliability, durability, ruggedness, performance under adverse condi-
tions, and ease of maintenance, the AR-15 is a significant improvement over
any of the standard weapons including the M-14 rifle. The M-14 rifle is
weak in the sum of these characteristics. . . .

It is significantly easier to train the soldier with the AR-15 than with the
M-14 rifle.

Three times as much ammunition can be carried on the individual soldier
within the standard weapon-and-ammunition load. . . .

Meanwhile, the Army Materiel Command, home of the ordnance corps, was conducting its own evaluations of the AR-15. In these, too, there was consistency. The corps found little to admire in the AR-15, and many technical objections to it. It had poor "pointing and night firing characteristics"; its penetration at long distance was also poor. The ordnance corps' recommendation was to stick with the M-14 until a "radically" better model, based on advanced technology, emerged from research programs that the ordnance labs had recently begun.

Early in 1963 with strong support from President Kennedy and Secretary of Defense Robert McNamara, the Special Forces (better known as the Green Berets) asked for and got approval to use the AR-15 as their standard issue, because they needed lightweight gear for mobility and stealth. The Army's airborne units in Vietnam also got it, as did some agents of the CIA. As the AR-15 attracted a greater and greater following among units actually operating in Vietnam, Secretary of the Army Cyrus Vance asked the Army's inspector general to look again at the reasoning and evidence that had led the Army Materiel Command to reject the AR-15. His investigation found that the tests had been blatantly rigged. The M-14s used in the tests were all handpicked, handmade, "matchgrade" weapons (suitable for marksmen's competitions), while the AR-15s were taken straight from the box. The ammunition for the M-14 had also received special care. The inspector found that various organizations of the ordnance corps had met beforehand to discuss how to fix the tests. They agreed to take a dry run through the tests, and then (according to the printed minutes of their meeting) include in the final evaluation "only those tests that will reflect adversely on the AR-15 rifle. . . ." The lines became more clearly drawn within the Pentagon, with the Air Force and the civilian leadership of the Defense Department (especially McNamara) in favor of the AR-15 and the Army ordnance establishment opposed.

As the fighting in Vietnam grew more intense, in late 1963, procurement of the rifle began, with 19,000 rifles for the Air Force and another 85,000 for the special Army units. Robert McNamara, in the interest of efficiency, designated the Army as the central procurement agency for all the services. It was at this point that the Army ordnance corps got hold of

Eugene Stoner's AR-15, declared it to be inadequately "developed," and "militarized" it into the M-16.

The first of several modifications was the addition of a "manual bolt closure," a handle that would permit the soldier to ram a cartridge in manually after it had refused to seat properly by itself. The Air Force, which was to buy the rifle, and the Marine Corps, which had tested it, objected vehemently to this change. An Air Force document said, "During three years of testing and operation of the AR-15 rifle under all types of conditions, the Air Force has no record of malfunctions that could have been corrected by a manual bolt closing device." Worse, they said, the device would add cost, weight, and complexity to the weapon, thereby reducing the reliability that had been its greatest asset.

Years later, during the congressional hearings, Eugene Stoner said that he had always opposed a closure device because "when you get a cartridge that won't seat in the rifle and you deliberately drive it in, usually you are buying yourself more trouble." Colonel Howard Yount, who had been a project manager at the Rock Island arsenal in 1963 and who throughout the hearings bore the burden of explaining the ordnance corps' decisions, was asked how this change could have been justified. Not on the basis of complaints or of prior tests, Colonel Yount said. It was justified "on the basis of direction." Direction from where? a congressman asked. Directions from his superiors on the Army staff, was all he would say. The widespread assumption was that the late General Earl Wheeler, then the Army's Chief of Staff, had personally ordered that the M-16 carry the useless handle, largely because previous Army rifles had had them. Eugene Stoner said that his only explanation for the Army's decision was that "the M-1, the M-14, and the carbine had always had something for the soldier to push on; [perhaps the Army thought] that this would be a comforting feeling to him, or something."

The next modification was to increase the "twist" of the rifle's barrel (the spiral grooving inside the barrel that gives the bullet its spin). The rate of twist was changed from one-in-14-inches to one-in-12. More twist made the bullet spin faster as it flew, and therefore made it hold a more stable path; but it likewise made the bullet more stable as it entered flesh, and thereby reduced, by as much as 40 percent, the shocking "lethality" that had so distinguished the AR-15. The Army's explanation for increasing the "twist" of the barrel was that otherwise the rifle could not meet its all-environments test. To qualify as "military standard," a rifle and its ammunition had to show that they would perform equally well at 65 degrees below zero and 125 above. On the basis of skimpy test evidence, an Artic testing team concluded that the AR-15 did not do well on the cold-weather portions of its test. Supposedly, the rounds wobbled in flight at 65 below. The Army's reaction was to increase the "twist" and thereby decrease the "lethality," even though the rifle was due for shipment to the steaming jungles along the Mekong.

The final change was the most important. Like the others, it was publicly justified by a letter-of-the-law application of technical specifications, but it was apparently motivated by two other forces: the desire of some Army bureaucrats to discredit the AR-15, and the widespread tendency to overlook the difference between meeting technical specifications and producing a weapon that would perform reliably in the real circumstances of combat.

Weapons designers speak of automatic rifles as "resonant mechanisms," in which several different cycles must all work in harmony. One of the determining factors for synchronizing these cycles is the explosive characteristic of the powder in ammunition. Some powders explode very quickly, others build up pressure more slowly. Certain decisions follow from the explosion pattern—for example, the location of the "gas port" or the proper cycling rate for inserting and extracting the bullets. Eugene Stoner had designed his AR-15 around a powder known as IMR 4475 ("improved military rifle"). It was produced by Du Pont, which sold it to Remington to fill the cartridges. It is made of nitrocellulose, sometimes known as guncotton. IMR 4475 ammunition had been used in all the early tests of the AR-15; it was the ammunition that had proven so reliable in all field trials and had won the acceptance of the Air Force.

In June of 1963, the Army Materiel Command conducted tests at Frankford Arsenal that discredited the original IMR powder and brought about the most consequential modification made to the AR-15—and the one that, nearly twenty years after the fact, is still the most difficult to explain. (The Army's Armament Research and Development Command extended, and then withdrew, an invitation for me to interview technicians who had participated in the decision to abandon IMR 4475. A spokesman for the organization said, "These were the Army's decisions, so we feel the Department of the Army at the Pentagon should explain them." At the Department of the Army, virtually no one is left who held authority at that time. The only official explanations now available are the ones, couched in bureaucratese, that Colonel Yount offered when he was asked time and again by Representative Ichord's committee to justify what the ordnance corps had done.)

The decision about ammunition turned on the detailed specifications, known as the "technical data package," that the Army drew up when it converted the rifle into the M-16. The data package included the requirements that the muzzle velocity of the rifle must average 3,250 feet per second (fps), plus or minus 40, and that the pressure within the firing chamber must not exceed 52,000 pounds per square inch.

Where had these specifications come from? Not from Eugene Stoner, or Armalite, or any users or testers of the rifle. Stoner had based his design on an off-the-shelf commercial cartridge packed with IMR powder, which had never attained the muzzle velocity that the Army now specified. Some Army officials claimed that the manufacturer advertised the bullet as having a 3,250-fps velocity; if so, they chose to believe commercials rather than the way the bullet actually performed. In all its previous tests, in the field trials that had made the Air Force and the Marines so enthusiastic about it, and in its successful performance in combat in Vietnam, the AR-15 with its original ammunition had produced a muzzle velocity about 100 fps below the newly specified level.

What, then, was the basis for the Army's decision? The congressional committee tried a dozen different ways to get Colonel Yount to answer that question. The closest thing to a response that the hearing records contain is the following paragraph, from the "Statement on Propellants for 5.56mm Ammunition," which the Army submitted after Yount's testimony:

> In the course of the 5.56mm ammunition program, the Army could have elected to reduce the specified velocity, thus avoiding the necessity of developing new propellants. . . . This would have reduced somewhat the range and effectiveness of the M-16 rifle. Instead, the Army chose to maintain the original [sic] ballistic performance, and utilize propellants which could meet these requirements consistently in mass production.

Once the Army had set these specifications, the result of its tests at Frankford Arsenal was predetermined: the original IMR powder would not do. To get the velocity up to 3,250 fps, it had to bring chamber pressure too close to the limit. In February of 1964, the Army sent out a request to the manufacturers to come up with substitute powders. A few months later, Du Pont said it would stop producing IMR, and Remington switched to the Army's supplier of "ball powder," Olin-Mathieson. By the end of 1964, Remington was loading only ball powder in its cartridges for the rifle, which had been renamed the M-16. (Another kind of IMR powder, with explosive characteristics different from the original's, was eventually produced as alternate ammunition for the M-16.)

Ball powder was first adopted by the Army early in World War II, for use in certain artillery rounds. It differs from IMR in being "double-based" (made of nitrocellulose and nitroglycerine) and in several other ways. Its most important difference is its explosive characteristics, for it burns longer and more slowly than IMR. Only one company in the United States produces ball powder and sells it to the Army. That is Olin Mathieson, which received contracts for some 89 million cartridges in 1964 alone, and far more as the war went on. More than 90 percent of the cartridges used in Vietnam were loaded with ball powder.

After the Army had made the decision to switch to ball powder, it sent a representative, Frank Vee, of the comptroller's office, to try to get Eugene Stoner to endorse the change. Stoner had not been consulted on any of the modifications to his rifle, not the bolt closure nor the barrel twist nor the ball powder, and he thought that all were bad ideas. He recalled for the congressional committee his meeting with Vee:

> *He asked me my opinion [about the specs requiring ball powder] after the fact. In other words, this was rather an odd meeting. . . . I looked at the technical data package and he said, "What is your opinion?" and I said, "I would advise against it. . . ."*
>
> *I asked, "So what is going to happen?" And he said, "Well, they already decided this is the way they are going to go," meaning the committee. I said, "So why are you asking me now?" and he said, "I would have felt better if you approved of the package."*
>
> *And I said, "Well, now we both don't feel so good."*

The reason for Stoner's concern was that the change of powders destroyed most of the qualities he had built into his rifle. With ball powder, the M-16 looked better on the Army's new specifications sheets but was worse in operation. There were two problems. One was "fouling"—a powder residue on the inside of the gas-tube chamber that eventually made the rifle jam. The AR-15 had been designed so that its gas port stayed closed through the combustion of the powder, but that was for a different powder. The new ball powder was inherently dirtier, and it burned longer; it was still burning when the gas port opened, so it burned into the gas tube. The other effect of ball powder was to increase the rifle's "cyclic rate." The AR-15, with all its interlocking mechanical cycles, had been designed to fire between 750 and 800 rounds per minute. When cartridges loaded with ball powder were used, the rate went up to 1,000 or more. "When the Army said, 'No, we are going to use our ammunition,' the cyclic rate of the weapons went up at least 200 rounds per minute," Stoner told the congressional committee. "That gun would jump from 750 to about 1,000 rounds a minute, with no change other than changing the ammunition."

The consequences of a higher cyclic rate were grave. What had been a supremely reliable rifle was now given to chronic jams and breakdowns. In November of 1965, engineers from Colt fired a number of rifles, some with the original IMR powder and some with ball. They reported: "For weapons such as those used in this experiment, none are likely to fail with ammunition such as [IMR], whereas half are likely to fail with ammunition such as [ball powder]." In December, the Frankford Arsenal conducted another test for malfunctions. When M-16s were loaded with IMR cartridges, there were 3.2 malfunctions per 1,000 rounds, and .75 stoppages.

When the same rifles were fired with ball propellant, the failure rates were about six times higher (18.5 and 5.2, respectively). Under the central procurement policy, the Army's decision also forced the Air Force to switch to ball powder. The Air Force protested, pointing out that the rifles had been extremely reliable when loaded with IMR. One Air Force representative described a test in which twenty-seven rifles fired 6,000 rounds apiece. The malfunction rate was one per 3,000 rounds, and the parts-replacement rate one per 6,200 rounds. The rifle and its original cartridge worked fine, the Air Force insisted, even though they didn't happen to meet the specifications of 3,250 fps from the muzzle.

In May of 1966, there was one more report, this one the result of an extensive and unusually realistic series of tests held by the Army's CDEC field test organization at Fort Ord. (For example, the soldiers fired as squads, not as individuals; the targets resembled real battlefield targets, in that they were hard to see and obscured by brush and other cover; there was simulated fire from the targets themselves, done in a pattern resembling that of combat; soldiers were run through the course only once, to avoid their having any familiarity with it.) The conclusion was that the M-16 was more effective than the M-14 or the Soviet AK-47 (which was also tested), but that it was an unreliable weapon. The reason for the fouling, the jamming, and the breakdowns, the testers said, was the switch to ball powder. By that time the Army was ordering ball powder in greater quantities than ever, and shipping it to Vietnam.

In 1965, after the years of the advisers and the Special Forces, American troops began full-fledged ground combat in Vietnam. The regular Army and Marine units carried the old M-14. On arrival, they discovered several things about their weapon. One was that in jungle warfare, the inaccurate, uncontrollable M-14 was no match for the AK-47, which their enemies used. Both were .30-caliber rifles, but the AK-47's cartridges had a lighter bullet and were packed with less powder, which reduced the recoil to an endurable range. They also saw that the old AR-15s that had been used by the Special Forces had been a big hit in Vietnam. Soldiers were willing to sacrifice several months' pay to get hold of one on the black market.

One of those who noticed these facts was William Westmoreland, then the commander of American forces in Vietnam. He saw that his men were doing very badly in the fire fights against the AK-47, and that the casualties were heavy. He also saw how the AR-15 performed. Near the end of December, 1965, he sent an urgent, personal request for the M-16, immediately, as standard equipment for units in Vietnam.

The ordnance corps met this request with grudging compliance. The rifle would be sent to Vietnam, but only as a special, limited purchase. It would not be issued to American troops in Europe or in the United States; it would not replace the M-14 as the Army's standard weapon. Nor would it go to Vietnam under circumstances likely to show off its merits, because there was no backing off the requirement that its cartridges be filled with ball powder.

The climactic struggle over ball powder had occurred one year before Westmoreland's request, in 1964. As test after test showed that ball powder made the rifle fire too fast and then jam, the manufacturing company finally threw up its hands. Colt said that it could no longer be responsible for the M-16's passing the Army's acceptance test. It could not guarantee performance with the ball powder. One of the test requirements was that the rifle's cyclic rate not exceed 850 rounds per minute, and six out of ten rifles were far above that when using ball powder. Don't worry, the Army said, *you can use whatever ammunition you want for the tests.* But we'll keep sending our ball powder to Vietnam.

The Technical Coordinating Committee, which represented all services using the M-16 but was dominated by the Army, formally gave Colt permission early in 1964 to use any ammunition it had in stock for the acceptance tests. Colt received no new shipments of the original IMR ammunition after May of 1964, but by that time the company had several million rounds on hand. Beginning in 1964, Colt used IMR powder so that its rifles would pass the acceptance tests. The Army promptly equipped those rifles with ball-powder cartridges and sent them to soldiers who needed them to stay alive. The Army's official reasoning on the matter was that since it did not recognize the theory that ball powder was the cause of the problems, why should it care which powder Colt used? Colt delivered at least 330,000 rifles under this agreement. After uncovering the arrangement, the Ichord Committee concluded:

> *Undoubtedly many thousands of these were shipped or carried to Vietnam,* with the Army on notice that the rifles failed to meet design and performance specifications and might experience excessive malfunctions when firing ammunition loaded with ball propellant [emphasis in original]. . . . *The rifle project manager, the administrative contracting officer, the members of the Technical Coordinating Committee, and others as high in authority as the Assistant Secretary of Defense for Installations and Logistics knowingly accepted M-16 rifles that would not pass the approved acceptance test. . . . Colt was allowed to test using only IMR propellant at a time when the vast majority of ammunition in the field, including Vietnam, was loaded with ball propellant. The failure on the part of officials with authority in the Army to cause action to be taken to correct the deficiencies of the 5.56mm ammunition borders on criminal negligence.*

The denouement was predictable and tragic. In the field, the rifle fouled and jammed. More American soldiers survived in combat than would have with the M-14, but the M-16's failures were spectacular and entirely unnecessary. When they heard the complaints, ordnance officials said it only proved what they'd said all along, that it was an inferior rifle. The official Army hierarchy took the view that improper maintenance was at fault. Officials from the Pentagon would go on inspection tours to Vietnam and scold the soldiers for not keeping the rifles clean, but there never seemed to be enough cleaning supplies for the M-16. The instruction leaflets put out by the Army told them that "This rifle will fire longer without cleaning or oiling than any other known rifle," and "an occasional cleaning will keep the weapon functioning indefinitely." Many in the ordnance establishment said the problem was that the rifle chamber was not lined with chrome—an expensive improvement that had not been necessary in the rifle's original version.

At last the soldiers began writing letters—to their parents or their girlfriends, and to the commercial manufacturer of a rifle lubricant called Dri-Slide. The Dri-Slide company received letters like the following:

December 24, 1966

Dear Sir:

On the morning of December 22nd our company . . . ran into a reinforced platoon of hard core Viet Cong. They were well dug in, and boy! Was it hell getting them out. During this fight and previous ones, I lost some of my best buddies. I personally checked their weapons. Close to 70 per cent had a round stuck in the chamber, and take my word it was not their fault.

Sir, if you will send three hundred and sixty cans along with the bill, I'll "gladly" pay it out of my own pocket. This will be enough for every man in our company to have a can.

—— ——, Spec. Fourth Class

Parents in Idaho received this letter from their son, a Marine:

Our M-16s aren't worth much. If there's dust in them, they will jam. Half of us don't have cleaning rods to unjam them. Out of 40 rounds I've fired, my rifle jammed about 10 times. I pack as many grenades as I can plus bayonet and K bar (jungle knife) so I'll have something to fight with. If you can, please send me a bore rod and a 1-1/4 inch or so paint brush. I need it for my rifle. These rifles are getting a lot of guys killed because they jam so easily.

One man wrote to a member of the Armed Services Committee staff, recounting what his brother had told him about his experience in Vietnam:

> He went on to tell me how, in battles there in Vietnam, the only things that were left by the enemy after they had stripped the dead of our side were the rifles, which they considered worthless. That when battles were over the dead would have the rifles beside them, torn down to attempt a repair because of some malfunction when the enemy attacked. . . . He said, "Part of me dies when I have to stand by and see people killed, and yet my hands are tied."

A letter that ended up in the office of Representative Charles W. Whalen, Jr., of Ohio:

> I was walking point a few weeks back and that piece of you know what jammed three times in a row on me. I'm lucky I wasn't doing anything but reconning by fire or I wouldn't be writing this letter now. When I brought the matter up to the Captain, he let me test fire the weapon—well in 50 rounds it double fed and jammed 14 times. I guess I'll just have to wait until someone gets shot and take his rifle because the Captain couldn't get me a new one.

Another, from a Marine officer, was referred to Senator Gaylord Nelson of Wisconsin:

> The weapon has failed us at crucial moments when we needed fire power most. In each case, it left Marines naked against their enemy. Often . . . we take counts after each fight, as many as 50% of the rifles fail to work. I know of at least two Marines who died within 10 feet of the enemy with jammed rifles.
>
> My loyalty has to be with these 18-year-old Marines. Too many times (yesterday most recently) I've been on the TF's awaiting medical evacuation and listened to bandaged and bleeding troopers cuss the M-16. Yesterday, we got a big one. . . . The day found one Marine beating an NVA with his helmet and a hunting knife because his rifle failed—this can't continue—32 of about 80 rifles failed yesterday.

When investigators from the congressional committee went to Vietnam, they confirmed another report: that one Marine, who had the only cleaning rod in his squad, had been killed as he ran up and down the line unjamming his comrades' rifles.

The technical data that came out of the congressional inquiry persuaded the members of the committee to release an unusually sharp report, charging that the M-16 had been sabotaged by the ordnance corps. Yet the most striking aspect of the testimony was its humdrum, routine tone. When representatives of the ordnance corps were pressed to explain their decisions, they fell back on citations from the rule books, like characters in a parody of bureaucratic life. They seemed to have a hard time remembering who was responsible for crucial decisions; they tended to explain things by saying, "the feeling was," or "the practice has been. . . ." They could list with careful, bureaucratic logic the reasonableness of each step they had taken: if you didn't have Arctic test requirements, you might not have adaptable rifles. If you didn't change to ball powder, you would have had chamber pressures over the allowable limits—which might have been dangerous for the troops. They seemed not to see a connection between these choices and the soldiers who were dying with jammed rifles in their arms. They were certainly aware of the M-16's troubles, and bowed to no one in their concern. What it proved, they said, was that the rifle had always been a risky experiment—especially (as they pointed out several times) when it was being used by the kind of soldiers the draft was scrounging up these days, who couldn't understand the importance of keeping their weapons clean. Four years after the hearings, in 1971, an M-16 project manager, Col. Rex Wing, wrote a history of the rifle in *Ordnance* magazine. The headline of the story said, "Although the Viet Cong greatly feared the M-16 when our soldiers were first equipped with it in Vietnam, malfunctions caused by improper maintenance led to its being downgraded in the press." This story contained no mention of the change in ammunition.

The committee could find no real evidence of corruption. Its report criticized one Nelson Lynde, Jr., a general who was in charge of the Army Weapons Command between 1962 and 1964. He approved purchases of the M-16 from Colt, and then accepted a job shortly after retirement with the parent company of Colt. The committee reprimanded General Lynde for an apparent conflict of interests—even though, as Lynde pointed out, the Army's counsel had not forbidden him to accept the job. The committee also urged an audit of the profits Colt had made on the rifle and of the "sole-source" relationship with Olin-Mathieson. In 1980, I asked the committee's investigator, Earl Morgan, whether actual corruption—bribes, kickbacks—had been involved. "Oh, I'd be amazed if there wasn't some, knowing how that business is done," he said. "But we never found anything we could prove."

Perhaps the truest explanation of why things happened as they did is the most ordinary: that human beings could not foresee the way that chance and circumstance could magnify the consequences of their acts. The military supply organization, like most other organizations, is always full of power plays and bureaucratic games, which distract attention from the goals that in a rational world would always be pursued. Only occasionally does chance make the effects of these games catastrophic. Doubtless, thousands of military intelligence officers have lapsed in their attention to urgent dispatches; the handful who lapsed on December 6, 1941, were just unluckier than the rest. The ordnance corps was similarly unlucky. In late 1963 and early 1964, when the crucial decisions about the M-16 were being made, few people could have known that the U.S. would soon have a half million land troops in Asia, or that the soldiers would depend for their survival on a weapon that was the product of small-time bureaucratic squabbles. Most other squabbles had come and gone without costing soldiers' lives. The forlorn tone of one of the Army's last submissions to the congressional committee suggested the way in which the situation had gotten out of control:

> *From the vantage point of retrospect, it has sometimes been suggested that the peculiar behavior of ball propellant in the M-16 system should have been predicted. . . . Had the Army anticipated these developments, it is most unlikely that the course chosen in January 1964 would have been the same. A decision to reduce the velocity requirement, and continue loading IMR 4475 propellant would probably have been made instead.*

The committee recommended that the Army immediately conduct a thorough, honest test of the two kinds of ammunition, with the strong suggestion that it should switch to IMR 4475. That never happened. Instead of going back to the original powder, the ordnance corps modified the ball powder and changed the mechanical "buffer" of the rifle, which slowed down the cyclic rate. That solved part of the jamming problem, but did not restore the rifle's original reliability or "lethality." (The change in the barrel "twist" was also never corrected.) Through every day of combat in Vietnam, American troops fired cartridges filled with the ball powder that was the legacy of the ordnance corps. And if American troops were sent in battle today, they would use the same kind of ammunition.

American soldiers in Grenada (United States Army Military History Institute). This photograph of five American soldiers was taken by an army public affairs photographer. The soldiers are on "R&R" (rest and relaxation leave), but they still carry their M-16s. Two of the soldiers are women. Federal law does not permit women to serve in combat branches, but they are allowed to defend themselves and they receive the same basic training as men. Although the American public might not want their mothers or daughters to fight in combat, clearly the modern woman is just as capable of defending herself as are her brothers.

THE GRENADA OPERATION

Successful military operations sometimes can uncover hidden problems. The best example of this was the Spanish–American War. Even the staunchest military advocates of that time realized that the war would have been a disaster had the United States fought any high-quality military power. Although the errors discovered when the United States invaded the small Caribbean island of Grenada in the fall of 1983 were not nearly as bad as those made during the Spanish–American War, they indicated some serious shortcomings in American military communications, transportation, and command.

The following document is part of a Senate study ordered by Republican Barry Goldwater of Arizona and Democrat Sam Nunn of Georgia. These senators and the Armed Services Committee which they headed, proceeded on the assumption that it was in the best interest of the United States to combine its armed forces into one uniformed service. Not surprisingly, most generals and admirals did everything in their power to prevent the merger of the services. However, to the senators, the "Grenada Operation" demonstrated the kinds of "foul-ups" that can occur in even the simplest and most successful military operation, when the services fail to properly coordinate training, communications, and strategy.

On October 25, 1983 elements of the U.S. Army, Navy, Air Force and Marine Corps assaulted the island of Grenada in the Caribbean. The operation, code-named URGENT FURY, must be viewed as a success. The principle [sic] missions—the rescue of the American medical students, the restoration of democracy and the expulsion of Cuban forces—were accom-

---

SOURCE: *Defense Organization: The Need for a Change,* Staff report to the Committee on Armed Services, United States Senate, October 16, 1985 (Washington, DC: 1985); Senate Doc. 99th Cong; 1st Session; S.Prt. 99–86.

plished rapidly and with relatively little loss of life (18 U.S. servicemen killed and 116 wounded).

The operation was planned and conducted with extraordinary speed. On October 14, the National Security Council instructed the Joint Chiefs to begin planning for the evacuation of American citizens from Grenada. Conditions on the island continued to deteriorate and on October 21 the National Security Council modified its guidance to add the "neutralization of Grenadan Armed Forces, stabilization and, as requested by the Organization of Eastern Caribbean states, restoration of democracy in Grenada." The operation was scheduled to begin before dawn on October 25.

Despite the success of URGENT FURY, after-action reports prepared by the Services and numerous articles in professional journals reveal serious problems in the ability of the Services to operate jointly. These problems have their roots in organizational shortcomings. . . .

1. Concept of the Operation

Grenada is located in the geographical area of responsibility of the Commander-in-Chief of the U.S. Atlantic Command (CINCLANT), Admiral Wesley McDonald, whose headquarters are in Norfolk, Virginia. On October 14, the JCS tasked CINCLANT to begin planning a possible evacuation of U.S. citizens from Grenada. CINCLANT's initial plan called for the operation to be conducted by a Marine Amphibious Unit (MAU) which was on its way to Lebanon and could be diverted. However, when that proposal was reviewed by the Joint Chiefs, it was determined that the Marines should take the northern half of the island and that U.S. Army forces should take the southern half of the island where the major targets were located, including the capital of St. Georges, the Point Salines Airfield, the medical schools and the major concentration of Cuban and Grenadan forces. Some have speculated that CINCLANT's plans were changed only because the Joint Chiefs insisted that each Service should have a piece of the action. There is no direct proof of that allegation, and the JCS have stated that CINCLANT himself discarded using only Navy and Marine Corps units because "the number, size and location of the various objectives exceeded the capability of a single Marine battalion. . . ."

The forces were organized under a Joint Task Force designated JTF 120 and commanded by Vice Admiral Joseph Metcalf, who was the Commander, Second Fleet. Because Admiral Metcalf had no Army personnel on his Second Fleet staff, one Army general officer and two majors were assigned to his staff on an emergency basis. There was no unified ground commander on the island, a matter which caused some problems. Additionally, some Air Force aircraft remained under the control of the Military Airlift Command.

A number of individuals have criticized the tactics and performance of some of the units involved. This analysis undertakes no such criticism but rather focuses on those problems which may be traced in whole or part to organizational shortcomings. American forces performed bravely and fought well. Because the operation was so hastily planned and conducted, subordinate and small-unit commanders were forced to make rapid adjustments and to improvise. One of the great strengths of the American Armed Forces has always been the initiative and leadership of small unit commanders. Grenada proved no exception. However, with better organizational arrangements, much of the need for improvisation could have been avoided. In a more serious fight against a stronger and more sophisticated enemy, these organizational failures could prove disastrous.

2. Communications

Probably the largest single problem was the inability of some units to communicate. Many Army and Navy units could not communicate with one another. There were also problems between the Army and Marine units on the ground. The root cause of this inability to communicate is that each Service continues to purchase its own communications equipment which all too frequently isn't compatible with the equipment of the other Services. On March 22, 1985, in response to a question from Senator Nunn as to why there was a lack of communications interoperability [sic] between the Services, General Wallace H. Nutting, then the Commander-in-Chief of the U.S. Readiness Command, stated:

> It is a function of the way we prepare for war and that is the fact that the law charges each military department to organize, train and equip forces to operate in a particular environment for which it is responsible. That is too simple an answer, but that is where it begins with the way we prepare for war.

For example, the Army elements initially on the ground were unable to speak to the Navy ships offshore to request and coordinate naval gunfire. It has been reported that one Army officer was so frustrated in his efforts to communicate with the Navy ships that he used his AT&T calling card to place a call on an ordinary civilian pay telephone to his office at Ft. Bragg in an attempt to coordinate fire support. It has also been reported that some of the early communications were conducted via a ham radio operator.

Officers from the 82nd Airborne Division flew by helicopter several times to the USS *Guam* (Admiral Metcalf's flagship) to coordinate naval gunfire; unfortunately these efforts were still unsuccessful. Another officer from the 82nd even borrowed a UHF radio from the Marine Headquarters on the *Guam* in order to be able to communicate directly with the Navy ships. However, subsequent efforts by that officer to request fire and to reposition the destroyers to more favorable locations failed in part because of the inability to authenticate requests using Navy codes. . . .

In a further example, certain messages failed to reach the Army on the ground in Grenada. This problem nearly proved disastrous as one of those messages contained information concerning the existence of a second campus where American students were located. The Army forces were unaware of the existence of the second campus until the students at that campus telephoned on the afternoon of the 25th to report they were surrounded and to request urgent rescue. The operation was mounted the next day, October 26, successfully rescuing 224 American students.

The JCS "Joint Overview" of the Grenada operation states that "several observations were made in the US CINCLANT report regarding communications difficulties. The observations centered around equipment and compatibility and procedural differences. . . ."

Communications failures were also acknowledged by Army Major General Jack Farris who was the Commander of U.S. Forces Grenada from October 29 until December 15, 1983. General Farris said that the inability of the Army and the Navy to work together "causes communications problems . . . components of the Joint Task Force being [not] able to talk to each other. . . . It affects the efficiency of all your operations—for example, intelligence operations. . . ."

3. Fire Support

By all accounts the fire support to the Marines was adequate and presented no problem. However, fire support from the Navy to the Army was a serious problem.

According to after-action reports, the coordination between the Army and the Navy ranged from poor to non-existent. The initial assault on the southern part of the island was made by U.S. Army Ranger elements. The Navy was not present at any of the Ranger planning sessions and when Navy aviators were briefed on their mission to support the ground troops, no Army representatives or Air Force Forward Controllers were present. According to an after-action report, Navy aviators

> went into combat the first day with absolutely no knowledge or coordination with the Ranger operation . . . due to this reason all [USS Independence-based] aircraft were initially prohibited from flying south of the northern sector without [special] permission until midday of day one. . . .

Likewise, representatives of the 82nd Airborne were not present at CINCLANT's planning sessions on Monday, October 24.

> *This conscious oversight proved to have several ill-effects, the most important of which was the failure to obtain critical information on the non-Army fire support assets in the area of operations. Procedures for requesting naval gunfire communications channels to be used, FSE [the 82nd Airborne Division fire support elements] coordination with the Supporting Arms Coordination Center (SACC), availability and munitions of air and naval assets are examples of the kinds of issues which were not fully resolved before deployment. These problems and others were dealt with on the ground. . . .*

4. Lack of a Unified Ground Commander

Other problems were apparently caused by the failure to appoint a single ground commander. The marines on the northern half of the island were designated as the 22nd MAU and the Army forces on the southern half were designated as JTF 123 (Rangers and Air Force gunships) and JTF 121 (82nd Airborne). These units reported directly to Admiral Metcalf, the commander of the Joint Task Force aboard the USS *Guam*.

At one point the boundary between the Marines and the Army was adjusted southward so that the Marines could conduct a helicopter and amphibious assault at Grand Mal near St. Georges. By all available accounts, the operation went well, but the absence of "unity of command" on the ground prompted General Farris to comment:

> *We never had a joint land [commander]. We never had a land forces commander in Grenada. Now, it wasn't necessary as long as the Marines were way up there in Pearls and the Army's way down there at Point Salines, but when the forces come into proximity—like they were there after the marines came in north of St. Georges—then you have forces operating in proximity and they must coordinate their efforts. And when you don't have a common commander, then what happens is that people have some disagreements and than [sic] they bicker and then they argue. And it takes time to do all that and to debate things and to decide what's going to be done. You don't have time for that in combat. There needs to be a guy there that can say here's the way we're going to do it, here's the resources we are going to use to do it with. . . .*

It is reasonable to assume that at least some of the organizational problems, such as the lack of coordination of fire support, could have been solved if a unified ground commander had been established.

5. Logistics

Similar organizational shortcomings caused serious logistics problems. The initial attack elements (the Rangers, the Marines and the 82nd Airborne Division) were deployed so rapidly and with such little planning that they arrived with only what they could load on the initial aircraft. . . .

There were problems even within the Services. For example, Lt. Col. Keith Nightingale, a battalion commander in the 82nd, said "we deployed with virtually nothing except what was in our rucksacks." The 82nd deployed with no vehicles. There was no room on any of the aircraft for the 150 transporters a battalion would normally take on a mission. Without its trucks, the 82nd has no long range communications gear. "No vehicles meant no radios" said Nightingale's executive officer. The 82nd arrived without any heavy anti-armor weapons. TOW missiles did not arrive until D+3. The 82nd did not have the ability to communicate sophisticated intelligence data because its radio teletype [was] "delayed because they earned a low ranking on the aircraft priority list. . . ." As a result, the Rangers and the 82nd had to commandeer local trucks and gasoline.

Once the Port Salines airstrip had been secured, a substantial airlift began but backups occurred almost at once. One principle [sic] reason was that the runway would only permit aircraft to land, unload, and take off one at a time. But there were other, more organic problems. Duffy writes:

> Many units deployed from U.S. bases to Grenada actually spent more time circling the Point Salines airfield than in transit. Some aircraft had to return to Puerto Rico and other locations to refuel. "Aircraft were stacked up to the ionosphere," says one commander, who added that lift operations might have been aborted had the enemy had longer range anti-aircraft capability.
>
> The airlift back-up was complicated by a number of factors. All requests for supplies and access to the island were channeled through the Military Airlift Command's liaison working with the task force commander. But many units, both in Grenada and in the United States, tried to obtain direct flights to the island regardless of the pecking order. The conflicting systems kept a lot of people in the air and probably delayed the arrival of needed equipment. . . .

In addition there were a number of other problems. Native food had to be bought in great quantities because much of the rations shipped to the island for U.S. soldiers had to be diverted to feed the more than 800 prisoners of war. The Army also had to create a unique supply system because its existing supply channels proved to be too cumbersome. According to reports, the 82nd Airborne Division resorted to using messengers who would return to Ft. Bragg and order supplies directly from various Army depots. The supplies would then be sent by Express Mail to Ft. Bragg where they were loaded on aircraft bound for Grenada. Even with this expedited process, the first delivery took eight days.

URGENT FURY revealed many shortcomings in the logistical support for the rapid deployment of joint forces. Vice Admiral William Cowhill, the Director of Logistics for the Joint Chiefs of Staff during the operation, has observed:

> You've got to get the logistics in early. You get different forces from different services and it causes overlaps and shortages. Unless you get the staffs together early, you can't do the proper coordinating. . . .

As in other areas examined in this analysis, it seems reasonable to conclude that better organization would have avoided many of these problems.

6. Conclusions

The operation in Grenada was a success, and organizational shortcomings should not detract from that success or from the bravery and ingenuity displayed by American servicemen.

However, serious problems resulted from organizational shortfalls which should be corrected. URGENT FURY demonstrated that there are major deficiencies in the ability of the Services to work jointly when deployed rapidly. The poor communications between the Army and the Navy are unacceptable. The Services are aware of some of these problems and have created a number of units and procedures to coordinate communications, such as the Joint Communications Support Element and the Joint Deployment Agency. However, in Grenada, they either were not used or did not work. More fundamentally, one must ask why such coordinating mechanisms are necessary. Is it not possible to buy equipment that is compatible rather than having to improvise and concoct cumbersome bureaucracies so that the Services can talk to one another? Are the unified commands so lacking in unity that they cannot mount joint operations without elaborate coordinating mechanisms? In a war, these mechanisms would probably be discarded in favor of a much more direct procedure, as happened in several instances in Grenada.

Similar problems arose because of differences in doctrine and training. The lack of understanding on the part of very senior commanders in all Services about the capabilities, assets and tactics of the other Services resulted in serious shortcomings. Far more attention must be paid to joint operations because employment of force by the United States in all but the most unusual circumstances will be joint. . . .

This inability to work together has its roots in organizational shortcomings. The Services continue to operate as largely independent agencies, even at the level of the unified commands. The failure of the Joint Task Force Commander in Grenada to be familiar with Army and Air Force tactics and assets, and the failure of the senior Army commanders to be aware of the problems of working with the Navy, clearly demonstrate this problem.

In future conflicts, we may not be so successful.

WOMEN CADETS AT WEST POINT

Helen Rogan

Many new challenges confronted the armed services because of the social revolution in the United States following the Vietnam War. Some enlisted men wanted to organize a servicemen's union to represent them. Homosexual rights groups contended that "gays" should not be automatically excluded from the military. Ethnic minorities demanded better representation in the officer corps. But possibly the greatest social change in the armed forces in recent years has been the integration of women into every aspect of military life except direct combat. Before the Vietnam War, women were excluded from almost all military specialties except nursing and clerical duties. Today, they are eligible for almost any job that does not require the firing of weapons at an enemy.

In one way or another, women have been in war zones in every American war. At first, they accompanied armies as laundresses or seamstresses. By the end of the Civil War, women served in a quasi-official capacity as battlefield nurses. In the twentieth century, the United States officially established in every service a branch for nurses and a special women's corps, designed primarily for clerical help. Still, women were largely segregated from men. They were trained in separate, all-female units and generally could not command men. These regulations limited any woman's chance to have a satisfying career in the military.

The Vietnam War brought female nurses and clerks into the fight. Because there were no front lines in Vietnam, women often found themselves under enemy fire. Old taboos disappeared at home where a sexual

SOURCE: Reprinted by permission of the Putnam Publishing Group from *Mixed Company: Women in the Modern Army* by Helen Rogan. Copyright © 1981 by Helen Rogan.

revolution changed American mores. Women's groups won case after case in the courts for equal rights and pay. The final bastion of male control fell in the summer of 1976 when the first female cadets entered the three service academies. The old guard did not make life easy for them, but many of these women survived, and some excelled. Their success opened new opportunities for women at all levels of military life. The following selection comes from Helen Rogan's book, *Mixed Company*, a study of women in the army. This chapter examines the experiences of the first female cadets at West Point.

Most of the cadets who arrived in July 1976 had visited the Academy only once or twice before. West Point at first glimpse is awesome, even frightening—a pile of granite buildings on high bluffs overlooking a bend in the Hudson River, two hours' drive north from New York City. It is a fortress, not a college. The ethos is rugged, based on a Spartan life of intense competition—particularly in athletics—arduous, continuous study, both academic and military, and, pervading everything, strict adherence to discipline and tradition as exemplified in the motto Duty, Honor, Country. The idea is to elicit real leadership from a well-rounded individual. West Pointers proudly think of the Academy as a combat school, even though about 15 percent of the graduates in any given year do not enter the combat arms. Typical graduates are not intellectuals—they are practical, dogged, and competent, and often very successful, as they move surely up the ladder to the top positions at the Pentagon, in the field, and in business.

There were cracks in the structure. In 1976 the Academy . . . weathered a rough period when its cherished ideals were publicly and loudly held up to question. Some attributed the worst mismanagement and excesses of the Vietnam war to the rigidly deterministic approach to warfare taught at West Point. A large cheating scandal had violated the Honor Code, one of the Academy's most valued traditions.

General Goodpaster became the new Superintendent in the spring of 1977. A four-star general with a Ph.D., he had been persuaded to come out of retirement and accept a demotion in rank in order to help the Academy through its morale crisis. Some of the changes he began to make in the system coincided with the arrival of the women. . . .

Of the hundred and nineteen women who entered the Academy on July 7, 1976, hardly any were pioneers. (Those who were found themselves poorly equipped for the long, slow struggle ahead, and had vanished by Christmas.) They hesitated to call themselves "feminists," partly because the word would have been inflammatory under the circumstances, but they were women who wanted their equal opportunity and were not ready to settle for anything less. However, in outlook they greatly resembled the men: they were conservative, serious, patriotic, and many came from military families. They had performed better in high school than many of the men, and had participated in more extramural activities. They tended to be less athletic, both in strength and in inclination, and, on average, smaller, lighter, and weaker. . . .

The male cadets of the class of '80 were confronted with some surprises. When required to deal with women as colleagues and fellow students in the art of war, they experienced a jolt of disorientation. . . . The shock was accompanied by bitterness, rage, and bewilderment, and the result was—as I heard from the class of '80, their teachers, and tactical officers—a collision between the young males and females and a sustained and violent outburst of hostility from the men.

The stories came out in the cafeteria over paper cups of coffee at 8:15 A.M.—which for a cadet is the middle of the morning—and they came out in halting, polite voices as people sat carefully on their narrow iron beds. Alice Sullivan, an articulate twenty-three-year-old who had been studying for a degree in marine biology at the University of Colorado when she decided to try for West Point, was, of all the candidates I met, most detached from what had happened, presumably because she is a little older and has a skeptical streak that developed into a tendency at the Academy. She is slight and pale, no athlete, and she smokes a pack a day. She calls herself a wimp.

Alice told me that the problems began with the uniform. It had no pockets, which made life impossible for plebes, who are constantly required to scribble down notes. All the buttons and zippers were on the wrong side, and the plastic zippers on the trousers would break. (A few of the women ventured out to formation in a skirt once, but only once.) Because the design and fabric of the bulky uniform did not flatter the female figure, and because the jackets fastened on the wrong side, in inspections the women never had a trim "gig line"—the line made by jacket edges and trouser seams when everything is correct. Irate upperclassmen, sniffing for perfume, would poke and peer at the quaking women, and, unable to find a violation, conclude that what was wrong was what they had suspected all along. The cadets were girls!

Every cadet makes war stories out of the rigors of Beast. Amy Branch sat with me one morning in Grant Hall, with gossip and laughter all around, and she began to tell me her war stories. . . .

Branch said, "I remember the first time I really cried," and she told me about it. "One guy said to me, 'I can see by your rosy glow you must have been ——,' and I said, 'Now, you wouldn't have said that to your mother, your sister, or your girlfriend or my roommate, so *don't say it to me.*' He said, 'Can't you see I'm joking?' I got so mad."

Most of the abuse of the women was expressed in these sexual terms. A quiet, graceful cadet called Joan Reeve said to me, "When we were in formation we had to stand at attention in silence. The guys would gather around and say sexual things about us that we couldn't respond to. They would surmise about our weekends and they'd talk about how many women they had gotten to bed. It was embarrassing." She looked for more effective words and said, "Just to be talked about as if you're not entirely human is a kind of terror." Alice Sullivan, sitting cross-legged on her bed, told me, "They would warn our classmates not to go out with us because we carried a lot of diseases." She laughed thinly at my horrified expression and said, "Of course it was just quite standard to be walking out to formation or class all neat and straight and say to an upperclassmen, 'Good morning, sir' and have him say, 'Hi, whore.'"

Upperclassmen expressed their rage through enforced haircuts. One of the [coaches] in the physical education department told me, "They would be sent to have their hair cut, sometimes daily, and it would be savagely chopped off in tiers, so that it looked quite terrible." Some cadets managed to ignore it or rise above it, some seemed to invite more. They told me about finding condoms overflowing with shaving cream stuffed into their beds, obscene slogans written all over their walls; they received vibrators in the mail; they were called terrible names.

Reeve told me, "A sexual double standard was operating. In the beginning it was the ones who were prettiest or the most feminine, who wore perfume and makeup in formation. The guys didn't like that at all; they felt that if the women had time to do that, they should have been polishing shoes. They turned on the pretty women because they felt they didn't belong at West Point. They wanted to drive them out."

Another cadet said, "A lot depended on the company. The ones without women were the worst, and so they moved some in." Sullivan said, "In my company six out of the eleven women would collapse on the floor and hyperventilate." She lit a cigarette and added, "This stuff was not supposed to be going on. And you wouldn't believe how terrified most of the women were. One was literally too scared to leave her room—as soon as they see you, you're a target—and so she would urinate in the sink at night rather than risk going out to the bathroom." Sullivan said wanly, "We could not let the authorities know what was happening, because if we did we would be harassed further. We were victims, and there was nothing we could do."

There were visits from upperclassmen in the night. One sober young woman said, "It never happened to me, so I feel nervous about telling you, but I *know* it happened a lot between one and four A.M. when everyone was asleep. There are no guards, no locks on the doors, so you can just wander wherever you want." She said firmly, "I know of some plebe women who had this happen, and they couldn't tell."

Ellen Davis did tell. She was pretty and feminine-looking, with a high, girlish voice. A basketball star, very competent and keen, she was one of several women moved into a previously all-male company in order to improve antifemale attitudes. Ellen proved to be a catalyst for the hostility. She weathered several incidents of minor harassment before the night when an upperclassman came into her room at 2:30 A.M., and she awoke to the feel of his fingers between her legs. A friend of hers told me, "She just froze. She went downstairs and spent the rest of the night on the floor of another girl's room, who, when she woke up in the morning, found Ellen just sitting there in shock. They took her to the hospital, and the regimental commander took care of it. He was well known for his attitude; he'd brag about how many women he'd lost from his regiment. He's still there," she added.

The proceedings that followed were like an old-fashioned rape trial before a board. Ellen was put through a lie detector test and asked about her previous boyfriends and whether she was a virgin. The assailant was allowed to graduate but not commissioned, which made the rest of the women furious. They felt he had received the honor of graduation without the obligation of service—almost a reward. Ellen did not come back from vacation. Alice Sullivan told me, "One of the most interesting things about that was the reaction of the guys. They kept saying, 'Why are you all so upset, why's she so upset? She was just finger-fucked.'" There was a long pause, and Alice said, "I look at them, and I don't believe they said it, that they don't understand what it means to have your body violated." As a result of the incident the women, who share rooms, were not allowed to spend the night alone. If their roommates were away, they had to move in with other women for the night. They bitterly resented this, and moaned, "Why should *we* have to move?"

The other side of the sexual double standard was also in operation. It was not only the very pretty women who were picked on. Many of the others were powerfully built and muscular, a tendency that the rigorous training increased. Professional athletes are probably the only women who are more fit than West Point cadets. The men like to date lissome, elegant types, and they judged the women as potential dates. So they sneered at the heftier women, saying they had Hudson hips, and indeed some of them did. There were serious weight problems among the women, and among the men too. Amy Branch told me, "The food is very good, and when the tension is great, which it was for at least the first year, we all tended to compulsively eat, for comfort." In addition, the daily menu, relentlessly adjusted to the needs of hulking male youth, the prospective infantrymen, consisted of 5000 calories a day, itemized on the printed menu.

The men did not understand the workings of female physiology. There were a few attempts to educate them, but they probably had as much effect as other "leader-prep" lectures with subjects such as "Women as Leaders in American Society." The scorn and the cruel jokes with which they tormented the women cannot, however, be attributed simply to ignorance. Their behavior was not comparable to that of construction workers whistling at girls on their lunch hour or callow fraternity boys slopping their grain alcohol down the front of a dowdy girl. Something more than casual cruelty was involved, because West Point's ethos was and still is, however much the benign General Goodpaster and his aides may have attempted to change it, centered on athletic prowess.

"The training on the athletic fields which produces in a superlative degree the attributes of fortitude, self-control, resolution, courage, mental agility and, of course, physical development, is one completely fundamental to an efficient soldier." This was the view of General MacArthur, who created the intensive program of athletics. As far as the men were concerned, nobody could be a good officer without being a good athlete, or, at the very least, a good runner. The fear of "wimping out" would cause the less brawny men to throw up in secret terror before a PT test. The program had been modified for the women—something that the men could not forgive. The rationale was that the women should try almost everything, and that the requirements would be adjusted to meet their level of potential achievement. This was the only way for the women to reach their capacity.

The exceptions and modifications were crucial. Rough sports—football, hockey, lacrosse, rugby—would not be integrated; the women were to wear chest protectors during pugil stick training and fight only other women; the flexed-arm hang replaced the pull-up. On the reveille rifle run, all cadets were to carry an M-16 instead of an M-14 (an M-16 weighs 6.5 pounds empty—2.5 pounds less than an M-14). To accommodate the smaller reach of the women, the M-14, used in drill, had its operating rod spring shortened.

The separate grading scale on the obstacle course and the three-mile run meant that a female could get a low score and pass, while a male who got the same score had to go to summer school to make up—and this in an institution that was making so much triumphant noise about equality.

Furthermore, since the women learned neither to box nor to wrestle, and their close-quarters training emphasized self-defense, they never had bloody noses. The men were outraged, since deep down they knew that war is about bloody noses. They felt that the women's presence at West Point was a total cheat and public relations exercise if they were not to be put on the line physically. In hand-to-hand sports the men were graded, but the women did not have to compete in their simulated combat lessons in self-defense. As the men saw it, they did not have to try so hard. West Point teaches competition, but it lets the women escape when they cannot cope.

It lets them get over. This was a visceral feeling so strong that nobody could miss it. Not all the men felt it, but the few who did not kept silent, because it was unwise to speak out in favor of the women. . . .

So, understandably, the women tried to be invisible, and they avoided making waves. They could never succeed as men. That is, however, what they attempted. They *never* wore skirts, they lowered their voices to avoid attention, and they always looked as military as they could. For some, these efforts to merge took an extreme form. One young woman had a breast reduction. Her big breasts were not simply uncomfortable through all the physical exercises, they caused her to be tormented as well. Many of the really pretty young women left West Point. The rest learned to adapt. Some of them became religious. As one said to me, "Nobody's told West Point men it's okay to express your feelings. There's such a lack of love here, even between your friends, and so people turn to God." A slew of cadets rushed into marriage, and by the day of graduation thirty out of the sixty-two remaining women were engaged. West Point men often marry after graduation, and the sociologists say it is because they are apprehensive of leaving the structured security of Academy life. As for the women, they wanted to withdraw. Being engaged to cadets made them at once attractive and protected.

A few women did not need to withdraw. Amy Branch told me, "Because I'm black I know how to deal with the pressure right from the start. I know what it is like to be a minority. I was talking about this the other day with my black classmate and she said, 'I'm sick of these white girls talking about pressure. They don't know what real pressure is.'"

After four years of stress and adjustment the Academy and its inmates grew more tolerant. Fennessy, sitting in a cloud of cigarette smoke in her shared bedroom, said, "It's not cool to display the hostility anymore. Those who feel it keep their negative feelings under cover." The word from BS&L [West Point's sociology department, the Behavioral Science and Leadership Department] was: "Flagrant, odious abuses are gone, and if they recur the administration will deal with them." As a result, male officers and cadets now complain in private about being silenced. One young male captain, asking to remain anonymous, told me, "It's galling, because if you express any negative opinions about the women, your career is ruined. But the women are out there complaining to the press about every tiny thing." We were sitting in the basement of a classroom building, in a library, and talking in low voices. He cleared his throat and said, "I must say that when I came here I had strong opinions about the women, and as I worked with cadets my opinion changed. And all credit goes to the cadets. I had felt that the women would be unable to command the respect of the typical soldier or have a command presence, or stand the job emotionally and physically." He continued, choosing his words very carefully, "Some of the women who are here are unable to fit these categories." This was not a ringing endorsement, but it was not at all bad for a West Point graduate.

Nowadays women are not an aberration. If one drops out, there is not a crisis, and fewer women are dropping out. They come in better prepared mentally, and they have had sports programs in school. The new women are cheerful, irrepressible.

Marines in Lebanon, 1983 (Marine Corps photo). In 1983, President Ronald Reagan sent a force of marines into Lebanon to help maintain the shaky peace in that war-torn country. This photograph shows marine sniper scouts using sophisticated surveillance equipment to study the countryside around Beirut. The marines had been sent to Lebanon as part of a multinational peace force to try to prevent further conflict between Israel and the Palestine Liberation Organization (PLO). Because U.S. interests in the Middle East are closely allied with Israel's, the Palestinians regarded the American marines as a further extension of the Israeli military. In November 1983, a PLO terrorist drove a truck loaded with explosives onto the grounds of the U.S. embassy. There it exploded, killing 229 marines and wounding 81 others. Although the marine involvement in Lebanon had been undertaken with the best of intentions, it failed. It was clear that any future commitment of American troops would have to be backed up with adequate firepower. When the decision was made five years later to escort oil tankers through the dangerous waters of the Persian Gulf, there was enough military force present to protect U.S. personnel. One naval captain, who had permitted an Iraqi plane to strafe his ship, was relieved of command for dereliction of duty. Another captain was praised by the Reagan administration after shooting down an unarmed commercial airplane loaded with civilians. This captain and his crew had mistaken the airliner for a hostile Iranian military fighter.

THE ALL-VOLUNTEER ARMY

Charles C. Moskos, Jr.

In 1973, President Richard M. Nixon ended military conscription. Although all the armed services were affected, the army had the greatest adjustments to make. All-Volunteer Service helped defuse student protest over the Vietnam War, but also made it increasingly difficult for the army to attract middle-class, white males into its combat branches (infantry, armor, and artillery).

Except for the year before World War II, peacetime conscription in the United States was new. It was first used in 1948 in response to the perceived threat of the Soviet Union. All males who were physically fit and over eighteen could be drafted, but there was a host of deferments available that could be used to delay or prevent service. It was easy for college-educated males from middle-class families to avoid military service. However, the increased manpower needs in Vietnam meant that conscription could draft them too. Many college-educated, middle-class draftees were placed in combat assignments because the more desirable specialties were reserved for volunteers. A lottery system was introduced to end the uncertainty, but it had the countereffect of increasing the certainty of military service for some men, regardless of background.

An All-Voluntary Force made military service voluntary and removed a primary objection to the Vietnam War. But it also meant that the enlisted ranks no longer included a broad cross-section of the American population. In the army, soldiers came from a background that was predominantly lower-class—Hispanics, blacks, and poorly educated whites. Critics with short historical memories complained that such an unrepresentative force

SOURCE: "Status of the All-Volunteer Armed Force." Hearing before the Subcommittee on Manpower and Personnel of the Committee on Armed Services, United States Senate, 95th Congress, 2nd Session, June 20, 1978 (Washington, DC: 1978).

was "un-American." In truth, enlisted military service had always attracted minorities and the undereducated. A government survey of army recruits before the Mexican War concluded that "the material offered in time of peace is not of the most desirable character, consisting principally of newly arrived immigrants, of those broken down by bad habits and dissipation, the idle, and the improvident."

The All-Voluntary Service did create some disquieting problems. The first and most important is the question of good citizenship: whether every citizen should give some time in national service. Second, Congress was faced with providing adequate career benefits for enlisted personnel so that they would not feel alienated from the society they were to serve and protect. Third, despite the military's frequently heard television commercial to "Be All That You Can Be," military service requires group identity and cooperation, not individual initiative. Many volunteers quickly become disenchanted with peacetime service, which may include meaningless tasks compounded by "Mickey Mouse" regulations. Last is the problem of effective control. When the military is only composed of volunteers, the public and its representatives tend to permit a wider latitude of toleration. This may lead to more frequent employment of the military, less concern over tactics used against enemies (as in the American Indian wars or the Philippine insurrection), and a general deterioration of enlisted morale compounded by drug or alcohol abuse.

The following reading was taken from a 1978 Senate hearing chaired by Democrat Sam Nunn of Georgia on the status of the All-Volunteer Service. Charles C. Moskos, Jr., is a professor of sociology at Northwestern University. He is an authority on enlisted life in the military and has written extensively on the All-Volunteer Army and voluntary national service.

Mr. Moskos.   Since January 1963, the United States has sought to accomplish what it has never attempted before—to maintain over two million persons on active military duty on a voluntary basis. Now into its 6th year, the All-Volunteer Force has been analyzed in a seemingly endless series of studies. The commentators tend to divide into two groups. On the one side, there are those who convey their belief that the All-Volunteer Force is a success which at most requires only certain changes in personnel management policies. On the other, there are those who see little prospect of a viable defense force short of returning to a form of compulsory military service. I place myself in neither camp.

The problems in the All-Volunteer Force are not found in the end of conscription, or in the efforts of service recruiters, who have accomplished a task of immense proportions. The grievous flaw has been a redefinition of military service in terms of the economic marketplace. This has contributed to moving the American military away from an institutional format to one more and more resembling that of an occupation.

I may add immodestly that I was the first person to draw to public attention the shift to an occupational format in the wake of the All-Volunteer Force. It has eroded the standard of military participation as a citizen's duty.

My statement focuses on that component of the All-Volunteer Force which relied most directly on the draft—the enlisted ranks of the Army. It must be immediately emphasized, however, that all services were beneficiaries of the Selective Service System. The draft was also the major impetus for recruitment into reserve/guard units. Recruitment objectives, moreover, will confront inescapable demographic constraints; in 1977, some 2.14 million males reached age 18; in 1980 the figure will decline slightly to 2.13 million, and then drop precipitously to 1.8 million by 1985, and 1.7 million by 1990.

We have already mentioned here the decreasing cohort of young persons turning age 18 over the next couple of years. We have also heard remarks about the drop in the educational levels of non-prior service [NPS] male enlistees in the All-Volunteer Force. What has not been stressed enough is a comparison point with the average education of the 19-year-old male. From this perspective we find the Army is recruiting almost double the proportion of high school dropouts than there is in the equivalent age group for the larger society.

It is a misjudgment to compare today's All-Volunteer Force with the last year's draft Army in 1972–73. That was the point when the American military was close to its lowest in its modern history. The more meaningful reference would be the peacetime draft of the pre-Vietnam era. In 1977 approximately 44 percent of the males did not possess a high school diploma entering the Army. In 1964 only 28 percent of the draftees were similarly high school dropouts. So, over the past 15 years there has been a tremendous increase in high school dropouts entering the Army.

One might also add that to be a high school dropout today means you are really trying.

We are not referring to the same kind of person who was a dropout a decade or two back. The census figures are clear that high school graduates have been increasing steadily over the past decade and a half. We have a situation today where the voluntary Army is going contrary to the national trend, recruiting lesser educated people when in society as a whole more people are finishing high school.

It is also remarkable we are only talking about high school diplomas being a major indicator. What about college people? In the pre-Vietnam

Army college people composed a large segment of the enlisted ranks. Army data show over 17 percent of drafted soldiers in 1963 had some college compared to less than 5 percent of All-Volunteer entrants.

The rising proportion of minority entrants has generated controversy in the debate on the All-Volunteer Army. In 1977 black accession exceeded 30 percent of NPS males. The rise in black content reflects the large increase in the proportion of blacks eligible for military service—through higher educational levels and better aptitude scores—the unprecedently high unemployment rate among black youth in the 1970's, and the appeal of an institution that has gone further than any other to attack racism. Although the number of other minorities is not as [reliably] tabulated, a figure of at least 5 percent, principally Hispanic, would be a cautious estimate. In other words, over one-third of the men now entering the Army's enlisted ranks are from minority groups. To take note of the minority composition of the Army must not misdirect attention away from the participation—or lack of it—of the larger white middle-class population.

It is important to stress that the decline in educational levels of NPS male recruits is not correlated with the rising number of black servicemen. Since the end of the draft, the proportion of black high school graduates entering the Army has exceeded that of whites, and this is a trend that is becoming more pronounced. In point of fact, today's Army is the only major arena in American Society where black educational levels surpass that of whites, and by quite a significant margin.

What is happening in the All-Volunteer Army is that whereas the black soldier is fairly representative of the black community, white entrants of recent years are coming from the least educated sectors of the white community. In my stays with Army line units I am most impressed by what I do not often find—urban and suburban white soldiers of middle-class origins. The All-Volunteer Army, that is, is attracting not only a disproportionate number of minorities, but also an unrepresentative segment of white youth, who, if anything, are more uncharacteristic of the broader social mix than are our minority soldiers.

An unanticipated consequence of the All-Volunteer Force has been a dramatic change in the marital composition of the Army. From 1965 to 1976, the proportion of married enlisted men increased from 36.4 to 56.9 percent. The figures are all the more remarkable in that they reflect almost entirely a change among junior enlisted personnel; thus in 1977, 43.7 percent of E-4's, the modal lower enlisted pay grade, were married. This has caused accompanying organizational and economic costs in the operation of the All-Volunteer Force. The sharp increase in the number of young enlisted marrieds runs directly counter to national trends where the clear pattern is toward later marriage.

Perhaps no change in the All-Volunteer Force has received as much media attention as the growing numbers and role of women service members. A strong argument could be made that it has been the female entrants, virtually all of whom possess a high school diploma, that are the margin of success in the All-Volunteer Force.

The crux of the issue remains the prohibition of women in the combat arms and aboard war ships. Leaving aside the considerable legal, normative, and organizational difficulties in the assignment of women to combat roles, a removal of the ban cannot be viewed as a solution to All-Volunteer recruitment. Certainly enlisted women are not clamoring for a major expansion of their numbers into combat roles—or even, for that matter, into heavy labor tasks. It is likely that the recruiting successes in attracting high quality women in the All-Volunteer Force would be reversed if combat assignment were given to females.

A metamorphosis has occurred in the enlisted ranks. There is no question of that. The real question is how high powered studies and well financed commissions can come up with the opposite conclusion—that is a remarkable thing—which argues that there has been no change in the social composition of the enlisted ranks. . . .

What other studies usually do is to merge all the services together. You have, for example, the Air Force which has a higher educational level and this ups the average. If you look at the Army, the force most affected by the absence of the draft, the evidence is incontrovertible that there has been a broad and basic change in the social composition of the enlisted ranks. When you figure over half of our white entrants do not possess a high school diploma, that alone is indicative of a tremendous social change.

The distinctive quality of the enlisted ranks in modern times has been a mixing of the social classes. This served to give less advantaged youth an opportunity to test themselves, often successfully, against more privileged youth. This was the elemental social fact underlying the enlisted experience. This is the state of affairs that has disappeared in the All-Volunteer Army.

To ask what kind of society excuses its privileged from serving in the ranks of its military is not to argue that the makeup of the enlisted ranks be perfectly calibrated to the social composition of the larger society. But if participation of persons coming from less advantaged backgrounds in leadership positions is used as a measure of democratic character, it is even more important that participation of more advantaged groups in the rank and file also be a measure of representational democracy.

The time is ready to reassess our stock of experience regarding the All-Volunteer Force. It ought not be constrained by policy alternatives—tinkering with the all-volunteer status quo versus bringing back conscription—that dominate the debate on the All-Volunteer Force. What are the relations between citizen participation, the kind of enlisted force that is desirable, and national security? Econometrically based analyses tend not to ask these kind of questions, but we must.

We have heard some talk about bringing the draft back in recent months but I think the possibility is remote. The most popular thing Richard Nixon ever did was to end the draft.

It is indisputable that public opinion strongly supports the all-volunteer concept. A return to the draft would also pose again the question of who serves when not all serve. . . .

You face the inevitable problem of who serves, if not all serve. Some people will try to stay out which will bring its own problems in its wake. What you can do is have the analog of the draftee in the all-volunteer framework. We cannot walk back down the road toward the draft. The problems would be severe if we did bring back the draft.

Granting conscription is not [feasible], what about management steps that could be taken to improve manpower utilization within the all-volunteer framework. Here we run into the difficulty that most proposals in this vein—a kind of suboptimal approach—do not address the core issue: Getting young men into the ground combat arms or onto warships. Neither lowering physical standards for men, nor increasing the number of women, nor greater reliance on civilian personnel suit the imperatives of combat assignments.

That increasing the proportions of such categories in support units will result in releasing more soldiers for assignment into the combat arms is also highly questionable. What would probably happen is that the All-Volunteer Force will experience even greater recruitment and attrition problems among its male soldiers than presently.

Large raises in military pay were the principal rationale to induce persons to join the All-Volunteer Force. This has turned out to be a double-edged sword, however. Youth surveys show that high pay motivates less qualified youth, for example, high school dropouts, those with poor grades, to join, while having a negligible effect on more qualified youth, those taking academic high school courses or college bound.

To use salary incentive as the primary motivating force to join and remain in the military can also lead to grave morale problems. If future military pay raises were to lag behind civilian scales, as seems likely, the present grumbling throughout the ranks now limited to preceived erosion of entitlements would then become a rumbling chrous of complaint.

The central issue remains: Is there a way without direct compulsion or excessive reliance on marketplace determinants by which a large and representative cross section of young men can be attracted into the combat arms. Or to put it another way, can we obtain the analog of the peacetime draftee in the all-volunteer framework? I believe there is. Several proposals are presented by consideration.

First, one step would be a 2-year enlistment option—the term of the draftee—to be restricted to the combat arms, low skill shipboard duty, and labor intensive fields. It is in these very low skill tasks that attrition problems are most severe in the modern Volunteer Force. If you say 4 out of 10 servicemen don't complete their enlistment, if you look at the low-skill jobs the figure would be much higher, well over half.

The quid pro quo for such assignment would be post service educational benefits along the lines of the GI bill of World War II. A college education in exchange for 2 years in the combat arms formula would be a means to attract highly qualified soliders who can learn quickly, serve effectively for a full tour, and then be replaced by similarly qualified recruits. Moreover, because there would be no presumption of acquiring civilian skills in the military, the terms of such short-term service would be unambiguous, you are not promising anything, thus alleviating a major source of post entry discontent in the All-Volunteer Force.

There are so many tasks in the military which cannot be gussied up as satisfying jobs or jobs that have civilian transferability.

A second proposal would go a step farther. The military could set up a two-track personnel system recognizing a distinction between a citizen soldier and a career soldier. Soldier is used here inclusively for airmen, sailors, and marines. The career soldier would be assigned and compensated in the manner of the prevailing system.

The citizen soldier, however, would serve a 2-year term in the combat arms or labor intensive tasks with a low active duty salary, few if any entitlements, but with deferred compensation in the form of post service educational benefits.

Third, for highly skilled technicians, the answer might be subsidized education in a civilian university with a prescribed pre-engineering or science curriculum. Such an educational program would entail attendance at a civilian university during freshman and sophomore years, along with military training during the interim summers. Upon completion of the sophomore year, the service member would be committed to 3 or 4 years in an active duty assignment in an earmarked technical position. A continuing inflow of such near-engineers would be one way of addressing the perennial problem of retraining highly skilled personnel in the military system.

Fourth, there has been some movement on Capital Hill and the administration to provide financial relief for middle-income families with children in college. Whether the student aid program takes the form of tax credits for parents or expansion of Federal grants to students, it is estimated this will cost at least $1.2 billion—some say more than $4 billion—

annually. It is amazing that no public leader has thought to connect such student aid with national youth service, civilian as well as military.

It could be said that those tax credits or grants could only be given to those youths who perform a service to their country.

The above are only sketchy proposals, but there is some evidence that many qualified youths would choose a term in the military under such conditions. In fact, for many in their late teens or early twenties, a deversion from the world of school or work would be tolerable and perhaps even welcome.

Post-service educational benefits, morever, could be tied to military obligations following active duty and thus bolster our sagging reserve forces. The only way of salvaging our reserve forces would be to get prior-duty service persons in those positions. If reserve duty were linked with post-service benefits, I think the solution would be well in hand.

The definition of military service in the all-volunteer era needs overhauling as badly as the machinery of selection. We must break the mind-set that sees the All-Volunteer Force as possible only in terms of the marketplace. Attracting a representative, including college-bound, cross section of American youth to serve in the military would help reinvigorate the ideal of military participation as a citizen's duty. In the final analysis, the market system is not the way to recruit an All-Volunteer Force, nor is it the way to strengthen a service institution. . . .

We must talk about redefinition of military service. We must not think of the present as peacetime waiting for a war to happen. The military is serving a positive deterrent and national security role as it is. We are now a force in being, not just a cadre force ready to grow in case of hostilities.

So, our servicemen and our citizenry should understand what they are doing today. Even in a nonhostility situation, our military is performing a vital national service. I am always constantly impressed by the fact that very few servicemen have any sense of higher mission and calling in their present duty, especially in the ground combat forces.

Senator Nunn.   What about Reserve Forces? How would your proposal affect Reserve Forces, the education benefits, and so forth?

Mr. Moskos.   Many people joined the Reserves or the Guard to stay out of active duty. That is the blunt truth of the matter. At the end of the draft one of the major motivations for joining the National Guard disappeared. We have to think of ways of linking post-service obligation with educational benefits and reserve duty. Indeed if one goes on to college, reserve duty dovetails quite nicely with that kind of life pattern [in] terms of weekends being free, summers being free, things of that sort.

This, I believe, would really answer the question. The thing about the Reserves being in such a shambles is that it has made the issue of the All-Volunteer Force come to the fore. If you ask me candidly I would give the active duty force about "C-plus" or "B-minus" in terms of a noninflated grade system. That is where they stand. It is not in a state of crisis. But it is not as good as it ought to be.

ANNOTATED BIBLIOGRAPHY

Books on contemporary military issues tend either to be sociological studies of military life or critiques of current military policy. Among the best in the former group are Morris Janowitz's *The Professional Soldier* (1960), Charles C. Moskos, Jr.'s, *The American Enlisted Man: The Rank and File in Today's Military* (1970), and Larry R. Ingraham's *The Boys in the Barracks: Observations on American Military Life* (1984). Less positive, but very readable and popular studies of the same subjects, are Ward Just's *Military Men* (1970) and Maureen Mylander's *The Generals* (1970).

Studies critical of the military-industrial complex began with C. Wright Mills's pioneering work, *The Power Elite* (1956), which took on the establishment before it had become popular to do so. Noam Chomsky's *American Power and the New Mandarins* (1969), Ralph E. Lapp's *The Weapons Culture* (1968), Clark R. Mollenhoff's *The Pentagon: Politics, Profits and Plunder* (1967), and James A. Donovan's *Militarism, U.S.A.* are recent works in the same genre. John Stanley Baumgartner takes on these critics in his proestablishment book, *The Lonely Warriors: Case for the Military-Industrial Complex* (1970). An important study of the role of the modern military officer as a manager (rather than as leader) may be found in Richard A. Gabriel and Paul L. Savage's *Crisis in Command: Mismanagement and the Army* (1978) and Robert Ellis and Robert Moore's *School for Soldiers: West Point and the Profession of Arms* (1974). Richard A. Gabriel continued his attack on the armed forces in *Military Incompetence: Why the American Military Doesn't Win* (1985). More objective and comprehensive than most studies is Adam Yarmolinsky's *The Military Establishment: Its Impact on American Society* (1971), a history of that relationship since the Second World War.

THE ROMANCE OF WAR

The question of whether war is a genetically determined or a culturally acquired trait in human beings has long challenged psychologists, sociologists, and anthropologists. Whether natured or nurtured, war is an often-condemned, but a much-loved, human activity. Earlier selections in this anthology have expressed man's fascination with war. Some psychologists have compared this attraction in males to the mothering instinct in females. Whether innate or acquired, one thing is certain—both emotions are strongly ingrained in the human species.

The following article does not attempt to answer academic or philosophical questions. Instead, it shows through one man's experiences the affection that most males have for war. By discussing his own love of war, William Broyles helps readers understand its universal attraction: Why men in all times and places have risked death, rather than miss the "beauty" and thrill of war.

WHY MEN LOVE WAR

William Broyles, Jr.

I last saw Hiers in a rice paddy in Vietnam. He was nineteen then—my wonderfully skilled and maddeningly insubordinate radio operator. For months we were seldom more than three feet apart. Then one day he went home, and fifteen years passed before we met by accident last winter at the Vietnam Veterans Memorial in Washington. A few months later I visited Hiers and his wife, Susan, in Vermont, where they run a bed-and-breakfast place. The first morning we were up at dawn trying to save five newborn rabbits. Hiers built a nest of rabbit fur and straw in his barn and positioned a lamp to provide warmth against the bitter cold.

"What people can't understand," Hiers said, gently picking up each tiny rabbit and placing it in the nest, "is how much fun Vietnam was. I loved it. I loved it, and I can't tell anybody."

Hiers loved war. And as I drove back from Vermont in a blizzard, my children asleep in the back of the car, I had to admit that for all these years I also had loved it, and more than I knew. I hated war, too. Ask me, ask any man who has been to war about his experience, and chances are we'll say we don't want to talk about it—implying that we hated it so much, it was so terrible, that we would rather leave it buried. And it is no mystery why men hate war. War is ugly, horrible, evil, and it is reasonable for men to hate all that. But I believe that most men who have been to war would have to admit, if they are honest, that somewhere inside themselves they loved it too, loved it as much as anything that has happened to them before or since. And how do you explain that to your wife, your children, your parents, or your friends?

SOURCE: *Esquire*, vol. 102 (November 1984). Courtesy of William Broyles, Jr.

That's why men in their sixties and seventies sit in their dens and recreation rooms around America and know that nothing in their life will equal the day they parachuted into St. Lo or charged the bunker on Okinawa. That's why veterans' reunions are invariably filled with boozy awkwardness, forced camaraderie ending in sadness and tears: you are together again, these are the men who were your brothers, but it's not the same, can never be the same. That's why when we returned from Vietnam we moped around, listless, not interested in anything or anyone. Something had gone out of our lives forever, and our behavior on returning was inexplicable except as the behavior of men who had lost a great—perhaps the great—love of their lives, and had no way to tell anyone about it.

In part we couldn't describe our feelings because the language failed us: the civilian-issue adjectives and nouns, verbs and adverbs, seemed made for a different universe. There were no metaphors that connected the war to everyday life. But we were also mute, I suspect, out of shame. Nothing in the way we are raised admits the possibility of loving war. It is at best a necessary evil, a patriotic duty to be discharged and then put behind us. To love war is to mock the very values we supposedly fight for. It is to be insensitive, reactionary, a brute.

But it may be more dangerous, both for men and nations, to suppress the reasons men love war than to admit them. In *Apocalypse Now* Robert Duvall, playing a brigade commander, surveys a particularly horrific combat scene and says, with great sadness, "You know, someday this war's gonna be over." He is clearly meant to be a psychopath, decorating enemy bodies with playing cards, riding to war with Wagner blaring. We laugh at him—Hey! nobody's like that! And last year in Grenada American boys charged into battle playing Wagner, a new generation aping the movies of Vietnam the way we aped the movies of World War II, learning nothing, remembering nothing.

Alfred Kazin wrote that war is the enduring condition of twentieth-century man. He was only partly right. War is the enduring condition of man, period. Men have gone to war over everything from Helen of Troy to Jenkins's ear. Two million Frenchmen and Englishmen died in muddy trenches in World War I because a student shot an archduke. The truth is, the reasons don't matter. There is a reason for every war and a war for every reason.

For centuries men have hoped that with history would come progress, and with progress, peace. But progress has simply given man the means to make war even more horrible; no wars in our savage past can begin to match the brutality of the wars spawned in this century, in the beautifully ordered, civilized landscape of Europe, where everyone is literate and classical music plays in every village cafe. War is not an aberration; it is part of the family, the crazy uncle we try—in vain—to keep locked in the basement.

Consider my own example. I am not a violent person. I have not been in a fight since grade school. Aside from being a fairly happy-go-lucky carnivore, I have no lust for blood, nor do I enjoy killing animals, fish, or even insects. My days are passed in reasonable contentment, filled with the details of work and everyday life. I am also a father now, and a man who has helped create life is war's natural enemy. I have seen what war does to children, makes them killers or victims, robs them of their parents, their homes, and their innocence—steals their childhood and leaves them marked in body, mind, and spirit.

I spent most of my combat tour in Vietnam trudging through its jungles and rice paddies without incident, but I have seen enough of war to know that I never want to fight again, and that I would do everything in my power to keep my son from fighting. Then why, at the oddest times—when I am in a meeting or running errands, or on beautiful summer evenings, with the light fading and children playing around me—do my thoughts turn back fifteen years to a war I didn't believe in and never wanted to fight? Why do I miss it?

I miss it because I loved it, loved it in strange and troubling ways. When I talk about loving war I don't mean the romantic notion of war that once mesmerized generations raised on Walter Scott. What little was left of that was ground into the mud at Verdun and Passchendaele; honor and glory do not survive the machine gun. And it's not the mindless bliss of martyrdom that sends Iranian teenagers armed with sticks against Iraqi tanks. Nor do I mean the sort of hysteria that can grip a whole country, the way during the Falklands war the English press inflamed the lust that lurks beneath the cool exterior of Britain. That is vicarious war, the thrill of participation without risk, the lust of the audience for blood. It is easily fanned, that lust; even the invasion of a tiny island like Grenada can do it. Like all lust, for as long as it lasts it dominates everything else; a nation's other problems are seared away, a phenomenon exploited by kings, dictators, and presidents since civilization began.

And I don't mean war as an addiction, the constant rush that war junkies get, the crazies mailing ears home to their girlfriends, the zoomies [pilots] who couldn't get an erection unless they were cutting in the afterburners on their F-4s. And, finally, I'm not talking about how some men my age feel today, men who didn't go to war but now have a sort of nostalgic longing for something they missed, some classic male experience, the way some women who didn't have children worry they missed something basic about being a woman, something they didn't value when they could have done it.

I'm talking about why thoughtful, loving men can love war even while knowing and hating it. Like any love, the love of war is built on a complex of often contradictory reasons. Some of them are fairly painless to discuss;

others go almost too deep, stir the caldron too much. I'll give the more respectable reasons first.

Part of the love of war stems from its being an experience of great intensity; its lure is the fundamental human passion to witness, to see things, what the Bible calls the lust of the eye and the Marines in Vietnam called eye fucking. War stops time, intensifies experience to the point of a terrible ecstasy. It is the dark opposite of that moment of passion caught in "Ode on a Grecian Urn": "For ever warm and still to be enjoy'd/ For ever panting, and for ever young." War offers endless exotic experiences, enough "I couldn't fucking believe it!"'s to last a lifetime.

Most people fear freedom; war removes that fear. And like a stern father, it provides with its order and discipline both security and an irresistible urge to rebel against it, a constant yearning to fly over the cuckoo's nest. The midnight requisition is an honored example. I remember one elaborately planned and meticulously executed raid on our principal enemy—the U.S. Army, not the North Vietnamese—to get lightweight blankets and cleaning fluid for our rifles, repeated later in my tour, as a mark of my changed status, to obtain a refrigerator and an air conditioner for our office. To escape the Vietnamese police we tied sheets together and let ourselves down from the top floor of whorehouses, and on one memorable occasion a friend who is now a respectable member of our diplomatic corps hid himself inside a rolled-up Oriental rug while the rest of us careered off in the truck, leaving him to make his way back stark naked to our base six miles away. War, since it steals our youth, offers a sanction to play boys' games.

War replaces the difficult gray areas of daily life with an eerie, serene clarity. In war you usually know who is your enemy and who is your friend, and are given means of dealing with both. (That was, incidentally, one of the great problems with Vietnam: it was hard to tell friend from foe—it was too much like ordinary life.)

War is an escape from the everyday into a special world where the bonds that hold us to our duties in daily life—the bonds of family, community, work—disappear. In war, all bets are off. It's the frontier beyond the last settlement, it's Las Vegas. The men who do well in peace do not necessarily do well at war, while those who were misfits and failures may find themselves touched with fire. U.S. Grant, selling firewood on the streets of St. Louis and then four years later commanding the Union armies, is the best example, although I knew many Marines who were great warriors but whose ability to adapt to civilian life was minimal.

I remember Kirby, a skinny kid with JUST YOU AND ME LORD tattooed on his shoulder. Kirby had extended his tour in Vietnam twice. He had long since ended his attachment to any known organization and lived alone out in the most dangerous areas, where he wandered about night and day, dressed only in his battered fatigue trousers with a .45 automatic tucked into the waistband, his skinny shoulders and arms as dark as a Montagnard's.

One day while out on patrol we found him on the floor of a hut, being tended by a girl in black pajamas, a bullet wound in his arm.

He asked me for a cigarette, then eyed me, deciding if I was worth telling his story to. "I stopped in for a mango, broad daylight, and there bigger'n hell were three NVA officers, real pretty tan uniforms. They got this map spread out on a table, just eyeballin' it, makin' themselves right at home. They looked at me. I looked at them. Then they went for their nine millimeters and I went for my .45."

"Yeah?" I answered. "So what happened?"

"I wasted 'em," he said, them puffed on his cigarette. Just another day at work, killing three men on the way to eat a mango.

"How are you ever going to go back to the world?" I asked him. (He didn't. A few months later a ten-year-old Vietcong girl blew him up with a command-detonated booby trap.)

War is a brutal, deadly game, but a game, the best there is. And men love games. You can come back from war broken in mind or body, or not come back at all. But if you come back whole you bring with you the knowledge that you have explored regions of your soul that in most men will always remain uncharted. Nothing I had ever studied was as complex or as creative as the small-unit tactics of Vietnam. No sport I had ever played brought me to such deep awareness of my physical and emotional limits.

One night not long after I had arrived in Vietnam, one of my platoon's observation posts heard enemy movement. I immediately lost all saliva in my mouth. I could not talk; not a sound would pass my lips. My brain erased as if the plug had been pulled—I felt only a dull hum throughout my body, a low-grade current coursing through me like electricity through a power line. After a minute I could at least grunt, which I did as Hiers gave orders to the squad leaders, called in artillery and air support, and threw back the probe. I was terrified, I was ashamed, and I couldn't wait for it to happen again.

The enduring emotion of war, when everything else has faded, is comradeship. A comrade in war is a man you can trust with anything, because you trust him with your life. "It is," Phillip Caputo wrote in *A Rumor of War*, "unlike marriage, a bond that cannot be broken by a word, by boredom or divorce, or by anything other than death." Despite its extreme right-wing image, war is the only utopian experience most of us ever have. Individual possessions and advantage count for nothing; the group is everything. What you have is shared with your friends. It isn't a particularly selective process, but a love that needs no reasons, that transcends race and personality and education—all those things that would make a difference in peace. It is, simply, brotherly love.

What made this love so intense was that it had no limits, not even death. John Wheeler, in *Touched with Fire*, quotes the Congressional Medal of Honor citation of Hector Santiago-Colon: "Due to the heavy volume of enemy fire and exploding grenades around them, a North Vietnamese soldier was able to crawl, undetected, to their position. Suddenly, the enemy soldier lobbed a hand grenade into Sp4c. Santiago-Colon's foxhole. Realizing that there was no time to throw the grenade out of his position, Sp4c. Santiago-Colon retrieved the grenade, tucked it into his stomach, and, turning away from his comrades, absorbed the full impact of the blast." This is classic heroism, the final evidence of how much comrades can depend on each other. What went through Santiago-Colon's mind for that split second when he could just as easily have dived to safety? It had to be this: my comrades are more important to me than my most valuable possession—my own life.

Isolation is the greatest fear in war. The military historian S. L. A. Marshall conducted intensive studies of combat incidents during World War II and Korea and discovered that at most, only 25 percent of the men who were under fire actually fired their own weapons. The rest cowered behind cover, terrified and helpless—all systems off. Invariably, those men had felt alone, and to feel alone in combat is to cease to function; it is the terrifying prelude to the final loneliness of death. The only men who kept their heads felt connected to other men, a part of something, as if comradeship were some sort of collective life-force, the power to face death and stay conscious. But when those men came home from war, that fear of isolation stayed with many of them, a tiny mustard seed fallen on fertile soil.

When I came back from Vietnam I tried to keep up with my buddies. We wrote letters, made plans to meet, but something always came up and we never seemed to get together. For a few years we exchanged Christmas cards, then nothing. The special world that had sustained our intense comdradeship was gone. Everyday life—our work, family, friends, reclaimed us, and we grew up.

But there was something not right about that. In Vietnam I had been closer to Hiers, for example, than to anyone before or since. We were connected by the radio; our lives depended on it, and on each other. We ate, slept, laughed, and were terrified together. When I first arrived in Vietnam I tried to get Hiers to salute me, but he simply wouldn't do it, mustering at most a "Howdy, Lieutenant, how's it hanging?" as we passed. For every time that he didn't salute I told him he would have to fill a hundred sandbags.

We'd reached several thousand sandbags when Hiers took me aside and said, "Look, Lieutenant, I'll be happy to salute you, really. But if I get in the habit back here in the rear I may salute you when we're out in the bush. And those gooks are just waiting for us to salute, tell 'em who the lieutenant is. You'd be the first one blown away." We forgot the sandbags—and the salutes. Months later, when Hiers left the platoon to go home, he turned to me as I stood on our hilltop position, and gave me the smartest salute I'd ever seen. I shot him the finger, and that was the last I saw of him for fifteen years. When we met by accident at the Vietnam memorial it was like a sign; enough time has passed—we were old enough to say goodbye to who we had been and become friends as who we had become.

For us and for thousands of veterans the memorial was special ground. War is theater, and Vietnam had been fought without a third act. It was a set that hadn't been struck; its characters were lost there, with no way to get off and no more lines to say. And so when we came to the Vietnam memorial in Washington we wrote our own endings as we stared at the names on the wall, reached out and touched them, washed them with our tears, said goodbye. We are older now, some of us grandfathers, some quite successful, but the memorial touched some part of us that is still out there, under fire, alone. When we came to that wall and met the memories of our buddies and gave them their due, pulled them up from their buried places and laid our love to rest, we were home at last.

For all these reasons, men love war. But these are the easy reasons, the first circle, the ones we can talk about without risk of disapproval, without plunging too far into the truth or ourselves. But there are other, more troubling reasons why men love war. The love of war stems from the union, deep in the core of our being, between sex and destruction, beauty and horror, love and death. War may be the only way in which most men touch the mythic domains in our soul. It is, for men, at some terrible level the closest thing to what childbirth is for women: the initiation into the power of life and death. It is like lifting off the corner of the universe and looking at what's underneath. To see war is to see into the dark heart of things, that no-man's-land between life and death, or even beyond.

And that explains a central fact about the stories men tell about war. Every good war story is, in at least some of its crucial elements, false. The better the war story, the less of it is likely to be true. Robert Graves wrote that his main legacy from World War I was "a difficulty in telling the truth." I have never once heard a grunt tell a reporter a war story that wasn't a lie, just as some of the stories that I tell about the war are lies. Not that even the lies aren't true, on a certain level. They have a moral, even a mythic, truth, rather than a literal one. They reach out and remind the tellers and listeners of their place in the world. They are the primitive stories told around the fire in smoky teepees after the pipe has been passed. They are all, at bottom, the same.

Some of the best war stories out of Vietnam are in Michael Herr's *Dispatches.* One of Herr's most quoted stories goes like this: "But what a story he told me, as one-pointed and resonant as any war story I ever heard, it took me a year to understand it:

"Patrol went up the mountain. One man came back. He died before he could tell us what happened."

"I waited for the rest, but it seemed not to be that kind of story; when I asked him what had happened he just looked like he felt sorry for me, fucked if he'd waste time telling stories to anyone as dumb as I was."

It is a great story, a combat haiku, all negative space and darkness humming with portent. It seems rich, unique to Vietnam. But listen, now, to this:

"We all went up to Gettysburg, the summer of '63: and some of us came back from there: and that's all except the details." That is the account of Gettysburg by one Praxiteles Swan, onetime captain in the Confederate States Army. The language is different, but it is the same story. And it is a story that I would imagine has been told for as long as men have gone to war. Its purpose is not to enlighten but to exclude; its message is not its content but putting the listener in his place. I suffered, I was there. You were not. Only those facts matter. Everything else is beyond words to tell. As was said after the worst tragedies in Vietnam: "Don't mean nothin'." Which meant, "It means everything, it means too much." Language overload.

War stories inhabit the realm of myth because every war story is about death. And one of the most troubling reasons men love war is the love of destruction, the thrill of killing. In his superb book on World War II, *The Warriors*, J. Glenn Gray wrote that "thousands of youths who never suspected the presence of such an impulse in themselves have learned in military life the mad excitement of destroying." It's what Hemingway meant when he wrote, "Admit that you have liked to kill as all who are soldiers by choice have enjoyed it at some time whether they lie about it or not."

My platoon and I went through Vietnam burning hooches (note how language liberated us—we didn't burn houses and shoot people; we burned hooches and shot gooks), killing dogs and pigs and chickens, destroying, because, as my friend Hiers put it, "We thought it was fun at the time." As anyone who has fired a bazooka or an M-60 machine gun knows, there is something to that power in your finger, the soft, seductive touch of the trigger. It's like the magic sword, a grunt's Excalibur: all you do is move that finger so imperceptibly, just a wish flashing across your mind like a shadow, not even a full brain synapse, and *poof!* in a blast of sound and energy and light a truck or a house or even people disappear, everything flying and settling back into dust.

There is a connection between this thrill and the games we played as children, the endless games of cowboys and Indians and war, the games that ended with "Bang bang you're dead," and everyone who was "dead" got up and began another game. That's war as fantasy, and it's the same emotion that touches us in war movies and books, where death is something without consequence, and not something that ends with terrible finality as blood from our fatally fragile bodies flows out onto the mud. Boys aren't the only ones prone to this fantasy; it possesses the old men who have never been to war and who preside over our burials with the same tears they shed when soldiers die in the movies—tears of fantasy, cheap tears. The love of destruction and killing in war stems from that fantasy of war as a game, but it is the more seductive for being indulged at terrible risk. It is the game survivors play, after they have seen death up close and learned in their hearts how common, how ordinary, and how inescapable it is.

I don't know if I killed anyone in Vietnam, but I tried as hard as I could. I fired at muzzle flashes in the night, threw grenades during ambushes, ordered artillery and bombing where I thought the enemy was. Whenever another platoon got a higher body count, I was disappointed: it was like suiting up for the football game and then not getting to play. After one ambush my men brought back the body of a North Vietnamese soldier. I later found the dead man propped against some C-ration boxes. He had on sunglasses, and a *Playboy* magazine lay open in his lap; a cigarette dangled jauntily from his mouth, and on his head was perched a large and perfectly formed piece of shit.

I pretended to be outraged, since desecrating bodies was frowned on as un-American and counterproductive. But it wasn't outrage I felt. I kept my officer's face on, but inside I was . . . laughing. I laughed—I believe now—in part because of some subconscious appreciation of this obscene linkage of sex and excrement and death; and in part because of the exultant realization that he—whoever he had been—was dead and I—special, unique me—was alive. He was my brother, but I knew him not. In war the line between life and death is gossamer thin; there is joy, true joy, in being alive when so many around you are not. And from the joy of being alive in death's presence to the joy of causing death is, unfortunately, not that great a step.

A lieutenant colonel I knew, a true intellectual, was put in charge of civil affairs, the work we did helping the Vietnamese grow rice and otherwise improve their lives. He was a sensitive man who kept a journal and seemed far better equipped for winning hearts and minds than for a combat command. But he got one, and I remember flying out to visit his fire base the night after it had been attacked by an NVA sapper unit. Most of the combat troops had been out on an operation, so this colonel mustered a motley crew of clerks and cooks and drove the sappers off, chasing them across the rice paddies and killing dozens of these elite enemy troops by the light of flares. That morning, as they were surveying what they had done and loading the dead NVA—all naked and covered with grease and mud so they could penetrate the barbed wire—on mechanical mules like so much garbage, there was a look of beatific contentment on the colonel's face that I had not seen except in charismatic churches. It was the look of a person transported into ecstasy.

And I—what did I do, confronted with this beastly scene? I smiled back, as filled with bliss as he was. That was another of the times I stood on the edge of my humanity, looked into the pit, and loved what I saw there. I had surrendered to an aesthetic that was divorced from that crucial quality of empathy that lets us feel the sufferings of others. And I saw a terrible beauty there. War is not simply the spirit of ugliness, although it is certainly that, the devil's work. But to give the devil his due, it is also an affair of great and seductive beauty.

Art and war were for ages as linked as art and religion. Medieval and Renaissance artists gave us cathedrals, but they also gave us armor, sculptures of war, swords and muskets and cannons of great beauty, art offered to the god of war as reverently as the carved altars were offered to the god of love. War was a public ritual of the highest order, as the beautifully decorated cannons in the Invalides in Paris and the chariots with their depictions of the gods in the Metropolitan Museum of Art so eloquently attest. Men love their weapons, not simply for helping to keep them alive, but for a deeper reason. They love their rifles and their knives for the same reason that the medieval warriors loved their armor and their swords: they are instruments of beauty.

War *is* beautiful. There is something about a firefight at night, something about the mechanical elegance of an M-60 machine gun. They are everything they should be, perfect examples of their form. When you are firing out at night, the red tracers go out into the blackness as if you were drawing with a light pen. Then little dots of light start winking back, and green tracers from the AK-47s begin to weave in with the red to form brilliant patterns that seem, given their great speeds, oddly timeless, as if they had been etched on the night. And then perhaps the gunships called Spooky come in and fire their incredible guns like huge hoses washing down from the sky, like something God would do when He was really ticked off. And then the flares pop, casting eerie shadows as they float down on their little parachutes, swinging in the breeze, and anyone who moves in their light seems a ghost escaped from hell.

Daytime offers nothing so spectacular, but it also has its charms. Many men loved napalm, loved its silent power, the way it could make tree lines or houses explode as if by spontaneous combustion. But I always thought napalm was greatly overrated, unless you enjoy watching tires burn. I preferred white phosphorus, which exploded with a fulsome elegance, wreathing its target in intense and billowing white smoke, throwing out glowing red comets trailing brilliant white plumes. I loved it more—not less—because of its function: to destroy, to kill. The seduction of war is in its offering such intense beauty—divorced from all civilized values, but beauty still.

Most men who have been to war, and most women who have been around it, remember that never in their lives did they have so heightened a sexuality. War is, in short, a turn-on. War cloaks men in a costume that conceals the limits and inadequacies of their separate natures. It gives them an aura, a collective power, an almost animal force. They aren't just Billy or Johnny or Bobby, they are soldiers! But there's a price for all that: the agonizing loneliness of war, the way a soldier is cut off from everything that defines him as an individual—he is the true rootless man. The uniform did that, too, and all that heightened sexuality is not much solace late at night when the emptiness comes.

There were many men for whom this condition led to great decisions. I knew a Marine in Vietnam who was a great rarity, an Ivy League graduate. He also had an Ivy League wife, but he managed to fall in love with a Vietnamese bar girl who could barely speak English. She was not particularly attractive, a peasant girl trying to support her family. He spent all his time with her, he fell in love with her—awkwardly, formally, but totally. At the end of his twelve months in Vietnam he went home, divorced his beautiful, intelligent, and socially correct wife, and then went back to Vietnam and proposed to the bar girl, who accepted. It was a marriage across a vast divide of language, culture, race, and class that could only have been made in war. I am not sure that it lasted, but it would not surprise me if, despite great difficulties, it did.

Of course, for every such story there are hundreds, thousands, of stories of passing contacts, a man and a woman holding each other tight for one moment, finding in sex some escape from the terrible reality of the war. The intensity that war brings to sex, the "let us love now because there may be no tomorrow," is based on death. No matter what our weapons on the battlefield, love is finally our only weapon against death. Sex is the weapon of life, the shooting sperm sent like an army of guerrillas to penetrate the egg's defenses—the only victory that really matters. War thrusts you into the well of loneliness, death breathing in your ear. Sex is a grappling hook that pulls you out, ends your isolation, makes you one with life again.

Not that such thoughts were anywhere near conscious. I remember going off to war with a copy of *War and Peace* and *The Charterhouse of Parma* stuffed into my pack. They were soon replaced with *The Story of O*. War heightens all appetites. I cannot describe the ache for candy, for taste; I wanted a Mars bar more than I had wanted anything in my life. And that hunger paled beside the force that pushed us toward women, any women; women we would not even have looked at in peace floated into our fantasies and lodged there. Too often we made our fantasies real, always to be disappointed, our hunger only greater. The ugliest prostitutes specialized in group affairs, passed among several men or even whole squads, in communion almost, a sharing more than sexual. In sex even more than in killing I could see the beast, crouched drooling on its haunches, could see it mocking me for my frailties, knowing I hated myself for them but that I could not get enough, that I would keep coming back again and again.

After I ended my tour in combat I came back to work at division headquarters and volunteered one night a week teaching English to Vietnamese adults. One of my students was a beautiful girl whose parents had been killed in Hue during the Tet Offensive of 1968. She had fallen in love with an American civilian who worked at the consulate in Da Nang. He had left for his next duty station and promised he would send for her. She never heard from him again. She had a seductive sadness about her. I found myself seeing her after class, then I was sneaking into the motor pool and commandeering a deuce-and-a-half truck and driving into Da Nang at night to visit her. She lived in a small house near the consulate with her grandparents and brothers and sisters. It had one room divided by a curtain. When I arrived, the rest of the family would retire behind the curtain. Amid their hushed voices and the smells of cooking oil and rotted fish we would talk and fumble toward each other, my need greater than hers.

I wanted her desperately. But her tenderness and vulnerability, the torn flower of her beauty, frustrated my death-obsessed lust. I didn't see her as one Vietnamese, I saw her as all Vietnamese. She was the suffering soul of war, and I was the soldier who had wounded it but would make it whole. My loneliness was pulling me into the same strong current that had swallowed my friend who married the bar girl. I could see it happening, but I seemed powerless to stop it. I wrote her long poems, made inquiries about staying on in Da Nang, built a fantasy future for the two of us. I wasn't going to betray her the way the other American had, the way all Americans had, the way all men betrayed the women who helped them through the war. I wasn't like that. But then I received orders sending me home two weeks early. I drove into Da Nang to talk to her, and to make definite plans. Halfway there, I turned back.

At the airport I threw the poems into a trash can. When the wheels of the plane lifted off the soil of Vietnam, I cheered like everyone else. And as I pressed my face against the window and watched Vietnam shrink to a distant green blur and finally disappear, I felt sad and guilty—for her, for my comrades who had been killed and wounded, for everything. But that feeling was overwhelmed by my vast sense of relief. I had survived. And I was going home. I would be myself again, or so I thought.

But some fifteen years later she and the war are still on my mind, all those memories, each with its secret passages and cutbacks, hundreds of labyrinths, all leading back to a truth not safe but essential. It is about why we can love and hate, why we can bring forth life and snuff it out, why each of us is a battleground where good and evil are always at war for our souls.

The power of war, like the power of love, springs from man's heart. The one yields death, the other life. But life without death has no meaning; nor, at its deepest level, does love without war. Without war we could not know from what depths love rises, or what power it must have to overcome such evil and redeem us. It is no accident that men love war, as love and war are at the core of man. It is not only that we must love one another or die. We must love one another *and* die. War, like death, is always with us, a constant companion, a secret sharer. To deny its seduction, to overcome death, our love for peace, for life itself, must be greater than we think possible, greater even than we can imagine.

Hiers and I were skiing down a mountain in Vermont, flying effortlessly over a world cloaked in white, beautiful, innocent, peaceful. On the ski lift up we had been talking about a different world, hot, green, smelling of decay and death, where each step out of the mud took all our strength. We stopped and looked back, the air pure and cold, our breath coming in puffs of vapor. Our children were following us down the hill, bent over, little balls of life racing on the edge of danger.

Hiers turned to me with a smile and said, "It's a long way from Nam, isn't it?"

Yes.

And no.

Hiroshima, 5 August 1945 (Smithsonian Institution Photo No. 3381). Some men may have a love affair with war, but few can rejoice in the horror brought to humankind by modern weapons. With the marriage of science and war, today's chemical, biological, and nuclear weapons threaten all life on earth. Although not every person would be killed in a nuclear war, what remains would not be worth the price. The destiny of the human race and the planet on which we live demands that such weapons never be used. The tragedy of humankind is that our fate lies in our own hands. Unfortunately, the history of our violent past offers us little hope for the future.